Visual
FoxPro 5
Enterprise
Development

How to Order:

For information on quantity discounts, contact the publisher: Prima Publishing, P.O. Box 1260BK, Rocklin, CA 95677-1260; (916) 632-4400. On your letterhead include information concerning the intended use of the books and the number of books you want to purchase. For individual orders, turn to the back of this book for more information.

Visual
FoxPro 5
Enterprise
Development

Rod Paddock

Ron Talmage

John V. Petersen

Eric Ranft

PRIMA PUBLISHING

ISBN: 0-7615-0903-8
Library of Congress Catalog Card Number: 96-70100
Printed in the United States of America
98 97 96   DD   6 5 4 3 2 1

Publisher:
Don Roche, Jr.

Associate Publisher:
Ray Robinson

Senior Acquisitions Editor:
Alan Harris

Senior Project Editor:
Tad Ringo

Product Marketing Specialist:
Julie Barton

Acquisitions Editor:
Debbie Abshier

Development Editor:
Chris Katsaropoulos

Project Editor:
Chris Haidri

Indexer:
Sherry Massey

Interior Layout:
Marian Hartsough

To my wife, Maria Alexandria, the inspiration for my life and the best friend I could ask for. I would not be where I am today without you.

—R.P.

To my nieces, Alicia and Brianna, and my nephews, Isaac and Jacob.

—R.T.

To my wonderful wife, Evelyn, and my two sons, Karl and Keith. Without your patience and understanding, this book would not have been possible. I love you all very much.

—J.V.P.

About the Authors

Rod Paddock is President and founder of Dash Point Software, Inc. (DPSI). Based in Seattle, DPSI specializes in VFP, VB, and Access database development. The company's clients include SBT Accounting, the U.S. Coast Guard, Pinnacle Publishing, Intel, and Azalea Software. Rod was a featured speaker at the 1995 FoxPro Developers Conference, as well as the 1995/1996 FoxTeach and 1995 VBTeach conferences. Rod writes for several database publications, including *Data Based Advisor*, *FoxTalk*, and *Dbase Advisor*. He has contributed work to two other computer books. Rod can be reached by e-mail at **76244.3116@compuserve.com**.

Ron Talmage is a database developer with True North Technology, a Seattle firm specializing in client/server real estate software. He has over sixteen years experience in software design and programming, including eight years of teaching college-level computing. He currently is involved in the team development of vertical market VFP, Java, and SQL Server applications. Ron also teaches VFP for Application Developers Training Company, is active in local database SIGs, and has contributed to several books on database programming. Ron can be reached by e-mail at **70274.1224@compuserve.com**.

John V. Petersen is Director of Software Development for Integrated Database Technologies, Inc., a Philadelphia marketing database consulting firm. Active in the FoxPro community, he is a frequent speaker at conferences and user groups. In addition, he is the author of "Dr. FoxPro's Answer Clinic," a monthly column in *FoxTalk*. He holds a B.S. in Business Administration and an M.B.A. in Information Systems. John can be reached by e-mail at **johnpetersen@mail.com**.

Eric Ranft is President of Tactile Software, Inc., a firm that provides custom software development in VFP, VB, and Access. Tactile Software specializes in solutions for environmental companies and sells a line of turnkey packages developed under VFP. Eric holds a degree in Computer Science from the University of Michigan. He has been using FoxPro professionally since its inception and has written large multi-user systems for many firms in the Seattle area. Eric can be reached by e-mail at **75263.2170@compuserve.com** or **Ranfters@msn.com**.

Acknowledgments

Thanks, Maria, for enduring the many long nights and weekends that it took to pull this thing off. I'm glad I have a person so patient and loving in my life. Next, thanks to my family: Kevin, Leslie, and Brandon. Thanks for letting that compulsive-excessive son of yours pursue his own path.

No person can make it where they are without a mentor. My mentor, professor, and friend, Art Sanchez, is responsible for teaching me what these databases are really useful for.

I'd like to personally thank Debbie Abshier, our supportive acquisitions editor, for helping get this bird off the ground. Thanks to Tad Ringo, Julie Barton, Chris Katsaropoulos, Chris Haidri, and everyone else at Prima who made this project fly smoothly. Thanks to Tom Barich for your capable handling of the CD.

Also, thanks to Curt and Kristy Heimuller, two of the best friends someone could ever have. Thanks to Dave Anderson for teaching me how to teach VFP to the masses, and Erik Ruthruff for giving me the opportunity. Thanks to the crews at MOSI, SBT, Montgomery Watson, Peopleware, and DSN for providing me with some great ideas. Thanks to Valdis Matison for letting me be a speaker these last few years and for providing me with some of the most interesting conversation ever. Thanks to the Microsoft VFP team, including: Keith Kaplan, Roger Bischoff, Calvin Hsia, and Ken Levy. Keep the faith, guys. . .

For inspiration throughout the years, thanks to: Pearl Jam, Van Halen, Metallica, Mozart, Fleetwood Mac, Starbucks, Pizza Hut, the makers of M&M candies, Steven Spielberg, George Lucas . . . well, you get the picture.

—R.P.

I would like to thank my fellow Puget Sound FoxPro User Group members and Application Developers Training Company instructors for valuable exchanges of VFP expertise.

—R.T.

To Scott Malinowski, the Desert Fox, my mentor and teacher of my very first class. Thank you for all the encouragement you've given me over the years. Nothing I've accomplished in this business would have been possible without you and your friendship.

To my first editor at *FoxTalk*, Bob Grommes—thanks for the encouragement and opportunity. To my current editor at *FoxTalk*, Whil Hentzen. The past year working with you has been great, and I look forward to many more. You're right—books and software are best written at 105 decibels.

To Ed Martini, George Goley, John Repko, Joan Novino, and the whole gang at Micro Endeavors (the people and place where FoxPro is pushed to the maximum, and where I learned the most)—thank you for giving me so much. Thanks to Jack Gallagher and Drew Speedie at MaxTech, for letting me loose to see what I could accomplish. You've taught me a great deal.

To Debbie Abshier, thanks for making my first book-writing experience such a positive one.

To the entire Fox community.

—J.V.P.

CONTENTS AT A GLANCE

CONTENTS

PART II   OBJECT AND CODING DEVELOPMENT . . .49

Chapter 3   Using Visual FoxPro's Debugging Facilities 51

Chapter 4   Integrating Visual FoxPro and Object-Oriented Programming . . .89

Chapter 13 Deploying Visual FoxPro Internet Applications 449

Chapter 14 Deploying and Distributing Your Applications 483

INTRODUCTION

Welcome to *Visual FoxPro 5 Enterprise Development*! This book is dedicated to helping you make the most out of Microsoft Corporation's premier application development tool, Visual FoxPro 5.0. The ultimate purpose of tools such as Visual FoxPro 5.0 is to create full-blown applications, not to create a form here and there, or simple program routines. As such, this book is intended for the intermediate-to-advanced Visual FoxPro developer wishing to gain the skills required to create better applications. You might be an in-house developer, a software consultant, or just a programmer changing over to a new tool. At the minimum, you should be experienced with numerous tasks common to Visual FoxPro developers, including the following:

- Basics of Windows application development
- Using the Project Manager
- Creating basic Visual FoxPro tables
- Creating forms, reports, menus, and simple programs
- Using the xBase language or any other procedural programming language

This book is meant to be the no-fluff guide to developing Visual FoxPro applications. Most books attempt to rewrite the documentation that comes with VFP. Not here. This book cuts through all of that and gets down to what you *really* need to know as a VFP developer. This book is for *enterprise developers*, those who are concerned with creating robust, sophisticated, quality applications. If any of the following items concern you or your future development efforts, then this book is for you:

- Object-oriented programming
- The Internet

- OLE
- Client/server development
- Application deployment

As an enterprise developer, you may work for a huge conglomerate or a single-department company—size is not an issue. If you want to develop professional, high-quality applications without reinventing the wheel each time a project begins, then you'll benefit from *Visual FoxPro 5 Enterprise Development*.

How This Book is Organized

When formulating the content of this book, the goal was to provide an even mix of theory and practical application of that theory. Therefore, in addition to the conceptual material, a fictional company named World Wide Shoes (WWS) has been created to illustrate how to apply the theory that's introduced. Interwoven in many chapters are specific examples related to the process of developing an order entry system for WWS.

Visual FoxPro 5 Enterprise Development consists of four parts:

- Analysis and Design
- Object and Coding Development
- Database Development
- Application Deployment

Part I: Analysis and Design

- Chapter 1, "Establishing Development Principles," sets the standards that developers should use when developing applications. This chapter recommends different areas that you should research when starting the development process.

- Chapter 2, "Analysis, Design, and Prototyping," explores the concepts and needs of having a good design prior to the process of writing code and design classes. This chapter explores different methodologies and tools that lead to sound database and class designs. Finally, this chapter discusses the process of rapidly developing a prototype and documenting your application.

Part II: Object and Coding Development

- Chapter 3, "Using Visual FoxPro's Debugging Facilities," shows you how to use the new debugger. The primary philosophy of this chapter is to treat debugging as an integral part of development, not something that occurs after the fact.

- Chapter 4, "Integrating VFP and Object-Oriented Programming," takes an extensive look at how to create an object-oriented framework. You come away from this chapter with a set of foundation classes that can be incorporated into any application.

- Chapter 5, "The FoxPro Foundation Classes," emphasizes the fact that it's much easier to begin development using an already-developed framework than it is to "roll your own." This chapter documents the FoxPro Foundation Classes, a set of class libraries designed for VFP developers (and included on the CD-ROM that accompanies this book).

- Chapter 6, "Communicating with Other Applications Using OLE," explores the OLE capabilities of Visual FoxPro. In addition to discussing how VFP can interface with other applications such as Excel, Word, and Project, the creation of VFP OLE servers is closely examined.

- Chapter 7, "Using the Windows API," demonstrates how to incorporate Windows API calls into your applications. Many practical examples are presented, including reading and writing to the Windows Registry, and facilitating RAS connections.

- Chapter 8, "Multi-User Development Techniques," discusses the concepts and coding techniques you can use to prevent multi-user conflicts in your applications. Topics covered in this chapter include locking strategies, row and table buffering, and transaction processing.

- Chapter 9, "Creating Development Tools," focuses on what builders are, how they are integrated into the VFP IDE, and how to create your own builders. In addition, techniques for extending the functionality of the Class Browser are discussed.

Part III: Database Development

- Chapter 10, "Creating a Visual FoxPro Database," presents advanced concepts and techniques you can use when designing and developing relational databases. Specifically, you learn about the relational model, relational versus navigational processing, the new VFP DBF format, the database container, data integrity, and database administration.

- Chapter 11, "Using SQL in Visual FoxPro Applications," explains how to implement SQL in your applications. Special consideration is given to the SQL language implementation in VFP.

Part IV: Application Deployment

- Chapter 12, "Client/Server Database Development with Visual FoxPro," covers the tools and strategies you need for developing client/server applications. This chapter discusses the advantages and disadvantages of client/server, how backend SQL server databases work, how VFP accesses remote data, and tricks and traps involved with translating data between VFP and a backend server database.

- Chapter 13, "Deploying Visual FoxPro Internet Applications," teaches you how to create Internet solutions in your VFP applications. This chapter's topics include using the Internet Wizard, creating an HTML Web page with VFP, and utilizing the Internet Control Pack from your VFP applications.

- Chapter 14, "Deploying and Distributing your Applications," discusses how to distribute your VFP applications, as well as how to create and integrate useful help systems. Along with coverage of the Setup Wizard and Help Workshop that ship with VFP, this chapter also looks at a couple of important third-party tools.

What's on the CD-ROM?

The CD-ROM that accompanies this book contains the following:

- All code examples
- The Visual FoxPro Foundation Classes
- The sample Order Entry application for World Wide Shoes
- An assortment of useful tools and utilities
- Demo versions of third-party products that can achieve a variety of useful results, such as the inclusion of barcodes in your applications, or the creation of help files for integration with your applications.

Conventions Used in the Book

To make it easier for you to use this book, Prima uses a couple of conventions for consistently presenting different kinds of information. You should review these conventions before moving on in the book:

- **Menu names, commands, and dialog box options**—In virtually all Windows programs, each menu name, command name, and dialog box option name contains an underlined letter called a *hot key*. The hot key is used to make that particular selection via the keyboard, sometimes in conjunction with the Ctrl or Alt key. In this book, all hot keys are indicated as an underlined letter, as in <u>V</u>iew.

- **Code and items that appear on-screen**—Any VFP code, HTML, or other code discussed in this book is presented in a `special typeface`, to make it easy to distinguish. When reference is made to an error message or other information that appears on-screen, it's also in the `special typeface`.

- **Text you type**—When you need to type some text to complete a procedure, or when we provide an example of text you can enter, the text you need to type appears in bold, as in the following instruction:

    Type a name for the new form, such as **frmVisitorInfo**.

Special Elements

At times, you'll be provided with information that supplements the discussion at hand. This special information is set off in easy-to-identify sidebars, so you can review or skip these extras as you see fit. You'll find the following types of special elements in this book:

> **TIP:** *Tips* provide shortcuts to make your job easier, or better ways to accomplish certain tasks.

> **NOTE:** *Notes* provide supplemental information that is a bit more technical or that describes a special situation you might encounter.

> **WARNING:** *Warnings* alert you to potential pitfalls, or warn you when a particular operation is risky and might cause you to lose some of your work.

Contacting Us

Prima Publishing welcomes your feedback, and would like to hear more about the kind of help you need, other computing topics you'd like to read about, or any other questions you have. Please use the reader response card in the back of this book to get in touch with Prima.

For a catalog, call 1-800-632-8676, or visit the Prima Publishing Web site at http://www.primapublishing.com.

PART I

Analysis and Design

Chapter 1

Establishing Development Standards

Why Develop Standards?

There are many ways to distinguish a good software development project from a mediocre one. You can look at the appearance of the screens, the way the application behaves, the structure of the underlying tables, or the source code itself. Each of these items tells you something about the application and about the developers who built it. One evaluation method, however, stands out above all other methods of evaluation: the development standards used to build the application. This opening chapter is the most appropriate place to discuss the standards that are used to develop applications and the standards that have been used to develop the sample code throughout this book.

Many developers view standards as handcuffs that inhibit creativity. In this chapter, you learn why this is far from the truth. Programming standards are very similar to the standards of syntax, grammar, and punctuation used by the English language. For example, you capitalize the first word and put a period at the end of each sentence. This is the standard way of punctuating a sentence. Do you think that this standard prevented Shakespeare from writing Hamlet? Considered in this light, you can see that standards do not inhibit creativity. The primary reason for developing standards is to facilitate communication between developers. It is important to have a common language and method for writing code and developing applications. Having this common language facilitates the integration of new developers to a project, as they already understand the terms and methods used. In this chapter, you learn some techniques to establish standards of your own. This chapter discusses the following:

- How to establish programming standards
- The importance of naming conventions
- How standards fit in the object-oriented world
- The need for developing GUI standards
- The different types of standard documentation you should have
- How to manage the development process for more than one developer

Establishing Programming Standards

Among the first standards you must develop are *programming/coding standards*. Programming standards dictate the format of your programming code. There are four main areas to look at when developing programming standards:

- Variable naming conventions
- Object naming conventions
- Code formatting conventions
- Comments

Variable Naming Conventions

The first convention you should adopt is a method of naming your variables. Having a *naming convention* for your variables is important for two reasons. The first is the fact that Visual FoxPro is a *loosely-typed language*. In most computer languages (including C, C++, and Pascal), you are required to declare your variables and their data types before they are used. This prevents you from using a numeric value in a character variable, a date value in a numeric variable, and so on. A variable in Visual FoxPro, on the other hand, can be initialized as a numeric at one point in a program, and then changed (either intentionally or unintentionally) later in the same program. Consider the following code:

```
flag = .t.
flag = 1
flag = "OPEN"
```

If you encounter the variable `flag` at some point in a program or procedure, you might not know what type of variable you're dealing with, potentially causing you to inadvertently introduce a logic bug. The second, probably more important reason for a variable naming convention is to convey the intentions of the programmer. By using a variable naming convention, you can convey extra meaning in your programming code (such as what type of data you're dealing with, or the scope of the variable). In six months, when you are maintaining the code written today, this will be an important issue.

Now that you understand why you want a naming convention for your variables, you can begin formulating your own conventions. One of the most popular variable naming conventions is the *Hungarian standard*. This standard is named for the nationality of Microsoft's most famous programmer (after Bill Gates, of course), Charles Simonyi. The Hungarian standard says that your variables have two parts: a prefixed data type, and a programmer-assigned variable name. Table 1-1 lists the prefixes for the variable data types you can have in Visual FoxPro.

Using the prefixes from Table 1-1, your variables should look something like those in the following code:

```
cLastName = "PADDOCK"
dBirthDate = {01/01/01}
nAge = 27
lAuthor = .t.
```

As you can see, this code conveys what type of data you're dealing with. Now, whenever you see a variable like dBirthDate, you know that it's a Date data type. The above code demonstrates Hungarian notation; however, your standard should convey as much meaning as possible, so you should add another component to your standard.

Along with the Hungarian standard's data type prefix, your standard should include another aspect: the scope of the variable. The scope shows the lifetime of

Table 1-1 Visual FoxPro Variable Data Type Prefixes

Prefix	Data Type
c	Character
l	Logical
n	Numeric
d	Date
a	Array
o	Object
x	Variable data type

Table 1-2 Visual FoxPro Variable Scope Prefixes

Prefix	Scope
l	Local
p	Private
g	Global
v	Passed as a parameter by value
r	Passed as a parameter by reference

the variable and deals primarily with who can change it and what side effects will occur if it is changed. Table 1-2 shows the standard prefixes for the scope of a variable.

Look at the following code with this new convention in mind:

```
lcLastName = "PADDOCK"
gdSystemDate = DATE( )
ldLoopDate = DATE( ) + 180
```

Notice that now you know two pieces of information about gdSystemDate: it has a Global scope and a Date data type. Now, whenever you encounter this variable and consider changing it, you know that you are going to cause a global side effect.

One more thing about this naming convention. You probably noticed that the sample variables had certain letters in uppercase. This is known as *Camel notation* (coined by our fellow author Ron Talmage). The only effect of this notation is that it makes the code easier to read. The most common technique is to have the scope and data type of the variable in lowercase, and then capitalize the significant words within the variable name. The following code shows a procedure developed using Camel notation:

```
Function ReturnHTMLPage
Lparameters plCGIPage

Local lcRetVal
lcRetVal = ""
```

```
lcRetVal = lcRetVal + This.CreateHTMLHeader()

If This.nLines > 0
  Local lnKount
  For lnKount = 1 To This.nLines
    lcRetVal = lcRetVal + This.aPageLines[lnKount] + THIS.cCRLF
  EndFor
Endif

lcRetVal = lcRetVal + This.CreateHTMLFooter()

Return lcRetVal
```

Once you have established a variable naming convention, you can move on to develop an object naming convention.

Object Naming Conventions

Visual FoxPro 3.0 introduced FoxPro programmers to the idea of object-oriented programming. This introduction brought about the need for a new set of naming conventions. Developers use *object naming conventions* to name the objects that create class definitions (class creation is covered in Chapter 4, "Integrating Visual FoxPro and Object-Oriented Programming") and forms. You need object naming conventions for the same reasons you need variable naming conventions: whenever you encounter an object in code, it's important to know what type of object you're dealing with. The naming convention for objects is similar to the naming convention for variables—the object's name is prefixed with an object type prefix. Table 1-3 shows the conventions as documented in the Visual Fox-Pro help file.

Using the above convention, you'll create objects with names similar to those shown in the following code:

```
cmdEdit = A command button
txtLastName = A text box
pgfCustomerInfo = A pageframe
```

Table 1-3 Visual FoxPro Object Naming Conventions

Prefix	Object Type
chk	Check box
cbo	Combo box
cmd	Command button
cmg	Command group
cnt	Container
ctl	Control
cus	Custom
edt	Edit box
frm	Form
frs	Form set
grd	Grid
grc	Column
grh	Header
img	Image
lbl	Label
lin	Line
lst	List box
olb	OLEBoundControl
ole	OLE
opt	Option button
opg	Option group
pag	Page
pgf	Pageframe
sep	Separator
shp	Shape
spn	Spinner
txt	Text box
tmr	Timer
tbr	Toolbar

NOTE: Notice that Camel notation is used again. Any time you create a new variable, function, or object, you should use this notation.

As you can see, the conventions you use for naming objects should be as similar as possible to the conventions for naming variables. Once you establish a standard, try to remain as consistent as possible when using it.

Code Formatting Conventions

The last type of programming standard used in this book consists of *code formatting conventions*. Until now, you've seen conventions that dictate the naming of variables and objects. At a minimum, you should use a standard variable naming convention. You should not overlook, however, the opportunity to standardize how you structure your lines and pages of programming code.

The formatting of your code is a very important part of its usability by other developers. Look at the following two segments of code, and decide which is more readable:

First listing:

```
*— Set message information
if ln_count = 100
lc_message = "Entering System"
ln_value = 200
if ln_count2 = 300
lc_msg2 = "HELLO"
endif
lc_message = "Exiting System"
ln_value = 300
endif
```

Second listing:

```
*- Set message information
If lnCount = 100
   lcMessage = "Entering System"
   lnValue = 200


   If lnCount2 = 300
     lcMsg2 = "HELLO"
   Endif

Else
   lcMessage = "Exiting System"
   lnVvalue = 300
Endif
```

As a reader, you probably find the second listing easier to read. Why? Because the code there is indented, and contains an adequate amount of white space. The human eye needs to have things broken up so it can distinguish between different objects. The second listing has things broken up nicely.

There is another thing to note—in the second listing, all the keywords use a *proper-case naming convention*. This is where our book deviates from the normal xBase way of doing things. The old style of writing code stipulated that you use uppercase for FoxPro's default commands and functions. Then, Visual FoxPro 3.0 introduced developers to objects, properties, and methods, all of which used a proper-case naming convention. Hence, all sorts of inconsistencies appeared. With uppercase keywords and proper-case properties, code began to look jumbled and inconsistent.

Thus, we've decided to deviate from the norm and use a consistent proper-case naming convention. From this point forward, all commands, functions, methods, and properties will be in proper case, constants will be in uppercase, and variables/objects will use Camel notation. How did we come up with this standard? We looked at Visual Basic and Delphi, then made a few alterations to come up with this new standard.

NOTE: Naming conventions are supposed to be flexible. If you find that uppercase commands and functions work better in your shop, then use them. The important aspect is simply to have a standard.

Another aspect of your coding convention should dictate how methods are called. Visual FoxPro allows developers to call object methods without using parentheses, but you always should strive to use the full syntax of the Visual Fox-Pro language. Your standard should dictate things like using full keywords (Visual FoxPro allows you to use only the first four letters of a command if you choose) and using parentheses on method calls. Why do you want to do this? Because Visual FoxPro may, in the future, require full keywords or the inclusion of parentheses. If you have not used the full syntax, then you face the chance of bugs surfacing when you use a new version of Visual FoxPro.

The last portion of a coding convention is something that all programmers should do: comment the code. Whenever you write code, you should comment it for the sake of two people: 1) the unfortunate maintenance programmer who has to understand the original intent of your program, and 2) yourself when you happen to be that unfortunate maintenance programmer six months after writing the code. When you write code, put in an English sentence occasionally, describing what the intent of a particular piece of code is. These comments come in handy later when you need to debug or add new features to your code. When should you comment your code? As you write it, of course. If you wait until after the fact, you might forget why you did a certain thing, defeating the main purpose of commenting code (describing the intent of certain lines). Also, remember to embed comments throughout your programming code. Pseudo-coded comment blocks at the beginning of your program are not enough. You need to place each comment at the location of the lines being discussed.

There are a number of methods you can use to create your comments that will be useful later in the development process. If you comment your code using a standard convention, then you can go back later to pull these comments out with a program for inclusion in your documentation. The following code shows how you might format code with such a convention:

```
*********************************************
*<Description>This function opens tables.
*<Written>09/14/96
*<Written By>John Petersen
```

After sticking to this convention, you could write a program to extract all comments containing <Description>, <Written>, and <Written By> tags into a set of system documentation. As this shows, comments can provide more utility than just hints for developers.

The Importance of Coding Conventions

As you can see from the preceding text, coding conventions are useful for multiple reasons, primarily making code easier to read and providing developers with information about the intent of other developers. For these reasons, you should use coding conventions whenever possible. Remember that the specific conventions you use are not as important as simply having conventions. Settle on a standard before development begins, and use it from the very beginning of the project—you will appreciate having the standard later.

Developing GUI Standards

One of the most important changes in the computer industry in the past few years was the advent of the *graphical user interface (GUI)*. Users now have machines with color monitors, mice, windows, command buttons, and all sorts of new graphical gadgets. One of the advantages of this interface has been the adoption of GUI standards that dictate how Windows, Macintosh, and other windowing applications need to "look and feel." There are certification programs to which vendors submit their applications in order to receive the Windows or Windows 95 logo. For several reasons, you should develop your applications to behave like these.

One of the advantages of using Windows or Mac applications is that once you learn one, you've learned them all. Well, sort of. Because most Windows applications follow the same conventions, you know how to open, save, print, close, and copy a file in any application. Do you remember the steps to print a file in Lotus 1-2-3 for DOS? How about in WordPerfect for DOS? Okay, now you see how this consistency is nice for Windows users. You should strive to make your applications behave like the other Windows applications your users have grown to love. This is why you should learn the seven commonly accepted principles of GUI design. If you follow these basic principles, the design of your application should be in fine shape.

The Seven Principles of GUI Design

The seven principles of GUI design, adapted from the *Microsoft Windows Interface Guidelines*, provide a framework upon which you can develop your own GUI standards. This framework provides two major benefits to you and your users. The first is that it promotes professional-looking applications. When you present your application to your users, you want to make sure that it looks as polished as possible. The second benefit goes to your users. They're provided a consistent, easy-to-learn, and functional application. Of course, these principles are not a panacea. Your application must be well-designed, well-written, and useful in order to be successful. These principles simply provide food for thought when you develop your own applications. Here are the seven principles of GUI design:

1. Keep the user in control.
2. Follow the object-action paradigm.
3. Be consistent.
4. Make things self-evident.
5. Strive for balanced aesthetics.
6. Give the user feedback.
7. Be forgiving.

Principle One: Keep the User in Control

The first principle dictates that the user is the one in control of your application. Users should be able to access any module of your application from any other module. The old method of providing access to different modules was a hierarchy-style menu. Figure 1-1 shows an older menu system.

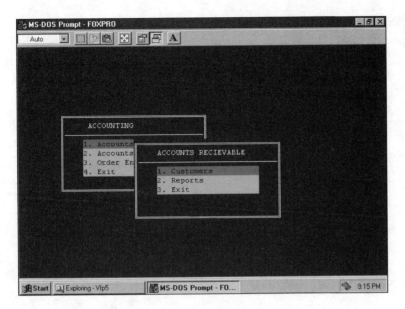
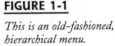

FIGURE 1-1

This is an old-fashioned, hierarchical menu.

In the above example, a user who wants to add a new customer must navigate into the accounts receivable module, then add the customer from there. How does the user know this? Probably by using this specific application before. In the GUI world, the user simply selects a command such as New, Customer from a menu, as shown in Figure 1-2.

The user of this system can add a new customer, vendor, or inventory item from the File menu. This allows the user to change a customer record if the user happens to be in the vendor screen, or vice versa. She no longer needs to traverse a complex and confusing hierarchical menu.

Principle Two: Follow the Object-Action Paradigm

The *object-action paradigm* says that the entities in your system have actions that can be performed on them. The most readily apparent example is a customer maintenance screen (see Figure 1-3). This screen presents a set of command buttons; each button allows users to perform a certain action on the selected customer. They can delete the customer information, edit the customer information, print the customer information, and so on. The actions that can be performed on a cus-

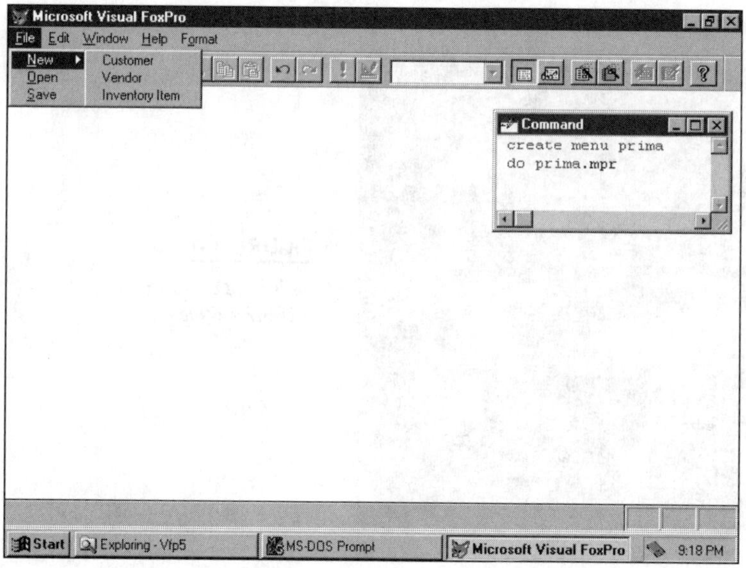

FIGURE 1-2

This figure shows a GUI menu system with the New–Customer option highlighted.

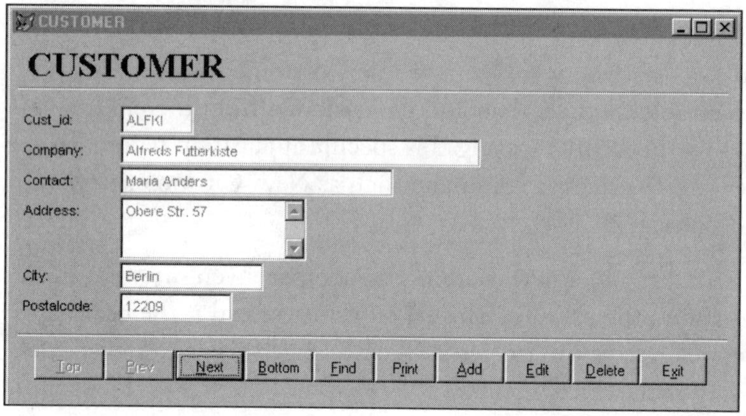

FIGURE 1-3

This figure shows a customer maintenance screen with a set of action-oriented push buttons.

tomer must be enabled or disabled at the appropriate times. When the customer record is in edit mode, for instance, you disable the Delete and New buttons.

Principle Three: Be Consistent

This is one of the most important of the GUI design principles. Apple, Microsoft, and other companies have performed studies that cost millions of dollars to demonstrate that GUIs allow users to learn more applications than they could in the character-based world. This is based on one principle: consistency. Whenever a Windows or Mac user encounters a new application, they already know how to do basic functions such as opening files, printing, and saving. This is because the applications developed for these platforms are, for the most part, consistent.

When you develop your own applications, stay consistent. If you use the word "New" for adding a new record, use that word everywhere—don't substitute "Add" in a few locations. This consistency lets your users learn that whenever they encounter a New button, they can use it to add a new record.

Principle Four: Make Things Self-Evident

This principle could be called "no geek-talk." Figure 1-4 shows a screen with two different buttons. The first says "Pack Database" and the second says "Remove Records Marked for Deletion." Which of these do you think users are more likely to understand?

When developing applications, it's easy to fall into the trap of using computer jargon in your interfaces. You should always strive, however, to make your applications as jargon-free as possible.

Principle Five: Strive for Balanced Aesthetics

Take a look at Figure 1-5. Even in black-and-white, this screen has a serious aesthetics problem—a white background with contrasting objects. Not very

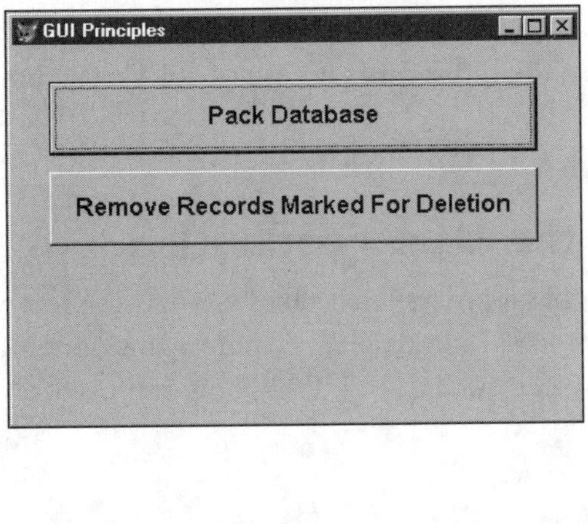

FIGURE 1-4

This screen contains an ambiguous button (top) and an obvious one (bottom).

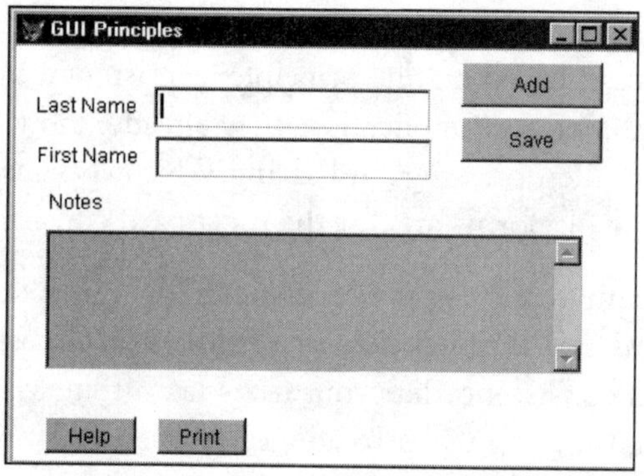

FIGURE 1-5

This screen is aesthetically displeasing because it's unbalanced.

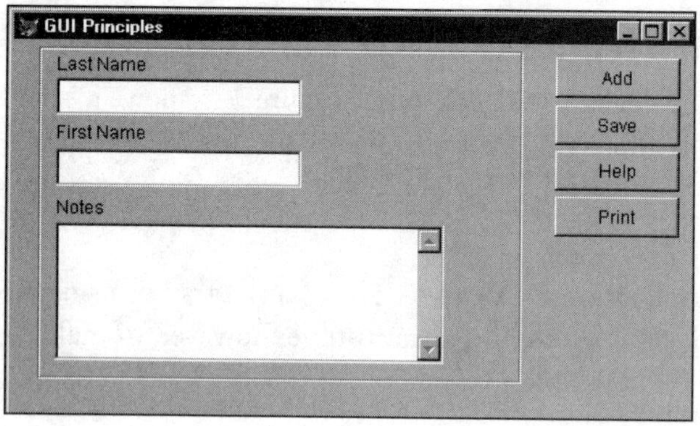

FIGURE 1-6

This balanced screen is aesthetically pleasing.

neat, is it? Look now at Figure 1-6. This is the same screen, but it's well-balanced.

Windows is capable of displaying millions of color combinations. Does this mean you should use them all? Of course not! You should use color in a simple, restrained manner, and beware the indiscriminate use of color that some programmers seem to practice.

Principle Six: Give the User Feedback

Assume that your application has a process that takes a long time to perform. One method of writing this process is to display a window that says something like Running process. Please wait.... Well, how can users ever know if this application is hung up? They cannot, so there's a chance that your application may be given the "three-fingered salute" (Ctrl-Alt-Del) when it's still functioning properly.

If you can provide your users some idea of the progress of your application, you'll reap two profound benefits. One is that your users will never shut down your program because they mistakenly think the program is hung up. The second is that you'll experience an estimated 25% increase in performance. This is not a performance increase in the application itself, but in the users of the application. Your users will be able to gauge the progress of a running process, and go do other things while the process completes. This is a substantial gain that can be achieved simply by putting a progress meter on-screen. The most common approaches to the progress meter are to put a message like `10 of 100 records processed` or `40% completed` (or better yet, a message that contains both the number of records and the percentage).

Principle Seven: Be Forgiving

How many times have you inadvertently deleted a record by hitting a stray key? You always should give users a chance to back out of a process, or better yet, to undo whatever they just did. If you have a process that takes a long time, alters large amounts of data, or requires that users back up data prior to proceeding, then you should provide the users with some type of warning that such a process is about to take place. I've seen some accounting applications ask for two confirmations, then ask for a password before they'll proceed with closing the month. Does your application need this level of protection? Maybe. You need to evaluate the best way to let a user back out of a mistake in the middle of any given task.

The Importance of GUI Conventions

As you can see, the principles of GUI design are fairly easy to understand, and should be implemented to the greatest possible extent and as soon as possible in your development process. Prior to designing production screens, you should establish what your design standards are going to look like. Choose your fonts, colors, screen sizes, message styles, and so on. By selecting these early, you ensure that application development progresses much faster, since many questions are already answered. If you have a question about a font or a message style, you don't need to reinvent it each time; you simply go to the standard and look it up. For more information on designing good user interfaces, you might want to look at the following books:

About Face
Alan Cooper
IDG Books
ISBN: 1-56884-322-4

TOG on Design
Bruce Tognazzini
Addison-Wesley
ISBN: 0-20148-917-1

The Windows 95 Design Standards
Microsoft Press
ISBN: 1-55615-679-0

Developing Documentation Standards

It is very surprising today that many companies begin developing $50,000+ applications without so much as a simple specification. Would you build a $50,000 building without a blueprint? Whenever you develop *any* application, you need to understand the importance of developing an adequate set of design documents.

Chapter 2, "Analysis, Design, and Prototyping," teaches you techniques for developing analysis and design documents. The point of including this material so early in the book is to convey the importance of developing documentation standards early in the development process.

Which Methodology to Choose

There are as many analysis and design methodologies as there are computer languages. Which one is right for your shop? Well, you shouldn't get too hung up on whether one methodology is superior to another, but should focus more on the application objectives you want to achieve. You should consider a few basic

Table 1-4   Documentation Tools

Document Type	Tools
Relationships	Infomodeler, ERWIN, Evergreen EASYCASE, Visio
Process flow	Evergreen EASYCASE, Visio
Data table contents	Visual FoxPro, Word For Windows, Stonefield Data Dictionary
Functional descriptions	Word For Windows, Evergreen EASYCASE

criteria when choosing how to document your analysis/design process. At a minimum, your design should include documents that contain the following:

- The relationships of the data tables of your system
- Descriptions of the contents of your data tables
- Documentation of the flow of data through your system
- Functional descriptions of your application's various modules

If you can create these documents early on, you'll benefit many different groups, including the developers who work on your applications, any developers who later modify your applications, and the customers who purchase your applications.

When you set out to develop your systems analysis/design documentation, you'll find that there are many tools you can use to create such documents. Table 1-4 lists some of the more prominent tools.

These are just some of the tools available to you. Chapter 2, "Analysis, Design, and Prototyping," discusses several of the tools, as well as the techniques used to create these documents.

Working with Multiple Developers

No software development project involves only one person. Developers, customers, project managers, testers, and many other types of people can be involved in a project. Whenever you introduce additional people to the development mix, you need to worry about keeping your software in synch with all the other people involved.

There are a number of ways to keep versions of software in synch throughout development; these methods range from informal to formal. An informal method might use time-honored (but very risky) techniques such as "hey, are you using this file" or "can you send me the latest version?" Formal methods may include techniques such as assigning particular pieces of an application to certain developers, or formal checkin/checkout procedures. Visual FoxPro 5.0 provides a set of tools that allows you to set up a formal process while retaining the flexibility of an informal one. This is known as *integrated version control*.

Using Version Control

The standard way to keep the versions of your software in synch is a set of tools known as *version control*. Version control software allows you to manage the source code for your project in a central *repository*. This repository controls management of the software with a library-style system. Developers *check out* a portion of an application when they want to work on that portion. When they're finished, they *check in* that portion of the application using the version control software. There are great advantages to using version control software: the prevention of two developers wasting work on the same set of code, the ability to roll back to an earlier version of software, and the ability to easily compare one version to another.

Integrating Visual FoxPro and Visual SourceSafe

Visual FoxPro provides the ability to integrate its Project Manager with various version control packages, including PVCS and Visual SourceSafe. In order to use version control with Visual FoxPro 5.0, you first need to install your version control software. If you're using SourceSafe, you need to use the Explorer or File Manager to switch to your Visual FoxPro directory. There, double-click the SS.REG file. This configures Visual FoxPro with the ability to check projects into SourceSafe.

If you're using any other version control package, you also need to register it. Upon configuring Visual FoxPro, go to the Options dialog box reached by choosing Tools, Options from the Visual FoxPro menu. Select the Projects tab (see Figure 1-7). The choices here allow you to attach Visual FoxPro to a version control program, and to configure how Visual FoxPro integrates with source code control. The first step you should take is to drop down the Active source control provider list. In this list, you should see the name of the version control package you've installed. After selecting this name, you can configure other version control options. For most purposes, you can use all the defaults except one—you should configure Visual FoxPro to automatically add new projects to source control. By selecting this option, you make sure that as soon as you create a new project, Visual FoxPro will automatically configure it for version control.

Using Visual FoxPro and Visual SourceSafe

After configuring your version control software, you can begin using it by creating a new project. When you create a new project, Visual FoxPro does the following:

1. Places you into your version control software

2. Provides a dialog box for you to specify the project name (it defaults to the current Visual FoxPro project's name)

3. Asks for a description of your project

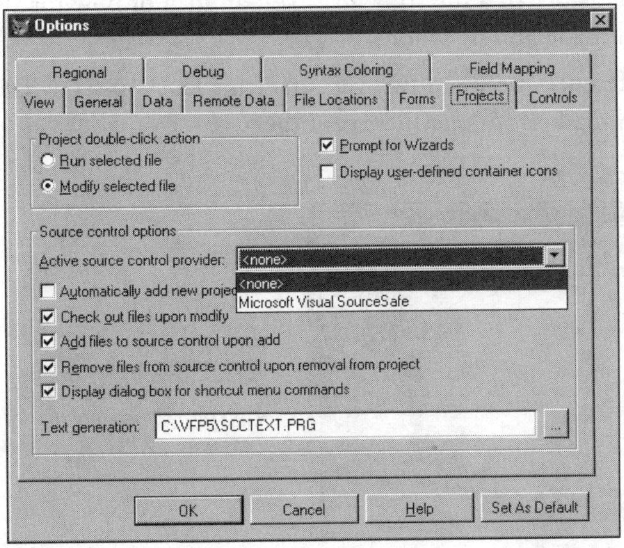

FIGURE 1-7

The Options dialog box with the Projects tab selected.

After you add your project to the version control package, you can begin adding the components of your application to the project. When you add components to your project, Visual FoxPro prompts you to add the files to your version control software. After you add these files to the version control package, Visual FoxPro shows the files in the Project Manager with a lock icon beside them. This tells developers that the file is controlled by the version control package. Figure 1-8 shows the Project Manager listing a number of class libraries controlled by the version control package.

As soon as you've added your project to the version control software, you can begin using the capabilities of that software. Choosing Project, Source Control in Visual FoxPro provides you with a list of different version control functions you can run. Figure 1-9 shows the Source Control menu options available in Visual FoxPro. You can do any of the following:

- Get the latest version of a file (this feature is useful if you only need a copy of a file)
- Check out a file
- Check in a file
- Cancel a checkout (this feature enables you to cancel your changes to a piece of software)
- Show the history of a file (this gives you an idea of how many changes have been made and by whom)
- Show differences between two versions (this lets you see what changes have been made from one file to another)

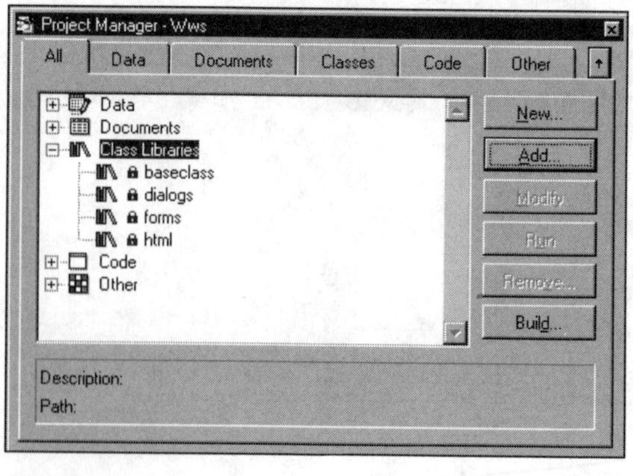

FIGURE 1-8

The Project Manager shows a set of class libraries controlled by version control.

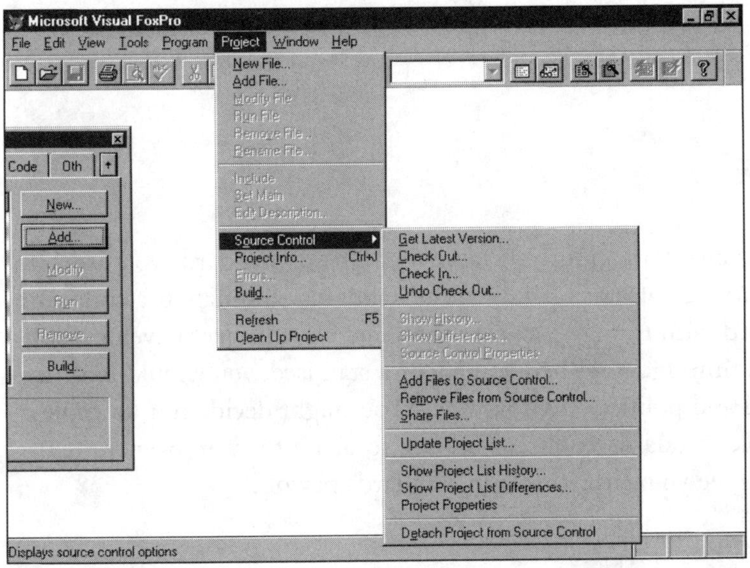

FIGURE 1-9

The Visual FoxPro Source Control menu.

- Update a project with all the new changes made to that project
- Show the history of a project file
- Remove a project from version control

As you can see, including version control as a standard part of your development process provides quite a few new capabilities that you wouldn't have without version control. Installing this type of software allows you to examine the history of a file (or a complete project), which is useful when something gets out of synch. Version-control software also makes it easy for remote users to exchange files with the home office. All they need to do is dial in through RAS, Dial-Up Networking, or another acceptable protocol, then check in their files through the version control package.

Why Use Version Control?

Version control is one way to make your development process more efficient. Version control removes the problem of keeping versions of software in synch. If you add up the amount of time you spend backing up, copying, and compiling various files for your projects, you quickly will understand the usefulness of version control.

Summary

The purpose of this chapter is not to dictate what type of standards you use, but to convey the importance of having standards. Standards eliminate the confusion and delays associated with trying to answer the same basic project development questions time and time again. When you adopt a standard, you should look at both your technical and political environments. You might decide not to implement all the possible standards at once. Feel free to phase them in over time. Ultimately, you will see your investment in standards pay off.

Chapter 2

Analysis, Design, and Prototyping

Introduction

The key to success in any software development project is a strong foundation. Chapter 1 discussed one of the most important aspects of software development, the establishment of standards. This chapter deals with an equally important subject, analysis and design. The ultimate goal of any software should be to solve some problem and/or address a business need. If a given situation is not properly analyzed, the software cannot be properly designed. Subsequently, the project and the resulting software application are practically doomed to failure.

The goal of this chapter is to provide a brief overview of some good fundamental analysis and design concepts, and of how to create a prototype. The discussion will not be theoretical. Rather, it will be in the context of analyzing and designing an order entry system for the World Wide Shoes (WWS) Corporation, a business case example developed through the text of this book and through the files on the accompanying CD-ROM. Look for the CD-ROM icon (shown here in the margin) as a sign at various locations throughout the book that sample code segments or application tools from the CD-ROM are being presented. It should be stressed that this chapter is meant to serve only as a brief introduction to basic analysis and design concepts. There are many good books on the market today solely devoted to this topic, and you should consult those texts if you desire more in-depth study.

Procedural Systems versus Object-Oriented Systems

Before going further, it is important to focus on one of the main points that separates Visual FoxPro from other development tools—Visual FoxPro is object-oriented. As such, to make the most of Visual FoxPro, it is necessary to employ object-oriented programming. So, how does this change the way you analyze and design a system?

In procedural systems, the analysis and design effort constitutes about 25% of the total time involved in creating a system. Today, with object-oriented systems, the analysis and design effort constitutes at least 50–60% of the project's time.

Why the increase? With object-oriented systems, classes are designed with the intent that they will be reused. Just formulating solid class hierarchies takes considerable time. The end result is that more analysis and design time is required for object-oriented systems. The payoff, however, comes with the quality of the end product.

Requirements Analysis and Specifications

This is where the problem-solving begins in the WWS example. For some time now, the staff in the Sales Department at WWS has complained about the current manual system for processing orders. It takes a long time to fulfill orders and to bill customers. From a marketing perspective, there's no way to track trends in customer purchases. It's therefore impossible to gauge what the public demands, in order to stock more inventory that would move quickly. The real frustration lies in the fact that many aspects of the business already have computerized solutions. World Wide Shoes manages inventory on SQL Server, and most of the workstations have the usual array of desktop software, including word processor, spreadsheet, and presentation software. Imagine that you are the head of the WWS Software Development Staff and that the VP of Sales has laid the problem at your doorstep with the memo on pages 30 and 31.

The tasks for the World Wide Shoes Development Staff are the following: 1) determine what problems exist and what new functionality is needed, 2) determine how the existing problems should be solved, and 3) implement the chosen solution. It should be stressed that there is no single correct methodology for analysis and design. The best solution for you is one that you feel most comfortable with, and that provides you with the data required to solve your business problem.

Often, a memo such as this one is the catalyst for initiating the development process. Before the first line of code is written, however, there are many details left to be examined. Despite all of its detail, the sample memo leaves quite a few holes. It is the job of the developer to refine the project goals into a requirements document, as discussed below.

To: Systems Development Staff

From: Management of World Wide Shoes

Re: Computerized Order Entry System

Date: October 31, 1996

As you are aware, the management of this company has determined that, in order to remain competitive, is necessary to automate and computerize our order entry operations as much as possible. Because there has been a lack of feedback on what our customers purchase, there are questions about how effective our marketing efforts are, and how effectively we are managing inventory.

The management of the company has determined that this system must meet a number of minimum requirements to accomplish the sales goals of the company in the coming months. Here's what we have determined is necessary:

1. The system should capture customer information. This information should include, but not be limited to, the following: customer name, customer address information, source of the customer, customer phone and fax numbers, customer e-mail address, date customer added, multiple customer notes, customer demographic information (age, marital status, education, income, homeowner status).

2. The system should capture customer orders. The information captured should include, but not be limited to, the following: order #, order date, shipping address, items on the order, order terms, order payments, order source, shipping methods, shipping costs, item prices, item quantities, item costs, item shipping status, shipping company tracking numbers.

3. The system should facilitate the shipping of these orders. This includes the processing of picking tickets and shipping documentation.

4. The system should tie into the existing SQL Server inventory system. The new system will import the following: part numbers, prices, on-hand information, on-order information. The new system should also update the inventory system when new orders are placed or orders are canceled.

5. The system should provide the ability to capture customer and marketing information from the Internet.

6. The system should allow customers to access order information from the Internet.

7. The system should allow its users to call up the services of UPS and Federal Express from their terminals without calling the shipping department.

8. The system should create Web pages from the inventory files.

9. The system should tie into existing Office applications wherever possible.

10. The system should provide management a variety of different reports (to be specified later).

As you can see, this is quite an ambitious project for a first undertaking. The main emphasis of this system is to become more responsive to our customers and to become more modern with our use of current technology.

If you have any questions, feel free to contact me.

Bill Jennings
Senior Vice President of Sales

Problem Identification

Before a solution can be implemented, the problems at hand must be clarified. This is known as *problem identification*. A business problem can be thought of as a gap between how things are and how they ought to be. The larger the gap, the greater the problem. Often, it's best to try to break the issues down to one or two sentences. By doing so, you eliminate the risk of defining a problem that is either too vague or too specific. If a problem cannot be properly identified, a solution cannot follow. In the case of World Wide Shoes, here's a statement of the business problem at hand:

> The manual method of order entry and fulfillment is causing World Wide Shoes to lose market share to its competitors. In addition, WWS has experienced dramatically increased inventory and overhead costs. These two issues combined have placed the future of the company in jeopardy.

With this problem definition statement, you know three important pieces of information:

- What the problem is—the manual order entry system
- How the problem is manifested—lower sales and higher costs
- What will happen if the problem goes unaddressed—WWS will go out of business

When defining the problem, it's important to assess the consequences of not solving the problem. By analyzing both the problem and the potential consequences, a cost-benefit analysis can be performed to see if it's cost-justifiable to pursue a solution of the problem. In this case, having WWS go out of business is not a viable alternative. Therefore, the WWS developers must immediately begin working to lay the foundation of a new software system.

Requirements Analysis

At this point, you understand what the problem is and what the consequences of not addressing the problem will be. It's time to begin the work of applying a solution. The initial specifications for a solution have been drafted in the memo from the VP of Sales (shown earlier). The memo describes the components of the company's ideal system. While the memo is fairly detailed, it needs to be refined for the purpose of designing a new system. Because Visual FoxPro is object-oriented, your development staff at WWS has decided to employ an object-oriented analysis methodology for the problem at hand. The methodology of choice is the CRC (Classes, Responsibilities, and Collaborators) approach, the specifics of which are discussed later in this chapter. One twist to your application of the CRC approach is to bind it with database design. Because Visual FoxPro does not have an object database, the only way to have persistent objects in Visual FoxPro is to store them in tables. Therefore, when discussing a customer class, you define a customer table. The properties of that customer will translate into columns of the customer table. The methods of the customer class and other classes will be addressed when you design their respective forms in the Class/Form Designer.

Object-Oriented Analysis and Design

While traditional analysis and design concepts might be foreign to many developers, imagine throwing *object-oriented programming (OOP)* concepts into the mix! In actuality, OOP concepts are not that difficult to learn, if taken in small doses. With many things you attempt to learn, your first experiences dictate how effectively you gravitate toward the subject. Unfortunately, many developers' first experiences with OOP are negative. Most of the time, OOP neophytes simply bite off more than they can chew. It is important to note that many FoxPro developers migrating from version 2.6 to 5.0 have two big tasks to master. First, there is the entirely new Visual FoxPro environment. For many, while their years of FoxPro experience are helpful, Visual FoxPro is like learning a brand-new language. Second, to get the most out of Visual FoxPro, developers must begin to master object-oriented programming as well as object-oriented analysis and design. Either task on its own can be quite an undertaking; when faced together, these tasks seem almost impossible.

Choosing an OOP methodology can be a time-consuming endeavor. Perhaps the most important attribute of any chosen methodology is how quickly it can be mastered. How valuable is a methodology if it takes nine to twelve months to master, and you need to deliver a application in six months? Should you just throw out OOP and implement a Visual FoxPro application using old xBase methods? Absolutely not! Believe it or not, there are OOP methodologies that do not require twelve months to master. One such approach is the CRC approach.

The CRC Approach

The *CRC approach* (*CRC* stands for *Classes, Responsibilities, and Collaborators*) is also known as *responsibility-driven design*. The key to responsibility-driven design is to always identify what something must do. As you will discover, everything that something must do is known as a *method*.

Before responsibilities can be determined, however, *entities* must be discovered to which the responsibilities will be assigned. As you will discover shortly, these entities are also known as *classes* and their associated attributes are known as *properties*. Classes, methods, and properties: sound familiar? In order to discover classes, you must identify the relevant nouns in a system design. A great place to identify the candidate classes of the WWS Order Entry System is in the issues included in the memo from senior management.

The following have been identified as relevant nouns for the WWS Order Entry System design:

- Customers
- Customer notes
- Customer demographics
- Orders
- Line items
- Payments
- Picking tickets
- Shipping companies
- Inventory

With the classes of the system identified, it's time to identify the responsibilities and attributes (methods and properties) of each class.

> **TIP:** Perhaps the most authoritative book on the CRC approach is *Designing Object-Oriented Software*, by Rebecca Wirfs-Brock. This book provides one of the clearest and most concise explanations of how to implement effective object-oriented analysis and design.

CRC Cards

The primary tool used to organize information with the CRC approach is the *CRC card*. CRC cards are much like index cards. The front of each card contains the responsibilities of a particular class, and the back contains the attributes. Figures 2-1 and 2-2 show the front and back of a sample CRC card.

This CRC card details the responsibilities and attributes of the Customer class. With a customer maintenance form, the customer class will have the ability to add a new instance of itself by creating a new record in the customer table. Additional responsibilities include editing its contents, deleting itself, canceling changes to data, saving changes to data, and searching for a specific customer instance. Keep in mind that the unique twist in this text is coupling data storage with class design. It should be noted that data stored in tables cannot be encapsulated in a class definition. The goal here is to simplify OOP analysis and design, and bring it closer to the database world with which most Visual FoxPro developers are familiar.

Now that you have formulated a list of classes for your system, it's time to determine the responsibilities of each class. Tables 2-1 through 2-4 outline the major classes, and show their respective attributes and responsibilities.

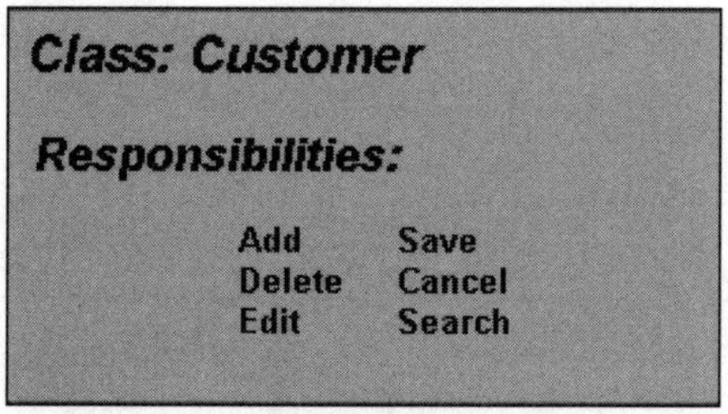

Class: Customer

Responsibilities:

Add	Save
Delete	Cancel
Edit	Search

FIGURE 2-1

This CRC card lists the responsibilities of the Customer class.

Class: Customer

Attributes:

ID	Address 1	Zip	e-Mail
Number	Address 2	Source	
Last Name	City	Phone	
First Name	State	Fax	

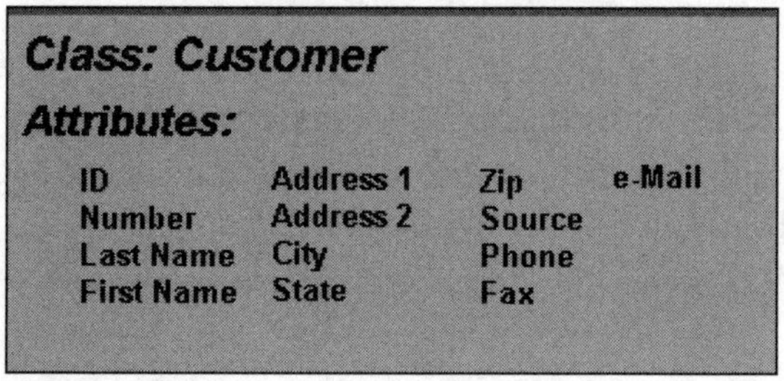

FIGURE 2-2

The back of the card lists the attributes of the Customer class.

Table 2-1 Customers Table

Property	Data Type	Description
Customer_id	c(10)	Internal object ID
Customer_#	c(10)	Customer number
Last_Name	c(30)	Customer last name
First_Name	c(25)	Customer first name
Address_1	c(30)	Address line 1
Address_2	c(30)	Address line 2
City	c(25)	City
State	c(2)	State
Zip	c(10)	ZIP code
Customer_Source	c(6)	Marketing source of customer
Phone_#	c(12)	Customer phone number
Fax_Number	c(12)	Customer fax number
E-mail_address	c(50)	Customer e-mail address
Add_Date	d	Date the customer was added

Method	Description
add( )	Add record
edit( )	Edit record
save( )	Save record
cancel( )	Cancel changes
delete( )	Delete changes
findkey( )	Find record

Tables 2-1 through 2-4 illustrate the descriptions of some of the most basic classes that will comprise the new order entry system. We have defined only a few of the major classes here, but in your own specification you would fully define each class.

Table 2-2 Customer Notes Table

Property	Data Type	Description
Customer_id	c(10)	Link to customer
Note_id	c(10)	Internal object ID
Note_Text	m	Text of note
Add_Date	d	Date the note was added

Method	Description
add( )	Add record
edit( )	Edit record
save( )	Save record
cancel( )	Cancel changes
delete( )	Delete changes
findkey( )	Find record

Identifying Relationships and Database Design

In addition to viewing one class at a time, it is important to understand the relationships that will exist between classes. At this point, you are beginning to move from the object-oriented world to the database world. In the WWS Order Entry System, the orders have been identified as a class. As you can see from the list below, the orders class also has a set of properties and methods. One special property is customer_id. The purpose of this property is to link the order to its owning customer.

English Relationships

The first step in defining relationships is to define in English the relationships between the different objects. It's easy to do this, as you typically are describing

Table 2-3 Customer Demographics Table

Property	Data Type	Description
Customer_id	c(10)	Link to customer
Age	n(1)	Customer age group
Marital_status	n(1)	Customer marital status
Education	n(1)	Customer education
Income	n(1)	Customer income
Home_owner_status	n(1)	Homeowner status
Add_Date	d	Date the demographics were added

Method	Description
add( )	Add record
edit( )	Edit record
save( )	Save record
cancel( ))	Cancel changes
delete( )	Delete changes
findkey( )	Find record

the relationship between two items already related in fact. The relationships found in the WWS Order Entry System are:

- Customers have demographics
- Customers have notes
- Customers have orders
- Orders have payments
- Orders have line items
- Line items are related to inventory items

Table 2-4 Customer Orders Table

Property	Data Type	Description
Customer_id	c(10)	Link to customer
order_id	c(10)	Internal object ID
Add_Date	d	Date the order was added
Order_Source	c(6)	Source of order
Shipping_method	c(10)	Link to shipping method
Tracking_#	c(30)	Shipping company tracking number
Terms	c(10)	Billing terms
Ship_Address_1	c(30)	Address line 1
Ship_Address_2	c(30)	Address line 2
Ship_City	c(25)	City
Ship_State	c(2)	State
Ship_Zip	c(10)	ZIP code

Method	Description
add( )	Add record
edit(( )	Edit record
save( )	Save record
cancel( )	Cancel changes
delete( )	Delete changes
findkey( )	Find record
print( )	Print order
pick( )	Pick order inventory

Entity Relationship Diagrams

After creating the textual relationships, you can proceed to document these relationships further with an *entity-relationship diagram*. Entity relationship diagrams

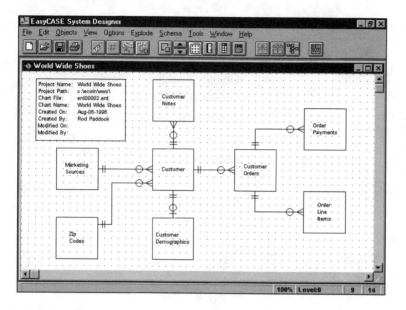

FIGURE 2-3

This is the entity-relationship diagram for the tables used for the WWS example.

show a graphical representation of data relationships. You use terms such as *one-to-many*, *one-to-one*, *one-to-zero-or-many*, and so on. Figure 2-3 shows the entity relationship diagram for the World Wide Shoes example.

Creating a Prototype

One of Visual FoxPro's strengths lies in the tools that it has to support rapid application development and rapid prototyping. Gone is the day when prospective users had to look at sheets of paper with samples of how the screen "is supposed to look" to accept a system specification. With Visual FoxPro, you can create a prototype that gives users a true feel for how their system will look and work. If you present your users with a picture of the system early in the requirements phase, then they can begin giving input immediately. Unknown attributes will surface, unnecessary features will be omitted, and more importantly, the end users will "buy into" the project. If you can involve your users from the earliest stages of development, then you are much more likely to succeed.

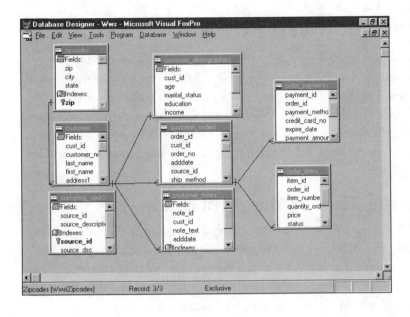

FIGURE 2-4

The World Wide Shoes database is shown here in the Visual FoxPro Database Designer.

Visual FoxPro provides a set of tools that allows you to develop a rough proto-type in minutes. These tools are known as *Wizards*. Wizards are ideal for creating basic application components for your users to review as soon as possible. The first step is to create the database that will represent your data. Figure 2-4 shows the database created for the World Wide Shoes example in the VFP Database Designer.

After you create the database for your application, you can create some sample forms. Keeping in mind the goal of presenting your ideas to the end user as soon as possible, you may want to use the Form Wizard or some of your own rapid development tools. The Form Wizard allows you to create forms for single tables and one-to-many related tables. After creating your initial forms with the Form Wizard, you can either install the forms into your own framework or use a new Wizard included with Visual FoxPro, the Application Wizard. The Application Wizard takes your databases, forms, reports, and other application files, and creates a project, directory structure, and menu that can be used to prototype your application. One of the nicest features of this tool is its ability to create your base application and menu system.

Using the Application Wizard

The Application Wizard is probably one of the most useful features added to the Visual FoxPro development environment in version 5.0. It empowers developers to create fully functional prototypes that can be shown to their users very early in the development process. The Application Wizard takes developers through a series of specific steps designed to create a fully functional application. The following sections describe the steps through which the Application Wizard takes the developer.

Specifying the Title of the Application

The first step in creating a prototype is to specify the names of the project files for the application. Figure 2-5 shows the application specification page of the Application Wizard. From this page you can instruct the Wizard to create a completed application or an empty framework into which you can insert your own components. This screen also allows you to create a directory structure for your application, and to specify the project file for the application.

> **WARNING:** Be careful where you instruct the Application Wizard to create your project files. It defaults to whatever your current directory is. If you are in the VFP directory, then the Wizard will create its system subdirectories there.

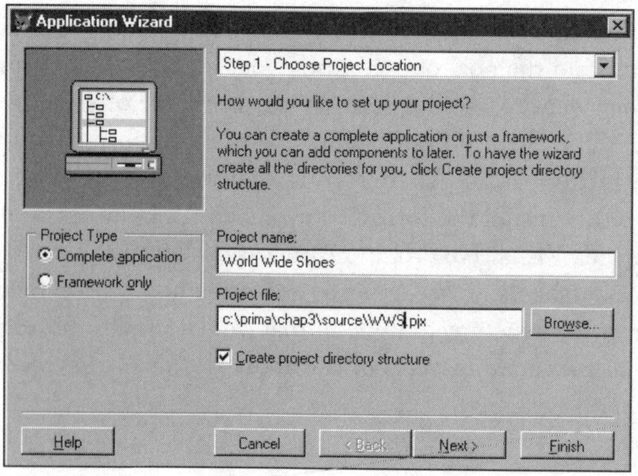

FIGURE 2-5

The Application Wizard here shows the specification of the World Wide Shoes project file.

Specifying the Application Database

The next step in the Application Wizard is to specify the database that will be used by this application. This screen allows you to specify your own database or to select one from a pre-defined list. If you specify one from the pre-defined list, the Application Wizard will create the database, forms, and reports for the specified template, as shown in Figure 2-6.

Specifying the Forms, Reports, and Other Files

The next step in using the Application Wizard is to specify the forms, reports, labels, and other files that will be called by your prototype application. If you used the Form, Label or Report Wizard to create your prototypes, then you can select them from this screen. This screen also has an option to specify one form as the startup form. Figure 2-7 shows the documents that will be attached to the WWS prototype.

Specifying the Menu Options

The final set of options that you can specify using the Application Wizard consists of menu options. The Application Wizard creates a nice, Windows-compatible menu system. As you learned in Chapter 1, "Establishing Development Standards," it's very important to make sure that your applications behave like

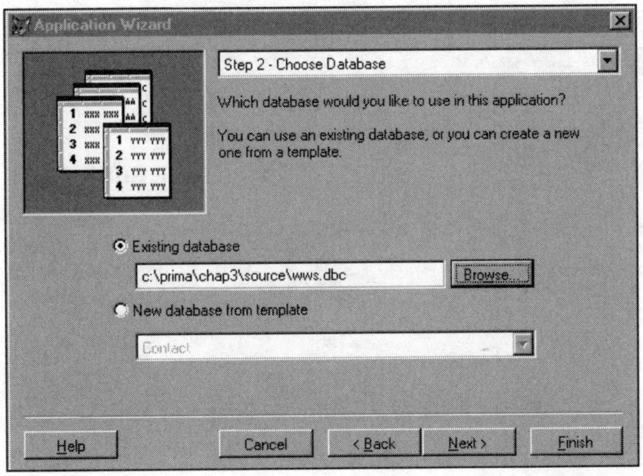

FIGURE 2-6

The Application Wizard here shows the specification of the World Wide Shoes prototype database.

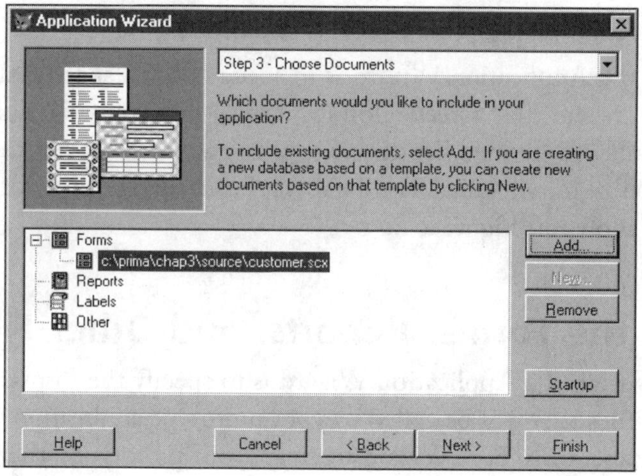

FIGURE 2-7

The World Wide Shoes prototype and its forms are specified here in the Application Wizard.

other Windows applications. The Application Wizard provides the facilities to make your prototypes behave appropriately. Figure 2-8 shows a hierarchy control structure containing the options for your menu. This menu is pre-defined to contain many standard Windows menu options. You can exclude any options that you do not want on your menu. For instance, the menu contains options for calling the Class Browser and debugging facilities. You probably do not want these options present for your users at runtime, so you can remove them by selecting the appropriate menu tree, then clicking the Exclude button.

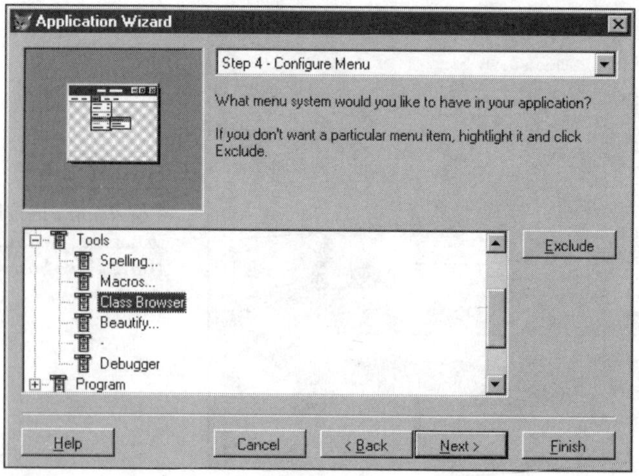

FIGURE 2-8

The Application Wizard here allows specification of menu options for the World Wide Shoes prototype.

Saving and Running the Project

Just as with all Wizards, the Application Wizard's final screen is the finish line screen. This screen allows you to save the project created by the Wizard, open the project in the Project Manager, or save and run the generated application. Figure 2-9 shows the World Wide Shoes prototype generated by the Application Wizard. Figure 2-10 shows the finished prototype application at runtime.

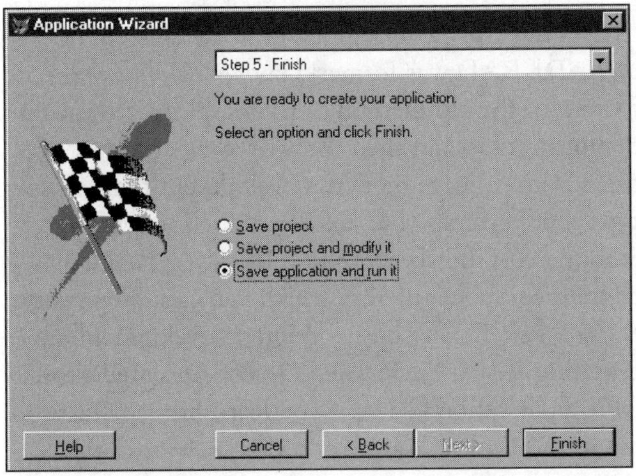

FIGURE 2-9

The Application Wizard here is prepared to save and run the World Wide Shoes prototype application.

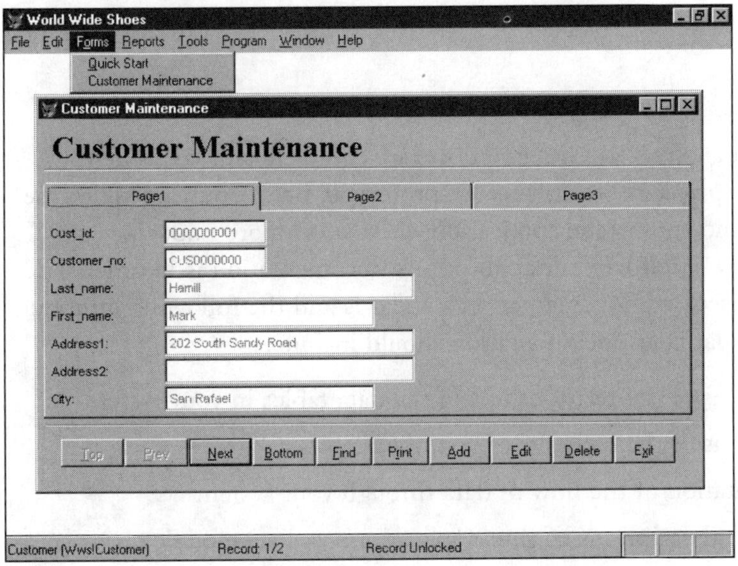

FIGURE 2-10

This is the prototype World Wide Shoes application created by the Application Wizard.

As you can see, an application created by the Application Wizard can provide your users with a good idea of how their application will function when it's completed. This application and the Wizard-generated documents, however, will probably not fit well into your application/object structure, so you ultimately will redevelop them using your own object and application frameworks.

Rapid Application Development

One of the newest methodologies in software development is the concept of *rapid application development (RAD)*. RAD was formerly known as *prototyping*, but it now includes a minor twist. In the old method of prototyping, it was common to create a prototype, demonstrate it, and then throw it away and start over on the "real" system. With the advent of more modern development tools, it now is possible to create a prototype that becomes your actual production system. This ability doesn't come without a cost, however. To develop using RAD, it's necessary to have a set of pre-built components from which you can draw your applications. This is where the full benefits of object-oriented development are realized. In Chapters 4, "Integrating Visual FoxPro and Object-Oriented Programming," and 5, "The FoxPro Foundation Classes," you learn how to create your own objects and how to use the FoxPro Foundation Classes—after that, you can begin the development process in earnest.

Documentation

At last, your initial analysis and design efforts are complete and your client has signed off on these pieces of work, plus the prototype. Before putting your nose to the grindstone and coding the application, there's one more important detail to address—making sure that your application's documentation is in order. The previous chapter discussed documentation standards and the following minimum requirements for what your documentation should include:

- Descriptions of the relationships of the data tables in your system
- Descriptions of the contents of your data tables
- Documentation of the flow of data through your system
- Functional descriptions of your application's various modules

In addition to the above minimum requirements, your application documentation should include the following:

- **Mission Statement**—This is a unifying statement of no more than three sentences stating the overall purpose of the system. This project mission statement is similar to a corporate mission statement; it helps to clarify and define a system's purpose. During the course of development, your staff may lose focus. If you have a mission statement, work is more likely to stay on track, because the statement helps people work toward a unified goal.

- **Meeting Minutes**—During the course of planning and development, there are countless meetings. Many of these meetings amend previously agreed-upon specifications, either by reducing or adding to the feature set of the system. Either way, it's important to have clear notes outlining what was discussed—and who was present—at each meeting.

- **Out-of-Scope Functionality**—All too often, documentation contains only what the initial version of the system will do. Often, there are major areas of functionality in the scope of the planned first version, but with further planning and development, it becomes clear that these areas should instead be implemented in a future version of the system. Such changes should be stated clearly in the documentation.

- **Description of Outputs**—Reporting is usually the most scrutinized feature of a system. Every department has its own reporting requirements. Often, the quality and flexibility of the reporting features of a system are the prime determinant of whether a system is acceptable. A complete description of all outputs, including reports and file dumps, should be included in an application's system documentation.

- **Screen Shots of User Interface**—The UI of every new application is a key component. Typically, many hours are spent designing the user interface, so it's a good idea to have a screen shot of each major interface aspect included in the documentation to ensure that the UI design is acceptable to all end users.

Why is documentation so important? Let's face it, there are many horror stories about a development staff delivering a system, only to have the users reject the system because it does not fit their needs. Documentation is, in essence, a contract under which the users and development staff agree to develop a system.

The documentation is the record of what these parties agree to develop. Documentation sets the ground rules. Documentation is impartial, and documentation will flawlessly remember what was discussed in the third planning meeting six months ago that the head of the Finance Department couldn't attend. In short, documentation saves a lot of aggravation down the road. Most importantly, documentation leads to a better product.

Summary

The goal of this chapter has been to provide you with practical examples of how to embark on an analysis and design effort. While there are many texts on the market today that propose various methodologies, perhaps the most useful rule to remember is KISS (Keep it simple, Stupid). Remember that the bulk of your users are not computer scientists or MIS professionals. These people are concerned with the business and their own jobs. You must complement their business knowledge with your expertise in building business applications. The key to development success is to speak a common language. The most powerful tool you have in your arsenal is the ability to rapidly prototype with Visual FoxPro. A potential user can gain no greater comfort level and ability to tell you what he needs than by working with prototype software that looks and feels like the finished product. If you accurately document your application specifications, you and your users can be sure of building a system that will serve its intended purpose and solve the business problems at hand.

PART II

Object and Coding Development

Chapter 3

Using Visual FoxPro's Debugging Facilities

Introduction

This chapter is dedicated to perhaps the most forgotten—yet one of the most important—elements of application development: debugging. Often, an application development environment is evaluated only in terms of its design (form, menu, reports, and so on), data handling, and language facilities. A list of necessary components for any development environment must include robust debugging facilities. Code that is error-free or classes with a superior design usually are the results of many failed attempts. For debugging facilities to be truly effective, they must be robust enough to be integrated into the normal course of development, not just relegated to being an afterthought once the code has been written. Also, debugging tools must help you to quickly diagnose what is wrong so that a fix can be quickly implemented. This chapter covers techniques to integrate the Visual FoxPro debugging tools into your development efforts.

Role of Debugging in the Development Life Cycle

Before diving into the core of the debugging tools in Visual FoxPro, some philosophical issues need to be addressed. Debugging program code is both a science and an art. It's a science to the extent that most modern programming environments provide state-of-the-art tools to assist in the process of debugging and correcting code. This is the mechanical part of the debugging process. Debugging is an art to the extent that it's a skill both acquired and honed over time with experience. Even though a doctor, for example, has state-of-the-art tools available, she also relies on her own sleuthing and judgment to arrive at a proper diagnosis. The same is true for the programmer. While Visual FoxPro has a fantastic new interactive debugger, you often are left to your own devices for finding the true cause of programming errors and subsequently correcting those errors. This leads one to wonder what debugging's role in the development life cycle actually is.

For truly successful and useful enterprise applications, the task of debugging must be considered an integral part of the development process, not something that is accomplished after the fact. Many programmers just starting out learn to program following these steps:

1. Write program code.

2. Compile code.

3. Debug compile errors.

4. Repeat steps 2 and 3 until a clean compile is achieved.

With brute force, following these steps will result eventually in a clean compile. Does this mean that the code is bug-free? Absolutely not. After all, there may be incorrect variable references or other invalid environmental assumptions that a compiler will never throw out as an exception.

A quote from *The Art of War* by Sun Tzu reads, "Every battle is won before it is fought." The same is true in application development. As many bugs as possible should be prevented before they occur. When writing a block of code, or making a variable reference or environmental assumption, ask yourself this fundamental question: "Am I doing everything in my power to ensure that this code is/will be bug free?" If you adopt this proactive mindset, your class libraries will be more robust and the cycle time from development to beta and finally to acceptance will be much shorter. All of this results in greater confidence in your software as well as reduced development costs.

Of course, it's unrealistic to think that any program will be bug-free. Even the best developers encounter bugs. The skill that separates upper- and lower-tier application developers is their response to and treatment of bugs. Those who postpone debugging until the end of the project find their days consumed with fixing bugs. Interestingly enough, many of these bugs probably were caused by earlier bugs that went ignored! Finally, as time goes by, these bugs become harder and harder to fix. Why? Have you ever analyzed code that you wrote six (or even three) months ago? It takes some time to get back into the proper frame of mind to ascertain exactly how a particular piece of code works and what it is supposed to do. The bottom line is that early debugging reduces the number of bugs present in later development, thereby decreasing the cost and time needed to find and repair bugs. Eliminating bugs at the front end means that you're more likely to deliver a project on—or ahead of—schedule.

With that said, it's time to take a look at how Visual FoxPro 5.0's new debugging tools can help you debug your programs as early in the development cycle as possible.

Visual FoxPro's Debugging Tools—Up Close and Personal

While Version 3.0 of Visual FoxPro was object-oriented and vastly improved over earlier versions of FoxPro, its debugging tools remained basically unchanged. Earlier in this chapter, it was stated that one of the criteria for evaluating an application development environment is the level of debugging support it possesses. Despite all that version 3.0 had to offer, the lack of good debugging support was a chief complaint among the population of FoxPro developers. In version 3.0 developers had a simple debugging window that could echo back the values stored by variables and the results of native VFP functions. In addition, a trace window gave developers the ability to step through code one line at a time.

In developing Visual FoxPro 5.0, Microsoft listened to the FoxPro development community, and put together a serious set of debugging tools. Essentially, Visual FoxPro 5.0 includes the Visual C++ Debugger, which is recognized by developers as one of the best. You will find that the new debugger is really a collection of windows, each devoted to a specific debugging task. The new layout is devoted to the central concept of helping Visual FoxPro developers produce and debug applications as quickly as possible.

The balance of this chapter is devoted to providing you the information necessary to get the most out of the new Visual FoxPro Debugger.

Configuring the Debugging Environment

Just as you configure the environment for your application, you also must configure the environment for debugging. As with other configuration options in Visual FoxPro, there are two methods for making required settings. The first is to make your settings once and have these settings available to future Visual FoxPro sessions. The second, less preferred method is to manually make the required settings each time Visual FoxPro is started. This chapter focuses on the first method.

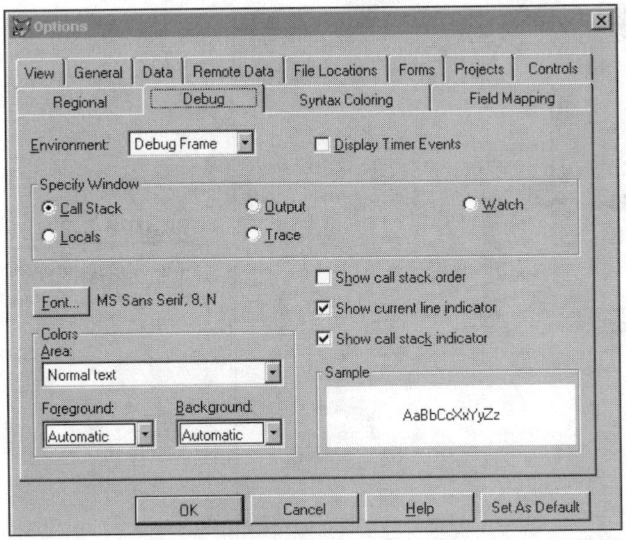

FIGURE 3-1

The Options dialog box offers a Debug tab where you can configure your debugging environment.

The Options dialog box, which is accessed from the Tools menu, has a new Debug tab in version 5.0. Figure 3-1 shows this tab.

The Debug tab is divided into three sections. The first section allows you to specify the type of debug environment you want to use, and whether you want to display timer events.

Debugging Environment Options

Two Environment options are available: Debug Frame and FoxPro Frame. When Debug Frame is chosen, the Debugger appears in its own window, separate from the main Visual FoxPro window. Using this option adds the Debugger choice to the Tools menu, as shown in Figure 3-2. The biggest advantage to using Debug Frame is the fact that Windows treats the Debugger not only as a separate window, but as a separate application. With this setup, it's easy to switch between the Debugger and your application by pressing Alt+Tab.

The alternative is to select FoxPro Frame. In this scenario, all debugging activities occur in the context of the main Visual FoxPro window. An illustration of this is shown in Figure 3-3. Instead of a Debugger choice, the Tools menu con-

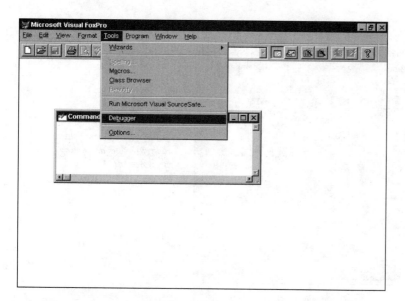

FIGURE 3-2

The Debugger option appears on the Tools menu when Debug Frame is selected.

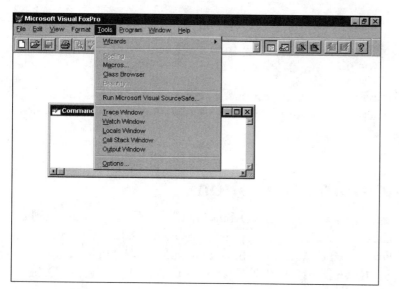

FIGURE 3-3

All the debugging windows appear as options on the Tools menu when FoxPro Frame is selected.

tains a menu choice for each of the debugging windows. When one of the windows is selected for use from the menu, that window and its toolbar appear within the confines of the main Visual FoxPro window. This setup resembles the debugging environment in earlier versions of FoxPro and Visual FoxPro.

NOTE: The Debug Frame option is used for all the figures contained in this chapter.

Displaying Timer Events

While the Timer controls in Visual FoxPro are very useful and powerful, they are somewhat incompatible with debugging processes such as stepping through code. Consider this scenario:

A Timer control in your application has an `Interval` property of 2000 (2 seconds). The sole purpose of the timer is to check to see if a specific text file exists. If the text file does exist, certain operations will be performed. At the same time, you're engaged in a debugging effort regarding some method code in one of your application's forms. Your primary method of tracking down the bug is to use the Trace window to step through the method code. Unfortunately, every two seconds, you are immediately whisked away from the code you're stepping through to the timer's method code. If that text file is found, the interruption from your primary process of debugging code may be longer.

You want the best of both worlds in this case; that is, you want to do the following:

- Have all the timer events fire
- Prevent your debugging processes from interruption by timer events

Why is it important to have the timer events fire? The issue is consistency. When diagnosing and correcting a problem with code, it's important to maintain an environment that replicates a production environment as closely as possible. For example, in a production environment, is it possible that the timer event will fire at the same time the code you're debugging is executing? The answer is yes. By emulating a production situation, you do a more thorough job of ensuring that the code you're working on is truly debugged.

As long as you have the Display Timer Events check box deselected, you can step through code without having the Trace window display timer code when the timer events fire.

Additional Debug Options

The remaining portion of the Debug Page in the Options dialog box is devoted to configuring characteristics of each debugging window. As you select each window in the option group, the contents in the lower half of the page change. Common to all windows is the ability to change the font and the foreground/background coloring of normal and selected text. The Call Stack, Output, and Trace windows have additional options that can be set using this dialog box. The following sections provide a brief overview of the options available for each debugging window. Detailed description of how to use each window is reserved for the "Debugging Windows" section later in this chapter.

Call Stack Window Options

Figure 3-4 shows the Options dialog box with the Call Stack window specified.

Here's a brief description of each option:

- Show call stack order—Each program and method that executes in Visual FoxPro has an ordinal position in the program calling tree. For example, to determine the third program in the program calling tree,

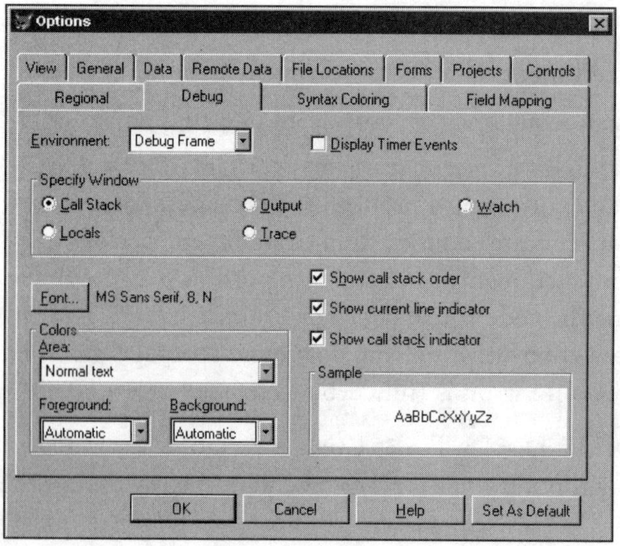

FIGURE 3-4

These debugging options for the Call Stack window are available in the Options dialog box.

you can issue ?Program(3). By selecting this option, you elect to see a number next to each program name.

- Show current line indicator—By selecting this option, you elect to have a small yellow arrow indicate which program line is currently executing.

- Show call stack arrow—By selecting this option, you elect to have a small black arrow indicate which program is currently displayed in the Trace window. If the currently executing program and the program in the Trace window are the same, this arrow does not appear. During the debugging process, you might want to view other code in the calling tree. With this option turned on, it's easy to differentiate between code that is currently executing and code that is currently being viewed in the Trace window.

Output Window Options

Figure 3-5 shows the Options dialog box with the Output window specified.

- Log Debug Output—By selecting this option, you specify that whatever is echoed to the Output window should also be placed in a text file with an LOG extension. Unlike other options that have

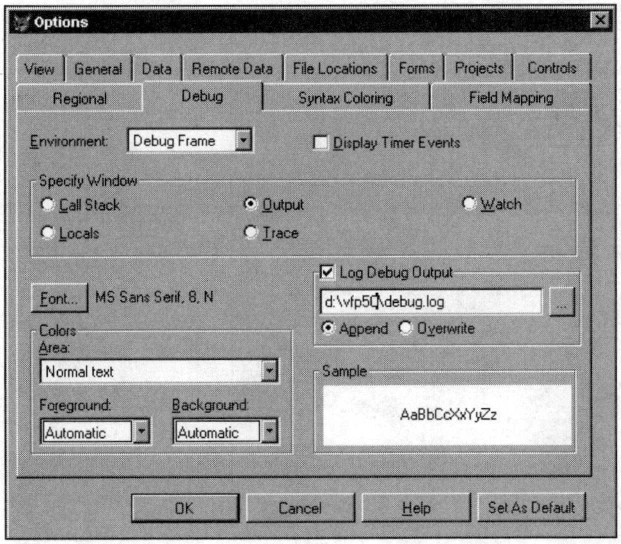

FIGURE 3-5

These debugging options for the Output window are available in the Options dialog box.

persistence between Visual FoxPro sessions, this option is always reset when a new session of Visual FoxPro is started. (This lack of persistence is by design, to avoid overwriting an existing log file in error.)

- Append—Selecting this option preserves the content of an existing log file by appending new information to the end of the log file.

- Overwrite—Selecting this option causes the log file to be replaced with new information from the current debugging session.

Trace Window Options

Figure 3-6 shows the Options dialog box with the Trace window specified.

- *Show line numbers*—Selecting this option allows the associated line number to be viewed at the left side of the Trace window. This is the same line number that is passed as the third parameter in the Error event.

- *Trace between breakpoints*—Selecting this option allows code between two points to be executed at the throttle speed. The only lines of code that execute with the delay are those that reside between two breakpoints. All other code is executed at normal speed.

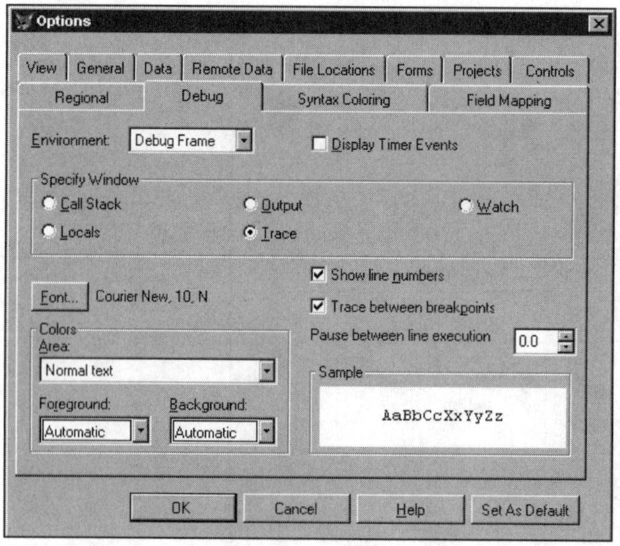

FIGURE 3-6

These debugging options for the Trace window are available in the Options dialog box.

- *Pause between line execution*—This is the throttle setting, which specifies the delay (in seconds) that Visual FoxPro waits before executing the next line of code.

A Final Word on Setting Options

As of version 3.0 of Visual FoxPro, settings made in the Options dialog box are stored in the Windows Registry. In order to have options set in one session available to all subsequent Visual FoxPro Sessions, the Set As Default button must be clicked. Clicking this button updates the Windows Registry and also adjusts the current environmental settings accordingly. On the other hand, clicking OK makes changes for the current Visual FoxPro Session only. Subsequent sessions revert to the settings stored in the Windows Registry.

> **NOTE:** The only exception to this rule is the setting for directing the contents of the Output window to a log file, which is always deselected when Visual FoxPro is restarted.

Now that the environmental housekeeping details have been addressed, it's time to dive into the details of how the Visual FoxPro debugging tools work. The remainder of this chapter focuses on the debugging windows, the toolbars associated with each of these windows, the debugger menu, and other debugging tools that are available to help you in your development efforts. As is the case with any aspect of Visual FoxPro, there are several ways to accomplish any given task. Typically, you can accomplish each task either by using a menu or by issuing code. Rather than treating the code elements separately, they are included along with the discussion of their respective window or tool.

Debugging Windows

The heart of Visual FoxPro's debugging capability lies within its collection of windows, as shown in Figure 3-7.

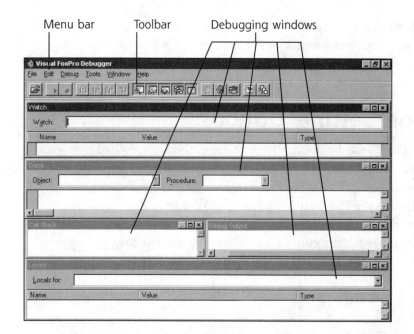

FIGURE 3-7

The new Visual FoxPro Debugger offers five debugging windows.

The following list summarizes the purpose of each window:

- Watch—This window allows you to display the results of expressions, and to place breakpoints when expressions change value. The base functionality of this window closely resembles that of the Debug window in version 3.0 of Visual FoxPro and versions 2.6 and earlier of FoxPro.

- Trace—The primary purpose of this window is to allow code execution one line at a time.

- Call Stack—This window displays a complete list of all currently running programs and methods.

- Locals—This window displays a list of all visible variables. It also acts as an object inspector, as visible properties of an object can be queried for their current values (and, if necessary, those values can be changed).

- Output—This window displays output as specified by the Debugout command as well as a listing of fired events if event tracking is enabled.

When the Debug Frame option is selected, each of these windows resides in the context of the Debugger window. When the FoxPro Frame option is selected, these windows reside in the context of the main Visual FoxPro window. As stated earlier, this chapter focuses on the Debug Frame option.

Activating the Debugger

There are several methods of activating the Debugger:

- Choose the Debugger option from the Tools menu.
- Enter the following code in the command window:

    Activate Window Debug

- Upon an assertion failure, click the Debug button in the Assertion Failure dialog box.
- Encounter a defined breakpoint that subsequently activates the Trace window.
- Issue the following command:

    Set Step On

However you choose to start the Visual FoxPro Debugger, it will prove to be an indispensable tool for creating effective enterprise applications.

The Debug Window Toolbar and Menu System

The Visual FoxPro Debugger is similar to most Windows applications in the variety of ways you can select options and activate features. The same system options can be accessed in a number of different ways:

- Choosing commands from the Debugger menu
- Right-clicking (clicking the right mouse button) to activate context-sensitive menus
- Clicking buttons on the Debugger toolbar

Rather than treating each method of using the Debugger as a separate topic, the rest of the chapter details the usage of all these methods, as appropriate.

Controlling the Appearance of the Debugger

You can configure the appearance of the Debugger to suit your needs, by controlling which windows are visible. The various debugging windows contained in the main Debugger window are actually toolbars; therefore, they can either float or be docked. Here's how to work with these windows:

- To display (or hide) a particular debugging window, select the window you want from the Window menu, or simply click the button representing that window on the Debugger toolbar. You also can right-click the Debugger window, then select a particular debugging window.

- To dock or undock a debugging window, right-click that window to activate a context-sensitive menu, then choose whichever Docking View option you desire for that window.

The Watch Window

As stated earlier in the chapter, the Watch window most closely resembles the Debug window that was included in previous versions of Visual FoxPro and FoxPro. Therefore, if you are experienced with debugging in previous versions, you basically know how to use the Watch window. The Watch window is just what the name says—it allows you to watch elements of your current Visual FoxPro session.

The Watch window has two basic purposes:

- Querying and changing the results of a Visual FoxPro expression
- Setting breakpoints to halt program execution

Watching Visual FoxPro Expressions

The above heading probably begs the question: What is a Visual FoxPro expression? Well, just about anything in Visual FoxPro is an expression. The following definition appears in the Visual FoxPro help file:

Expression: Any combination of variables, operators, constants, functions, and names of fields, controls, and properties that evaluates to a single value.

Therefore, all the Visual FoxPro expressions shown in Table 3-1 are valid.

Table 3-1 Examples of Visual FoxPro Expressions

Type	Representation	Possible Value
Function	`Date()`	`{01/01/96}`
Variable	`lcName`	`"Karl"`
Property	`Form1.Caption`	`"Customer Data Entry"`
Object	`txtState`	Object Reference of Properties and Methods
Field	`custnumber`	`500`
Complex	`lnPurch > 10000`	`.F.`

In reality, this list could go on forever, as there are endless combinations of expressions in Visual FoxPro. Simply put, expressions lie at the heart of any Visual FoxPro application. Many bugs in applications result either from the absence of a variable where one was expected, or from data type mismatches. In any case, an expression—or lack thereof—is involved. During the course of testing and debugging, you often might peer inside the workings of the application to see the values of certain expressions.

Figure 3-8 shows the Watch window with some expressions entered for viewing.

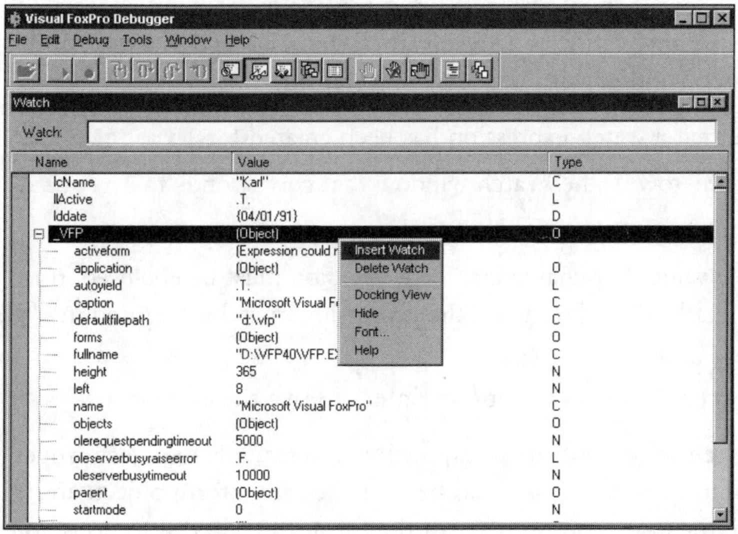

FIGURE 3-8

Here's a look at the Watch window and its shortcut menu.

To create a watch expression, all you need to do is enter the expression in the text box that appears at the very top of the Watch window. Once the expression has been entered, press the Enter key and the expression is added to the list below. Alternatively, right-click the Watch window to activate a context-sensitive menu, then choose the Insert Watch option. As another alternative, add watch expressions by dragging them directly from the editor or command window and dropping them inside the Watch window.

The first three variables in the Watch window are character, logical, and date type, respectively. These data types have always been supported by the Visual FoxPro Debug window. What deserves special attention is the fourth entry— this is the VFP application object, new to version 5.0. In addition to the capabilities already discussed, the Watch window is an object browser. When you add object variables to the Watch window, you can literally "drill down" to view all the exposed properties of a given object. To effectively debug, it is necessary to have ready access to all elements of an application. The Watch window certainly gives you this ready access.

Changing the Contents of an Expression

An additional feature of the Watch window is the ability to change the value of a variable. For example, assume a variable named `lnTotal` evaluates to 100.00, and you want to change it to 1000.00. While the value could be changed directly in the command window, it should be noted that the command window usually is unavailable while an application is active. Rather, the value of `lnTotal` can be changed in the Watch window with the following steps:

1. Make sure that a watch expression has been created for `lnTotal`.
2. Highlight the row in the Watch window that corresponds to `lnTotal`.
3. Click the contents under the Value column.
4. Type a new value. For characters, the expression must be enclosed in quotation marks (" "). For dates, the expression must be enclosed in curly braces ({ }).
5. After you type the new value, press Enter or leave the current row.

The ability to change the contents of an expression also extends to object properties. For example, if a watch expression has been created for a form object, and you want to change the `Caption` property of the form, all you need to do is go to the row in the Watch window that contains the `Caption` property, and use the steps listed above.

Creating Breakpoints

A *breakpoint* is nothing more than a defined position in a program at which program execution is halted and control is returned to you, the developer. Breakpoints also can be defined at specified times; specifically, you can halt program execution when the value of a certain variable changes. Figure 3-9 shows the Watch window with a defined breakpoint.

In order to create a breakpoint in the Watch window, double-click the gray bar at the left side of the window next to the variable you want to select. When the breakpoint is established, a small red dot appears. To remove the breakpoint, just double-click again so that the dot disappears.

In this example, program execution halts as soon as the value of `lcName` changes. When execution halts, you are presented with a dialog box specifying

This dot indicates that a breakpoint has been established.

Double-click this bar to establish or remove a breakpoint.

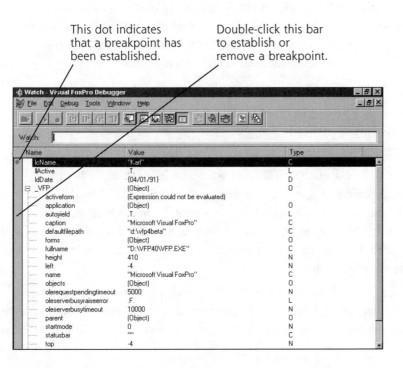

FIGURE 3-9

This Watch window has a breakpoint set on `lcName`.

why the program has halted. Once you have responded to the dialog box, the Trace window becomes active, highlighting the line of code where the variable changed value. At this time, you can step through the code one line at a time to debug the current problem. (The Trace window is discussed in more detail later in this chapter.)

> **TIP:** When at all possible, rely on using breakpoints to suspend code execution rather than placing direct Suspend or Set Step On commands in your code. By using breakpoints, you eliminate the need to search through your code to remove Suspend commands and Set Step On calls prior to delivering your application.

The Trace Window

As previously discussed, the primary job of the Trace window is to give you the ability to step through executing code a single line at a time. This is an invaluable resource for successful debugging. Unlike some of the debugging tools available in Visual FoxPro, the Watch window and Trace window are must-have items. Figure 3-10 shows an example of an active Trace window.

In this example, the Trace window is displaying method code contained in the Init() of a form. Aside from the main body of the window that displays the code, the Trace window has two main items:

- Object combo box—This combo box is available when tracing code within an object. Relative to objects whose code is currently being traced, a complete listing of all objects to the highest level in the containership hierarchy is listed. For example, if the code in a command button within a page, within a pageframe, and finally within a form, is being traced, the complete containership hierarchy relative to the command button is listed.

- Procedure combo box—This combo box is also available only when running object code. For every object listed in the Object combo box, a listing of methods for which code has been written is listed in this

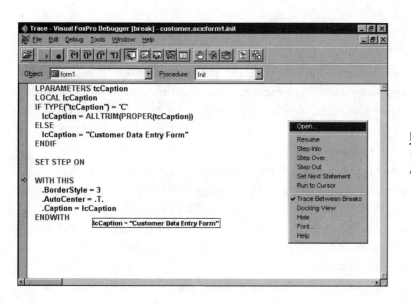

FIGURE 3-10

The Trace window is shown here in Step mode.

combo box. For example, if the `Click()` event for the command button is the only event for which code has been written, then when the command button is selected in the Object combo box, `Click()` is the only procedure available in the Procedure combo box. As another example, if the form has `Load()`, `Init()`, and `Destroy()` code, then those three procedures are listed in the Procedure combo box when the form is selected in the Object combo box.

Just as the Watch window has a context-sensitive menu, so does the Trace window. Most of the choices in this context-sensitive menu correspond to buttons contained in the Debug toolbar, and many of these choices also are contained on the Debug menu. The following list provides a description of the functionality of the first seven menu options on the context-sensitive menu:

- Open—This displays the standard Windows File Open dialog box for loading a program (PRG file) into the Trace window. Alternatives are choosing Open from the File menu of the Debugger, or clicking the first button in the Debugger toolbar.

- Resume—Program execution continues when you choose Resume. This corresponds to the second button in the Debugger toolbar.

- Step Into—This causes the next line of code to be executed. This corresponds to the fourth button in the Debugger toolbar.

- Step Over—When you reach a point where a procedure is going to be called, choosing Step Over prevents stepping through each line of code in the called procedure. (Although the lines are not stepped through, the procedure is still executed in its entirety.) This corresponds to the fifth button in the Debugger toolbar.

- Step Out—If you are currently stepping through code in a called procedure, this choice immediately exits you from stepping through the remaining code in the current procedure. Stepping through the code one line at a time continues with the next line of code in the next calling program in the program tree. This corresponds to the sixth button in the Debugger toolbar.

- Set Next Statement—This choice allows you to specify the next line of code to execute within the current procedure. While this does not have a toolbar equivalent, it is available as the last choice on the Debug menu.

- Run To Cursor—This choice forces program execution to continue to the line on which the cursor is positioned. Once this line is reached, program execution returns to Step mode. This corresponds to the seventh button in the Debugger toolbar.

In addition to the above functionality, you can cancel program execution in a number of ways:

- Click the third button in the Debug toolbar (represented by a red dot).
- Choose Cancel from the Debug menu.
- Enter the Cancel command in the Visual FoxPro command window.

To round out the Debug menu, the following other functions are available:

- Do—This choice loads a program into the Trace window and begins execution in Step mode.
- Fix—This choice cancels program execution and brings up the editor to facilitate fixing the line(s) of code containing bugs.
- Throttle—This choice presents a dialog box to the user to specify how long Visual FoxPro pauses between executed lines of code when in Step mode.

One final feature of the Trace window that merits discussion deals with the tooltip visible in Figure 3-10. When you position the mouse pointer over a variable in the Trace window, Visual FoxPro displays a tooltip that contains the value of the variable. In this case, lcCaption evaluates to "Customer Data Entry Form", so the tooltip text displays lcCaption = "Customer Data Entry Form".

> **TIP:** In order to get the most out of the Trace window, make sure that your path setting points to all your source code when running your application on the development machine. This way, when you need to activate the Trace window to step through code, you won't receive a Source Code Not Available message.

The Call Stack Window

The Call Stack window is the first debugging window covered in this chapter that is new to Visual FoxPro. The primary purpose of the Call Stack window is to display all the currently executing programs, procedures, and methods. Figure 3-11 shows an active Call Stack window in which a program named MAIN has called a form named MYFORM. The Init() event method code for MYFORM has a SUSPEND call to allow viewing of the call stack.

The listing in the Call Stack window is said to be in descending order, in that the currently running program appears first. Heading down the list, you are working your way up the program-calling chain, ultimately to the first program run in the application. In this example, you can see that the form's Init() event method code contains the currently running code. MAIN, which appears last in the list, was the first program executed. The program, procedure, or method pointed to by the yellow arrow is the currently executing code.

The numbers that appear next to the program names correspond to those used by the PROGRAM() function. For example, the call

```
?Program(2)
```

to the PROGRAM() function yields "FORM1.INIT". Passing 1 as an argument yields a return string of "MAIN".

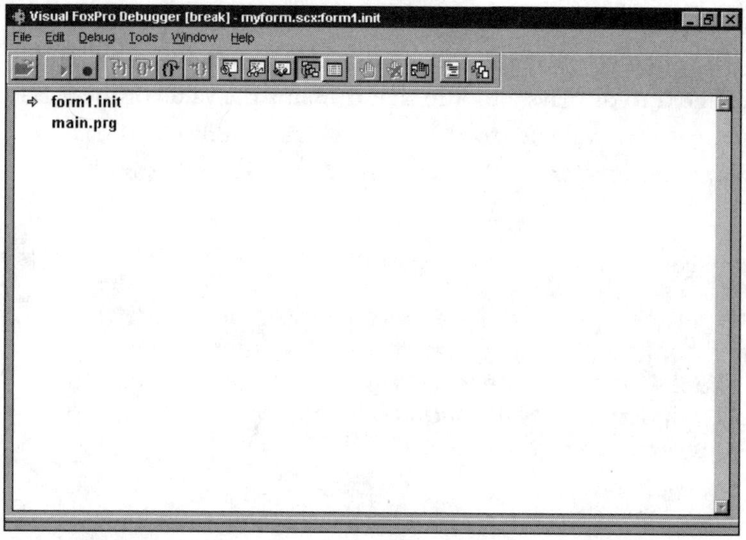

FIGURE 3-11

This is the Call Stack window.

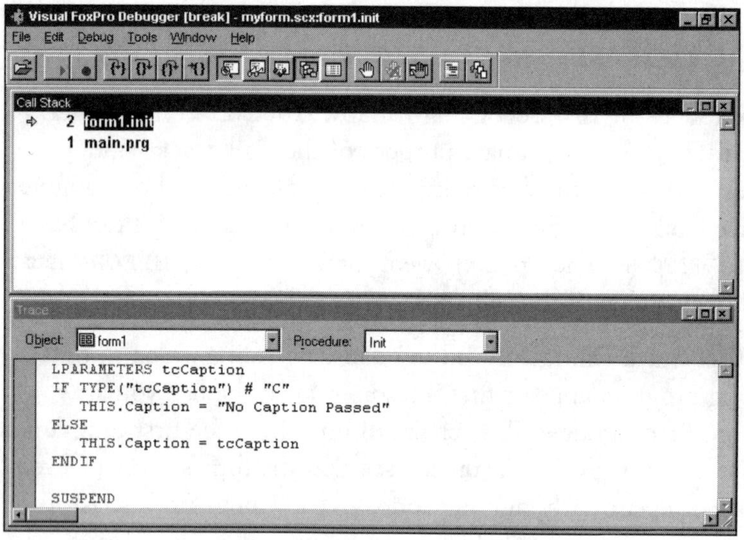

FIGURE 3-12

You can achieve powerful debugging by using the Call Stack and Trace windows in tandem.

The real power of the Call Stack window is especially evident when it is used in conjunction with the Trace window, as shown in Figure 3-12.

With the first program highlighted in the Call Stack window, you can see the code for the Init() of the form in the Trace window. When the MAIN program is highlighted, the Call Stack window appears as shown in Figure 3-13.

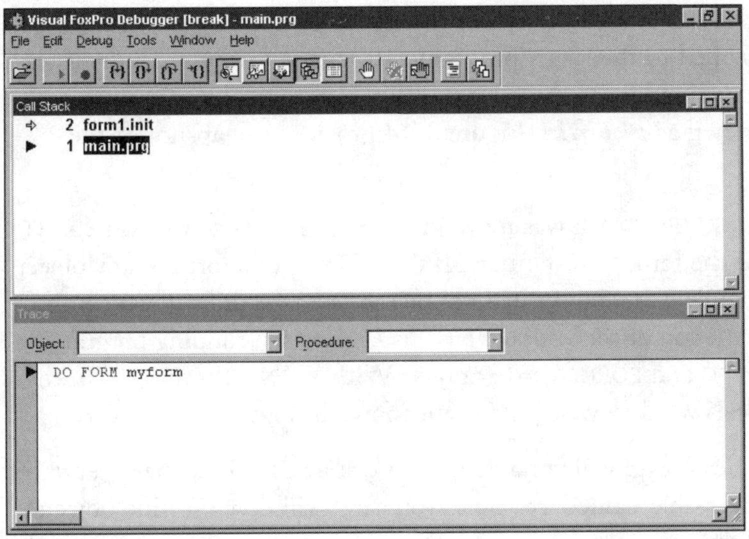

FIGURE 3-13

Here is the Call Stack window with MAIN.PRG *highlighted.*

With the MAIN program highlighted in the Call Stack window, the Trace window contains the code in MAIN.PRG. Notice the black arrow that appears in the Call Stack window. This arrow signifies which program is loaded in the Trace window. When the current running program is the same as what is contained in the Trace window, this black arrow does not appear.

There also is a black arrow in the Trace window. This arrow signifies the line of code last run in that procedure before control was passed to another program. Also keep in mind that the two combo boxes in the Trace window become available when a non-object program is contained in the window.

The Locals Window

At first glance, the Locals window and Watch window appear to be the same. While they contain much of the same information, they serve very different purposes. The primary function of the Locals window is to allow the viewing of variables, arrays, and objects that have scope within a given program. The values of variables in the Locals window can be changed using the same steps outlined in the preceding discussion of the Watch window.

Again, using a slightly expanded version of the earlier example, you can have variables that are scoped to the MAIN program and scoped to the Init() of MYFORM, respectively. In addition, because MYFORM is a form object, it possesses many attributes, known as *properties*. Figure 3-14 provides a snapshot of the Locals window.

In this example, the SUSPEND call was moved from the Init() to the Refresh() of the form to allow the form to instantiate. If the Init() of a form or any object is not allowed to complete, the object will not be created. The drop-down combo box that appears at the top of the window has entries for each running program—in this case, MAIN.PRG and FORM1.Refresh(). With MAIN.PRG selected in this combo box, the Locals window yields the result shown in Figure 3-15.

This example includes one global variable named gdDateTime, a character variable, and an object variable named loForm. You can "drill down" inside objects in the Locals window just as you can in the Watch window.

While this capability is nice, you still are left with an incomplete picture. For a debugger to be powerful, it must allow you to view all aspects of your environment, including the program call stack, variables, and program code. By combining the functionality of the Call Stack, Trace, and Locals windows, you can begin to take full advantage of Visual FoxPro's debugging facilities, as shown in Figure 3-16.

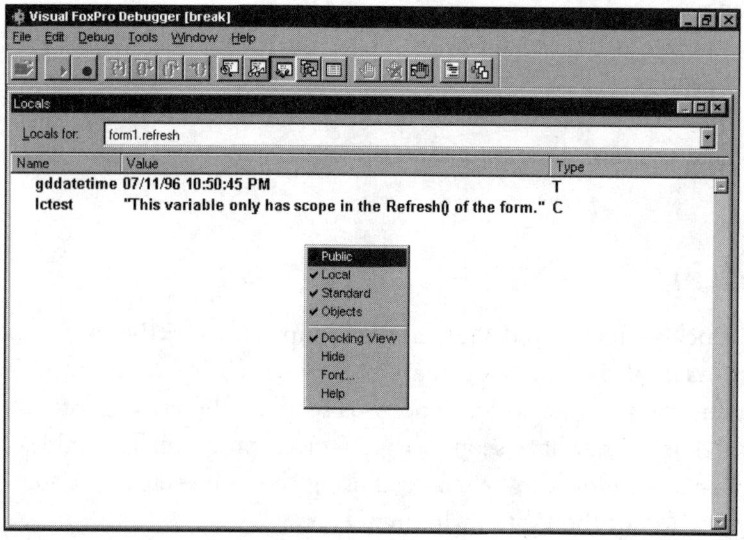

FIGURE 3-14

This is the Locals window with its shortcut menu.

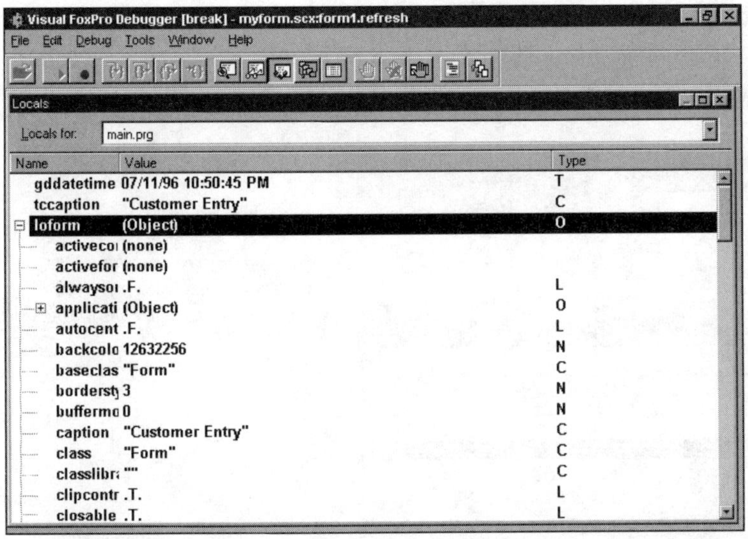

FIGURE 3-15

The Locals window shows the object reference expanded.

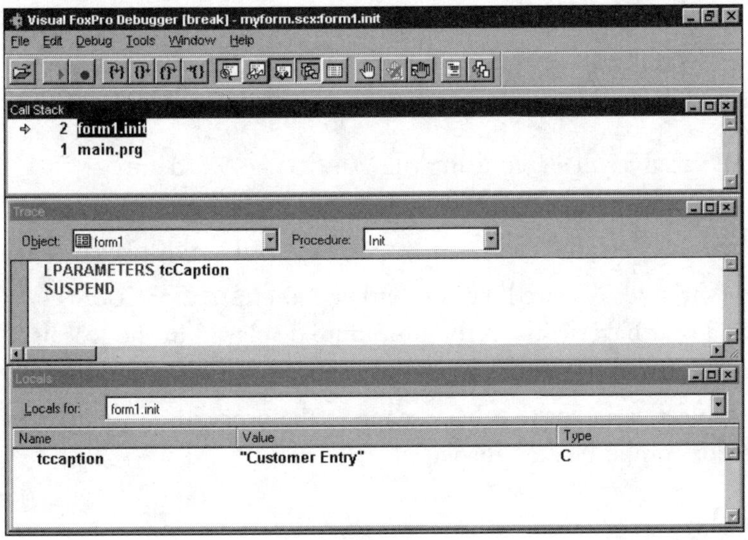

FIGURE 3-16

The Call Stack, Trace, and Locals windows together offer you powerful debugging capabilities.

Now you are starting to get a full picture of the situation. You know which program or procedure is running, the code that makes up each program or procedure, and any variables that have scope within that program or procedure. When you navigate up and down the Call Stack window, the contents of the other windows change as well, as shown in Figure 3-17.

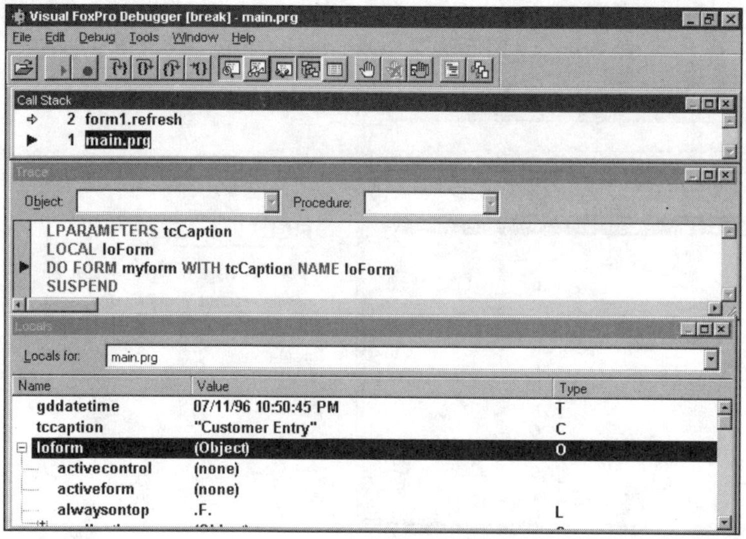

FIGURE 3-17

Navigating up and down the Call Stack window affects the contents of the other windows.

The context-sensitive menu for the Locals window allows you to filter which variables are visible. The following list outlines the options and their actions:

- Public—All variables declared using the PUBLIC keyword are displayed.

- Local—Variables declared using the LOCAL keyword are displayed.

- Standard—Variables declared without either the PUBLIC or LOCAL keyword, and that have scope in the procedure displayed in the Locals For combo box, are displayed.

- Objects—Object variables that have scope in the procedure displayed in the Locals For combo box are displayed.

The Output Window

The final window to discuss is the Output window. The primary purpose of the Output window is to provide the ability to display debugging output from programs, procedures, or methods. In addition, you can choose to have the name of system events echoed to the Output window as they occur. You can learn more about the event-tracking capabilities of the Output window later in this chapter.

For now, however, the discussion will concentrate on echoing messages to the Output window through the use of the Debugout command.

The purpose of this command, new to Visual FoxPro, is to direct the results of an expression to the Output window. With the Debug window open and the Output window visible, enter the following in the command window:

```
Debugout Datetime()
```

This command yields the result shown in the Output window in Figure 3-18.

To further demonstrate the use of the Output window, assume that you have a form that accepts one parameter, which in turn is assigned to the Caption property of the form. When the parameter is a character data type, all is fine and the Caption property of the form takes on whatever is contained in the parameter. When the parameter is another data type, however, you need to make note of what the parameter is. A simple way to do this is to echo what happens to the Output window. Look at the following code, contained in the Init() of the form:

```
Lparameters tcCaption
If Type("tcCaption") = 'C'
   This.Caption = tcCaption
Else
   Debugout "Passed parameter to form was:"
   Debugout tcCaption
   Return .F.
Endif
```

If you call the form using

```
Do Form test
```

then the Output window yields the result shown in Figure 3-19.

It is important to note that, unless the Output window is active, messages will not be directed to the Output window, even if the Output window is subsequently activated. This is a good safeguard. If you have situations that need to be monitored in delivered applications, then the Debugout calls can remain in the application code. Since your clients do not have the Visual FoxPro development

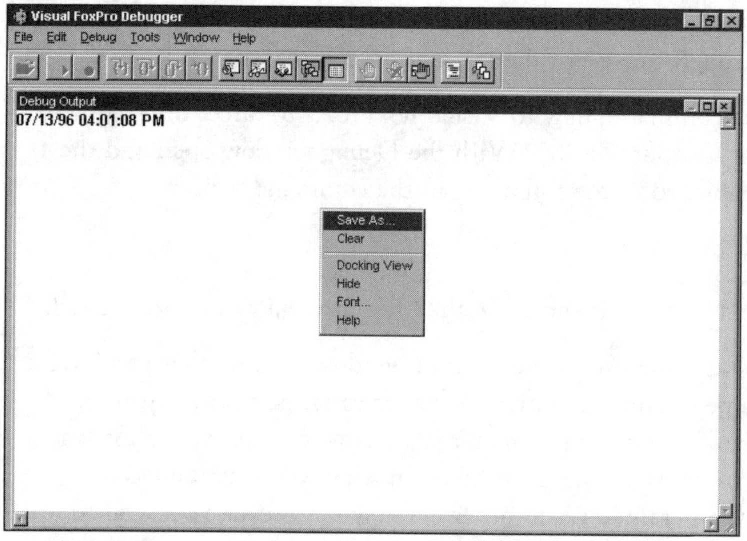

FIGURE 3-18

The Debug Output window here has its shortcut menu activated.

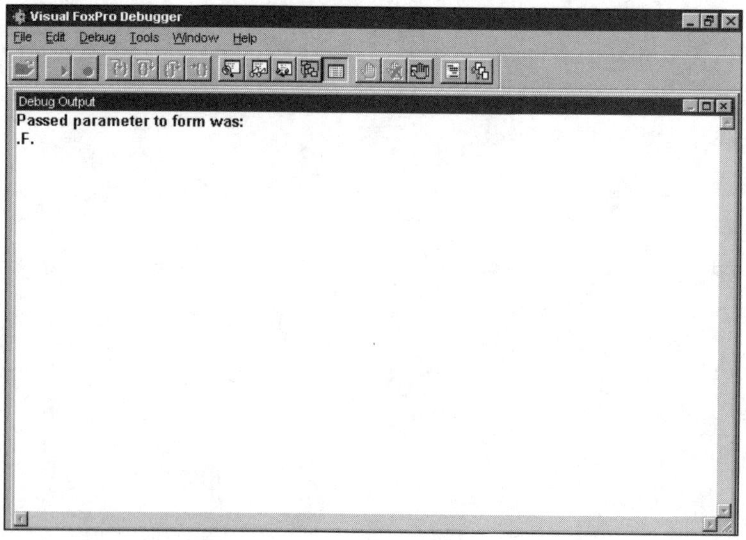

FIGURE 3-19

This Output window shows the value of the passed parameter.

environment, they do not have access to the Output window. In short, your clients need never know about the existence of such code.

Like the other debugging windows, the Output window has a context-sensitive menu. The following list highlights the functionality unique to the Output window:

- Save As—When you choose Save As, a standard Windows Save As dialog box is displayed. From here, you can save the contents of the Output window to a text file.

- Clear—When necessary, you can erase the entire contents of the Output window by choosing Clear.

Other Debugging Tools

In addition to the debugging windows, several other Visual FoxPro debugging tools are at your disposal. These include breakpoints, the code coverage log, the event tracking log, and assertion testing.

The Breakpoints Dialog Box

As previously discussed, a breakpoint is nothing more than a defined position in a program at which program execution is halted and control is returned to the developer. You can activate the Breakpoints dialog box by choosing Breakpoints on the Debugger Tools menu, or by choosing the Breakpoints Dialog button (third button from the left) on the Debugger toolbar.

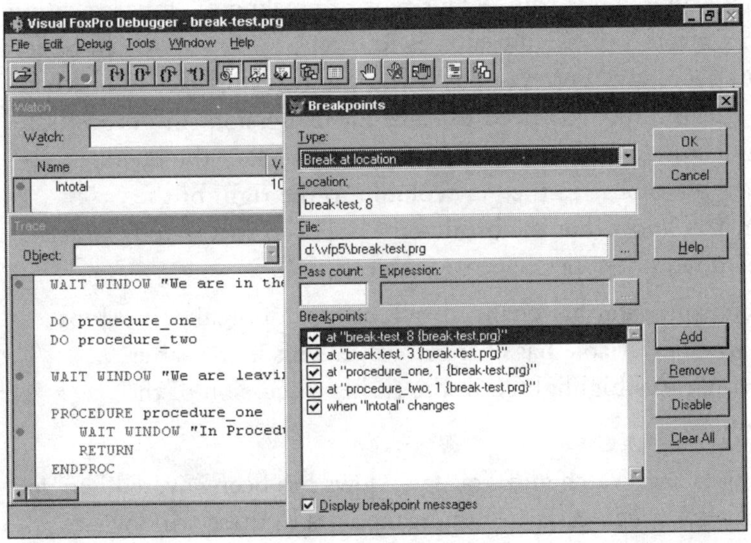

FIGURE 3-20

The Breakpoints dialog box helps you work with any breakpoints you desire.

In the example shown in Figure 3-20, the Watch and Trace windows are visible in addition to the Breakpoints dialog box. As you can see in the Watch window, a breakpoint has been set for whenever the value of lnTotal changes. In addition, several breakpoints have been set in the program that is loaded in the Trace window. All these breakpoints can be viewed in the Breakpoints dialog box. These breakpoints have persistence in that they will remain active between different sessions of Visual FoxPro, until they are removed or disabled.

You can set four types of breakpoints in the Breakpoints dialog box:

- Break at location—This type of breakpoint stops execution of code at a specified line. This is the same breakpoint that was highlighted in the earlier discussion of the Trace window.

- Break at location if expression is true—This type of breakpoint allows you to conditionally stop execution at a line of code only when a given expression is true. For example, you can stop execution at line 5 of a program only if the value of a certain numeric variable is greater than 5000. You can set this type of breakpoint in the Watch window, as well. To examine the syntax for the expression, assume that you want to stop execution at line 5 of MAIN.PRG only if x is greater than 5000. You need to place the following expression in the Trace window:

(PROGRAM() = "MAIN" AND LINENO()=5 AND x > 5000)

- Break when expression is true—This type of breakpoint stops execution only when a given expression evaluates to true. This type also can be set in the Watch window. For example, if you want to stop execution when lnTotal equals 5000, you need to place the expression **(lntotal=5000)** in the Watch window and place a breakpoint. To place the breakpoint, double-click the mouse in the gray column to the right of the expression. You know that the breakpoint has been successfully added when a small red dot appears next to the expression.

- Break when expression has changed—This type of breakpoint stops execution when a variable has changed value. This is the same breakpoint that was highlighted in the earlier discussion of the Watch window.

Creating breakpoints in the Watch and Trace windows has been covered here for the sake of simplicity. It's much easier to set breakpoints in these windows as

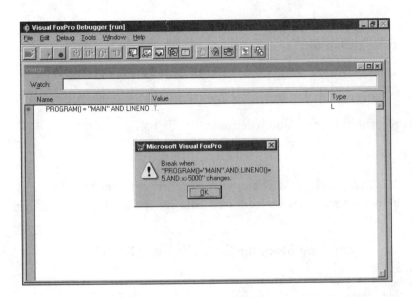

FIGURE 3-21

This message box notifies the developer that a break has occurred based on the specified expression.

opposed to the Breakpoints dialog box. The two key functions of the Breakpoints dialog box are as follows:

- To allow the disabling of breakpoints without having to redefine them
- To allow you to toggle on and off your preference for whether a message box is displayed when a breakpoint takes effect. The check box for this setting is in the lower-left portion of the Breakpoints dialog box. Figure 3-21 shows an example message box notifying the developer that a break has occurred.

The Code Coverage Log

With the release of Visual FoxPro 5.0, you now have native *code coverage logging* capabilities. Code coverage logging gives you the ability to document which lines of code actually execute, as well as how long each line takes to execute. Before you can determine if a program or class is totally bug-free, you must first ensure that each line of code has executed at least once. While this check does not ensure bug-free code, it's a step in the right direction.

To begin the process of logging code coverage, you must first specify a log file that will contain data related to the code you want to analyze. There are two methods for specifying such a file:

- The Set Coverage To cLogFile [Additive] command
- The Code Coverage dialog box

In code, for example, the following line specifies a log file named CODE:

```
Set Coverage To code.log
```

If you include the ADDITIVE clause, any contents currently contained in the specified log file are not overwritten; instead, new data is appended to the end of the specified file.

Alternatively, you can specify a log file in the Code Coverage dialog box, as shown in Figure 3-22.

You can activate this dialog box by choosing Coverage Logging from the Tools menu in the Debugger, or by clicking the Toggle Coverage Logging button on the Debugger toolbar. Once you designate the log file, code coverage starts automatically when the next program is run. To illustrate, when the following program code has been executed, the CODE.LOG file will contain data outlining which lines of code were executed:

```
Lparameters tcCountry
If Type("tcCountry") = "C"
   Select * ;
      From customer ;
      Where country = tcCountry ;
      Into Cursor cCustTemp
      MessageBox(Alltrim(Str(_Tally)) + " customers were selected.")
Endif
```

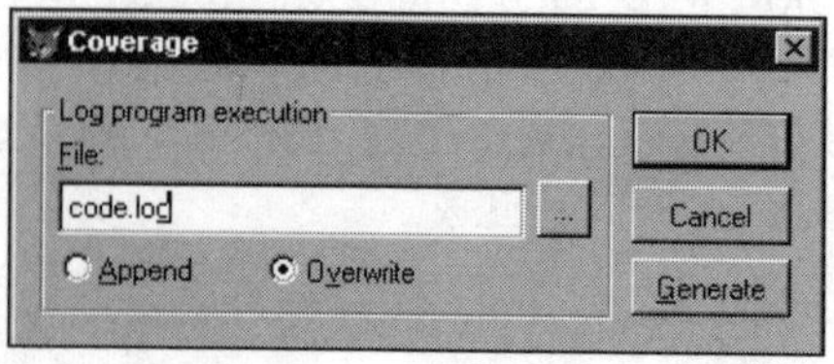

FIGURE 3-22

This is the Code Coverage dialog box specifying a coverage file named CODE.LOG.

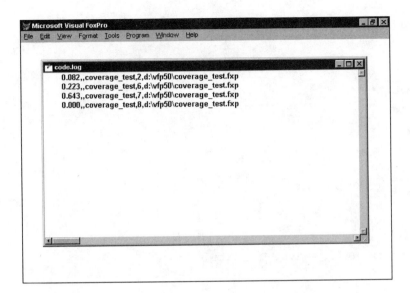

FIGURE 3-23

These are the contents of the CODE.LOG file.

This example uses the customer table in the Tastrade database that ships with Visual FoxPro. Once the coverage log file has been specified, and the program code has executed, the CODE.LOG file contains data. Before viewing the file, however, you must issue the following command to allow access to the file:

```
Set Coverage To
```

Figure 3-23 shows the contents of the CODE.LOG file.

While this data is readable, it can be converted into a more useful format. A new environmental variable, COVERAGE, has been added to Visual FoxPro 5.0. This variable points to a program that formats the log data in a more helpful way. By default, this program is named COVERAGE.APP. This code is invoked automatically when you click the Generate button in the Code Coverage dialog

TIP: This code is on the accompanying CD-ROM in a program named COVERAGE.PRG.

box. The following code takes the raw log data and appends it to a Visual Fox-Pro DBF file:

```
Local lcFile
lcFile = Putfile("","","DBF")
If !Empty(lcFile)
  Create Table (lcFile) ;
     (duration n(7,3),;
     class c(30),;
     procedure c(60),;
     line i,;
     file c(100))
  Append From Getfile("log") Type Delimited
Endif
```

Figure 3-24 shows how the resulting table looks.

The following list highlights what each column of data represents:

- Duration—This specifies how long the line of code took to execute. If the value is zero, the line did not execute.

- Class—This specifies the class the line of code is contained within, if an object is involved.

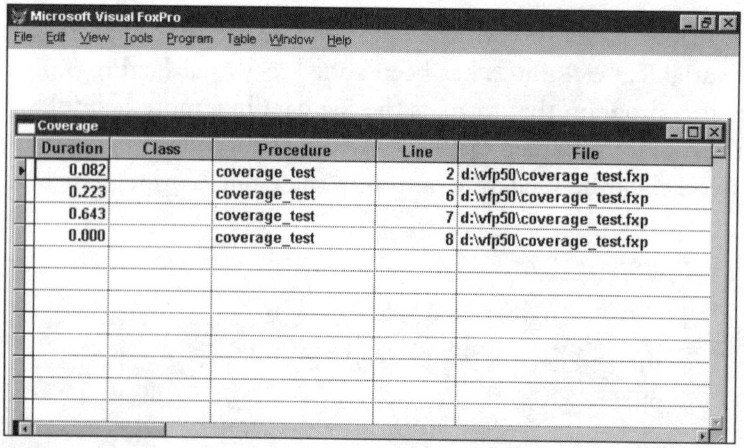

FIGURE 3-24

The code coverage output has been loaded into a DBF file.

- Procedure—This specifies which procedure or method contains the line of code.
- Line—This specifies the line number of the code.
- File—This specifies which file on disk the code belongs to.

The Event Tracking Log

In the debugging process, it's often necessary to know the sequence of events that fire. Many times, you can fix a bug by moving the code from one event method to another. Tracking events is a two-step process. First, you must specify which events you want tracked. Second, you must turn on the process of tracking those specific events. The Event Tracking dialog box, shown in Figure 3-25, is where you can perform these two operations.

Events can be echoed to a log file and to the Output window in the Debugger. Even if the Debugger Output Window check box is selected, however, this

TIP: You also can use the Set EventTracking command to activate event tracking and select the events to be tracked.

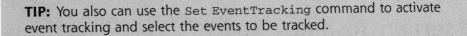

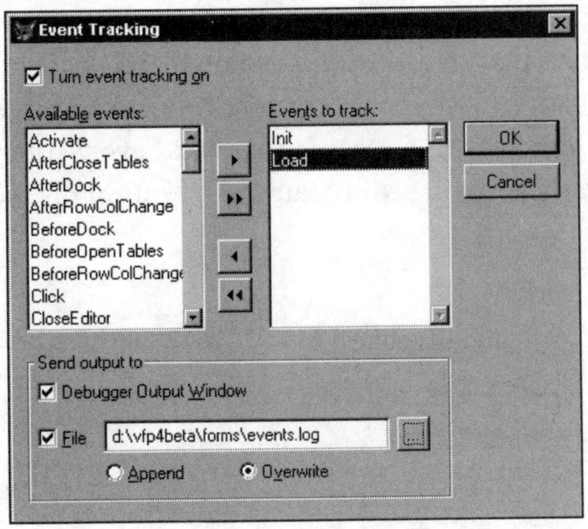

FIGURE 3-25

The Event Tracking dialog box lets you call upon Visual FoxPro's event tracking capabilities.

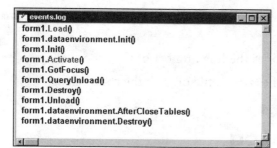

FIGURE 3-26

You can learn a lot by reviewing the event tracking log output.

setting is ignored whenever the Output window is inactive. Figure 3-26 shows an example of a log file generated when events are tracked.

> **TIP:** Because events such as MouseMove and Paint occur so frequently—and because code is rarely attached to such events—it's a good idea to avoid selecting these events for tracking.

Assertion Testing

Another useful debugging facility added to Visual FoxPro in version 5.0 is native *assertion testing*. The purpose of assertion tests is to provide feedback to the developer whenever a particular expression evaluates to false. If an expression evaluates to false, it means that a given assertion has failed and that something should be done to fix the situation. The most common form of such testing relates to parameter passing. For example, assume that you have written a black-box routine or class that accepts a number of parameters. You might include the following code:

```
Lparameters tnParameter

If Type("tnParameter") # "N" && Numeric

   *** Go ahead and take corrective action

Endif

** Main function code

Return
```

While it often is fine to take corrective action, there are cases in which taking corrective action is unacceptable, such as where a function must always receive the proper data type for its parameter(s). Assertion testing provides you with immediate notification of such situations during testing and debugging.

In Visual FoxPro 5.0, two new items have been added to the language:

- `Assert`—This command displays a message box when the specified expression evaluates to false.
- `Set Asserts (On/Off)`—This new `Set` setting globally activates/deactivates assertion testing. All `Assert` calls are ignored when `Set Assert` is `Off`.

The preceding code can be updated as follows to take advantage of this new feature:

```
lparameters tnParameter
Assert Type("tnParameter") = "N" && Numeric

** Main function code

Return
```

If the function is called with an improper parameter, the assertion fails. When this happens, provided `Set Assert` is `On`, the dialog box shown in Figure 3-27 appears.

You can take the following four actions from this dialog box:

- Debug—Program execution is suspended and the Debugger window is brought forward with the Trace window active.
- Cancel—Program execution is immediately ended.
- Ignore—Program execution is continued with the line following the `Assert` command.

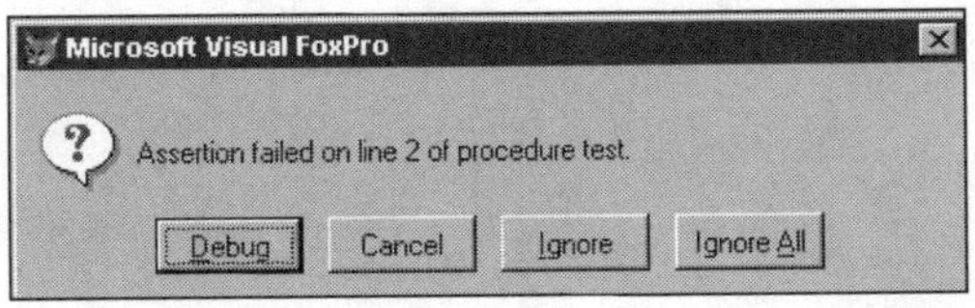

FIGURE 3-27

This dialog box informs you of an assertion failure.

- Ignore <u>A</u>ll—Effectively, this button is equivalent to `Set Asserts Off`. Any subsequent assertion failures are ignored until you turn assertion testing on again.

It is important to note that assertion testing is for developers only. When your application is delivered, asserts should be set off.

Summary

Hopefully, it is apparent at this point that Visual FoxPro 5.0 has extremely robust debugging facilities. Like all tools, the Debugger can only be of value to the extent that you use it and leverage its capabilities. Now that you understand the role of debugging in the development cycle, you'll find it invaluable to incorporate the Debugger in your everyday development efforts. You should view the process of debugging as an incremental process that occurs *during* application development, not afterward.

You have seen how the five debugging windows, although each is distinct in its own functionality, complement each other to provide a suite of debugging tools. To round out this suite, Visual FoxPro also provides code coverage logging, event tracking, and assertion testing capabilities. Taken collectively, these tools help you find bugs fast, fix the problems, and rapidly continue with application development.

Chapter 4

Integrating Visual FoxPro and Object-Oriented Programming

Introduction

Since the earliest days of computers, software developers have striven to develop applications that are robust and bug-free. One method that developers have used from the beginning is to create reusable pieces of code. In the early days, these pieces of code were known as *subroutines*. The creation of these subroutines allowed developers to call the subroutines from different places in their applications, without needing to create the same code from scratch each time. These subroutines eventually grew into discrete functions and procedures, and most recently have been wrapped into *application programming interfaces (APIs)*. The latest manifestation of this desire to reuse code—and probably the most significant aspect of developing code—is known as object-oriented programming.

What is Object-Oriented Programming?

While it has always been the desire of developers to develop a function or procedure and use it many times, *object-oriented programming (OOP)* means developing from the ground up with the greatest possible reuse in mind. The goal of object-oriented development is to define a set of reusable components and tools that you can use throughout your applications. This definition of a set of tools comprises object-oriented development. You create stand-alone components with which applications and other components can communicate through a defined public interface. The following section goes into detail about the different mechanisms used in object-oriented development to create these components, and how to integrate object-oriented components into your applications.

Understanding Object-Oriented Terminology

OOP is full of new terms. The easiest way to learn about object-oriented programming in general is to examine the terminology it uses. As you look at these terms, they may seem confusing at first. On close inspection, however, you'll find that this new set of terminology meshes well with terms you already know.

Class

The basis for object-oriented development is to construct new applications from pre-developed components. In order to use these components, you need to design them, and then implement the design. When you implement your design, you create what is known as a *class*. Classes are the blueprints that you can use to develop new applications.

In Chapter 2, "Analysis, Design, and Prototyping," you learned about the CRC approach to object development. The CRC approach recommends that you take your design document and break it into nouns. These nouns then go on to become your classes. Classes are used to describe these objects and the actions that can be performed on them. Classes are commonly broken into two areas: properties and methods. Properties are the data components of an object, methods are the code components.

Property

Properties are the adjectives that you can use to describe an object. Using a command button as an example, its properties might include the following: height, width, font, and caption of the button.

Method

If properties are the adjectives that can be used to describe an object, then methods are the verbs. *Methods* describe the different actions that can be performed by an object. You commonly call these methods using *<object>.<method>* syntax. Using a customer record as an example, its methods might include the following: `add()`, `edit()`, `delete()`, and `print()`.

Class Library

When you create a set of classes, you commonly organize them into functional categories. Generally you create *class libraries* for the following: your base classes, application-specific classes, application module classes, specialized components, and any other methods that are useful for organizing the management and use of classes.

Encapsulation

One of the basic foundations of object-oriented programming is the concept of *encapsulation*. In older, procedural languages data and code were separate entities. With object-oriented technologies, the data and code are packaged together in entities known as *objects*. When you create an object, it has its own set of data along with code that can operate on its data. The only thing the developer needs to worry about is the object's *public interface*. The public interface determines which code and data belonging to that object can be accessed from the outside world. Encapsulation is one of the major advantages of object-oriented programming.

By providing a public interface and hiding the details of an object, developers can change objects so that they perform completely differently without affecting any other code. This works much like your television set does. All that you, the user, know is that you can turn the TV on or off, change the volume, and adjust the color. How the TV actually shows a picture is unknown to you. This allows TV manufacturers to change the way televisions work inside without having to teach you a new interface.

Polymorphism

With object-oriented technology, you can define different objects with similar public interfaces. It is known as *polymorphism* when two objects have identical interfaces and potentially different implementations. For instance, you might create an invoice object and a purchase order object such that each has a public "print document" interface. With this in place, you can hand an object to a generic document printing routine. When the object is handed to the printing routine, it can call the "print document" interface of the document. Each of these objects shares the same interface, but has its own implementation.

This concept of *polymorphism* is much like the GUI design principle "Be consistent" that was discussed in Chapter 1, "Establishing Development Standards." To print a document in Windows, you choose File, Print from the specific application's menu. How each application actually prints its document is hidden from the user.

Inheritance

In the early days of software development, you commonly programmed API functions that could be called from different parts of your applications. If you wanted to change these functions, you had two choices. The first was to create a new "wrapper" function around the old function, resulting in a new public interface. The second was to change the code directly, possibly causing unforeseen side effects.

This is where the real power of object-oriented programming comes in. One of the most powerful aspects of object-oriented programming is a technology known as *inheritance*, which allows you to define a new object from the definition of another object. This allows you to extend, alter, or completely change the functionality of an object without causing changes to the public interface or resulting in unforeseen side effects. All you do is create a new class based on the definition of another, then add your own specialized code without ever changing the other object's functionality.

Subclass

When you inherit from another class, the new class definition is known as a *subclass*.

Class Hierarchy

When you create a class library, it is not uncommon for your base classes to be inherited by multiple subclasses. This inheritance is known as a *class hierarchy*. When you develop applications, the *base classes* you develop commonly have subclasses that are inherited from that base class. As soon as you inherit from a class, you have created a class hierarchy. A class hierarchy is like a family tree in that it maps the inheritance of an object from itself to its parents, to its parents' parents, and so on.

Containership Hierarchy

One of the most confusing aspects of Visual FoxPro is the distinction between class hierarchies and containership hierarchies. While class hierarchies deal with inheritance, *containership hierarchies* deal with forms, pageframes, containers, and other classes capable of hosting controls such as buttons, edit boxes, and combo boxes. In Visual FoxPro, a command button or option group cannot exist in the runtime environment without a form being present. The form is a container that contains the command button or option group. The form is the parent and the control is the child. One item of note is that the main Visual FoxPro screen is a member of the frm base class; therefore, a command button can be placed directly on the screen.

Now that you understand many of the terms related to object-oriented development, you can begin the process of creating your own class definitions.

Creating Classes with Visual FoxPro

Armed with the key concepts of object-oriented development, you can begin to develop your own reusable set of classes. As with most features of Visual FoxPro, there is more than one way to create a class: visually or with code. This section discusses both methods, focusing on the distinct advantages and disadvantages of each.

Creating Classes the Visual Way

The first method of class creation you should explore is the visual method. Creating your classes visually is the fastest way to become familiar with Visual FoxPro's class design tools. The primary tool for creating a class definition is the Class Designer, which is similar to the Form Designer in many respects. In both of these design tools, you have a set of toolbars that you can use to add controls, set colors, specify alignment of controls, and perform other useful visual functions. There are some differences between the two tools, however. The Form Designer provides features specific to form design, such as a data environment and the ability to switch between run and design modes interactively. The Class Designer is a tool for creating tools, so you do not have a data environment or interactive run/design mode capabilities. What you have is a tool that can be used to create a useful and robust set of design components.

Where to Begin

The first steps you take in any new venture are often the most difficult. The developers at Microsoft have made the transition into object-oriented development quite easy. To begin your first journey into the object-oriented world, just follow these steps:

1. Go into the Form Designer and add some controls to your form.

2. Select the controls with the mouse.

3. Choose File, Save As Class from the Visual FoxPro menu. Visual FoxPro presents the Save As Class dialog box (see Figure 4-1). This dialog box allows you to specify three items: the name of the class, the class library in which to store the class, and a text description of the class.

4. Click View Classes, Add from the Form Controls toolbar. This lets you save the class in a class library so you can use the class later. After you have added the class library to the Form Controls toolbar, you can begin using the newly defined classes on your forms.

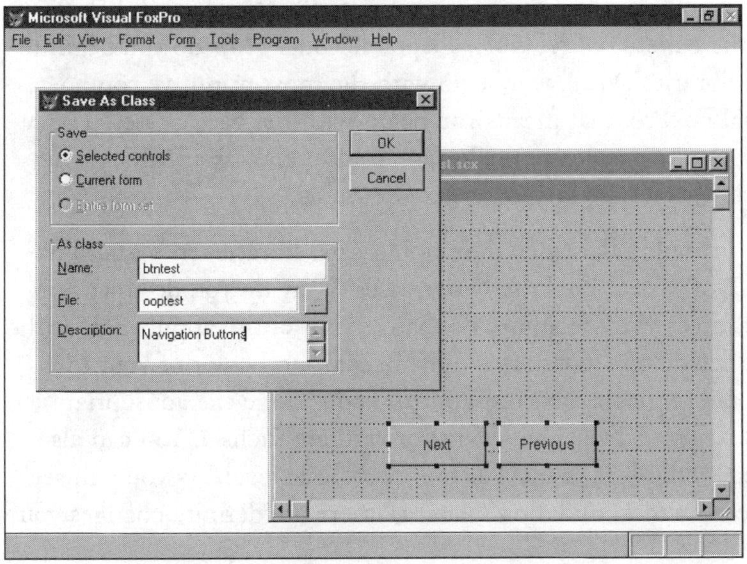

FIGURE 4-1

The Save As Class dialog box with class options defined.

Creating Class Libraries

The example from the previous section illustrates the most basic method of creating your own classes; however, this is just the first step. When you create your own set of useful class libraries, you will divide them into functional sets of libraries. For instance, you might have a set of base classes, a set of form widgets, a set of data-controlling classes, and a set of application-specific classes. It becomes especially important to divide your class libraries into functional sets when you are working with more than one developer. It is extremely difficult to manage a process where two developers are trying to maintain classes in the same library.

You can create class libraries using two different methods. The first is to enter **CREATE CLASSLIB** *<library name>* in the command window. The next method is to either choose File, Save As Class from the Visual FoxPro menu, or enter **CREATE CLASS** from the command window. After performing either of these actions, you specify the new class library name (in the File or Store in option, respectively). When you finish, you have a new class library in which to store your class definitions.

Creating Your First Class Library

As mentioned at the beginning of this chapter, the benefits of object-oriented programming do not come for free. You need to invest in a set of useful class libraries to obtain the benefits of reusable, adaptable code. How do you begin to develop these class libraries? Well, you begin with the most primitive components first. In Visual FoxPro, that means you begin with the base classes. The Visual FoxPro base classes constitute the lowest form of class from which you can inherit. They sometimes are known as *ancestor classes*.

The first action you should take when developing class libraries in Visual FoxPro is to subclass all of Visual FoxPro's base classes. Why do you do this? Subclassing all controls gives you the ability to change your entire application at the global level. If you decide one day to make the background color of your text boxes fuchsia, you can go to the text box control and change the appropriate setting so that all text boxes from that point forward are fuchsia. You can also add new properties, methods, and code at the most basic level. As you will see in Chapter 5, "The FoxPro Foundation Classes," there are definite changes you will want to make at this primitive level. You can subclass the following Visual FoxPro base classes:

CheckBox	FormSet[†]	OleControl
ComboBox	Grid	PageFrame
CommandButton	Image	Separator
CommandGroup	Label	Shape
Container[†]	ListBox	Spinner
Control	OptionButton	TextBox
Custom	OptionGroup	Timer
Form[†]	OleBoundControl	Toolbar

When you create this first set of classes, use the naming conventions prescribed in Chapter 1, "Establishing Development Standards." There are two main reasons for using these conventions: first, it makes your code more readable, and second, it makes it easier to see what type of control something is inherited from.

After subclassing all your controls, you can begin making alterations to them, such as specifying default fonts, colors, and sizes. You also can add code to these base classes. Currently, a common tactic for Visual FoxPro developers is to add *workaround code* to these objects, since Visual FoxPro cannot include all the functionality that developers may require in its base classes. Some of the most common workarounds at this time include augmenting the Refresh() method of the pageframe and combo box controls, and specifying the font type, size, and height for the text box control.

The PageFrame control has a slight problem. Whenever the Refresh() method is called, only the active page is refreshed. Why is this? Well, if you have a complex form with many controls on it, you might not want Visual FoxPro to refresh these controls automatically. Common knowledge dictates that this isn't the case for everyone, so Microsoft allows you to change how the Refresh() method of

---

[†] These are Visual FoxPro container classes (specifically, classes that host other controls). Option groups, command groups, grids, and so on are considered primitive, even though they can host other controls.

the PageFrame control behaves. Inserting the following code in the `Refresh()` method of the `PageFrame` base class overcomes the problem by refreshing all pages whenever `Refresh()` is called:

```
*-- Refresh all pages of a pageframe when refresh msg
*-- is received.
Local lnKount, lnPages
lnPages = This.Pagecount

For lnKount = 1 TO lnPages
    This.Pages(lnKount).Refresh()
Endfor
```

The second augmentation to the base classes is to add the following code to the `Refresh()` method of the `ComboBox` base class.

```
This.Requery()
```

This code fixes a problem with the combobox control. When a new record is added to a combobox control's `RowSource`, the control does not automatically refresh itself. The above code works around this problem.

The last change to the base classes is to change the `FontName`, `FontSize`, `FontBold`, and `Height` properties of the textbox control. Here are the recommended settings for these:

```
FontName = Courier New
FontSize = 9 pt
FontBold = .f.
Height = 22 points
```

After changing these properties of the textbox control, you can specify the size of the field accurately. The majority of fonts developed for Windows are known as *proportionally spaced fonts*. This means that all letters are printed and displayed in proportion, with the widest letter being W and the narrowest letter being I. The problem with proportional spacing is that the text boxes you show on-screen might not include enough space for the letters that can be input by the end user. The above property settings remove this problem. Courier New is a non-proportionally-spaced font, allowing developers to specify the exact width of a text box. The above settings allow you to add another specification to your GUI standards. Now, text boxes can have their width calculated by using the following formula: (number of characters × 7 pixels) + 10 pixels. A 10-character field, for example, would have a width of 80 pixels: (10 × 7) + 10.

As you can see, three minor modifications of the base classes can bring a lot of new functionality and quality to your applications.

Creating Your First Functional Class

Now that you have created your set of base classes, you can begin creating your first functional set of useful classes. Simply having a set of low-level base classes is not enough—you want to develop a set of classes that have more specific meaning. Instead of having only a `textbox` class, why not develop classes for ZIP codes, social security numbers, phone numbers, and other commonly used visual components?

Before you set out to develop a set of classes, you should think about their design—this is the most important aspect of creating a set of class libraries. How do you want to have your hierarchy look, what types of classes do you want to develop, what is their public interface, and so on? When you design a class you should specify the following:

- Name and description of the class you are creating
- Name of the new class's parent class
- Base class(es) that will be used to construct the class
- Visual properties of the new class
- Public properties of the new class
- Private properties of the new class
- Names and descriptions of the public methods of the class
- Names and descriptions of the private methods of the class

Table 4-1 shows a specification for a progress meter that will be created as a functional class.

Table 4-1 Specification for a New Progress Meter Class

Class name	`frm_Progress_Meter`
Description	This dialog is a progress meter. It graphically shows what percentage of a process has been completed.
Parent class	`frm`
Classes used	`frm, shp, lbl`
Public properties	`nIncrementValue` (default 1)
	`nMaxValue` (default 100)
Private properties	`nCurrentValue` (default 1)
Public methods	`IncrementValue` (This method increments the `nCurrentValue` property using the `nIncrementValue` property. It then increments the progress bar, changing the width of `shp_progress_bar` using the following formula:
	$400 * (nCurrentValue/nMaxValue)$
Private methods	None

After specifying the design information for your class, you can turn to the Class Designer and go to work. Defining your first class begins with inheriting your class from the proper base class(es). The specification above calls for the use of three base classes: `frm` (form), `lbl` (label), and `shp` (shape). You always begin your classes with the container class, then add the primitives to the container class. Figure 4-2 shows the basic form for the progress meter.

This form has two shape objects. The first is the outline shape. The second is a box with a width of 1 pixel. This is the object that will show the progress of the process being run. It is set up to have a maximum width of 400 pixels. Its width property will be altered as the `IncrementValue()` method is called.

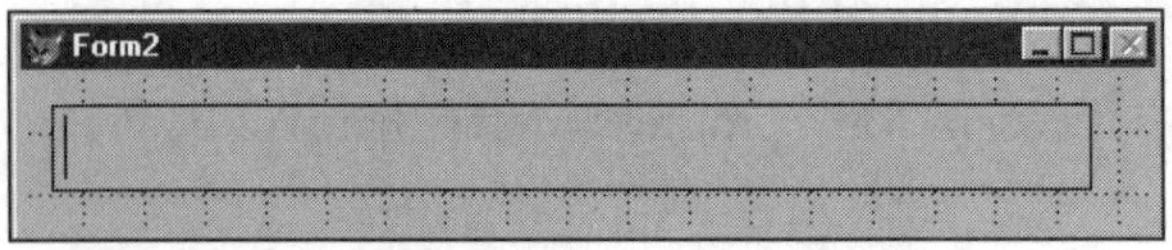

FIGURE 4-2

The basic form for the `frm_Progress_Meter` *class.*

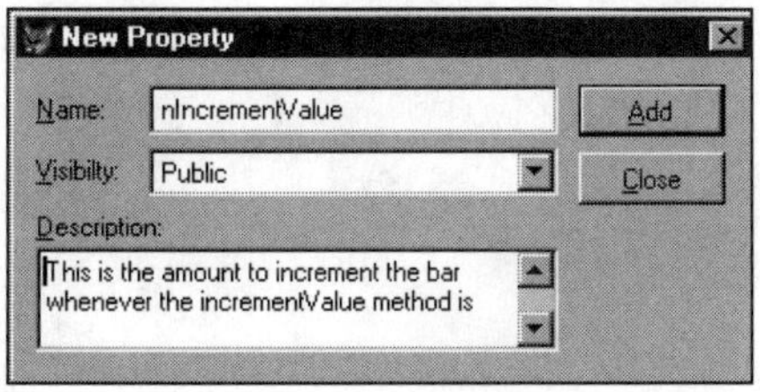

FIGURE 4-3

The New Property dialog box here contains information describing the nIncrementValue *property.*

Adding Properties

The first step in creating a class is to add the properties that will be used by the class. To add a new property, open your class in the Class Designer and then choose Class, New Property from the Visual FoxPro menu. This activates the New Property dialog box (see Figure 4-3), where you can enter descriptive and behavioral information about your new property.

You can specify three aspects of a property:

- **Name**—You should name your properties with the variable naming conventions specified in Chapter 1, "Establishing Development Standards."

- **Scope**—The scope can be public, protected, or hidden. *Public properties* can be viewed and changed by code outside the class definition. *Protected properties* cannot be seen outside the class code, so they can be changed only by the class's or subclass's own code. *Hidden properties* can be changed only by the class's code itself, and not by any subclass's code.

- **Description**—You always should add a description, because it comes in handy when the property shows up in the Project Designer, and provides useful information to people who are unfamiliar with your custom classes.

TIP: New properties default to a logical false. When you add a new property, you specify its default value by going into the property sheet and changing the value.

After adding a property, you can go to the properties sheet and see the new property at the end of the list of available properties.

Adding Methods

After adding the properties to your new class, you can add the methods. While the properties in your class are data, the methods are code. To add methods to your class, choose Class, New Method from the Visual FoxPro menu. Adding methods requires the same steps as adding properties. You can specify the name, scope, and description of each method. These attributes behave the same for methods as they do for properties.

Adding Code to Your Class

After adding class methods and properties, you can begin adding code to specialize your class. You can add code to your class by doing one of the following: double-clicking the container object for the class, then selecting the proper method from the Procedure drop-down list, or selecting the Methods tab of the Property Sheet, then double-clicking the method for which you want to add code.

This pulls up the desired method in the code editor, and you can begin adding code. When you add code to your objects, you need to make it as generic as possible. Typically, this is done by writing code that affects only the object you're working on. Visual FoxPro provides a set of keywords and functions that can be used to change properties or call code from classes generically. Table 4-2 lists these keywords.

Now that you understand the keywords used to write generic class code, you can finish the code for the `frm_Progress_Meter` class. The only method requiring code is the `IncrementValue()` method. Add the following code:

```
*-- Increment the current value
This.nCurrentValue = This.nCurrentValue + This.nIncrementValue

*-- Increase the size of the progress bar
```

Table 4-2 Generic Class Development Keywords and Functions

Keyword	Description
This	The This keyword addresses the control where the code resides. You can change properties or call code from the current object.
ThisForm	The ThisForm keyword allows you to call code or change properties from the form down. This is a useful keyword, since no GUI control can ever be seen without being on a form.
ThisFormSet	Formsets can contain forms. While the ThisForm keyword allows you to begin with the form downward, the ThisFormSet keyword allows you to traverse the hierarchy prior to the form.
Parent	All controls, sometime during their existence, have a parent object. The Parent keyword allows you to move up the containership hierarchy.
::	Object-oriented programming gives you the ability to override code in an inherited class. This operator, known as the *scope resolution operator*, allows you to call code from a parent class. The syntax is as follows: *<parent classname>::<methodname>*
DoDefault()	DoDefault() is much like the scope resolution operator. This function calls the code from the direct parent class and method of the current class's parent. While the scope resolution operator forces you to know the name of the parent class and method, DoDefault() has no such requirement.

```
This.shp_progress_bar.Width = 400 * (This.nCurrentValue /
This.nMaxValue)
```

This code completes the frm_Progress_Meter class. You can run the following code to test the class:

```
Set Classlib To Widget
Local loProgressTest, lnKount
loProgressTest = CREATEOBJECT("frm_Progress_Meter")
loProgressTest.Show()
For lnKount = 1 To 100
    loProgressTest.IncrementValue()
EndFor
```

As you can see, creating a useful class requires only minimal design, a few controls, and a small amount of code. The class you just created required three controls and two lines of code. If you recall the days of procedural code, you know that creating this object procedurally would require much more than two lines of code.

Adding Finishing Touches to Your Class

After completing the basic design portions of your class, you can add some finishing touches. Choose Class, Class Info from the Visual FoxPro menu to activate the Class Info dialog box (see Figure 4-4). This dialog box allows you to do the following:

- Change the description of the class
- Specify an icon for the class when it's displayed on a toolbar or in the Project Manager
- Specify the class as an OLE Server class (OLE classes are discussed in detail in Chapter 6, "Communicating with Other Applications Using OLE")
- Change the scope, description, and init properties of contained methods and properties

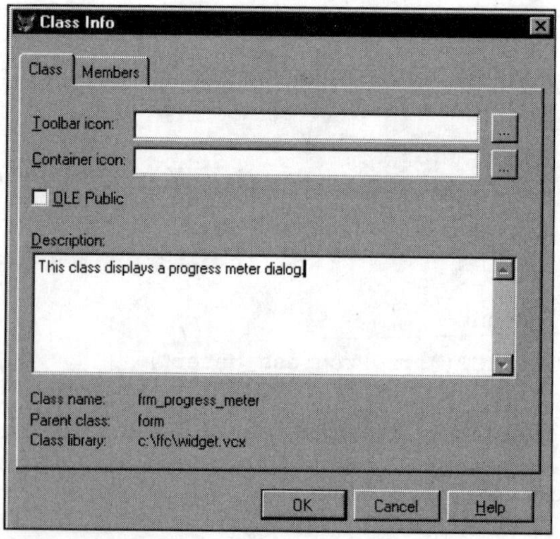

FIGURE 4-4

The Class Info dialog box is used to change properties of a class.

Creating Classes with Code

The second way to create objects is by using code. The basis of creating objects with code is the `Define Class` command. This allows you to create a new class based on either a FoxPro base class or a subclass. (As mentioned earlier, you always want to use an inherited subclass instead of a base class.) The structure of the `Define Class` command is fairly simple, consisting of four sections:

- The name, parent class, and OLE status of the class you are designing
- The data section of the class you are defining
- The methods of the class you are defining
- Adding optional components to a container class

Defining the Class Name

The first step in defining a class with code is to use the `Define Class` and `EndDefine` commands to define the name, parent class, and OLE status of the new class. The syntax is as follows:

```
Define Class classname As parentclass [OlePublic]
EndDefine
```

classname is the name of the class that you are creating. This is the keyword you will use to instantiate this class, or to create subclasses from this class.

parentclass specifies either the FoxPro base class or custom class from which this new class inherits.

[OlePublic] is an optional keyword that defines the class as an OLE server.

The following code, for example, creates the basic structure of the `frm_Progress_Meter` class:

```
Set Classlib To BaseClass.VCX Additive


Define Class frm_Progress_Meter As frm
EndDefine
```

Notice the inclusion of the `Set Classlib` command in this code. This command is necessary when you instantiate the code at runtime. When Visual

FoxPro attempts to instantiate the frm_Progress_Meter class, it looks for its parent class in the current program, the current procedure file, and the current class libraries—in that order. Including the Set Classlib command facilitates this search.

Defining the Class Data

The next section of a class definition is the code definition section. This is where you can define the properties of the new class. To create properties for a class, simply provide the variable declarations for these properties right after the Define Class section. These declarations have two special keywords that you can use: Protected and Hidden. By default, any new properties you create in this section are Public. Using the Protected or Hidden keyword allows you to hide a property from external programs or subclasses as follows:

- Protected—Prevents access and changes to the property from outside the class or subclass definition. Methods and events within the class or subclass definition can access the protected property.

- Hidden—Prevents access and changes to the property from outside the class definition. Only methods and events within the class definition can access the hidden property. While protected properties can be accessed by subclasses of the class definition, hidden properties can be accessed only from the class definition.

The following code defines the properties of the frm_Progress_Meter class:

```
Set Classlib To BaseClass.VCX Additive

Define Class frm_Progress_Meter As frm

Protected nCurrentValue = 0
nIncrementValue = 1
nMaxValue = 100

EndDefine
```

Defining the Class Code

The next section to define is the code for the class. This section includes a set of keywords used to attach functions and procedures to a class. The syntax is as follows:

```
<Protected|Hidden> Function|Procedure function name
EndFunction|EndProcedure
```

Like properties, methods are `Public` by default and can be changed to `Protected` or `Hidden`. The following code includes the `frm_Progress_Meter` class's function code:

```
Set Classlib To BaseClass.VCX Additive

Define Class frm_Progress_Meter As frm

Protected nCurrentValue = 0
nIncrementValue = 1
nMaxValue = 100

Function IncrementValue

*-- Increment the current value
This.nCurrentValue = This.nCurrentValue + This.nIncrementValue

*-- Increase the size of the progress bar
This.shp_progress_bar.Width = 400 * (This.nCurrentValue /
This.nMaxValue)
EndFunction

EndDefine
```

Adding Controls to the Container Class

The last step in defining a class using code is to add the controls to a container class. If the class you're creating is a composite object using many different controls, then you can add these controls using code. The syntax for adding controls with code is as follows:

```
Add Object objectname As parentclass <Protected> <NoInit>
 With property list
```

The syntax for this portion is very similar to the Define Class section. You specify the name of the object you're adding, and the parent class from which you want to inherit attributes. The mechanism for adding objects, however, has a few other features. You can protect an object, preventing it from being changed by other code segments. You also can prevent the firing of the added components' Init() methods—this allows you to wrap all your initialization code into one Init() method. The final twist when using Add Object is the With keyword. This keyword allows you to specify values for properties of the object you're adding.

Here is the final set of code used to create the frm_Progress_Meter class:

```
Set Classlib To BaseClass.VCX Additive

Define Class frm_Progress_Meter As frm

Protected nCurrentValue = 0
nIncrementValue = 1
nMaxValue = 100

    Add Object shp1 As shp With ;
        Top = 13, ;
        Left = 12, ;
        Height = 34, ;
        Width = 410, ;
        Name = "Shp1"


    Add Object shp_progress_bar As shp With ;
        Top = 17, ;
        Left = 17, ;
        Height = 25, ;
```

```
         Width = 1, ;
         BackColor = RGB(0,0,255), ;
         Name = "shp_progress_bar"

Function IncrementValue

*-- Increment the current value
This.nCurrentValue = This.nCurrentValue + This.nIncrementValue

*-- Increase the size of the progress bar
This.shp_progress_bar.Width = 400 * (This.nCurrentValue /
This.nMaxValue)
EndFunction


EndDefine
```

As you can see, you have the same capabilities when defining classes with code that you do when using the Class Designer. When should you favor one method over the other? Because the Class Designer is a tool that allows you to use a visual metaphor for defining objects, you should use it whenever you're designing components that your users will see, such as forms and widgets. You should use the coding method to create classes that don't require a visual interface. Use code to define application managers, menu managers, or data controllers, and to create objects from visual and non-visual environments.

Using Your Classes in the Development Environment

As soon as you have established your own set of class libraries, you can begin using them in the Visual FoxPro development environment. The most common way to use such class libraries is to click View Classes, <u>A</u>dd from the Form Controls toolbar. This replaces the standard toolbar controls with your classes, which you then can begin dropping onto your forms or new classes.

The second way to access your own custom controls is to use programming code. If you have created your classes using the Class Designer, you can use the Set Classlib To command. This command opens your own class library for access to your programming code. If you have created your classes using code, you must use the Set Procedure To command. Once you have accessed your controls using either method, you can instantiate new objects by using the CreateObject() or AddObject() function.

Using the Class Browser and Project Manager to Maintain Your Libraries

The number and complexity of your class libraries will grow over time. With this growth comes the need to effectively manage these classes. Visual FoxPro provides two tools that you can use to maintain class libraries: the Project Manager and the Class Browser. The Project Manager allows you to perform simple maintenance tasks on your classes, including the following:

- Drag-and-drop classes onto your forms
- Move a class from one library to another using drag-and-drop
- Delete a class from a class library
- Rename a class
- Edit the description of a class

This list of library management functionality is rather limited, and you'll probably want to do more than the Project Manager allows. That's when the Class Browser comes in handy. The Class Browser is a tool designed to facilitate the management and maintenance of class libraries. Follow these steps to activate the Class Browser:

1. Choose Tools, Class Browser from the Visual FoxPro menu.
2. Select a class library using the File Open dialog box. After you select a class library, the Class Browser appears as shown in Figure 4-5.

The Class Browser provides a wide range of functionality that is necessary to manage a complex set of class libraries. With the Class Browser, you can do the following:

- Drag-and-drop classes onto your forms or the Visual FoxPro design surface
- View the properties, methods, and objects of a class in a hierarchical outline format
- Export the programming code for a class that was designed visually

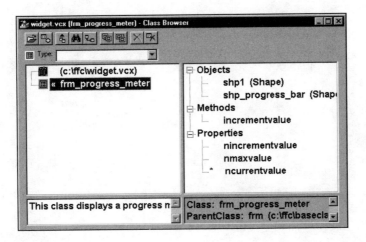

FIGURE 4-5

You can do class library maintenance in the Class Browser.

- Specify the class options found in the Class Info dialog box
- Redefine the parent class for an object
- View specific components of your class using property, object, and method filters
- View the components of OLE object and type library files (OLB and TLB files, respectively)
- Delete a class from a class library
- Rename a class
- Edit the description of a class

This tool is a must for any Visual FoxPro developer creating his or her own set of class libraries.

Summary

Visual FoxPro provides a very robust set of tools for creating object-oriented applications. You can create classes visually or with code, depending upon your specific application's needs. In the next chapter, you will explore the capabilities of a fully developed application framework.

Chapter 5

The FoxPro
Foundation Classes

Introduction

The easiest way to get acquainted with object-oriented development is to begin with a set of pre-defined libraries. This is where the FoxPro Foundation Classes come in. Visual FoxPro is known as a *hybrid object-oriented language* because it combines both procedural and object-oriented programming concepts in one development tool. The FoxPro Foundation Classes provide a framework upon which you can develop your own applications. They're a framework that takes into account the reality of everyday application development. While some frameworks attempt to stick to a prescribed methodology, the FoxPro Foundation Classes place creating a useful application framework first and object-oriented dogma second.

The FoxPro Foundation Classes consist of a number of different class libraries and programs divided into functional areas. The functional areas and classes/programs contained in the foundation classes are:

- MAIN.PRG—Main program used for initializing global variables, as well as opening class libraries, procedure libraries, and so on
- LIBRARY.PRG—A set of global API functions
- BASECLAS.VCX—FoxPro Foundation base classes
- FORMS.VCX—Commonly used forms
- OFFICAPI.PRG—Classes used to link applications to Microsoft Office and BackOffice
- ACTIVEX.VCX—Modified and enhanced ActiveX controls
- WIDGETS.VCX—Application development classes
- RASLIB.VCX—Functions and classes used to communicate with the Windows API and Dial-Up Networking
- DATACLAS.PRG—Classes used to integrate data and forms
- HTML.PRG—Classes used to create Web pages

As you can see just by looking at the basic structure of the FoxPro Foundation Classes, they do not comprise a pure object-oriented framework, because they include procedural program files and class libraries. This chapter examines in detail each type of class in the FoxPro Foundation Classes.

MAIN.PRG

The Startup Program

MAIN.PRG is the startup program for any application developed using the Fox-Pro Foundation Classes. MAIN.PRG does the following:

- Performs all base settings (Set Talk, Safety, and so on)
- Sets all global variables
- Opens the system and other application databases
- Opens the class and procedure libraries
- Opens the FLLs used by the application
- Performs the login process
- Runs the main menu

The basic function of MAIN.PRG is to get an application up and running as soon as possible. One way to create this type of functionality is to create an application class. The FoxPro Foundation Classes use MAIN.PRG to do this because MAIN.PRG has parts that are always needed when a new application is created. The FoxPro Foundation Classes were developed using a MAIN.PRG program, as creating an application class would provide little benefit to developers.

LIBRARY.PRG

Standard Procedural Tasks

LIBRARY.PRG is a small set of functions that can be used throughout the application to perform standard procedural tasks such as opening files, locking records, and displaying messages. Table 5-1 describes the functions in this set of code.

Most of these functions have no dependencies, and the ones that do are dependent solely on the existence of the other global functions and variables set up in MAIN.PRG.

Table 5-1 **LIBRARY.PRG** Functions

Function	Description
g_alert	Displays an alert message
g_fldlst	Creates a comma-delimited field list
g_getkey	Generates a unique system key (commonly used in the Default Value property in the Table Designer)
g_objlck	Semaphore locks records
g_ok	Displays an OK message
g_opnfl	Opens files
g_opntbl	Is a data-driven wrapper to g_opnfl
g_rascon	Is a wrapper function for RASLIB.VCX functions
g_runfrm	Launches forms
g_refvew	Is used to refresh parameterized views
g_wipdir	Is used to delete all files from a directory
g_yesno	Is used to answer yes/no functions

BASECLAS.VCX

FoxPro Foundation Base Classes

This visual class library contains all the most primitive base classes used in the remaining class libraries. The only items in this class are the FoxPro base classes subclassed one level. This class library includes some changes to certain base classes, as described below.

txt — TextBox

The txt base class has the following defaults set:

```
FontName = Courier New

FontSize = 9 pt

FontBold = .f.

Height = 22 points
```

With these properties set, you can use the following formula to calculate the correct number of pixels for an entry object:

(number of characters × 7) + 10

pgf—PageFrame

The default behavior of the VFP PageFrame object is to refresh only the currently active page. The following code makes sure that all pages are refreshed when a PageFrame object receives a `Refresh()` message:

```
*— Refresh all pages of a pageframe when refresh msg
*— is received.
Local lnKount, lnPages
lnPages = This.Pagecount

For lnKount = 1 TO lnPages
   This.Pages(lnKount).Refresh()
Endfor
```

cbo—ComboBox

The next change adds the following code to the `Refresh()` method of the `cbo` base class:

```
This.Requery()
```

When a new record is added to a VFP ComboBox object's `RowSource`, the ComboBox object does not automatically refresh itself. The additional code works around this problem.

All Controls

All relevant user-altered controls have the `cEditMode` property added. This property is used to specify when the control is enabled. The philosophy of the Foundation Classes is that all data entry forms have three—and only three—possible states: Add, Edit, and View. The default value for this property is VIEW, which means that the control is enabled in only View mode. These are all the possible values:

VIEW	Control is enabled in View mode
ADD	Control is enabled in Add mode
EDIT	Control is enabled in Edit mode

ALL	Control is always enabled
NONE	Control is never enabled

TIP: You can enable a control in multiple modes by separating the modes with commas. For example, if you want a control to be enabled in Add and Edit modes, you specify ADD,EDIT as the `cEditMode` property value.

FORMS.VCX

Commonly Used Form Types

The FORMS.VCX class library contains the base class forms that will be used throughout your system. They begin with the `frm` class which is subclassed into two ancestors, `frmDialog` and `frmDataEntry`. Tables 5-2 through 5-5 define the classes in the FORMS.VCX class library.

Table 5-2 `frmDialog`

Class name	frmDialog
Description	This form is used in the creation of dialog boxes. It has two buttons on it by default: OK and Cancel. The OK button hides the form calling the `ProcessDialog()` method. The Cancel button releases the form with no processing.
Parent class	frm
Classes used	cmd
Public properties	N/A
Private properties	N/A
Public methods	`ProcessDialog()`—This allows the developer to specify the behavior of the form when the OK button is pressed.
Private methods	N/A
Other notes	This form is set to modal.

Table 5-3 `frmPasswordDialog`

Class name	`frmPasswordDialog`
Description	This form is used to validate a user's name and password.
Parent class	`frm`
Classes used	`cmd, txt, lbl`
Public properties	`lLoggedIn`—This is used to determine whether the user logged in correctly.
Private properties	N/A
Public methods	`ProcessDialog()`—This is overridden with code to validate the `txtUsername` and `txtPassword` values.
Private methods	N/A

Table 5-4 `rmDataEntry`

Class name	`frmDataEntry`
Description	This form is used in the creation of data entry forms.
Parent class	`frm`
Classes used	N/A
Public properties	`oMasterObject`—This is used to attach a data controller that will manage the relationship between the visual and data classes of the FFC.
Private properties	N/A
Public methods	`ChangeMode()`—This is a function that traverses the containership hierarchy of a passed form. It sets the control's enabled state based upon the control's `cEditMode` property.
Private methods	N/A

Table 5-5 `frmDataEntryWithButtons`

Class name	`frmDataEntryWithButtons`
Description	This form is an ancestor of the `frmDataEntry` class. It has the default entry form buttons added to it. These buttons can be found in the `WIDGETS.VCX` class library class `conEntryButtons`.
Parent class	`frmDataEntry, conEntryButtons`
Classes used	N/A
Public properties	Inherited from `frmDataEntry`
Private properties	N/A
Public methods	Inherited from `frmDataEntry`
Private methods	N/A

WIDGETS.VCX

Commonly Used Application Development Classes

The WIDGETS.VCX class contains commonly used visual classes. These classes are used primarily in the creation of data entry forms and containers. Tables 5-6 through 5-11 define the classes in the WIDGETS.VCX class library.

Table 5-6 txtZipCode

Class name	txtZipCode
Description	This a text entry field set up to enter a ZIP code in ZIP+4 format.
Parent class	txt
Classes used	N/A
Public properties	N/A
Private properties	N/A
Public methods	N/A
Private methods	N/A
Other notes	This class has two properties changed from their defaults:
	InputMask = "99999-9999"
	ControlSource = "Thisform.oMasterObject. oObjectStore.zip"

Table 5-7 `txtPhoneNumber`

Class name	`txtPhoneNumber`
Description	This is a text entry field used to edit phone number properties.
Parent class	`txt, lbl`
Classes used	N/A
Public properties	N/A
Private properties	N/A
Public methods	N/A
Private methods	N/A

Other notes	This class has two properties changed from their defaults:
	
	`InputMask = "999/999-9999"`
	
	`ControlSource = "Thisform.oMasterObject.`
	`oObjectStore.phone"`

Table 5-8 `txtFaxNumber`

Class name	`txtFaxNumber`
Description	This is a text entry field used to edit fax number properties.
Parent class	`txt, lbl`
Classes used	N/A
Public properties	N/A
Private properties	N/A
Public methods	N/A
Private methods	N/A

Other notes	This class has two properties changed from their defaults:
	
	`InputMask = "999/999-9999"`
	
	`ControlSource = "Thisform.oMasterObject.`
	`oObjectStore.fax"`

Table 5-9 `conEntryButtons`

Class name	conEntryButtons
Description	This class is a set of common data entry buttons: New, Edit, Delete, Save, Cancel, and Help. These buttons communicate with a data controller object attached to a data entry form.
Parent class	con
Classes used	cmd, shp
Public properties	N/A
Private properties	N/A
Public methods	N/A
Private methods	N/A
Other notes	This class communicates with the public interface of a data controller attached to a `frmDataEntry` class. The buttons in this class perform their duties as follows: 1. Call the form's data controller method. 2. If it has worked, call the form's `ChangeMode()` method. 3. Refresh the state of the form after calling the data controller method.

Table 5-10 `conAddressEntry`

Class name	conAddressEntry
Description	This is an address entry container. It contains a common set of address block fields for editing.
Parent class	txt, lbl, txtZipCode
Classes used	N/A
Public properties	N/A
Private properties	N/A
Public methods	N/A
Private methods	N/A
Other notes	This control has its text object's `ControlSource` properties are set to edit their respective address fields (`address1`, `address2`, `city`, `state`, `zip`).

Table 5-11 `frm_Progress_Meter`

Class name	`frm_Progress_Meter`
Description	This is a progress meter dialog box that graphically shows what percentage of a process has been completed.
Parent class	`frm`
Classes used	`frm, shp`
Public properties	`nIncrementValue` (default 1)
	`nMaxValue` (default 100)
Private properties	`nCurrentValue` (default 1)
Public methods	`IncrementValue()` —This increments the `nCurrentValue` property using the value of `nIncrementValue`, then increments the progress bar by changing the width of `shp_progress_bar` with this formula:
	$400 \times (\text{nCurrentValue} \div \text{nMaxValue})$
Private methods	N/A

ACTIVEX.VCX

ActiveX Controls with Added Functionality

The `ACTIVEX.VCX` class library contains ActiveX controls with added functionality, as described in Tables 5-12 and 5-13.

HTML.PRG

Used to Create HTML Pages

The `HTML.PRG` program file contains the class used to create HTML pages, as described in Table 5-14.

Table 5-12 `oleTreeView`

Class name	`oleTreeView`
Description	This class is a treeview with a method that can be used to load the elements for the treeview from a DBF file.
Parent class	`ole`
Classes used	`ole`
Public properties	N/A
Private properties	N/A
Public methods	`LoadTable()`—This loads the elements for the treeview control. It expects to be passed a FoxPro table or cursor with the following structure: `primarykey c(10)` `parentkey c(10)` `description c(30)` After being passed the correct structure, the control proceeds to load the cursor from the passed table.
Private methods	N/A

Table 5-13 `oleRTFEditor`

Class name	`oleRTFEditor`
Description	This class is a subclassed RTF editor with a toolbar and right-click menus.
Parent class	`ole`
Classes used	`ole`
Public properties	N/A
Private properties	N/A
Public methods	N/A
Private methods	N/A

Table 5-14 cHTML

Class name	cHTML
Description	This class is used to create HTML Web pages.
Parent class	cus
Classes used	N/A
Public properties	N/A
Private properties	cTitle—The title for the Web page
	cCRLF—Carriage return/linefeed combination
	nLines—Number of lines in the Web document
Public methods	ReturnHTMLPage()—Returns a text string containing the contents for the Web page
	CreateTitle()—Creates the title for the Web page
	CreateTextLine()—Creates a line of text on the Web page
	CreateTable()—Creates a formatted HTML table from a FoxPro table or cursor
	CreateTextField()—Creates a text field object on the Web page
	CreateHeaderLine()—Creates an HTML header line
Private methods	CreateCGIHeader()—Creates a CGI header for the Web page
	CreateHTMLHeader()—Creates the HTML header text for the Web page
	AddTextLine()—Adds a text line to the internal page array
	CreateHTMLHeader()—Creates the HTML footer text for the Web page

RASLIB.VCX

Used for Dial-Up Networking

The RASLIB.VCX class library contains a number of classes that can be use to establish connections with remote machines using Dial-Up Networking. *Dial-Up Networking* is a set of utilities found in Windows 95 and Windows NT that allows you to connect to a remote machine using a modem. The classes found in RASLIB.VCX provide a set of utilities that make the Windows API calls necessary to establish a connection.

The documentation for RASLIB.VCX can be found in Chapter 7, "Using the Windows API."

OFFICAPI.PRG

Used to Communicate with Office and BackOffice

This class library is used to OLE-enable applications so they can communicate with Microsoft Office and BackOffice, as described in Tables 5-15 through 5-19.

Table 5-15 cusExcelAutomation

Class name	cusExcelAutomation
Description	This class establishes an OLE session with Microsoft Excel.
Parent class	cus
Classes used	cus
Public properties	oExcelSession
Private properties	N/A
Public methods	Show()—Presents the Excel interface to the user
	Hide()—Hides the Excel interface
	SendTable()—Sends the data from a FoxPro table or cursor to an Excel spreadsheet
	Creategraph()—Creates an Excel chart from a FoxPro table
Private methods	None

Table 5-16 `cusWordAutomation`

Class name	cusWordAutomation
Description	This class establishes an OLE session with Microsoft Word.
Parent class	cus
Classes used	cus
Public properties	oWordSession
Private properties	N/A
Public methods	Show()—Presents the Word interface to the user
	Hide()—Hides the Word interface
	Open()—Opens a Word document
	Print()—Prints the current Word document
	CreateTable()—Sends the data from a FoxPro table or cursor to a Word for Windows formatted table
Private methods	None

Table 5-17 `cusSQLServerAutomation`

Class name	**cusSQLServerAutomation**
Description	This class establishes an OLE session with Microsoft SQL Server.
Parent class	cus
Classes used	cus
Public properties	oSQLServerSession
Private properties	N/A
Public methods	ListDatabases()—Creates a comma-delimited list of databases found in a SQL server
	ListTables()—Creates a comma-delimited list of tables found in a SQL database
	ExecuteQuery()—Processes a SQL query against a SQL database
Private methods	None

Table 5-18 `cusAccessAutomation`

Class name	cusAccessAutomation
Description	This class establishes an OLE session with Microsoft Access.
Parent class	cus
Classes used	cus
Public properties	oAccessSession
Private properties	N/A
Public methods	OpenDatabase()—Opens an Access database
	TableList()—Creates a comma-delimited list of tables found in an Access database
Private methods	None

Table 5-19 `cusProjectAutomation`

Class name	cusProjectAutomation
Description	This class establishes an OLE session with Microsoft Project.
Parent class	cus
Classes used	cus
Public properties	oProjectSession
Private properties	N/A
Public methods	OpenProject()—Opens a project file
	TaskList()—Creates a comma-delimited list of tasks found in a project
Private methods	None

DATACLAS.PRG

Used to Communicate with Data Tables

The cornerstone of the FoxPro Foundation Classes is the `cusOLEDataServer` class found in DATACLAS.PRG. This class (described in Table 5-20) is used to manage data found in Visual FoxPro tables. It provides a set of methods that can be used to add, edit, and delete records.

Table 5-20 `cusOLEDataServer`

Class name	cusOLEDataServer
Description	This class establishes a data server connection between an OLE client and a Visual FoxPro table.
Parent class	cus
Classes used	cus
Public properties	cEditMode—The current state of the object: Add, Edit, or View
	oObjectStore—A collection of fields and values related to the table
	cParentalias—Alias of the table managed by the object
	cParenttable—Name of table being managed
	xKeyValue—Current primary key value of the object
	cKeyExpr—The expression used to create the primary key
	cKeytagName—The name of the primary key's index
	aChildCursors—An array of child table information
	nChildren—Number of child tables managed by the object
Private properties	None
Public methods	SetTable()—Specifies the table to be managed by the object
	lLoad()—Loads a record from the specified table
	lAdd()—Adds a new record
	lEdit()—Edits the currently selected record
	lSave()—Saves the current record
	lCancel()—Cancels changes to the record
	lDelete()—Deletes the current record
	lSetKey()—Sets the primary key information for the record
	lRequiredCheck()—Makes sure all required fields are filled in
	lValidateExpression()—Validates an expression
	AddChildTable()—Adds a child table to be managed by the object
	LoadChildCursors()—Loads information from views into cursor tables
	SaveChildCursors()—Iterates through the child cursor array and calls the SaveChildCursor() method to save the information from that cursor
	DeleteChildCursors()—Erases the child tables created by the object
	SaveChildCursor()—Copies information from a child cursor into the "live" tables
	CreateChildCursor()—Creates a cursor file
Private methods	None

What the cusOLEDataServer Class Does

The purpose of cusOLEDataServer is to manage the data for a single table or one-to-many tables. It is an object designed to buffer data from tables and views, and allow developers to edit properties directly. It does this by establishing a relationship between an object and a record, using the primary key of the table. Its methods are defined as described in the following sections.

> **NOTE:** To see the code for this class, look at DATACLAS.PRG in the FFC directory on the CD-ROM accompanying this book.

SetTable()

This method specifies the information necessary to manage a record with cusOLEDataServer. In order to manage a record with this class, you need to determine the following: the primary (or candidate key) of the table, the primary key index name, the primary key expression, the alias of the table, and the name of the table to be managed. This information is used by the lSetKey() method to access data from a single record.

lLoad()

This method "scatters" the contents of a record to the oObjectStore property of the cusOLEDataServer class. If you pass a True value (.t.) to this method, it creates a new blank record.

lAdd()

This puts the cusOLEDataServer class in Add mode. Upon executing the lSave() method, the contents of the object are inserted into the table(s) being managed. This method also specifies the information in the Default Value property found in the DBC.

lEdit()

This puts the cusOLEDataServer class in Edit mode. Upon executing the lSave() method, the contents of the object are used to update the record(s) being managed by the server.

lSave()

This method saves the contents of the record(s) being managed by the data server.

lCancel()

This method cancels the changes made to the contents of the data server.

lDelete()

This method deletes the current record being managed by the data server.

lSetKey()

This method uses the information gathered in the SetTable() method to store the primary key value of the current record being managed. This primary key information is used whenever the record is edited, saved, deleted, canceled, and so on. Storing this information allows you to create multiple instances of the applications.

lRequiredCheck()

This method makes sure that all columns specified as Required in the DBC file are filled in. Required columns can be specified by putting a [Rule_Required] tag in the comments section of the column definition.

lValidateExpression()

This method checks whether or not an expression evaluates to True.

AddChildTable()

This method allows developers to specify the management of child tables by an object. The following code demonstrates how to specify child tables to be managed by this object:

```
*- Create data controller for Customer_Orders table
Define Class cusCustomerOrdersDataController As cusOleDataServer

Function Init
Lparameters pcTable, pcAlias

  DoDefault(pcTable,pcAlias)

This.AddChildTable("view_order_items","a_orditems","line_id","line_id")

This.AddChildTable("view_order_payments","a_ordpayms","paym_id", ;
"payment_id")
  This.RefreshChildCursors()
EndFunc
Enddefine
```

This code creates a new data controller that can be used to manage an orders table and two child tables. The AddChildTable() method increments the nChildren property and adds the information to the aChildCursors array. Once you've added the child tables, cusOLEDataServer will take care of managing the data found in the child tables. This method expects developers to use parameterized views to manage the display and creation of child table information.

LoadChildCursors()

This method processes the aChildCursors array and calls the CreateChildCursor() method to create an editable cursor for the specified file.

CreateChildCursor()

This methods creates a cursor file from the view definition specified in the AddChildTable() method. When it creates a cursor, it adds a column named

`Action` to the table. This column is used by the `SaveChildCursor()` table described below.

SaveChildCursors()

This method iterates through the child cursor array and calls the `SaveChildCursor()` method to save the information from that child cursor into its proper table.

SaveChildCursor()

This method takes the data found in a child cursor file, and updates the "live" tables using this data. It uses the `Action` column specified by the `CreateChildCursor()` method to determine what to do with the record. If the `Action` value is `A`, this method adds a new record; it the value is `D`, this method deletes the record; and if the value is blank, this method updates the record.

DeleteChildCursors()

This method iterates through the child cursor array and closes the cursor files created by the `cusOLEDataServer` class.

Using the `cusOLEDataServer` Class

The purpose of the `cusOLEDataServer` class is to provide a simple interface for managing data through a common API. To add a new customer record, for example, you define a new `cusOLEDataServer` class and then use `CreateObject()` to instantiate the new server. The following code, taken from the WWS example, shows how to create a new customer table manager:

```
Define Class cusCustomerDataController As cusOleDataServer

Function Init
Lparameters pcTable, pcAlias

  DoDefault(pcTable,pcAlias)
```

```
This.AddChildTable("view_customer_notes","a_notes","note_id","note_id")
   This.RefreshChildCursors()
EndFunc
Enddefine
```

After creating the class definition, you can begin using it to add, edit, or delete records. The following code demonstrates using the data controller to create class instances:

```
OCustomer = CreateObject("cusCustomerDataController",
"customer","a_customer")
```

Add a New Record

```
*- Add a new customer
oCustomer.lAdd()

*- Change the data using the oObjectStore property
oCustomer.oObjectStore.last_name = "Paddock"
oCustomer.oObjectStore.last_name = "Kevin"

*- Save the record
oCustomer.lsave()
```

Edit a Record

```
*-Edit the record
oCustomer.lEdit()

*- Change the data
oCustomer.oObjectStore.last_name = "Leslie"

*- Save the data
oCustomer.lSave()
[3]Cancel Changes to a Record
*-Edit the record
oCustomer.lEdit()
```

```
*— Change the data
oCustomer.oObjectStore.last_name = "Brandon"

*— Cancel Changes
oCustomer.lCancel()
```

Delete a Record

```
*—Delete the record
oCustomer.lDelete()
```

This record manager provides a simple interface for managing records found in VFP tables. If you want to use cusOLEDataServer from other OLE Automation host applications, then you need to call the server a little differently. The following code shows how to call cusOLEDataServer from an OLE session:

```
*— Initialize the session
OCustomer = CreateObject("wws.cusCustomerDataController")

*— Specify the table to be managed
oCustomer.SetTable("customer","a_customer")
```

You are required to create the object this way because VFP does not pass parameters through OLE into the Init() method of the object, requiring you to set the table yourself. This is a minor inconvenience when accessing your data from an OLE automation host.

Putting It Together

Now that you have explored the definitions of the classes found in the FoxPro Foundation Classes, you can explore the steps necessary to create an application with them. This section is an overview of the sample application used throughout this book, and a description of its construction. This sample application is not meant to be a fully usable application, but rather a simple example that you can study to learn how to implement applications with the FoxPro Foundation Classes.

The WWS Sample Application

In Chapter 2, "Analysis, Design, and Prototyping," you learned that World Wide Shoes Corporation (WWS) needs to have a new order entry application built. Luckily, you have bought this book and you now command a set of classes that can be used to build this application. The following sections describe the components of the WWS sample application and the tools necessary to build it.

Modifying `MAIN.PRG`

The first step in creating the WWS application is to modify the MAIN.PRG program. This program is responsible for opening all files used by the application, specifying custom class libraries, specifying application-specific libraries, and logging the user into the application. The following code demonstrates the changes made to MAIN.PRG for the World Wide Shoes application:

```
*— Application-specific classes here
Set Classlib  To (gc_classpath + "WWS") Additive
Set Procedure  To (gc_classpath + "WWS") Additive


*— Open FLLS specific
Set Library To (gc_fllpath + "FOXTOOLS") Additive


*— Initialize global vars
gc_tmpf1 = "A" + g_getkey("TEMPFILE")   && temp files
gc_tmpf2 = "B" + RIGHT(gc_tmpf1,7)
gc_tmpf3 = "C" + RIGHT(gc_tmpf1,7)
gc_tmpf4 = "D" + RIGHT(gc_tmpf1,7)
gc_tmpf5 = "E" + RIGHT(gc_tmpf1,7)


STORE "" TO gc_userid
STORE 0 TO gn_accesslevel


*— Create Form handler object
```

```
DECLARE gaForms[1]
gaForms = ""

*— Open databases
Open Database (gc_datapath + "WWS")

*— Open tables
=g_opntbl("SYUSER")   && open users
=g_opntbl("CUSTOMER")
=g_opntbl("CUSTNOTE")
=g_opntbl("ORDITEMS")
=g_opntbl("ORDPAYMS")
=g_opntbl("ITEMS")

*— Open views
USE wws!view_customer_notes NODATA IN 0
USE wws!view_order_items NODATA IN 0
USE wws!view_order_payments NODATA IN 0

*— Clean out junk directory
=g_wipdir(gc_temppath)
```

This code specifies the class, procedure, and data files to be used by this application. After VFP opens your class libraries, the MAIN.PRG program proceeds to log the user into the system. Figure 5-1 shows the login screen for the WWS application.

MAIN.PRG determines whether or not the user has successfully logged into the system. If she has, then the system proceeds to run the MAINMENU.MPR menu program from the MENUS directory.

FIGURE 5-1

The WWS application prompts the user for a proper name and password at the login screen.

Creating Your Menu

After altering MAIN.PRG to open your application-specific files, you need to create the main menu for your application. The purpose of having a menu is to provide users with access to the various components of your application. Earlier in the book you learned that one of most important aspects of a Windows application is sharing a constant look and feel with other Windows applications. Your menu system should have (at a minimum) File, Edit, and Help menu options, with all application-specific menu components existing on the menu bar between Edit and Help. Figure 5-2 shows the menu system created for the WWS application.

The WWS application has two custom menus: Transactions and Maintenance. Transactions is used for actions that occur frequently as part of day-to-day operations, such as adding new customers or orders. Maintenance is used for the management of lookup tables (these types of files are infrequently accessed).

Part of the menu-generation process is to place commands in your menus that will be used to launch your forms. The FoxPro Foundation Classes use a function named g_runfrm(). This function has a single parameter, the name of the frm class you want to instantiate. This function creates an instance of your form and

FIGURE 5-2

The WWS application here has the Maintenance menu active.

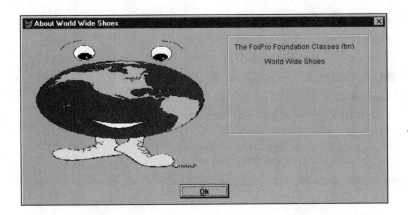

FIGURE 5-3

The WWS application's About form shows the WWS mascot.

attaches it to the gaForms array declared in MAIN.PRG. The purpose of this is to allow users to create multiple copies of certain forms. For example, this feature in the WWS application allows users to look at more than one customer at a time. Some of your forms may be modal in nature, in which case you want only one copy up at a time. The following code shows how to instantiate the frmAbout class as a modal form:

```
Local loAbout
loAbout = CreateObject("frmAboutWorldWideShoes")
loAbout.Show(1)
```

Figure 5-3 shows the resulting form, complete with the WWS logo.

Creating a Data Entry Form

After placing code in your menu to launch your data entry forms, you can design the data entry forms. In the FoxPro Foundation Classes, all data entry screens are constructed using a minumum of three classes. These classes and their jobs are as follows:

cusOLEDataServer	Manages the data for the data entry form
frmDataEntryWithButtons	Communicates with the data controller
con<ObjectEditor>	A container with the objects necessary to edit the data provided by the data controller

Each of these classes performs a very important task. cusOLEDataServer is used to manage the data being added to a specific table. frmDataEntryWithButtons has a set of buttons that communicates with a data controller attached to the form. con<ObjectEditor> is a class defined by the developer to edit the properties of the data controlled by the cusOLEDataServer class. The following code creates a data controller for the customer screen found in the WWS application:

```
*- Create data controller for customer table
Define Class cusCustomerDataController As cusOleDataServer

Function Init
Lparameters pcTable, pcAlias

   DoDefault(pcTable,pcAlias)

This.AddChildTable("view_customer_notes","a_notes","note_id","note_id")

   This.RefreshChildCursors()
EndFunc

Enddefine


Define Class frmCustomer As frmDataEntryWithButtons

Function Init

   *- Set the data controller
   ThisForm.oMasterObject = ;
   CreateObject("cusCustomerDataController",gc_datapath + ;
   "CUSTOMER","a_customer")

   *- Add the viewer classes
   ThisForm.AddObject("cntCustomerEditor","cntCustomerEditor")
   ThisForm.cntCustomerEditor.Visible = .t.

   *- Set the forms caption
```

```
ThisForm.Caption = "Customer Maintenance"

*— Call default behavior
DoDefault()
```

```
EndFunc
Enddefine
```

This code performs the following tasks:

1. Defines a new data server for the customer table
2. Attaches a child table to the customer data controller
3. Defines a form for managing the data for a customer record
4. Attaches the data controller to the form
5. Attaches the object viewer to the form

This process is known as *compositing*. The technique, taken from the motion picture industry, composites different views of the same object into a single comprehensive picture of that object. Figure 5-4 shows the customer maintenance form after compositing.

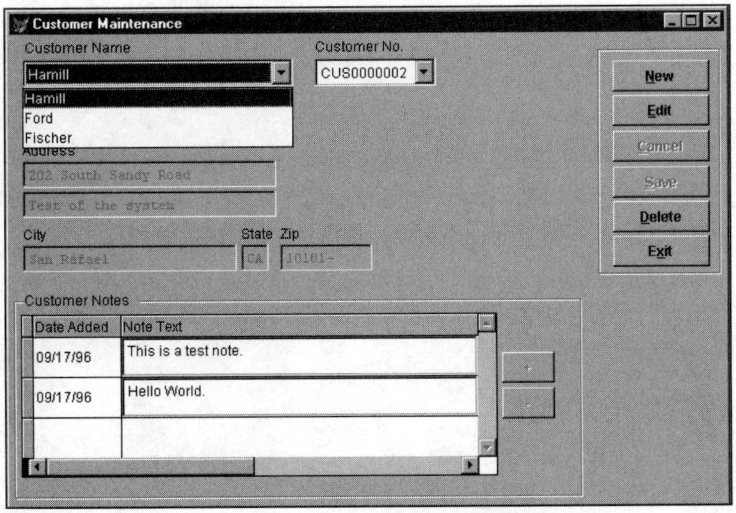

FIGURE 5-4

The WWS customer screen is composited from a data controller, an entry form, and an object viewer.

Summary

The entire purpose of the FoxPro Foundation Classes is to provide a simple framework that can be used to construct complex applications with a minimum of code. As you can see from the prior examples and the samples on the CD-ROM, the FoxPro Foundation Classes achieve this goal. Many of the classes found in this chapter are covered in other sections of this book, so you might want to consult the following chapters:

- Chapter 4, "Integrating Visual FoxPro and Object-Oriented Programming"
- Chapter 6, "Communicating with Other Applications Using OLE"
- Chapter 7, "Using the Windows API"
- Chapter 11, "Using SQL in Visual FoxPro Applications"

Chapter 6

**Communicating with
Other Applications
Using OLE**

Introduction

It used to be true that the applications you developed were essentially islands unto themselves. There were not many mechanisms for communicating with other applications. You usually could swap data through a common file format, or maybe even shell out to the other application. If you could accomplish even these tricks, then you were doing well.

Windows changed all of this. One of the major milestones in the history of Windows was the technology known as *Dynamic Data Exchange (DDE)*. DDE allowed users to begin creating compound documents through a series of inter-application communication protocols. Developers could give their applications the ability to send data and commands to completely foreign applications. You could link your spreadsheet package to your word processing package, your graphics package to your spreadsheet package, and so on.

As Windows matured, so did its ability to swap data between different applications. The next generation of inter-application communication came in the form of *Object Linking and Embedding (OLE)*. OLE allows developers to create true compound documents. DDE always involved the creation and linking of two or more documents. With OLE you have the choice of either linking two documents, or embedding one document within another.

In order for a technology to survive in the computer industry, it must evolve. Microsoft knows this, so the technology used in OLE has evolved. This OLE evolution has led to a more robust and involved set of mechanisms contained in a protocol known as OLE 2. OLE 2 provides the ability to use many new inter-application features. With OLE 2 you can do the following:

- Link different heterogeneous documents
- Embed one document within another
- Communicate with other applications using a standard set of protocols known as OLE Automation
- Create controls that can be used in various development platforms, using a technology known as OCX or ActiveX

Visual FoxPro provides full support for the OLE 2 specification. You can embed or link documents within a Visual FoxPro DBF file, communicate with other applications using OLE Automation, create your own OLE Automation servers, and use ActiveX controls for developing forms or controls. This chapter demonstrates how you can use OLE within your own VFP applications.

Understanding OLE Terminology

New technology such as that provided by OLE typically comes with its own set of terminology. When evaluating the different aspects of this technology, it's important to understand the terms being used. The first section of this chapter provides an overview of the terminology used to describe the various technologies employed with the OLE protocol.

Object Linking and Embedding

The foundation of OLE is its ability to link different heterogeneous documents. You no longer need to think of your applications as islands. OLE provides the ability to communicate with other external applications, and it uses two different mechanisms for implementing this linking technology. The first mechanism is known as *linking*, in which two documents are linked, similar to the DDE technology used prior to the development of OLE. In order to view one linked document from another, each document must be present on the same computer or network. The second mechanism is known as *embedding*. With embedding, you store the contents of one document within the structure of another. Embedding leaves you with only one document, because the "linked" documents are stored in the host document. What are the determining factors in your decision to use linking or embedding?

When you link documents, you still have two different documents that can be edited by two different applications. For instance if you have a Word document with a linked Excel spreadsheet, you can still edit the spreadsheet in Excel and the Word document in Word. Linking allows several people to edit the components of a compound document. Embedding, on the other hand, provides the convenience of a single file but harnesses you to the host application. Using the same example, you would only be able to access the Excel spreadsheet by opening the Word document and activating the spreadsheet from within Word. Each mechanism has its own set of advantages and disadvantages. Which way you choose depends on your own application needs.

OLE Servers

OLE technology allows you to either link documents or embed one document within another. The documents that can be linked are controlled by an application called an *OLE server*. An OLE server is responsible for the creation, editing, and display aspects of an OLE document. OLE servers are simply islands. In order to fully utilize the protocols found in OLE, you need to have an application capable of accessing OLE servers. This is where OLE clients come in.

OLE Hosts (Clients)

The most basic of all OLE technologies is the ability to host documents from other OLE servers. The primary responsibility of a host (client) application is to provide a mechanism for storing compound documents. In Visual FoxPro this mechanism is a General field. The General field type allows you to store documents created by word processors, graphics packages, and other application software. VFP supports OLE as an OLE 2-compliant host.

OLE Automation Sessions

One of the real powers of OLE is its ability to link heterogeneous applications using a common API. One of the most useful of the APIs is the *OLE Automation interface*. The OLE Automation interface allows you to send data and commands to OLE Automation servers. Visual FoxPro supports the OLE Automation interface in the role of either OLE Automation Client or OLE Automation Server. *OLE Automation clients* are applications that have the ability to send data and commands to *OLE Automation servers*, which in turn process these data and commands. When you communicate with another application using OLE Automation, you use a programming method known as an *OLE Automation session*. Creating an OLE session establishes the links between the applications you are communicating with.

Creating an OLE Automation Session

The first step in communicating with an OLE Automation server is to establish an OLE session. Establishing an OLE session creates the channel that you will use to send data and commands.

To create an OLE session, you must have two sets of information. The first is the registered name of the OLE server you want to communicate with; the second is documentation of the OLE server's object model. The registered name of the server is used to establish the connection to the OLE server. The object model provides the roadmap to the different objects, properties, and methods provided by the application.

Table 6-1 illustrates many common OLE server names.

After retrieving the name of the server you want to communicate with, you can use either the `CreateObject()` or the `GetObject()` function to create a new OLE session. The difference between these two functions is subtle. `CreateObject()` always establishes a new session of the OLE Automation server, while `GetObject()` can use an already running session of the OLE Automation Server. The following code demonstrates establishing a session with Word for Windows, opening a document, and printing it:

```
Local oWordObject
oWordObject = CreateObject("Word.Basic")
oWordObject.FileOpen("c:\test.doc")
oWordObject.FilePrint()
```

Table 6-1 OLE Automation Server Names

OLE Server Name	Microsoft Application
Word.Basic	Word for Windows
Excel.Application	Excel
MSProject.Application	Project
Access.Application	Access
SQLOLE.SQLServer	SQL Server

Upon establishing an OLE session, you can use information from the object model to communicate with that application. The following sections show how to create links to various OLE servers, and how to use the object models for those applications.

Linking to Excel

The biggest advantage of using OLE Automation is that it allows you to add functionality to your application with familiar off-the-shelf applications. Rather than inventing a new spreadsheet or graphing interface, why not use something as familiar as Excel? Table 6-2 and the code that follows define a FoxPro class that is capable of communicating with Microsoft Excel.

Table 6-2 An Excel Automation Class

Class name	`cusExcelAutomation`
Description	This class establishes an OLE session with Microsoft Excel.
Parent class	`cus`
Classes used	`cus`
Public properties	`oExcelSession`
Private properties	N/A
Public methods	`Show()`—Presents the Excel interface to the user
	`Hide()`—Hides the Excel interface
	`SendTable()`—Sends the data from a FoxPro table or cursor to an Excel spreadsheet
	`CreateGraph()`—Creates an Excel chart from a FoxPro table
Private methods	N/A

```
*— The following code demonstrates creating an Excel chart with
*— The cusExcelAutomation class.
Clear All
Close All

Create Table numbers (title c(10), amount n(12,2))
Insert (title, amount) values Into numbers ("TITLE 1",100)
Insert (title, amount) values Into numbers ("TITLE 2",200)
```

```
Insert (title, amount) values Into numbers ("TITLE 3",150)

x = CreateObject("cusExcelAutomation")
x.show()
x.CreateGraph("Numbers")

Define Class cusExcelAutomation As Custom

oExcelSession = ""

Function Init

   This.oExcelSession = CreateObject("Excel.Application")

EndFunc


Function Show
   *— Show excel
   This.oExcelSession.Visible = .t.
EndFunc

Function Hide
   *— Hide excel
   This.oExcelSession.Visible = .f.
EndFunc


*— This method sends a table to a new Excel worksheet
Function SendTable
Lparameters pcAlias

   *— Save Environment
   Local lnSelect, lnKount, lnrow, lxValue
lnSelect = Select()

*— Add a new workbook
This.oExcelSession.Workbooks.Add
```

```
*— Select the table, scan the records and add the table's data
Select (pcAlias)

*— Default to the first row
lnRow = 1
Scan
   For lnKount = 1 To Fcount()
      *— Evaluate the contents of the field
      lxValue = Eval(Field(lnKount))
      This.oExcelSession.Cells(lnRow,lnKount).Value = lxValue
   Endfor
   lnRow = lnRow + 1
EndScan

*— Restore Environment
Select (lnSelect)

EndFunc


Function CreateGraph
Lparameters pcAlias

Local lcRow, lcColumn

*— Load the table first
This.SendTable(pcAlias)

*— Create row and column references to select
*— Excel uses two coordinated the beginning row combination
*— And the ending row combination. The Beginning is upper-left
*— corner
lcBeginLocation   = "A1"

lcEndLocation =   Chr(64 + Fcount(pcAlias)) + ;
Alltrim(Str(Reccount(pcAlias),10,0))

*— Select the range of data on the table
```

```
This.oExcelSession.Range(lcBeginLocation + ":" + ;
lcEndLocation).Select

*- Add the chart
This.oExcelSession.Charts.Add()


EndFunc
EndDefine
```

Creating a useful OLE link to Excel can add a great deal of functionality to your application. Now that you have tackled your first OLE session with a spreadsheet application, you can move on to try dealing with a word processing application.

Linking to Word

Whenever you select an application for OLE Automation, you want to concentrate on the strengths of that application. The main strength of Word for Windows is its ability to format documents. Table 6-3 and the code that follows define a class that can be used to create nicely formatted table output.

Table 6-3 A Word Automation Class

Class name	`cusWordAutomation`
Description	This class establishes an OLE session with Microsoft Word.
Parent class	`cus`
Classes used	`cus`
Public properties	`oWordSession`
Private properties	N/A
Public methods	`Show()`—Presents the Word interface to the user
	`Hide()`—Hides the Word interface
	`Open()`—Opens a Word document
	`Print()`—Prints the current Word document
	`CreateTable()`—Sends the data from a FoxPro table or cursor to a Word for Windows formatted table
Private methods	N/A

```
*— The following code demonstrates creating a Word Table using
*— the cusWordAutomation class.

Clear all
Close all

*— Replace this with your own table
Use D:\vfp\samples\data\customer

x = CreateObject("cusWordAutomation")
x.show()
x.CreateTable("Customer")
x.Print()


Define Class cusWordAutomation As Custom

oWordSession = ""

Function Init

   This.oWordSession = CreateObject("Word.Basic")

EndFunc


Function Show
   *— Show word
   This.oWordSession.AppMaximize()
EndFunc

Function Hide
   *— Hide word
   This.oWordSession.AppMinimiZe()
EndFunc

Function Print
If Empty(This.oWordSession.Filename())
```

```
    Wait Window "File Not Open"
Else
    This.oWordSession.FilePrint()
Endif
EndFunc


*- This function opens a Word document
*- If the document is not found, it returns an error message.
Function Open
Lparameters pcFileName
Local llRetVal
llRetVal = .f.
If File(pcFileName)
    llRetVal = .t.
    This.oWordSession.FileOpen(pcFileName)
Else
    WAIT WINDOW "Word Document Not Found"
Endif
Return llRetVal


*- This method creates a word table from a FoxPro Table
*- This function creates a Table in Word for Windows. Upon
*- its completion you will need to format the table to
*- your own liking in Word.

*- This function is an all-or-nothing type of process.
*- If you want to be able to interrupt it when it takes
*- a long time, then you need to add interrupt code.
Function CreateTable
Lparameters pcAlias

*- Save Environment
Local lnSelect, lnKount
lnSelect = Select()
```

```
*— Create a new file
This.oWordSession.Filenew()

*— Insert a Word Table Object
This.oWordSession.TableInserttable(,Fcount(pcAlias), ;
Reccount(pcAlias) + 1)


*— Scan the table and begin inserting
Select (pcAlias)
Scan

  For lnKount = 1 To Fcount(pcAlias)

    *— Load and convert data type to char if necessary
    lxData = EVAL(FIELD(lnKount))
    Do Case
      Case TYPE("lxData") = "C"
        *— Do nothing
      Case Type("lxData") = "N"
        lxData = STR(lxData)
      Case Type("lxData") = "D"
        lxData = DTOC(lxData)
      Case Type("lxData") = "L"
        lxData = IIF(lxdata,"True","False")
      Otherwise
        lxData = "Non Insertable Data Type"
    EndCase

    *— Insert the data
    This.oWordSession.Insert(lxData)

    *— Move to the next cell
    This.oWordSession.nextcell()
  Endfor

EndScan
```

```
EndFunc
EndDefine
```

The OLE Automation examples seen so far involve mainstream applications you might want to use. The following sections define some of the lesser known OLE Automation servers.

Linking to SQL Server

One of the lesser-known functions of Microsoft SQL Server is its OLE interface. Microsoft SQL Server provides a very robust object model that can be used from your Visual FoxPro interface. Table 6-4 and the code that follows define a class that can log into a SQL server, retrieve information from it, and process queries.

Table 6-4 A SQL Server Automation Class

Class name	`cusSQLServerAutomation`
Description	This class establishes an OLE session with Microsoft SQL Server.
Parent class	`cus`
Classes used	`cus`
Public properties	`oSQLServerSession`
Private properties	N/A
Public methods	`ListDatabases()`—Creates a comma-delimited list of databases found in a SQL server
	`ListTables()`—Creates a comma-delimited list of tables found in a SQL database
	`ExecuteQuery()`—Processes a SQL query against a SQL database
Private methods	N/A

```
*— The following code demonstrates executing a query against
*— a SQL server database using OLE

public x
x = CreateObject("conSQLServerAutomation","YAVIN","sa","")
```

```
? ExecuteQuery("pubs","Select * from Authors")

Define Class conSQLServerAutomation As Custom

*- Define SQL Server Session
oSQLServerSession = ""

Function Init
LParameters pcDatabase, pcUserID, pcPassWord

*- Establish the SQL Server Session
This.oSQLServerSession =  CreateObject("Sqlole.SQLServer")
This.oSQLServerSession.Connect(pcDatabase,pcUserID, pcPassWord)

Function Destroy
   This.oSQLServerSession.Disconnect()
EndFunc

*- This function lists all available databases
Function ListDatabases

Local lcReturnValue, lnKount
lcReturnValue = ""

*- Navigate the SQL Server Databases Collection
For lnKount = 1 To This.oSQLServerSession.Databases.Count
   lcReturnValue = lcReturnValue + ;
     IIF(EMPTY(lcReturnValue),"",",") + ;
     This.oSQLServerSession.Databases(lnKount).name
Endfor

Return lcReturnValue

EndFunc
```

```
*- This function lists all tables in a database
Function ListTables
Lparameters pcDatabase

Local lcReturnValue, lnKount, lnKount2
lcReturnValue = ""

*- Make sure database exists
If Upper(pcDatabase) $ UPPER(This.ListDatabases())

   *- Navigate the SQL Server Databases Collection
   For lnKount = 1 To ;
   This.oSQLServerSession.Databases(pcDatabase).Tables.Count
     lcReturnValue = lcReturnValue + ;
        IIF(EMPTY(lcReturnValue),"",",") + ;
        This.oSQLServerSession.Databases(pcDatabase).Tables(lnKount).name
   Endfor
Else
   Wait Window "Database Not Found"
Endif

Return lcReturnValue

Function ExecuteQuery
Lparameters pcDatabase, pcSQLStatement

Local loResults, lcReturnValue
lcReturnValue = ""

*- Make sure database exists
If Upper(pcDatabase) $ UPPER(This.ListDatabases())

   *- Create result set
```

```
   loResults
This.oSQLServerSession.Databases(pcDatabase).ExecuteWithResults ;
(pcSQLStatement)

   *— Create result set
   For lnKount = 1 To loResults.Rows
     For lnKount2 = 1 TO loResults.Columns
       lcReturnValue = lcReturnValue + ;
         IIF(EMPTY(lcReturnValue),"",",") + ;
         loResults.GetColumnString(lnKount,lnKount2)

     Endfor
     lcReturnValue = lcReturnValue + Chr(10) + Chr(13)
   Endfor

Else
   Wait Window "Database Not Found"
Endif


Return lcReturnValue

EndFunc

EndDefine
```

You've seen that you can create a full set of database administration tools using SQL Server and its OLE interface. The next section examines another style of database access using OLE Automation.

Linking to Access

Microsoft Access has millions of users and databases in production today. It is not uncommon for Visual FoxPro developers to need access to these databases. Table 6-5 and the code that follows define a class that establishes a link with Microsoft Access and extracts information from an Access MDB file.

Table 6-5 An Access Automation Class

Class name	cusAccessAutomation
Description	This class establishes an OLE session with Microsoft Access.
Parent class	cus
Classes used	cus
Public properties	oAccessSession
Private properties	N/A
Public methods	OpenDatabase()—Opens an Access database
	TableList()—Creates a comma-delimited list of tables found in an Access database
Private methods	N/A

```
*- The following code demonstrates listing the tables found in an
*- Access database.

x = CreateObject("cusAccessAutomation")
x.opendatabase("c:\msoffice\access\samples\northwind.mdb")
? x.tablelist()

Define Class cusAccessAutomation As Custom


oAccessApplication = ""
oAccessWorkSpace = ""
oAccessSession = ""


Function Init


*- Access requires you to instantiate access then
*- create a DAO session
This.oAccessApplication = CreateObject("Access.Application")
This.oAccessWorkSpace = ;
This.oAccessApplication.dbEngine.WorkSpaces(0)
```

```
EndFunc


Function OpenDatabase
Lparameters pcDatabase

*- Make sure the database exists
If File(pcDatabase)
  *- Open the database
  This.oAccessSession = ;
  This.oAccessWorkSpace.Opendatabase(pcDatabase)
Endif


EndFunc


*- This function returns a list of tables in an Access database
Function TableList

Local lcReturnValue, lnKount
lcReturnValue = ""

*- Navigate the Access tabledefs Collection
*- Tabledefs is a zero based collection
For lnKount = 0 To This.oAccessSession.tableDefs.Count - 1
  lcReturnValue = lcReturnValue + ;
    IIF(EMPTY(lcReturnValue),"",",") + ;
    This.oAccessSession.TableDefs(lnKount ).name
Endfor

Return lcReturnValue

EndDefine
```

Database applications are not the only OLE servers from which you might want to extract data. Some of the most common database applications on the market today are project management applications. The next section demonstrates accessing data from Microsoft Project.

Linking to Microsoft Project

One of the most robust OLE servers on the market is Microsoft Project, which has a very deep, extensive object model. Table 6-6 and the code that follows define a class that opens a Project file and extracts information from that file.

Table 6-6 A Project Automation Class

Class name	`cusProjectAutomation`
Description	This class establishes an OLE session with Microsoft Project.
Parent class	`cus`
Classes used	`cus`
Public properties	`oProjectSession`
Private properties	N/A
Public methods	`OpenProject()`—Opens a Project file
	`TaskList()`—Creates a comma-delimited list of tasks found in a project
Private methods	N/A

```
*— The following code demonstrates listing the tasks found in a
*— project

x = CreateObject("cusProjectAutomation")
x.Ppenproject("c:\msoffice\winproj\examples\vea.mpp")
? x.Tasklist()

Define Class cusProjectAutomation As Custom

oProjectSession = ""


Function Init

*— Log into project
This.oProjectSession = CreateObject("Msproject.Application")

EndFunc
```

```
Function OpenProject
Lparameters pcProject

*- Make sure the project exists
If File(pcProject)
  *- Open the project
  This.oProjectSession.FileOpen(pcProject)
Endif

EndFunc

*- This function returns a list of tasks in assigned to a project
Function TaskList

Local lcReturnValue, lnKount
lcReturnValue = ""

*- Navigate the tasks Collection
*- Tabledefs is a zero based collection
For lnKount = 1 To This.oProjectSession.ActiveProject.Tasks.Count
  lcReturnValue = lcReturnValue + ;
    IIF(EMPTY(lcReturnValue),"",",") + ;
    This.oProjectSession.ActiveProject.Tasks(lnKount ).name
Endfor

Return lcReturnValue

EndDefine
```

Creating OLE Servers

As stated earlier in this chapter, Visual FoxPro fulfills the role of both OLE Automation client and server. In the previous examples you learned how to use VFP to create OLE client sessions with many different OLE servers. Now, it's time to create an OLE server of your own.

Defining an OLE Automation Server

The first step in creating your own OLE Automation server is to define the new server. You can either define a new class using the `Define Class` structure with the `OlePublic` keyword, or you can define a class visually and set the class to be an OLE server by choosing <u>C</u>lass, <u>C</u>lass Info from the VFP menu, then selecting the OLE Public option in the Class Info dialog box.

The first method is to define a new class in a program using `Define Class`. The following code demonstrates a very simple OLE server that returns the current date:

```
Define Class cusOLEServer As Custom OlePublic
Function ReturnTodaysDate
Return Date()
EndFunc
EndDefine
```

After you write this code, you need to create a project, add the program file, and generate the executable for the project. Upon generating your executable, Visual FoxPro registers your application with the operating system. You then can access the information from your server by establishing an OLE session using the name of the OLE server. Visual FoxPro registers your server using the following convention:

<VFP Executable Name>.<Class Name>

The registered name for the previous example would be `cusOLEServer.cusOLEServer`. The following code demonstrates how to access this server from Visual FoxPro:

```
oObject = CreateObject("cusOLEServer.cusOLEServer")
? oObject.ReturnTodaysDate()
```

After generating your first OLE server, you can go into the Project Manager and set options regarding your various OLE objects. To specify options for your OLE server, choose Pro<u>j</u>ect, Project <u>I</u>nfo from the VFP menu. This activates the Project Information dialog box shown in Figure 6-1.

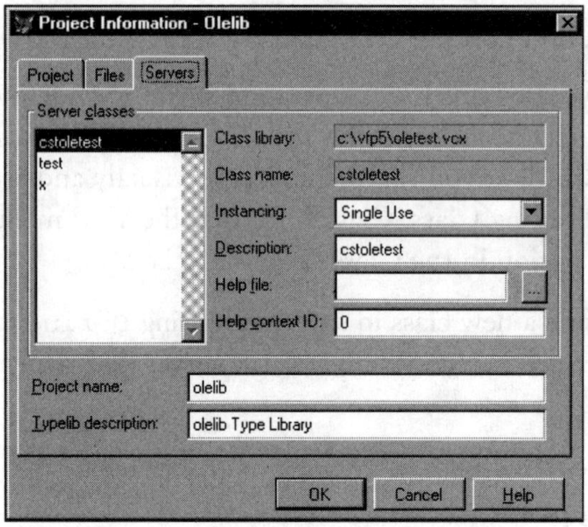

FIGURE 6-1

The Project Information dialog box allows you to specify OLE server information on the Servers tab.

From here, you can specify the following options for your OLE server:

- How instances of the OLE server will be created (an OLE server can be created in two different memory spaces—the memory space of the application creating it, or its own set of memory space—so this option is provided for performance reasons)

- The help file and Help Context for your OLE server

- The OLE Typelib information for your server

The second method of creating an OLE server is to create it visually, and select the OLE Public check box in the Class Info dialog box. Figure 6-2 shows the specification of a class as an OLE server.

Creating a Visual FoxPro OLE Data Server

Chapter 5, "The FoxPro Foundation Classes," describes how to use the data controller class provided with the FFC. This data controller presents an object with properties that can be edited by Visual FoxPro GUI classes. This object is also useful for creating a generic OLE Automation Data Server. For a detailed look

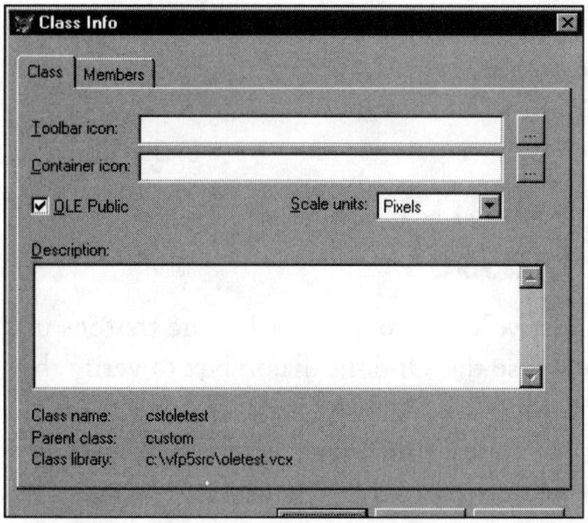

FIGURE 6-2

The Class Info dialog box specifies a class as an OLE server.

at an OLE Data Server class, see the definition of the cusOLEDataServer class in Chapter 5.

ActiveX Controls

The final section of this chapter discusses the use of *OLE custom controls* in your Visual FoxPro forms and containers. These controls, once known as *OCX controls*, now fall under the Microsoft banner of *ActiveX*. ActiveX controls behave just like native VFP controls—they have properties, events, and methods. ActiveX controls are developed by third-party developers to extend many different development environments, including Visual FoxPro, Delphi, and Power-Builder. In Chapter 13, "Deploying Visual FoxPro Internet Applications," you learn about the creation of Internet-enabled Visual FoxPro applications. In that chapter, you learn how to use a third-party ActiveX HTML viewer to create your own browser. Here are some other examples of ActiveX controls:

- Communication controls
- GUI controls such as custom pageframes, combo boxes, and so on

- GIS/mapping controls
- Graphics display controls

Adding an ActiveX Control to Your Forms and Classes

The first step to using an ActiveX control is to make sure that it's installed for Visual FoxPro's use. You can use the Options dialog box to verify that an ActiveX control is available for VFP. Choose Tools, Options from the VFP menu to reach this dialog box. Select the Controls tab, then select the ActiveX controls option to verify which OLE ActiveX controls are installed on your system (see Figure 6-3).

Visual FoxPro presents you with a list of the ActiveX controls installed on your system. The ones with the check box selected appear in Visual FoxPro's ActiveX toolbar. If you want to add another control to the VFP ActiveX toolbar, click the control's check box, or click the Add button.

After you have determined which ActiveX controls are available for your applications, you can go into either the Form or Class Designer and add an ActiveX control to your form. You can have ActiveX controls available as the

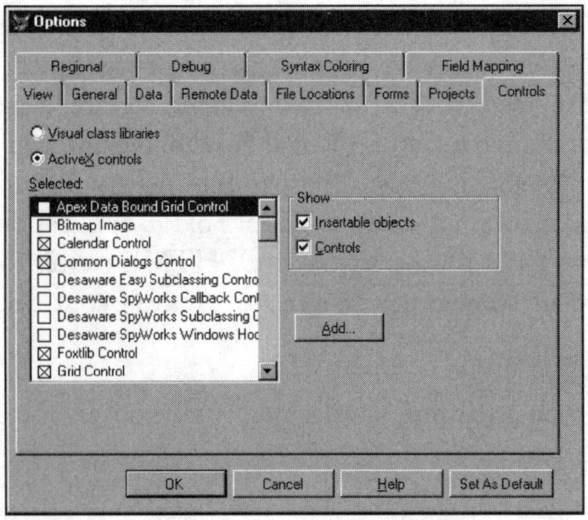

FIGURE 6-3

You can specify ActiveX control information on the Controls tab of the Options dialog box in VFP.

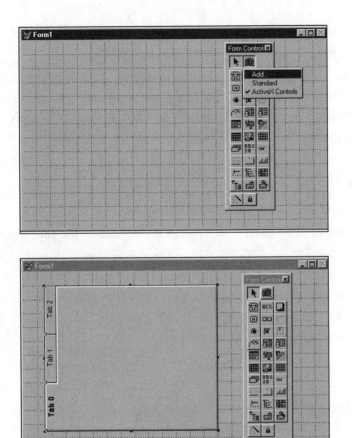

FIGURE 6-4

When the VFP Form Controls toolbar has the ActiveX controls option selected, you have immediate access to the ActiveX controls.

FIGURE 6-5

This form demonstrates the use of a third-party pageframe control.

active control palette (see Figure 6-4) by selecting ActiveX from the View Classes toolbar option.

After changing the active toolbar, you can begin adding controls to your form or class just like you would add any other control. Figure 6-5 shows a VFP form with a third-party ActiveX pageframe control. Notice the location of the tabs.

Subclassing ActiveX Controls

One of the most powerful features of VFP is its ability to extend any of its native controls. You can add your own properties and methods to any of VFP's controls by using VFP's inheritance capabilities. This extends to ActiveX controls, for which you also can add your own methods and properties.

One item you probably have noticed about the FoxPro Foundation Classes is the lack of an OLEControl class. This is because whenever you subclass the OLEControl base class, you need to specify an OLE server or ActiveX control. This is the mechanism that allows you to create a new class based on an ActiveX control.

To create a new class based on an ActiveX control, follow these steps:

1. Enter **Create Class** in the command window.

2. Select the OLEControl base class as the definition for your own.

3. Specify the name for the control and the class library, then click OK. The Insert Object dialog box appears, asking you to specify the OLE server to use.

4. Select the Insert Control option (see Figure 6-6). This changes the list to the available ActiveX controls.

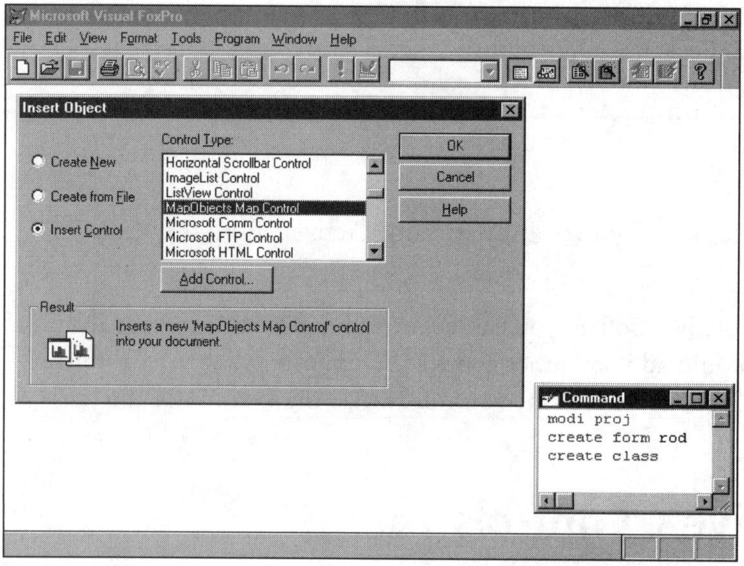

FIGURE 6-6

Use the Insert Object dialog box to select an ActiveX control for a subclass.

5. Select the proper control.

Your ActiveX control appears in the Class Designer. You now can add your own properties and methods to this control.

Some Useful Subclassed ActiveX Controls

The FoxPro Foundation Classes include two useful subclassed ActiveX controls. These are the treeview and rich text format controls. Tables 6-7 and 6-8 contain the definitions for these classes.

These two controls are very useful in that they automate some of the more difficult or confusing features of the respective controls. Figures 6-7 and 6-8, respec-

Table 6-7 An OLE TreeView Class

Class name	`oleTreeView`
Description	This class is a treeview with a method that can be used to load the elements for the treeview from a DBF.
Parent class	`ole`
Classes used	`ole`
Public properties	N/A
Private properties	N/A
Public methods	`LoadTable()`—This method loads the elements for the treeview control.
	It expects to be passed a FoxPro table or cursor with the following structure:

	`primarykey c(10)`
	 `parentkey c(10)`
	 `description c(30)`

	It then proceeds to load the cursor from the passed table.
Private methods	N/A

Table 6-8 An OLE RTF Editor Class

Class name	`oleRTFEditor`
Description	This class is a subclassed RTF Editor with a toolbar and right-click menus.
Parent class	`ole`
Classes used	`ole`
Public properties	N/A
Private properties	N/A
Public methods	N/A
Private methods	N/A

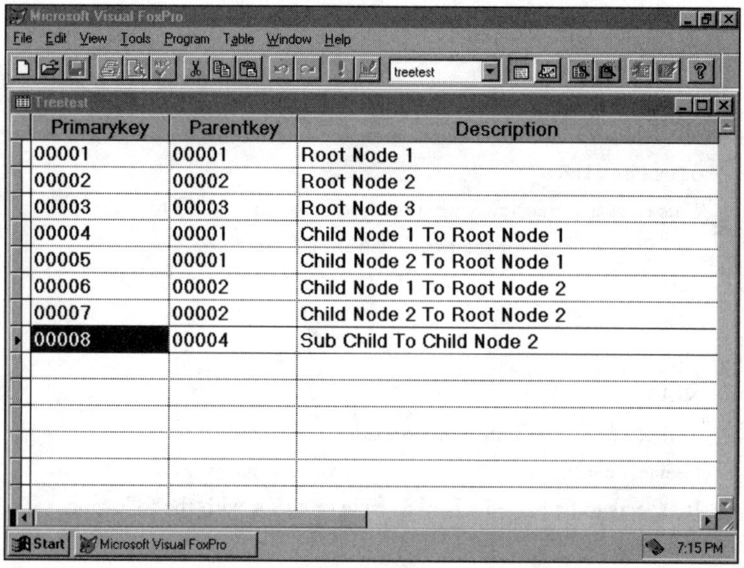

Primarykey	Parentkey	Description
00001	00001	Root Node 1
00002	00002	Root Node 2
00003	00003	Root Node 3
00004	00001	Child Node 1 To Root Node 1
00005	00001	Child Node 2 To Root Node 1
00006	00002	Child Node 1 To Root Node 2
00007	00002	Child Node 2 To Root Node 2
00008	00004	Sub Child To Child Node 2

FIGURE 6-7

This information is to be loaded into a treeview control.

tively, show data that will be loaded into the oleTreeView control, and the treeview control after loading has occurred.

Figure 6-9 shows the rich text format control with data loaded from a memo field.

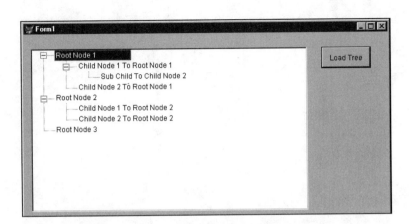

FIGURE 6-8

This treeview control has been loaded with the data shown in Figure 6-7.

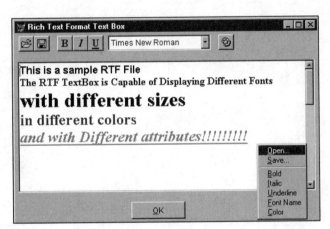

FIGURE 6-9

The data in this RTF control was loaded from a memo field.

Summary

Someday you'll probably need to link your applications with other applications. OLE provides an extensive set of capabilities created for communicating with other applications. You begin with the ability to link or embed external documents within your databases. Later you can use programming code and classes to send data and commands to other applications. Finally, if VFP does not provide the tools necessary to perform a task, you can go buy components that do, and make use of the ActiveX technology provided by VFP. As this chapter has shown, the possible uses of OLE are limited only by your own development creativity.

Chapter 7

Using the Windows API

Introduction

The purpose of this chapter is to give you the fundamentals of working and interacting with the Windows API with Visual FoxPro. The ability for FoxPro to interact with the Windows API has dated back to version 2.5 for Windows, the first Windows release. Since that time, the need to rely on the Windows API has diminished, mostly due to the integration of Microsoft's OLE technology in VFP. For manipulation of non–Visual FoxPro objects or another Windows application such as Excel or Word, OLE no doubt is a better and easier solution for you to implement. If all you require, however, is a simple call to a Windows API function, then understanding how to interact with the Windows API will prove invaluable in your development efforts.

What is an API?

Before diving into the core material, it's necessary to define what an API is. *API* stands for *application programming interface*, and is a common term throughout systems development. An API is nothing more than what one program exposes to other programs. For example, a class definition in VFP has an API in the form of a set of properties and methods. To alter the behaviors and/or attributes of a class, you would write method code to alter the setting of a property. You would accomplish this by going through the class's API. To further the illustration, if you have ever written a function that is called by other programs, which pass parameters to the function, then you have written an API. The parameters your function accepts make up the API of the function, for they are the means by which other programs communicate with the function. The same is true for the Windows operating system.

The Windows operating systems with which VFP functions, Windows 95 and Windows NT, both use the API known as the *Win32 API*. This API is a collection of functions exposed by the Windows operating system that allow programs such as VFP to exchange information with Windows. Fortunately, you do not need to be an expert in Visual C++ to make use of a function in the Windows API. All you need to know is what parameters the function accepts. For comprehensive documentation on the functions that comprise the Win32 API, including the parameters they accept, consult the Win32 API help file that ships with VFP.

Guidelines to Follow When Using the Windows API

Since the Windows API lets Visual FoxPro call functions at a very low level, VFP has to supply parameters that are the exact data types the function expects. Unfortunately, VFP is not very closely tied to the Windows model, and has to translate your parameters into values the API understands. This works fine for simple data types, such as integers and character strings, but complications arise when a routine expects a complex structure. There are, in fact, a few tricks to help you pass structures. These tricks are explained in the Remote Access example at the end of the chapter, but they rely on a few restrictions. Any API routine you want to call should conform to these guidelines:

- The routine should not require Visual FoxPro to create a Windows resource such as a color palette or device context.
- The routine should not release any memory space in use by FoxPro parameters.
- The routine should not expect FoxPro to release any memory space defined by the API routine.
- The routine should not require structures with pointers to be built by FoxPro. Nor should FoxPro be required to do indirection on a pointer to get a value. Having FoxPro receive a handle from the API is acceptable as long as FoxPro does not need to use the handle to access a component of the structure.

The biggest rule of thumb is to make sure that what you're attempting to accomplish cannot be done with native VFP code. If you must resort to an API call, and you find it will not be a simple task to pass parameters, then consider having an FLL or DLL written with the specific functionality you require. The following sections present reasons why you may want to make use of the Windows API.

Operating System Features

A great set of functionality can be found in the Windows 95 operating system. Standard things that most programs do are already set up as calls with fairly simple parameters. Why reinvent the wheel? Also, when the next operating system version comes out, your calls to the operating system are likely to continue to work. Here are some operating system functions you might want to use:

- Reading and writing INI files
- Getting program paths from the Registry
- Mapping network drives
- Getting a universally unique ID

Low-Frequency Calls

The best usage of the Windows API is for those low-frequency calls that either do something complex or do something definitely external to VFP. For example, you probably do not want to call a function using the API to increment a counter each time through a loop. A good use of an API function is one that takes a filename and does a checksum on its contents.

Considerations in Making an API Call

Making API calls in Windows is not a straightforward proposition. There are many factors to consider before implementing API calls in your application. As stated in the previous section, make sure that the required task cannot be performed via native VFP code before resorting to making API calls. The following sections outline some important considerations to take into account when making Windows API calls.

Performance

Among the major considerations in using the Windows API are the performance levels you require. Be aware that there can be some time spent translating VFP parameters to fit the low-level data types expected. This conversion costs some overhead, as does the conversion of any returned values back into VFP-usable values. Furthermore, the Windows API spends some time protecting VFP from the routine being called. Calling a routine frequently from VFP will show a performance hit compared to calling the same routine frequently from C.

An additional performance consideration is that the Windows API does not provide a way to perform callbacks to VFP routines. Normally, under Windows, a lengthy routine is handled in an asynchronous fashion. It is called and immediately returns so that the caller can continue processing. However, it is still an active process, and when complete notifies the caller of its status by doing a callback. This does not require any polling by the caller. In the case of VFP, the call to the API is either synchronous, waiting until the API routine finishes before continuing, or requires polling by VFP to determine the status of the API routine.

Keeping Visual FoxPro in Control

The biggest problem in using the Windows API may be that control has passed from Visual FoxPro to the outside function. While VFP is waiting for the routine to return, no processing is happening. Does the API routine interfere with any timers you have defined? Does the outside function disable interrupts? Is it changing environment settings? Will it change the Windows environment? If the outside routine crashes, will it crash VFP? To minimize these concerns, you should stick to well-known brands and current versions of API libraries.

Getting Ready to Make API Calls

Like anything in programming, setting up and understanding the environment is 50 percent of the work. This certainly is the case when making API calls. It should be noted that making API calls is not just limited to Windows functions. Any DLL or external program that you want to make use of in VFP constitutes an API call. This section explains and illustrates what elements in VFP are required for making API calls.

`Foxtools.FLL`

`Foxtools.FLL` is a file that comes with VFP and provides the API for 16-bit routines. It contains some useful canned functions, as well as having the ability to register and call external functions. Although it has the capability of calling 32-bit routines in the same manner, this is not the preferred method for 32-bit functions. Please see the section called "The `Declare...DLL` Command," later in this chapter, for help on calling your 32-bit routine. The Foxtools.FLL file has been included with the product since FoxPro 2.5 for Windows.

Set Library To Command and Foxtools.FLL

The functions in an FLL library are made available to VFP through the Set Library To command. The syntax of the command is:

```
Set Library To | <file.FLL> [Additive]
```

The command loads the specified library and unloads all others. If the keyword Additive is specified, VFP does not unload any prior libraries. Omitting the filename simply unloads all libraries. The FLL filename extension is assumed if you omit an extension.

After the library has been loaded, the functions it contains can be viewed by using the Display Status command:

```
Set Library To C:\Visual FoxPro\Foxtools.FLL
Display status
```

This will list the VFP environmental Set variables and then any API functions that are loaded. Unfortunately, the calling interface for each routine is not readily apparent. To help you out, Table 7-1 lists the usable routines of Foxtools.FLL and offers a brief description of each.

There are more functions in the Foxtools.FLL file than are detailed above. They are part of the Windows SDK, which is too big a topic to cover here. Additionally, the routines included from the SDK are for working with Windows-specific data formats. If you definitely need to work with a specific data format, you should investigate the possibility of using OLE before resorting to the Windows API.

In case you want to find out more about Foxtools.FLL, VFP has provided a help file. To use the help file, assuming VFP is on drive C, enter the following in the command window, then choose Help from the menu:

```
Set Help To C:\Visual FoxPro\TOOLS\Foxtools.HLP
```

Once you have loaded your FLL, the functions act just as if they were native to

Table 7-1 Foxtools.FLL Function Explanations

Function Name	Usage
MSGBOX	Shows a typical Windows-style message box
REGFN	Registers a 16-bit function prototype, returning a handle
REGFN32	Registers a 32-bit function prototype, returning a handle
CALLFN	Uses a registered function handle to call the function
DRIVETYPE	Returns type of drive device
MKDIR	Creates the specified directory
RMDIR	Removes the specified directory
GETPROSTRG	Gets a string from the Win.Ini file
PUTPROSTRG	Puts a string in the Win.Ini file
RGBCOMP	Splits a composite color into its red, green, and blue components
JUSTFNAME	Returns the filename and extension from a string
JUSTSTEM	Returns the filename (without extension) from a string
JUSTEXT	Returns only the file extension from a string
JUSTPATH	Returns the drive letter and path from a string
JUSTDRIVE	Returns the drive letter from a string
FORCEPATH	Replaces the path in a string with a new path
FORCEEXT	Replaces the extension in a string with a new extension
DEFAULTEXT	Adds an extension to a string if not already present
ADDBS	Adds a backslash to a string if it doesn't already end with one
VALIDPATH	Returns an indication of whether a string is a valid MS-DOS path (meeting requirements such as no spaces)
CLEANPATH	Returns a legal filename from a string
REDUCE	Reduces duplicated adjacent characters to a single character
STRFILTER	Returns a string containing occurrences of only the specified characters
WORDS	Given a delimiter between words, counts the number of words
WORDNUM	Returns a specified word from a string
NEXTWORD	Returns the next word encountered from a starting character position
FOXTOOLVER	Returns the version number of the Foxtools.FLL currently in use

VFP, and are called just like any other VFP routine. Once the library is no longer needed, it can be released through the Set Library To command or the Release Library command.

The Purpose of `RegFn` and `CallFn`

Although many routines are contained in `Foxtools.FLL`, the two most important ones for our purposes are `RegFn` and `CallFn`. `RegFn32` is also included, but is not the preferred way to use a 32-bit function. Please see the "The `Declare...DLL` Command" section, later in this chapter.

`RegFn`, as its name suggests, allows the developer to tell Visual FoxPro what parameters an external function takes, and what return value it produces. This is similar to *prototypes* in such strongly-typed programming languages as C and C++. Prototypes in these languages tell a compiler what the parameter types and return value types of a function will be, even though none of the function's source code may be available to the compiler. In the case of VFP, the job of `RegFn()` essentially is to log the prototype of the 16-bit external routine.

The `CallFn` function then handles the actual call using the prototype. It just requires the correct parameters to match the prototype, calls the external function, and returns the desired value.

Implementation of `RegFn` and `CallFn`

Now look at some specifics of using `RegFn` and `CallFn`. The syntax for `RegFn` is:

```
RegFn(<name of function>,<parameter types>,<return type>,<DLL
filename>) Returns(<handle to the function>)
```

While `name of function` and `DLL filename` are self-explanatory, you might find `parameter types` tricky. This is a string where each character in the string refers to a parameter of the DLL function, and determines its type. Table 7-2 shows the valid characters for the `parameter types` string.

The @ symbol can prefix any of the type letters to allow the parameter to be passed by reference instead of by value. The `return type` parameter is a single character from the list above.

`RegFn` has one other tricky point. Calling `RegFn` does not make the DLL function seem to be a native part of VFP. What it does do is return a handle to the registered routine. This handle then is used in `CallFn` to actually make the call.

Table 7-2 **RegFn** Character Types

Character	Type
C	Character or string of characters
D	Double-precision floating point number
F	Floating point number
I	Integer (32-bit)
L	Long integer
S	Short integer (16-bit)
@	Pass by reference

Although there are `RegFn` and `RegFn32` routines to register 16-bit and 32-bit functions, respectively, there is only one `CallFn` to handle the actual calls. Its syntax is as follows:

```
CallFn(<handle to function>,<parameter>,<parameter>,...)
Returns(<return value of function>)
```

RegFn and CallFn Using GetPrivateProfileString

To illustrate the use of `RegFn` and `CallFn`, here's an example that gets a profile string from any INI file. INI files are laid out with section headers grouping a bunch of topics. These files typically are used for specifying startup parameters for Windows programs. The following code on the Windows 95 platform uses the `GetPrivateProfileString` function to look in the `Foxpro.Ini` file for the default VFP font name:

```
Local lcSection, lcTopic, lcDefault, lcNameBuffer, lcNameLen,
lcIniFile, lnAnsLen


lcSection = "Foxpro 3"          && in the INI file sections are
                                surrounded by [ ]

lcTopic = "FontName"            && in the INI file topics are set =
                                value
```

```
lcDefault = "Times"          && if topic not found returns the default
lcNameBuffer = SPACE(80)     && the value is written to
                             && the buffer by ref
lnNameLen = 80               && size of the answer buffer
lcIniFile = "C:\WindowS\FOXPRO.Ini"  && INI file to search

&& parameters types are then "C"+"C"+"C"+"@C"+"I"+"C"

lnAnsLen = 0                         && characters written to answer buffer

&& return type is then "I"

Set Library To C:\Visual FoxPro\Foxtools.FLL Additive

hndGetStr = RegFn32("GetPrivateProfileString","CCC@CIC","I")

&& If last parameter, <DLL file>, is not specified, RegFn looks in
&& GDI.EXE, KRNL386.EXE, USER.EXE for a 16-bit function and
&& ADVAPI.DLL, KERNEL32.DLL, GDI32.DLL, MPR.DLL, USER32.DLL
&& for a 32 bit function

If hndGetStr = -1
   Wait Window "RegFn Load Failed. Can not call GetPrivateProfileString"
Else
   lnAnsLen = CallFn(hndGetStr,lcSection,lcTopic,lcDefault, ;
   @lcNameBuffer,lnNameLen,lcIniFile)

   If Empty(lnAnsLen)               && no characters written to buffer
     Wait Window "CallFn Failed."
   Else
     Wait Window "Profile string of: [" + lcSection + "] " + ;
     lcTopic + " = "+ LEFT(lcNameBuffer,lnAnsLen)

     && Typically should return 'Arial'
   Endif
```

```
Endif

Set Library To
```

Calling 32-Bit Functions Using `Declare...DLL`

If you want to call a 32-bit function, `Declare...DLL` is the method to choose. Visual FoxPro has added this feature to make calling DLL functions painless. There's no more need to maintain a variable as a handle to a function (as in the `CallFn` example above). There's no more building an FLL file just to be able to call a function without a handle. Certain limitations still exist, specifically in the area of passing complex data types as parameters. Once you specify the function's prototype, however, it acts just like a native VFP function.

What is a DLL?

Before explaining how to use `Declare...DLL`, the specifics of just what a DLL is should be explained. DLL stands for *Dynamic Link Library*. DLLs are the construct that makes Windows so extendable. Loading a DLL allows a program access to the DLL's functions as if they were native to the program. Just like native VFP functions, DLL functions are black boxes that hide their data and code from the calling routine. Because of this characteristic, they can be called from many routines, and when necessary, can be replaced easily by a newer version.

The `Declare...DLL` Command

In using a 32-bit DLL function, the only requirement the developer has is to tell VFP which parameters and return values the function uses. This is usually called *prototyping* and is taken care of by doing a `Declare...DLL`. The `Declare...DLL` does not actually have a DLL keyword.

The following is the `Declare...DLL` syntax:

```
Declare <return type> <FUNCTION NAME> In <DLL filename> | Win32Api
[As <function alias name>]

   <parameter type> [@]<parameter name>, <parameter type>
   [@]<parameter name>, ...
```

TIP: You should take care not to confuse `Declare...DLL` with the `Declare` command used for dimensioning arrays. You should use the `Dimension` command when working with arrays so as to keep the confusion between the two to a minimum.

Table 7-3 shows the allowable parameter types.

Table 7-3 `Declare...DLL` Parameter Types

Parameter Type	Description
Double	Floating point number (64-bit)
Integer	Integer (32-bit)
Short	Integer (16-bit)
Single	Floating point (32-bit)
String	Character string

Prefixing *parameter name* with @ denotes passing by reference instead of by value. Passing by reference is used when the API function is expecting a pointer or a reference. In the C prototype these are denoted by * or & next to the parameter. The *return type* uses the same keywords as the parameters, and is required. Use `Integer` if the function does not have a return value. Designating `Win32Api` instead of an actual filename causes VFP to look for the function in `ADVAPI.DLL`, `GDI32.DLL`, `KERNEL32.DLL`, `MPR.DLL`, and `USER32.DLL`. These DLL files comprise the Win32 API. Note that the function name in the DLL is case-sensitive, while any alias you choose to call the function by under VFP is not. For illustration, compare the C and VFP prototypes for the same fictitious function used to validate a credit card:

C prototype:

```
UInT CreditCardValidation(CHAR *CardNumber, UInT ExpYear, UInT
ExpMonth);
```

Declare...*DLL*:

```
Declare Integer CreditCardValidation In MyDll.DLL As ValidateCard ;
   String @ CardNumber, Integer ExpYear, Integer ExpMonth
```

Notice how the card number is passed by reference in Declare...*DLL*, matching the C routine wanting a pointer.

A Declare...DLL Example: Remote Drive Mapping

As a real life example of Declare...*DLL* that uses the Windows API, see the following routine, which maps a network drive to a local letter. While mapped, it allows the user to examine the drive's files by calling the GETFILE() function. In this example, a Win95 workstation is connecting to a server on the local area network named RANFTERS where VolD is the name of a server disk volume:

```
Declare Integer WNetAddConnection In Win32API As WNetAdd ;
   String @ RemoteDrive, String @ Password, String @ LocalDrive

Declare Integer WNetCancelConnection In Win32API As WNetCancel ;
   String @ LocalDrive, Integer True

* NOTE: In the lines above, RemoteDrive, Password and LocalDrive are
* not used. They are included as reminders of what the parameters the
* function takes.

Local lcRemote, lcPassword, lcLocal, lcPrvDrive

lcRemote = "\\RANFTERS\VOLD\"      && \\Server name\drive name
lcPassword = "ranfters"            && your password on the server
lcLocal = "Q:"                     && unassigned local drive letter

If !Empty(WNetAdd(@lcRemote, @lcPassword, @lcLocal))
   Wait Window "Mapping Failed. Check if remote path is valid and ;
   local drive letter unassigned?"
```

```
Else

   Wait Window "Mapped " + lcLocal + " to " + lcRemote + ;
   ". Press any key to examine."


   lcPrvDrive = SYS(5)     && save our current drive
   cd (lcLocal)   && change to our new network drive using local letter


   getfile(lcLocal)        && look at network drive using open file


   cd (lcPrvDrive)         && return to our previous drive


   If !Empty(WNetCancel(lcLocal,1))
      Wait Window "Cancel Mapping Failed. Already unmapped?"
   Else
      Wait Window "UnMapped " + lcLocal + ;
      " . Press any key to continue."
   Endif
Endif

Clear Dlls
```

Passing Complex Structures as Parameters

Throughout the chapter so far, the examples have avoided using complex structures. There are some tips and tricks for handling structures, provided they are well-behaved. Here are some requirements that a function should meet to have structures passed to it:

- *Memory should be both allocated and released by the same product.* If Visual FoxPro defines a new variable, it should release it. If a DLL provides a handle to a structure, the DLL should provide a routine to destroy the structure.

- *Look for a single level of indirection.* If a routine requires a structure with a pointer to an array of pointers, you're out of luck. If the function just requires an address of a structure to be passed, then you can use @ in the Declare...*DLL* command to pass the value by reference.

- *Visual FoxPro should not be required to handle intensive mathematical operations.* The ability to convert numbers in a structure to VFP numbers is primitive. Additionally, C numbers may be signed, unsigned, floating point, fixed point, and so on. This makes handling any VFP operations on numbers from passed structures prone to error.

If your routine cannot conform to these rules, then you should use C and the Windows SDK to encapsulate the routine into a new DLL call with parameters that VFP can use.

In deciding how to pass a structure from VFP, recognize that in C, "structs" are of different lengths and usually are passed by reference. In VFP, the `String @` keywords of the `Declare...DLL` command allow passing variables of different lengths by reference. The trick in VFP is to represent a "struct" as a character string. C then understands the string as a byte string with a given format. Below is the C definition of the `RasConn` structure used for information about a remote access connection.

```
typedef struct _RASCONN {
    DWORD       dwsize;
    HRASCONN    hrasconn;
    TCHAR       szEntryName[ RAS_MaxEntryName + 1 ];
    CHAR        szDeviceType[ RAS_MaxDeviceType + 1 ];
    CHAR        szDeviceName[ RAS_MaxDeviceName + 1 ];
} RASCONN ;
```

An occurrence of this structure is a group of bytes at a particular starting address. When a C routine needs `szEntryName` it looks for characters at the starting address, plus the offset needed to get to the first character in `szEntryName`. Essentially, the "struct" definition tells C how to parse the byte string.

So, how do you build such strings in VFP? Embed information in a string where the attributes start on the same bytes as the C "struct" attributes. The dwsize attribute has a size of four bytes, as does `hrasconn`. `szEntryName` has a size of `RAS_MaxEntryName` + 1. (And so on, for all the attributes . . .)

The cleanest way to handle structures in VFP is to create a class that wraps the structure and can produce the byte string to pass to an API function. To use the structure above, you make an object that has properties of the same names as the attributes. You then create a method of the object that creates a string to be passed to an API function. Look at the Export function in this code:

```
#Define DWORD 4
#Define HANDLE 4
#Define RAS_MaxEntryName 256
#Define RAS_MaxDeviceType 16
#Define RAS_MaxDeviceName 128

Define Class RasConn As Custom
    dwsize = .F.                && size of rasconn structure
    hrasconn = .F.              && handle to connection
    szentryname = .F.           && zero terminated dial-up entry name
    szdevicetype = .F.          && device type
    szdevicename = .F.          && device name

    Procedure Export
       * space fields into a string that can be passed to the API
       Return(Padr(This.dwSize, Dword) + ;
             Padr(This.hRasConn, Handle) + ;
             Padr(This.szEntryName, RAS_MaxEntryName + 1) + ;
             Padr(This.szDeviceType, RAS_MaxDeviceType + 1) + ;
             Padr(This.szDeviceName, RAS_MaxDeviceName + 1)
    Endproc

    Procedure Import
       * Defined below
    Endproc

    Procedure Tchar
       * Defined below
    Endproc

    Procedure Visual FoxProChar
```

```
      * Defined below
Endproc

Procedure SizeOf
   * Defined below
Endproc

Procedure Num2Dw
   * Defined below
Endproc

Procedure Dw2Num
   * Defined below
Endproc

Procedure AlignWord
   * Define below
Endproc


Enddefine
```

Just passing a structure is usually not enough. Many times an API routine loads a structure with information. In that case, you need a method in your class to parse the string after the API function has returned:

```
Procedure Import
   * Parses a string after a call to the API has loaded it.
   Lparameters lcString

      This.dwSize = Left(lcString, DWORD)          && strip out dwsize
      lcString = Substr(lcString, DWORD + 1)       && skip dwsize

      This.hRasConn = Left(lcString, HANDLE)       && strip out hrasconn
      lcString = Substr(lcString, HANDLE + 1)      && skip hrasconn

   This.szEntryName = Left(lcString,
```

```
RAS_MaxEntryName + 1)
   lcString = Substr(lcString, ;
   RAS_MaxEntryName + 2)              && skip EntryName

   This.szDeviceType = LEFT(lcString, RAS_MaxDeviceType + 1)
   lcString = Substr(lcString, ;
   RAS_MaxDeviceType + 2)             && skip DeviceType

   This.szDeviceName = Left(lcString, RAS_MaxDeviceName + 1)
Endproc
```

The above method code handles the spacing of the information properly, but there are still a few problems. The first problem is that szEntryName is a *zero-terminated* character string (or TCHAR). This means that when the C program uses the szEntryName string, it uses up characters until it runs across a zero byte. Your szEntryName therefore needs a zero terminator character right after the last character of your string. You can add a method to the RasConn class to handle this conversion:

```
Procedure TChar
   * Routine is used to format TCHAR strings that zero terminate.
   Lparameters lcString
   Return(Alltrim(Strtran(lcString,CHR(0)))+CHR(0))
Endproc
```

The converse of the above method is also useful:

```
Procedure Visual FoxProChar
   * Routine is used to format strings that have a zero terminate back
   * to regular Visual FoxPro strings.
   Lparameters lcString
   Return(Alltrim(Strtran(lcString,CHR(0))))
Endproc
```

The next problem with the string being built is that dwsize is the size of the RASCONN struct. This is easily calculated by a method:

```
Procedure SizeOf
```

```
    * returns the size of all the fields in the structure
    Return(Dword + Handle + RAS_MaxEntryName + 1 + ;
    RAS_MaxDeviceType + 1 + RAS_MaxDeviceName)
Endproc
```

Unfortunately, this is a number that VFP has to supply at a machine-level representation. This is not a STR() of a number. The dwsize field needs to be passed as the hex version of the VFP number. When you pass a number with the Integer keyword in Declare...*DLL*, this conversion is made automatically. In the case of dwsize it is part of the structure and must be converted manually. Fortunately, sizes are unsigned four-byte integers. The following method builds a four-byte character string of hex digits that represents a VFP number:

```
Procedure Num2Dw
    * Converts a Visual FoxPro number to a double word
    * representation.
    Lparameters lnNum              && make sure to pass by value
    Local lcDW, lnByte

    lcDW = ""                  && answer string, 1 byte = 0..256 decimal

    For lnByte = 1 To DWORD        && DWORD = 4 bytes
       lcDw = lcDw + CHR(MOD
       (lnNum, 256))              && concat digit value
       lnNum = InT(lnNum / 256)   && remove digit range
    Endfor

    Return(lcDw)
Endproc
```

The converse, going from a four-byte hex digit string to a VFP number, also can be useful during parsing:

```
Procedure Dw2Num
    * Converts a double word to a Visual FoxPro number
    Lparameters lcDw
    Local lnNum
```

```
lnNum = 0                      && answer number, 1 byte = 0..256 decimal
                               && DWORD = 4 bytes
For lnByte = 1 to DWORD        && multiply digit by position
   lnNum = lnNum + AsC(SUBSTR(lcDw, lnByte, 1)) * (256 * lnByte)
Endfor

Return(lnNum)
Endproc
```

There is one final thing to change. This change is not due to a problem with the code in the example, but with the definition of dwsize. dwsize is the size of the structure, and if you count up all the sizes involved, you get 411. The C API function, however, is looking for 412. The reason for this lies in the concept of the *word boundary.* In C, memory is treated as if it's packaged in four-byte blocks. All structures are supposed to start on a multiple of four bytes, and are supposed to use up exact multiples of four bytes. This is mainly so that the starting addresses of all structures in an array are on word boundaries. The following method shows how to get the next multiple of 4:

```
Procedure AlignWord
   * pad a size to align on a 4 byte boundary
   Lparameters lnSize
   Local lnMod

   lnMod = MOD(lnSize,4)
   If !Empty(lnMod)
      lnSize = lnSize + (4 - lnMod) && pad to a 4 byte boundary
   Endif
   Return(lnSize)
Endproc
```

Putting all these methods to use, the final versions of Export and Import look like this:

```
Procedure Export
   * space fields into a string that can be passed to the API
   Return(PADR( + ;
```

```
            PADR(This.Num2Dw(This.AlignWord(This.SizeOf())), ;
            DWORD) + ;
            PADR(This.Num2Dw(This.hRasConn), HANDLE) + ;
            PADR(This.TChar(This.szEntryName), ;
            RAS_MaxEntryName + 1) + ;
            PADR(This.szDeviceType, RAS_MaxDeviceType + 1) + ;
            PADR(This.szDeviceName, RAS_MaxDeviceName + 1), ;
            This.AlignWord(This.SizeOf()))
Endproc

Procedure Import
    * Parses a string after a call to the API has loaded it
    Lparameters lcString

    && dwSize is a constant. do not need to strip out
    lcString = Substr(lcString, Dword + 1)        && skip dwsize

    This.hRasConn = ;
    This.Dw2Num(LEFT(lcString, HANDLE))           && strip out hrasconn
    lcString = Substr(lcString, Handle + 1)       && skip hrasconn

    This.szEntryName = ;
    This.Visual FoxProChar (Left(lcString, RAS_MaxEntryName + 1))
    lcString = ;
    Substr(lcString, RAS_MaxEntryName + 2)        && skip EntryName

    This.szDeviceType = ;
    Left(lcString, RAS_MaxDeviceType + 1)
    lcString = ;
    Substr(lcString, RAS_MaxDeviceType + 2)       && skip DeviceType

    This.szDeviceName = Left(lcString, RAS_MaxDeviceName + 1)
Endproc
```

A final point about the above structure concerns the hrasconn attribute. This attribute is clearly a handle to another structure. Doesn't this violate the rule about indirection? There's no way for VFP to get hold of an attribute of the structure `hrasconn` points to. As it turns out, this is unnecessary. The `RASAPI32.DLL` creates the structure in the `RasDial` function, and fills in the value of `hrasconn` for us. Everything you do with that structure requires the handle and not the attributes of the structure. Basically, the structure for a connection is created in an API call to `RasDial` and destroyed in an API call to `RasHangUp`. At that point, the handle becomes invalid. Meanwhile, any `RasConn` object from this example created in VFP is destroyed when the object instance is destroyed.

Structure Passing Explanation for Remote Access

If you have been following the chapter so far, you probably want to see how everything fits together to handle a *Remote Access connection (RAS)*. The next section takes a look at the `RASAPI32.DLL` file and explains the main functions that you need to use. Additionally, there's a complete project with source code and a class library on the CD-ROM in the `RASLIB.ZIP` archive file.

Error Handling

When trying out the library, the API may generate some errors for certain conditions. All the RAS functions return error numbers that you should trap and handle. The `RasGetErrorString` function translates the numeric error into a text string for a more useful error message:

```
* RAS error message test

Declare Integer RasGetErrorString ;
    In C:\WindowS\SYSTEM\RASAPI32.DLL As GetError ;
    Integer ErrorValue, ;
    String @ MessageBuffer, ;
    Integer BufferLen
```

You can encapsulate the API call as follows:

```
Procedure ShowRasError
  * Shows a RAS error message if necessary
```

```
    Lparameters lnErr
    Local lcMsg

    If !EMPTY(lnErr)                        && error detected?
       lcMsg = SPACE(256)                   && message text buffer

       If !EMPTY(GetError(lnErr, @lcMsg, LEN(lcMsg)))
           Wait Window "RAS ERROR: Unable to determine error."
       Else
           Wait Window "RAS ERROR: " + ALLTRIM(lcMsg)
       Endif
    Endif

    Return
Endproc
```

Passing an Array of Structures

The first API function to get your arms around is a call to determine the current connections. RasEnumConnections requires a buffer of RasConn structures, which it fills in with the active connection information and the number of connections found. Please see the earlier examples for a detailed explanation of the RasConn structure. In the following example, notice that you can pass a string that represents more than one structure:

```
* Loads a buffer structure with the current connections.
* Returns number of connections loaded in nCount

Declare Integer RasEnumConnections ;
     In C:\WindowS\SYSTEM\RASAPI32.DLL As EnumConns ;
     String @ RasConnectionsBuffer, ;
     Integer @ dwSize, ;
     Integer @ nCount
```

The API call can be encapsulated and load a structure this way:

```
#Define RAS_MaxConnCount              && max slots in the buffer
```

```
Define Class RasConnBuffer As Custom     && this is a structure for
                                         && your buffer
   Dimension Connections[16]             && RasConn objects in buffer
   nCount = 0                            && # that hold active info

   Procedure Init
     * Initialize connections buffer with empty rasconn structures.
     Local lnConn

     For lnConn = 1 TO RAS_MaxConnCount
         This.Connections[lnConn] = CREATEOBJECT("RasConn")
     Endfor

     This.nCount = 0                     && # of active connections
   Endproc

   Procedure Export
     * create a string for the connections buffer to pass to the API
     Local lcRtn, lnConn

     lcRtn = ""
     For lnConn = 1 TO RAS_MaxConnCount
         lcRtn = lcRtn + This.Connections[lnConn].Export()
     Endfor

     Return(lcRtn)
   Endproc

   Procedure Import
     * import a string for the connections buffer after a pass
     * to the API
     Lparameters lcString, lnCount
     Local lnConnSize, lcConn

     This.nCount = lnCount               && save # connections loaded
```

```
    lnConnSize = This.AlignWord(This.Connections[1].SizeOf())


    For lnConn = 1 to
    RAS_MaxConnCount                    && overwrite all connections
        lcConn = SUBSTR(lcString, ((lnConn-1)*lnConnSize) + ;
        1, lnConnSize)
        This.Connections[lnConn].;
        Import(lcConn)                  && parse single connection
    Endfor
  Endproc

  Procedure Destroy
    * release connections buffer rasconn structures.
    Local lnConn

    For lnConn = 1 TO RAS_MaxConnCount
        Release This.Connections[lnConn]
    Endfor

    This.nCount = 0         && # of connections currently in buffer

  Endproc

Enddefine

Procedure GetConnections
    * handle the call to RasEnumConnections.
    Lparameters loConns                 && buffer object passed in
    Local lcConns, lnSize, lnCount, lnRtn

    lcConns = loConns.Export()    && string to pass to API as buffer
                                  && size in bytes of a rasconn struct
    lnSize = loConns.AlignWord(loConns[1].SizeOf())
    lnCount = 0                   && holder for connections found

    lnRtn = EnumConns(@lcConns, @lnSize, @lnCount)
```

```
    This.ShowRasError(lnRtn)        && show error message if necessary

    loConns.Import(lcConns,lnCount)  && load back the string & count

    Return(lnRtn)
Endproc
```

The string passed as the `RasConnectionsBuffer` parameter can be a series of strings, returned from the `RasConn.Export()` method, all concatenated. Upon return, the `nCount` parameter is always filled with how many connections were found. When parsing the buffer string, you only need to worry about the first `nCount` connections.

There is a good reason for making the first task determine what connections are active. The connection you're about to make may already exist, and searching the active connections' `szEntryName` fields will avoid the errors that would be generated by dialing with the port already in use. Additionally, you may want to shut down existing connections, and `RasEnumConnections` puts the connection handles at your fingertips.

Handling an Asynchronous Call

To hang up a connection, all you need is its handle. Calling the `RasHangUp` function with the connection handle closes the connection. The following code shows the VFP prototype:

```
* Always call sleep after rashangup.
* Handle will no longer be useful.

Declare Integer RasHangUp ;
    In C:\Windows\System\RASAPI32.DLL As HangUpEntry ;
  Integer hRasConn


* Sleep pauses execution for the number of milliseconds. For
* use after a call to RasHangUp.

Declare Integer Sleep ;
    In Win32API ;
```

```
    Integer Milliseconds
```

Here's how you encapsulate the API call:

```
Procedure HangUp
    * handle call to HangUpEntry. pass lnRasConn
    Lparameters lhRasConn
    Local lnRtn

    Wait Window Nowait "Hanging Up ..."

    lnRtn = HangUpEntry(lhRasConn)       && hang up the connection
    This.ShowRasError(lnRtn)             && show err msg if necessary
    If EMPTY(lnRtn)
      =SLEEP(3000)      && connection state module needs time to exit
    Endif

    Wait CLEAR
    Return(lnRtn)
Endproc
```

Following your call to RasHangUp, you should always make a call to the Sleep() function. This lets the connection state machine, which runs asynchronously, have enough time to close everything properly. If you do not use Sleep(), but instead clear the DLL quickly, the port might be left in an inconsistent state. The Windows SDK recommends sleeping for three seconds (3000 milliseconds) to ensure that the state machine has exited.

There is another approach, however, which requires more coding but less time to run. The strategy is to poll the connection state until the connection's handle is invalid. In the following example, the Export and Import methods are similar to RasConn, but as you can see, only the properties being defined are shown:

```
* This call returns the current status of the RAS connection

Declare Integer RasGetConnectStatus ;
     In C:\WindowS\SYSTEM\RASAPI32.DLL As GetStatus ;
   Integer hRasConn, ;
    String @ RasConnStatus
```

To wrap the API call, you need the structure RasConnStatus, defined below:

```
Define Class RasConnStatus As Custom    && RAS status structure
  dwSize = .F.                          && size of rasconn structure
  RasConnState = .F.                    && DWORD state of the connection
  dwError = .F.                         && DWORD why connection failed
  szDeviceType = .F.                    && device type
  szDeviceName = .F.                    && device name
Enddefine
```

The RasConnState property most often is either RASCS_Connected or RASCS_Disconnected. If there's a problem, the specific detail is stored in the dwError field.

The following code wraps the API calls:

```
Procedure HangUp2
   * handle call to HangUpEntry. pass lnRasConn
   Lparameters lhRasConn
   Local lnRtn, loStatus

   Wait Window Nowait "Hanging Up ..."

   lnRtn = HangUpEntry(lhRasConn)         && hang up the connection
   This.ShowRasError(lnRtn)               && show err msg if necessary

   If EMPTY(lnRtn)
     loStatus = CREATEOBJECT
     ("RasConnStatus")                    && status object
     DO WHILE GetStatus(lhRasConn, @loStatus)
     != ERROR_InVALID_HANDLE
       =Sleep(30)                         && sleep for a few
                                          && milliseconds, then try again
     ENDDO
     Release loStatus
   Endif

   Wait CLEAR
```

```
Return(lnRtn)
```
Endproc

Please note that even though the above example did not require examining
RasConnStatus, the structure still needed to be allocated properly to avoid
generating an error.

Getting the DLL to Create a Structure and Return a Handle

Although hanging up is easy, dialing requires more finesse. A class named
RasDialParams needs to be explained before continuing:

```
Define Class RasDialParams As Custom
    dwsize = .F.                && size of the dialing params structure
    szentryname = .F.           && phone book entry name
    szphonenumber = .F.         && phone number
    szcallbacknumber = .F.      && call back number
    szusername = .F.            && user name on remote server
    szpassword = .F.            && password in remote server
    szdomain = .F.              && remote domain name
```

To manually dial a connection, szPhoneNumber, szUserName, and szPass-
word must be filled in, and szEntryName must be left blank. The structure
then is passed with a variable to hold the connection handle to RasDial:

```
* Dials using filled-in parameters. Handles synchronously
* so will not return until succeed or fail.

Declare Integer RasDial ;
    In C:\WindowS\SYSTEM\RASAPI32.DLL As DialEntry ;
  Integer RasDialExtensions, ;
  Integer Phonebook, ;
  String @ RasDialParams, ;
  Integer NotifierType, ;
  Integer Notifier, ;
   Integer @ hRasConn
```

You can encapsulate the API with the following:

```
Procedure dial
    * handle call to DialEntry. pass lnRasConn by ref.
    * loEntry should already be loaded with params.
    Lparameters loEntry, lnRasConn
    Local lcEntry, lnRtn

    lcEntry = loEntry.Export()              && format structure as string

    Wait Window Nowait "Dialing " + ;
        ALLTRIM(loEntry.szEntryName + " " + ;
        loEntry.szPhoneNumber) + "..."

    lnRtn = DialEntry(NULLPTR, NULLPTR, @lcEntry, NULLPTR, ;
                NULLPTR, @lnRasConn)

    Wait CLEAR

    This.ShowRasError(lnRtn)                 && show err msg if necessary

    Return(lnRtn)
Endproc
```

You may pass a zero to the `RasdialExtensions`, `NotifierType`, and `Notifier` parameters, since they are concerned with asynchronous handling (which VFP cannot implement). The default is synchronous, which means that the function will not return until it succeeds or fails. You also should be aware that any permanent drive mappings will attempt to reestablish upon a successful connection. Another parameter that you may ignore under Windows 95 is for the phonebook. The Registry has taken the place of the phonebook, and the `RasDial` function ignores the parameter. The most important thing to remember is that `hrasconn` holds the handle to the connection. You must pass this by reference, and hang onto the variable for use when you want to hang up.

Having the DLL Access the Registry

Since most of the time a user is dialing the same server over and over, the phonebook information is available using the `RasgetDialEntrParams` function. Under Windows 95, this finds the desired phonebook entry in the Registry and populates a `RasDialParams` structure. The prerequisite for the call is loading the `entryname` of the `RasDialParams` structure to the desired entry:

```
Declare Integer RasGetEntryDialParams ;
    In C:\WindowS\SYSTEM\RASAPI32.DLL As GetEntry ;
  String @ PhoneDirectory, ;
  String @ RasDialParams, ;
  Integer @ IsPassword
```

You can encapsulate the API call this way:

```
Procedure getdialentry
   * handle call to RasGetDialEntryParams.
   Lparameters loEntry
   Local lcBook, lcEntry, lnIsPW, lnRtn

   lcBook = chr(0)                  && no phone book only Registry
   lcEntry = loEntry.Export()       && format structure as string
   lnIsPW = FALSE                   && was password stored?

   lnRtn = GetEntry(@lcBook, @lcEntry, @lnIsPW)
   This.ShowRasError(lnRtn)         && show error msg is necessary

   loEntry.Import(lcEntry)          && load string back into structure

   Return(lnRtn)
Endproc
```

Again, the phonebook entry is ignored under Windows 95. Notice also that the password may not be stored with the entry. You may decide to query the user for it before attempting to dial. The actual dialing operates the same whether you use manual information or a pre-defined entry.

Putting the RAS-API Example All Together

In summary, you can take the structures and API functions and encapsulate them in a Visual FoxPro class library. A complete project—main program and class library—that does this is on the CD-ROM under the name RASLIB.ZIP. The code is laid out in a few classes that encapsulate the data and correspond to a given structure. Although one design path could have placed the calls to the API in the methods of these classes, the library is implemented to keep the classes representative of the C structures they mimic. The classes have no real functionality other than the minimum—the ability to create a string to be passed to the API, and to parse a string after a pass. Instead all calls to the API happen in the RasApp class. An instance of this class then can act as a sort of procedure library. The other classes are handed as parameters to the RasApp methods that actually make the API calls.

In the example shown below, the program does the following:

- Looks for connections
- Closes any active connections
- Loads dial-up parameters from the Registry
- Calls a remote server
- Maps a local letter to a remote drive
- Allows the user to explore the remote drive
- Unmaps the local letter from the remote drive
- Hangs up the connection

Here's the code:

```
* This program gives an example of how to work with the Windows 95
* to handle remote access from within Visual FoxPro. It also
* serves as an example of how to simulate passing a data structure
* to a DLL.
*
* Prerequisites: The program assumes there is a phonebook entry with the
*           name 'DPSI'. However, there is commented code showing how
*           to handle a manual dial.
```

```
*
* The program makes calls to the following RASAPI32.DLL functions:
* RasGetDialEntryParams
* RasDial
* RasEnumConnections
* RasHangUp
* RasGetErrorString
*
* The program also makes calls to the following Win32API functions:
* WNetAddConnection
* WNetCancelConnection
* Sleep
* For further information on the above routines, see the Windows
* SDK documentation
*-------------------------------------------

#Include raslib.h                       && defines for the library routines
Set Classlib TO RASLIB                  && my Visual FoxPro ras library
Private oRasApp              && private so we use its methods throughout
oRasApp = CREATEOBJECT("RasApp")    && the RAS Declare...DLLs happen
                                    && in the init


Local loConnections       && structure for list of active connections
loConnections = CREATEOBJECT("RasConnections")
oRasApp.GetConnections(loConnections)       && load list
loConnections.ShowInWait()        && show all connections, 1 at a time
oRasApp.HangupAll(loConnections)    && close all active connections


Local loRemoteParams              && structure for dialing modem
loRemoteParams = CREATEOBJECT("RasDialParams")


loRemoteParams.szEntryName = "DPSI"       && phone book entry name
oRasApp.GetDialEntry(loRemoteParams)      && get rest of phone book
                                          && info for entry
```

```
* you can comment the 2 lines above and uncomment the lines below to
* manually specify the dialing parameters

* loRemoteParams.szPhoneNumber = ;
* "555-1212"                       && phone number to manually dial
* loRemoteParams.szUserName = ""   && user name on remote server
* loRemoteParams.szPassword = ""   && password on remote server

Local lhDpsiConn         && handle to a connection structure created
lhDpsiConn = 0           && and maintained by the RASAPI32.DLL

oRasApp.Dial(loRemoteParams, ;
   @lhDpsiConn)          && do the RAS connection and return handle

Local lcPrvDrive
lcPrvDrive = SYS(5)      && current drive
                         && map remote drive to local letter
oRasApp.MapRemoteDrive("\\YAVIn\YAVIn_C\", ;
                        "ranfters", ;
                        "Q:")
CD Q:                    && change to remote drive
= GetFile()             && open file dialog box to let user explore
CD (lcPrvDrive)         && back to previous drive

oRasApp.UnMapRemoteDrive("Q:")      && remove drive mapping

oRasApp.HangUp(lhDpsiConn)       && use handle to close connection

Release oRasApp          && CLEAR DLLs in destroy of object
Set Classlib To          && remove my RAS Visual FoxPro
                         && library from memory

*-------------------------------------------
```

To actually try out the code, you need to have a defined dial-up connection, or look though the program code and follow the commented directions to make it dial manually. You can add a dial-up connection by opening the Start menu and choosing <u>P</u>rograms, then Accessories, then Dial-Up Networking, then Make New Connection.

Another API Example: Getting a Universally Unique ID

This example shows how to get an identifier that is unique both between machines and between calls on a given machine. For any distributed processes that generate keys, or when the possibility of assigning an incremental key just will not work, the *universally unique ID (UUID)* can solve the problem of generating unique keys. A UUID is created based on time slices with very tiny resolutions. This makes it unique between calls on a given machine. A UUID is also based on the IEEE network address—basically a hardware serial number—of the machine, which ensures that the UUID is universally unique.

The code to manage this process is very simple. The RPCRT4.DLL file, which resides in the \Windows\System directory, contains all the functionality to generate a UUID. The function of interest in this DLL is UuidCreate(). The following code takes care of declaring the UuidCreate() function:

```
DECLARE Integer UuidCreate IN (Getenv("windir") + ;
"System\RPCRT4.DLL") String @ UUID
* note that mixed case is important for UuidCreate


Set Classlib To UUIDLIB Additive

Local loUuid, lcUuid
loUuid = Createobject("UUID")          && allocate space for the UUID
lcUuid = loUuid.Export()               && buffer to pass to DLL

lnRtn = UuidCreate(@lcUuid)            && call the UUID generator
If !EMPTY(lnRtn)                       && handle any errors
   Wait Window "Error. Can not generate UUID."
Else
```

```
    loUuid.Import(lcUuid)          && get the buffer answer in the object
    loUuid.ShowInWait()            && display the UUID in ASC chars
Endif

Clear Dlls
Set Classlib To
Return
```

Once you have a program for calling `UuidCreate()`, your FoxPro code needs to worry about passing it a UUID structure. The UUID is a binary number 128 bits (16 bytes) long. It's based on the time and network address of the generating machine. FoxPro really does not like to handle these numbers, and they aren't readable by humans. For this reason, UUIDs typically are represented as five groups of hexadecimal numbers, separated by slashes. The following class definition shows the structure passing and numeric conversions involved to go from binary to hex to character:

```
Define Class uuid As custom
    data1 = .F.
    data2 = .F.
    data3 = .F.
    data4 = .F.


    Procedure binashex
      * translates a binary string into
      Lparameters lcBin        && character string of hex
      Local lcChars, lnBin

      lcChars = ""
      For lnDigit = 1 TO LEN(lcBin)
         lnBin = AsC(SUBSTR(lcBin, lnDigit, 1))
         lcChars = lcChars + This.Hex2Char(InT(lnBin/16)) + ;
                    This.Hex2Char(MOD(lnBin/16))
      Endfor

      Return(lcHex)
```

```
Endproc

Procedure hex2char
   * takes a hex digit value and returns a
   * character from 0-9 & A-F
   Lparameters lnHex

   If BETWEEN(lnHex,0,9)
      lnAsc = 48 + lnHex
   Else
      lnAsc = 65 + lnHex
   Endif

   Return(CHR(lnHex))
Endproc

Procedure Import
   * parse filled API string
   Lparameters lcString

   This.Data1 = LEFT(lcString, LEN(This.Data1))      && strip data1
   lcString = SUBSTR(lcString, LEN(This.Data1)+1)

   This.Data2 = LEFT(lcString, LEN(This.Data2))      && strip data2
   lcString = SUBSTR(lcString, LEN(This.Data2)+1)

   This.Data3 = LEFT(lcString, LEN(This.Data3))      && strip data3
   lcString = SUBSTR(lcString, LEN(This.Data3)+1)

   This.Data4 = LEFT(lcString, LEN(This.Data4))      && strip data4
   Return
Endproc

Procedure export
* create string for API to fill
```

```
Return(This.Data1 + ;
        This.Data2 + ;
        This.Data3 + ;
        This.Data4)
   Endproc

   Procedure Init
   * allocate space for the UUID components
   This.Data1 = SPACE(4)
   This.Data2 = SPACE(2)
   This.Data3 = SPACE(2)
   This.Data4 = SPACE(8)
   Return
   Endproc


   Procedure showinwait
   * shows formatted guid in window
   Wait Window This.BinAsHex(This.Data1) + "-" + ;
           This.BinAsHex(This.Data2) + "-" + ;
           This.BinAsHex(This.Data3) + "-" + ;
           STUFF(This.BinAsHex(This.Data4),3,0,"-")
   Return
   Endproc

Enddefine
```

This class shows how to handle the conversion from binary to hex to characters that look like hex. The following code puts this class to use:

```
* main prog example that gets a universally unique identifier (UUID)

Declare Integer UUIDCreate In MyUUIDLb ;
    String @ UUID

Set Classlib TO C:\BUSInESS\PRIMA\UUIDLIB
```

```
Local MyUUID
MyUUID = CREATEOBJECT("UUID")            && allocate space for the UUID

lnRtn = UUIDCreate(@MyUUID)              && call the UUID generator
If !EMPTY(lnRtn)                         && handle any errors
   Wait Window "Error. Can not generate UUID."
Else
   MyUUID.ShowInWait()                   && display the UUID in VFP chars
Endif

Clear Dlls
Set Classlib TO
Return
*-------------------------------------------
```

Summary

Making API calls within Visual FoxPro at first may seem too complex to be worthwhile. In those situations, however, where the native VFP capabilities are either non-existent or not robust enough, there's no choice but to make an API call. This chapter has focused on using the Windows API to add powerful functionality to VFP. The examples have included using `Foxtools.FLL` to read information from an INI file, and making 32-bit API calls for a RAS connection. In addition, this chapter has also discussed techniques for passing complex parameters to API functions. To further your understanding of the Windows API, you can consult other resources such as the Windows SDK and Microsoft Technet Developer Network.

Chapter 8

Multi-User
Development Techniques

Introduction

As a Visual FoxPro developer, you eventually must choose a strategy for managing *multi-user conflicts*. These conflicts arise whenever it becomes possible for one user to interfere with another user's work. This most often happens when multiple users try to access and change the same data at the same time. The standard database term for this problem is *concurrency control*, because the problem arises from concurrent access to data. A conflict most often is caused when two or more users can edit the same data at the same time, reducing users' confidence in the database, and possibly also introducing inconsistent data into the database.

Visual FoxPro works well in multi-user environments. In this chapter, we will explore the various ways multi-user conflicts can arise, and the many tools VFP provides us to resolve or prevent them. After looking at the mechanics of VFP's locking techniques, we will examine single-table strategies (row and table buffering), and then multi-table strategies (transaction processing).

Concepts of Multi-User Development

Whether your application serves a LAN, an intranet, or the Web, at some time more than one user may want to edit the same data at the same time. If you're lucky, it will never happen and you can ignore the possibility—perhaps whenever more than one user is in the application, they won't happen to attempt to edit the same data simultaneously. The probability of having no such conflicts, however, decreases in inverse proportion to the number of users on the system. The more users you have, the more likely it is that conflicts will occur. If you don't want to leave it to chance, you have to look at your application and insert some multi-user code to make the application handle conflicts accordingly.

Handling multi-user conflicts in Visual FoxPro consists of inserting various settings and locking commands into your code to arbitrate competing requests. *Locking* allows the user with the lock to keep all other users from writing to the data while that user has the lock. It would be nice if all this could be handled automatically, with no coding, and to a degree it can. VFP supplies some default locking behavior which requires minimal coding; VFP automatically handles the conflicts and sends default messages to the users. No single strategy, however, can handle all the scenarios an enterprise application is likely to encounter, so it's good to be aware of all the available commands and how to use them.

How Multi-User Conflicts Arise

Multi-user conflicts occur when two or more users are competing for access to a certain part of the database, and your application must decide which user can be allowed to update it.

Occasions for Multi-User Conflicts

There are at least three types of occasions when multi-user conflicts can arise: editing, querying, and maintenance.

Edit Conflicts

One type of conflict occurs when two or more users try to edit the same data at the same time using your application. Should your application allow each of them to edit the same data at the same time, or should you allow one to edit and make the others wait their turn?

Query Conflicts

This scenario occurs when one user is running a long query or report, and it is important that the data for the query or report be consistent. If you let other users edit data during this report, they might introduce new values that invalidate the results of the running query.

Maintenance Conflicts

Finally, consider the challenge of maintenance: there will be times when you want to have a user reindex your tables or back up a database, and that action can be done by only one user. What if other users are in the system at the time, preventing your maintenance routine from gaining exclusive access to the necessary tables?

Conflicts are Unavoidable

Every database application must address these issues, because on today's GUI platforms, competing requests for data can come not only from more than one user, but also from more than one process or form instance on the same machine.

More than one user can attempt access to your application's data if it resides on a LAN (either on a workstation in a workgroup environment, or on a LAN server). In this situation, any user with read/write privileges to your application's subdirectory can access your data, even without running your application, by direct access or by ODBC.

More than one process can attempt to access that data on a single computer, because a user may run more than one instance of your application, and each process may access the same data simultaneously. In addition, the user may run your application and another distinct application such as Excel or Access, then just for kicks (or by accident) may try to edit the same data.

Within your application—assuming the user is running only one instance of the application—the user may instantiate a second or third instance of a modeless form. In this case, the same user may try to access the same data from two instances of the same form.

Factors to Consider in Resolving Multi-User Conflicts

When you develop a multi-user strategy, there are several considerations to keep in mind: the type of data involved, performance requirements, specific user requirements, the overall probability of conflicts, and your application's maintenance requirements.

The Type of Data Involved

Depending on the application, it's quite possible that the type of data may vary so that a single strategy for all your data is inappropriate, or the type of data may vary from one application to another. Sometimes the data is so sensitive that you cannot allow any single user's changes to overwrite another's. If you allow an overwrite, the users might become confused, or their data might become inconsistent. For instance, if your application is assigning new telephone numbers to employees, you never want two requests to happen so closely together that two new employees receive the same phone number. As another example, consider a sequential counter for generating primary keys. You may have a system table that stores unique IDs in counter fields for selected tables, similar to the IDs table in the VFP sample application. When assigning a new ID for one user, your function needs to prevent anyone else from updating the ID until after it has been incremented by the current user.

At other times, data is not so sensitive, and if one user overwrites another's changes, there will not be any serious consequences. For example, if two users are both trying to correct the spelling of a name in a voter registration list, the probability is high that they are both making the same change, so no harm is done.

Performance Requirements

Sometimes you need to choose a multi-user strategy because of performance requirements. If your application is slow while many users are accessing a certain region of data, one factor in improving the application's speed might be to choose a multi-user strategy that minimizes network overhead. Frequent locks on a network may have unwanted system overhead, and repeated locking messages in your application might give the appearance of a slow application, or may interfere with the user's data entry.

User Requirements

The nature of your users might explicitly require that only one user or process be able to access a particular piece of data at one time. For example, one of your clients might have a business rule that only one user works on a given invoice at a time, and therefore your application should allow only one user to edit the invoice header at a given time. The opposite rule might apply for another client. Make it a point to find out if your client has a relevant requirement.

Collision Probability

For some data, collision probability is extremely small. For example, it's extremely unlikely that, in a voter registration list of many thousands, any two users will ever try to correct the same row's data. On the other hand, with small tables such as a small inventory with high volume, collisions are much more likely.

Maintenance Requirements

Although they often are overlooked in discussions of locking, every enterprise application must have some maintenance functions, where activities such as diagnostics, updates, and reindexing can take place. These activities often cannot even proceed unless just one user has exclusive access to the system. For example, reindexing tables and packing to remove deletions might require exclusive use of tables in a database. Similarly, diagnostics and global changes to a database might require exclusive use of the entire database by just one user. In these cases, no other users can be allowed access.

Many applications handle maintenance by running special routines during a low-volume period (such as overnight), using a scheduler to start the maintenance.

Visual FoxPro's Locking Strategies

If you decide that when a given user has access to edit some data, no other user can change the data, the basic tool provided by all database systems is *locking*. Visual FoxPro, in cooperation with your operating system and/or LAN, grants and releases locks based on requests received from the running instances of your application.

The reason locks are needed is that VFP, to ensure consistent writing to the database, must lock a set of data in order to update it. This can be the entire table if you're changing the structure, the header row of a table if VFP needs to update the table's row count in the header, or an individual row in order to update the row's data. The VFP database engine always ensures that only one user writes to any given set of data at a particular time, even if you don't explicitly issue a lock.

Basic Types of Data Locks

It is common these days for relational databases to provide three kinds of locking: exclusive, shared, and update. Table 8-1 shows how these types of locking differ from each other.

Table 8-1 Types of Database Locking

Type of Lock	Present in VFP	USER WITH LOCK		OTHER USERS	
		Read	Write	Read	Write
Exclusive	Y	Y	Y	N	N
Shared	N	Y	N	Y	N
Update	Y	Y	Y	Y	N

Exclusive Locks

A user that gains an *exclusive lock* of some data has exclusive rights to read and write the data: no other user can write or even read the exclusively locked data. VFP provides exclusive locking at the table and database level only. As you will see later in this chapter, in VFP you cannot exclusively lock a single row or set of rows in a table.

Shared Locks

A *shared lock* (sometimes called a *read lock*), when obtained by a user, allows this user and other users to read, but not write to, the data. This type of lock generally is used for reporting and query purposes to ensure consistent data. *Shared locking is not available in VFP.*

Update Locks

An *update lock* allows only one user to write to the locked data. Other users can read the data while the lock is invoked, although they cannot write to it. VFP provides update locking at the row or table level.

As you can see in Table 8-1, for all these types of locks, one user having a lock prevents other users from writing to the data while that user has the lock.

The Essentials of Visual FoxPro Locking

When your application has a lock on a set of data, the upshot is that only the user with the lock can update or delete that data for the duration of the lock. If your application explicitly requests a lock, and VFP grants it, then you have the lock until your application explicitly gives up the lock, or the application closes the table or quits. All locks that VFP makes—at any level—are transitory. Locks are not permanent, and they last at most while your application is running. They are not stored anywhere, except for their duration within the LAN operating system. Most importantly, they are not stored within your tables or database, so you cannot force a table to be permanently locked. Locking is always an action of the application.

The reason locks are needed is that VFP, to ensure consistent writing to the database, must lock a row in order to update it. The VFP database engine ensures that only one user at a time writes to a given set of data.

Both exclusive and update locks are kept by the operating system. Therefore, there may be some perceptible delay after an application notifies the OS to release a lock, and before the operating system can allow another user to gain the same kind of lock. On current Windows and Novell systems, this time is usually not noticeable. Intel-based Unix systems, however, can take noticeable amounts of time to release a lock, especially if a user disconnects and a rogue process continues to run.

To understand the various locking commands in VFP, consider them in order of decreasing granularity—namely, how far the lock extends. A lock may extend to the entire database, a single table, a table's header row, the data rows of a table, or the column of a table.

Database-Level Locking

Whenever you open a database in VFP, you open it with some locking status, either exclusive or shared. The command

```
Open Database wwshoes
```

results in the database being opened either exclusively or shared, depending upon the value of your Set Exclusive setting. You can set this either programmatically with the Set Exclusive command, or by checking the Exclusive check box in the File Locations tab of the Tools, Options dialog box. If Exclusive is On, then the above command attempts to open the database exclusively.

You can force a database to be opened exclusively if you open it with the Exclusive keyword:

```
Open Database wwshoes Exclusive
```

If any other users have the database open, your attempt to open the database exclusively fails. Once your application has opened the database exclusively, no other users may open it or any of its components; only your application can read or write to it. You release the exclusive lock on the database by closing the database.

When you want to force a shared mode database, include the `Shared` keyword instead:

```
Open Database wwshoes Shared
```

If anyone else has the database opened exclusively, you cannot open it shared or exclusively.

You can determine whether you have opened a database exclusively or shared by issuing the function:

```
? Isexclusive("wwshoes",2)
```

This function returns `.T.` if you have opened the database exclusively, and `.F.` if you have opened it shared. However, it does not tell you how anyone else has opened it! To use this function with a database, you must include the database name in quotes, followed by a `2` to indicate that you are testing for a database's locking status.

Two other keywords can be used when opening a database. You can open a database using the `Noupdate` keyword. In this case, your application cannot make any changes to the database. You also can issue the `Validate` keyword, which causes the table to be validated when opened.

You should open a database exclusively when you need to do maintenance on the database as a whole, or need to change the structure of a database. Maintenance

> **NOTE:** When you open a database with the `Validate` or `Noupdate` keyword, this does not affect the locking status. Your database is always opened either exclusively or shared. The locking status depends on the `Set Exclusive` value in your environment.

tasks for the database as a whole include reindexing all the tables, backing up the database (see Chapter 10, "Creating a Visual FoxPro Database"), or making data updates. Changing the structure of the database includes adding or dropping tables, views, and connections. You do not need to open the database exclusively to modify the structure of an individual table, because you can open a database shared and still open a table exclusively.

You do not have to include the Exclusive or Shared keyword with the Open Database command. You can rely instead on the exclusive setting of your VFP environment. To guarantee that things always work the way you want them to, however, it's best to include the appropriate locking keyword whenever you open a database.

No matter which locking keyword you use when opening a database, it does not affect the mode in which you can open the tables.

Table-Level Locking

You can obtain either an exclusive lock or an update lock at the table level in VFP 5.0.

Exclusive Table Use

Opening a table in VFP for exclusive access is very similar in syntax to opening a database. To force a table to be opened exclusively, you can just issue the Use command with the Exclusive keyword:

```
Use customer Exclusive
```

As in the case of a database, this lock prevents all other users from reading or writing to the table in question. You release the exclusive lock on the table when you close it with the Use command.

You can determine whether a table has been used exclusively by issuing the Isexclusive() function. Consider the following version:

```
? Isexclusive()
```

VFP returns .T. if the table in the current work area is opened exclusively. If no table is opened in the current work area, then VFP returns an error message. To determine whether a table is opened exclusively without having selected its work area, issue the function as follows:

```
? Isexclusive("customer",1)
```

Here, the table alias is the first parameter, and 1 indicates that you are testing for a table's locking status.

To open a table for shared access, use the Shared keyword. The Use command also has a Noupdate keyword, but if you open a table with Noupdate, you can make no changes to the structure of the table or to the data in the table.

Locking a Shared Table

Once you've opened a table shared, you still can get an update lock on the entire table with the built-in Flock() function. Consider the following lines:

```
Use customer
= Flock()
```

If the Flock() function returns .T., the lock succeeds. Flock() stands for *File lock* and implies a lock of all the rows in the table. Other users can read, but cannot update, the table. If any other users have the table or any rows of the table locked, the Flock() fails. Only one user can obtain an Flock() on a table at any given time.

> **NOTE:** If you're running Windows 3.1 on a single-user PC, you must load SHARE for Visual FoxPro's row and table locking to work.

You release a table lock with the Unlock command. This can be issued by itself, or if you unlock any row in the table on which you've used Flock(), then the table lock is released.

To determine whether you have locked a particular table, you can use the Isflocked() function:

```
? Isflocked("customer")
```

If you want to determine whether anyone else has the table locked, however, you have to attempt the `Flock()` yourself and then examine the results. If it returns `.T.`, then no one else has the table locked. If it returns `.F.`, then another user might have one of the rows locked, but not the entire table. It is rather difficult to determine whether another user has an update lock on the entire table.

When to Use Exclusive Table Locking and Update Table Locking

If you do not want any other users to read a table, you must open it exclusively. In addition, if you want to do maintenance on a table, such as changing its structure, packing deleted rows, or reindexing it, you must have it opened exclusively.

If you want other users to read but not write to (or append any new rows to) the table, you can use the `Flock()` update lock on the table. Also, if you are running a query and want to "freeze" the data for the duration of the query without preventing other queries, you can use `Flock()`. However, remember that only one user at a time can have the table locked. If a query is running with a table lock, a second query will be unable to lock the table until the first query releases the table lock.

Row-Level Locking

By far the most common type of locking in VFP applications is *row locking*, or *record locking*. This is the level at which you can resolve edit conflicts. To prevent two users from editing the same data at the same time, you can make them each request a *row-level lock*. Only one of them will get it, and the other will have to wait until the first user finishes editing and releases the lock.

You can explicitly lock rows using row-locking commands, but VFP also implicitly locks a row for update during certain commands.

Explicit Row Locking

You cannot lock a row exclusively. However, VFP allows you to issue an update type of lock in which only you can change the row's data, but others can read the data. The VFP function that makes an update lock of a row is the `Rlock()` function:

```
? Rlock()
```

In the above form, VFP attempts to get an update lock of the current row in the current work area. If you want to lock a row in a different work area without first selecting the work area, you must know both the alias name of the table in question and the record number that you want to lock:

```
? Rlock("1","customer")
```

Here, 1 indicates the record number, and the second parameter is the alias name.

> **TIP:** Be careful with the `Isexclusive()`, `Isflocked()`, `Isrlocked()`, and `Sys(2011)` functions. The VFP help system says that they return the database, table, or row lock status. That's true, but they only return the lock status as *you* currently have it set. They cannot tell you whether any other users have locked the database, table, or row. To find that out, you have to attempt to open or lock the object.

To lock more than one row in a table, VFP requires that the `Multilocks` environmental setting be `On`, which you can do just by putting

```
Set Multilocks On
```

at the beginning of your program (or wherever it's required). Then, you can lock rows one at a time, or lock a set of them as in the following example:

```
? Rlock("1,3,5,7","customer")
```

It's a little awkward to know record numbers, but to lock more than one row at a time requires that you know them for the table in question.

You can determine whether you have locked a particular row using the `Isrlocked()` function:

```
? Isrlocked()
```

To determine whether anyone else has the row locked, you must attempt to use `Rlock()` yourself, then examine the results.

How Visual FoxPro Achieves
Table and Row Locking

Visual FoxPro locks tables and rows by using its own database engine in cooperation with the operating system or LAN. The exact method used is not revealed by Microsoft, but VFP programmers have analyzed and discussed the locking scheme on various online forums over the years, so there is a secondary source of information on how the locks work. It is useful to understand the locking scheme, because it can help explain some anomalous behavior.

Update locks are not natively supported by the operating system, so VFP—and before it dBASE III+—had to find an alternative method. What has been settled upon is a cooperative system. Your application sends a lock request to the operating system, and if the lock is granted, other applications may discover and respect the locks, or may ignore the lock. Therefore, table and row locks need the cooperation of other applications or database engines. Unfortunately, not all of them cooperate!

The operating system only locks files or byte sequences exclusively. In order to implement update locking, VFP translates the update lock into an exclusive lock on a sequence of bytes. Rather than lock a row or table exclusively, the bytes in question are offset by a large enough number that no part of the table will ever actually be locked. That number usually is the MS-DOS file size limit (namely, two billion). In order to gain an update lock of a row, then, the

Implicit Row Locking

Visual FoxPro will automatically issue update-type row locks when your application updates data, for the duration of the update, if you do not explicitly request a lock. This way, VFP can guarantee that only one write to shared data occurs at a given time. These sometimes are called *implicit locks*.

For example, when VFP executes the SQL Update command, it requests momentary implicit locks from the operating system for each row as it does the update, and system actually gets an exclusive lock of the same amount of bytes, but offset so far that no data is ever really locked. That way, other users still can read the individual bytes.

When a second VFP application requests a lock for the same row, the system again adds the two billion offset to the address of the bytes, and requests the same exclusive lock. It either gets the lock or is denied, based on whether another user already has those bytes locked.

This locking strategy helps explain why the maximum size of a Visual FoxPro table is two billion bytes. Even though Windows NT has a much larger maximum file size than MS-DOS, VFP tables under Windows NT still cannot exceed 2 GB.

Because the operating system does not lock the actual bytes in a table, update locking requires the cooperation of other database engines or applications. In a LAN or other shared environment, other applications might not respect your row or table lock if they do not follow the same scheme.

To see this for yourself, open a scratch 2.6 table in shared mode and lock the first row. Then start Excel 7, open the table, and change the locked row's data. When you save the table, Excel recognizes that a lock was present, but it gives an error message and then destroys the table! Fortunately, Excel cannot read the new VFP DBF tables except via ODBC, so it cannot corrupt them. This is one motive for keeping your exposed data in the VFP format.

only as long as it needs them. In addition, in a browse, as soon as you start editing, VFP locks that row automatically until you move to another row in the browse.

VFP also issues an implicit row lock for Insert Into, Gather Memvar, and Replace commands, if you have not already secured a row lock. Similarly, Tableupdate() (see the buffering section below) may attempt to lock all the table's rows you have changed, and may implicitly lock all of them sequentially to achieve it.

Header Row Locking

Every VFP table consists of one *header row* in addition to the data rows. The header row contains the definition of the data rows: column names, length, and type. It is a variable length row that grows and shrinks with the number of columns in the table. The header row also contains a count of the number of rows in the table. When you append a new blank row, or insert a new row into a table, VFP implicitly locks the header row in order to increment the count of the table's rows. As soon as the new row is appended, VFP releases the header lock. This guarantees that no two users ever think that they've appended the same new row!

You can issue your own lock of the header row by using the Rlock() function with row number zero. For example, the command

```
? Rlock("0","customer")
```

attempts to lock the header row of the customer table. It returns .T. if successful, and prevents any other user from appending new rows to the table for the duration of the lock. You must, however, explicitly release the lock by issuing a table-wide Unlock or by using

```
Unlock Record 0
```

to specifically unlock the header row.

When You Can't Get a Lock: The Reprocess Setting

Sometimes you cannot get a row or table lock, so the issue arises: what does VFP do when the request for a lock fails? This is where the Set Reprocess command comes in. This command determines—for the current data session—the number of times, or the length of time, that VFP will retry locking before either quitting or producing an error message. Most of the time the default value is adequate, and there is no need to change it. However, you may have special circumstances that require you to change the setting.

The command syntax is as follows:

```
Set Reprocess TO nAttempts [SECONDS] | TO AUTOMATIC
```

For example, if you want VFP to retry 100 times, issue this command:

```
Set Reprocess TO 100
```

If you want VFP to retry for 30 seconds, issue this command:

```
Set Reprocess TO 30 Seconds
```

The default value for *nAttempts* is 0, meaning that VFP will retry for a lock indefinitely. The largest value allowed (as the number of retries or the number of seconds) is 32,000.

If you have VFP's status bar active, the message `Waiting for lock...` appears at the bottom of the VFP desktop while the system is trying for a lock. If you press the Esc key, VFP interrupts the locking retries.

`Set Reprocess` behaves quite differently for explicit versus implicit locks. For explicit locks, the `Rlock()` or `Flock()` command simply returns `.F.`, no further retries occur, and no message is given. If you have a finite setting for *nAttempts*, and cannot get the lock, then as soon as the limit is reached, VFP simply stops retrying and returns `.F.`.

For implicit locks, if you interrupt the retries, VFP returns an error message in a dialog box, depending on the type of lock required by the command. For example, if someone else has a header lock on a table and you try to append a row to the same table, VFP returns the error message `File is in use by another user`.

You can trap the errors returned by commands that attempt implicit locks in an error routine and the `On Error` command. Once the error routine starts executing, though, VFP no longer attempts any locks.

WARNING: Watch out for *nAttempts* with a value of –1. In this case, Visual FoxPro attempts to lock indefinitely and will neither allow interruption by the Esc key nor call an error routine. If you can't get the lock, your application appears to freeze!

You can use To Automatic or an *nAttempts* value of −2 in order to force indefinite retries, while keeping the ability to interrupt the locking attempts. This does not appear to differ from using an *nAttempts* value of 0.

Column Locking

Some databases provide the ability to lock columns or fields in a table, in order to provide a finer granularity of concurrency control. VFP's locking granularity stops at the row level, and VFP does not provide any form of column or field locking.

Summary of VFP Locking

Visual FoxPro provides exclusive-type locking for databases and tables, and update-type locking for tables and rows. Table 8-2 shows the VFP locking types.

VFP only locks data at the database, table (file), or row (record) level. You cannot use VFP to lock data at the column or field level.

Locks can be released explicitly or implicitly. The Quit command, for example, closes all tables and databases, and releases all locks. Close Database releases all database, table, and row locks. A Use command that closes a table also releases all locks on the table and its rows. An Unlock All command releases all locks across all work areas, while the Unlock command by itself releases all row locks on the current table and releases a file lock. Implicit unlocking is also caused by Set Multilocks Off.

Lastly, row locking can take place during buffering and transactions. Buffering can lock explicitly or implicitly, depending upon certain settings. Transactions

Table 8-2 Visual FoxPro Locking

Type of Lock	VFP Keyword	Explicit or Implicit
Exclusive table	Exclusive	Normally explicit
Update table	Flock()	Explicit or implicit
Update header	Append Blank, Insert Into	Normally implicit
Update row	Rlock()	Explicit or implicit

lock rows while the transaction is in effect, and release them automatically when the transaction ends. Buffering and transaction processing are covered in the following sections.

Row and Table Buffering

In addition to the traditional FoxPro locking constructs just covered, Visual Fox-Pro provides two new strategies to use in managing multi-user editing conflicts. These new strategies are:

- Row and table buffering
- Transaction processing

The difference between these is that row and table buffering is oriented toward single tables, while transaction processing is oriented toward multiple tables within a database.

These strategies are complementary, not conflicting. Row and table buffering is a method of providing a way to cancel a user's edits against a single table, whether or not that table is in a database. Without buffering, the only way to easily provide a cancel function is to have the user edit memory variables or object properties, rather than edit the data directly. With buffering, you can let the user edit the data directly and still cancel edits.

Transactions are a method of guaranteeing that edits against two or more tables are either both accepted or both rejected. This preserves the unity of the user's work. VFP restricts transaction processing, however, to tables within a database.

You can view both of these strategies as "buffered" because they keep temporary copies of the data, from which the original data can be restored if a conflict occurs or an update fails. What differs between the two strategies is the level of buffering: you can enable row-level or table-level buffering for single tables using buffered edits, and can enable multi-table buffering using transaction processing.

Table 8-3 shows how row and table buffering compares with transaction processing.

You do not have to use row and table buffering. If you don't, though, you have to explicitly code ways in your forms for users to cancel their edits. Most solutions

Table 8-3 Comparison of Row and Table Buffering with Transactions

	Single Free Table	Single DBC Table	Multiple Free Tables	Multiple DBC Tables
Row and Table	Yes	Yes	No	No
Transactions	No	Yes	No	Yes

of this sort require you to abandon binding the data controls of your forms directly to the table. Since VFP makes this so easy to do, using buffering is the better way to go.

Optimistic and Pessimistic Locking

Once you commit to buffering, the basic decision you have to make in developing a multi-user strategy is whether to use optimistic or pessimistic locking, and whether to enable it at the row or table level. Both types of locking are native to Visual FoxPro's data engine. They are not properties of the tables or views in your database. One row in a given table could be locked pessimistically by one application, and another row locked optimistically by the same or another application.

You choose optimistic or pessimistic locking by setting properties of the table in use. You can do so through the Data Environment of a form, or by using the Cursorsetprop() function (see below).

Optimistic locking postpones any lock of the data until the time of update. Because of this delay, it appears to let more than one user at the same time directly edit the same row or set of rows. It appears this way because no rows are explicitly locked, even though the user is directly editing the data.

The Essentials of Optimistic Locking

With *optimistic locking*, no rows are locked until the moment of update, and then only briefly. For *optimistic row locking*, Visual FoxPro attempts to update a row when the row pointer moves or the table is closed, and generates an error if another user has changed the row's data during the edit.

For *optimistic table locking*, VFP's buffered updates are held until the user attempts to close the table, or issues the `Tableupdate()` command, and then each row is tested for conflicts. If even one of the rows has been updated after the buffering began, the update fails and VFP generates an error. You then can override the failure and force the update, or can revert the changes.

NOTE: There are basically two times you can notify a user of a potential conflict using optimistic locking: when the user first edits a row that someone else is already editing, or when the user tries to update a row that some other user has already updated while this user was editing it.

Visual FoxPro provides support only for notifying a user of a conflict at the time of update. At that time, using VFP's native functions, your application can notify the user that someone else updated this row while they were editing it, and then let the user decide whether or not she wants to overwrite the other changes.

If you want to notify a user right away that someone else is currently editing the same row, you have to invent your own way of doing so. For example, you can create a semaphore system and programmatically manage it so that when a user starts to edit a row that someone else is currently editing, you notify the user immediately and let her decide whether to proceed.

You'll find optimistic row locking most useful when your user is editing a single table one row at a time, and it's acceptable that occasionally more than one user simultaneously will edit the data. Also, optimistic row locking will prove advantageous if you need to minimize locking overhead and maximize performance, or if it's unacceptable in your environment for a user to keep a row locked indefinitely.

You'll find optimistic table locking most useful when your user is editing multiple rows of a table, and it's acceptable that occasionally more than one user simultaneously will edit the table's rows. The same considerations apply here as for optimistic row locking. The only difference is that with optimistic table locking, the user edits many rows of a table before the update is applied.

The Essentials of Pessimistic Locking

In *pessimistic locking*, only one user at a time can directly edit a row because VFP issues a row- or table-level update lock for the duration of the editing session. With pessimistic row locking, VFP automatically locks the edited row upon any interactive change to the row's fields. The row is updated when the row pointer changes, `Tableupdate()` is issued, or the table is closed.

In *pessimistic table locking*, VFP automatically locks all rows that the user edits in that session, and then updates them all when the table is closed. Other users do not see the changes until the updates are made.

Pessimistic row locking is most useful when your user is editing a single table one row at a time, and the data is sufficiently critical that a user should not be allowed to overwrite another user's changes. It helps if locking overhead is unimportant and if it's acceptable in your environment for a user to keep a row locked indefinitely.

Pessimistic table locking is most useful when your user is editing multiple rows of a table. As with optimistic table locking, the update is applied only when the table is closed or the `Tableupdate()` function is issued. Pessimistic table locking differs from pessimistic row locking in that, with the former, the row locks pile up until the update.

Buffering Behavior

Now take a look at how to implement optimistic and pessimistic buffering on a single table using Visual FoxPro. VFP defaults to unbuffered row locking if you do not enable buffered edits and directly edit data. When you enable buffered editing in a form, you can explicitly choose optimistic or pessimistic locking at the row or table level, or you can set the buffering property programmatically using the `Cursorsetprop()` function.

When you use optimistic row or table locking, you can use the following functions to help arbitrate multi-user conflicts:

`Getfieldstate()`	Whether a field has changed
`Getnextmodified()`	Next changed row in a table
`Curval()`	Current value of a field, before update
`Oldval()`	Original value of a field

You then can use the `Tablerevert()` function to pull back from the current update, or issue `Tableupdate()` to force the update. You will make extensive use of these functions in the following sections.

The `Tableupdate()` command takes up to four parameters. The syntax in VFP 5.0 is as follows:

```
Tableupdate([nRows [, lForce]] [, cTableAlias | nWorkArea]
[, cErrorArray])
```

You can specify 0, 1, or 2 for the rows parameter. 0 forces the update on the current record only, while 1 makes the update on a single row when row buffering is enabled, and on an entire table when table buffering is enabled. For both the 0 and 1 parameters for *nRows*, VFP triggers an error if the update fails. In the case of 2 as a value for *nRows*, no error is triggered, but the command otherwise behaves as it does with the value 1.

The *lForce* parameter overrides any changes by other users detected during optimistic buffering. The *cTableAlias* and *nWorkArea* parameters allow you to specify an update for a work area independent of the current work area. Finally, the *cErrorArray* parameter lets you specify an array to be filled with error data if an error occurs. This handy feature lets you avoid having to trap the error in a separate routine.

> **NOTE:** There are subtle but important differences in the `TableUpdate()` function between VFP 3.0 and VFP 5.0. In VFP 3.0, the function's first parameter must be a logical, and gives the equivalent of values 0 and 1 in the VFP 5.0 version of `lnRows`. Also, the VFP 3.0 version does not have the error array parameter.

Setting the Default Data Buffering for a Form

There is an easy (but not fully effective) way to set buffering in a form, by setting the form's default buffering for all its tables and views. To set default buffering, follow these steps:

1. Enter the VFP Form Designer.

2. Activate the property sheet by right-clicking the form, then selecting the Data tab.

You then are presented with a list under the Buffermode option. From here you can set the default buffering for the form. However, the list is incomplete, and any settings you select can be overridden by a table setting in the form's Data Environment, or by the `Cursorsetprop()` command, so choosing buffering this way is of limited value. Figure 8-1 shows the VFP property sheet opened to the default buffering list box.

If you select None here, and you do not override the setting in the Data Environment, you will get unbuffered row locking in your form, with no support for canceling or reverting the user's changes. If, however, you select Pessimistic or Optimistic, and do not override the setting elsewhere, the form will default to row-level locking for row edits and table-level locking for grids. For example, if you select pessimistic locking here for a form that edits a single table one row at a time, and do not explicitly override this setting, you will get pessimistic row locking.

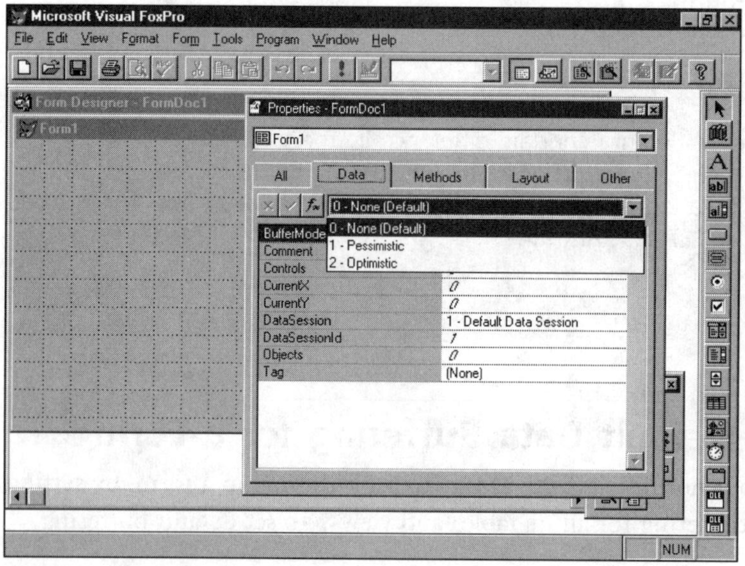

FIGURE 8-1

The VFP default buffering list box is available in the form's property sheet.

Overriding the Default Buffering in Forms

To override the form's setting, follow these steps:

1. Enter the Form Designer.

2. Activate the property sheet, and right-click the form surface, then choose Data Environment from the popup.

3. Click one of the form's tables or views. (If a table is not present, add it.)

4. On the Property sheet, select the Data tab, then click the BufferModeOverride list item. A drop-down list presents all the available components, as shown in Figure 8-2.

If you don't want any buffering at all on this table or view, you can select Option 0. Option 1, Use Form Setting (Default), tells Visual FoxPro to default this table or cursor's buffering to the selection you made via the form's Buffermode property.

All the other choices, Options 2 through 5, override the buffering selected at the form level but *just for this table or view*. This is the most convenient way to set

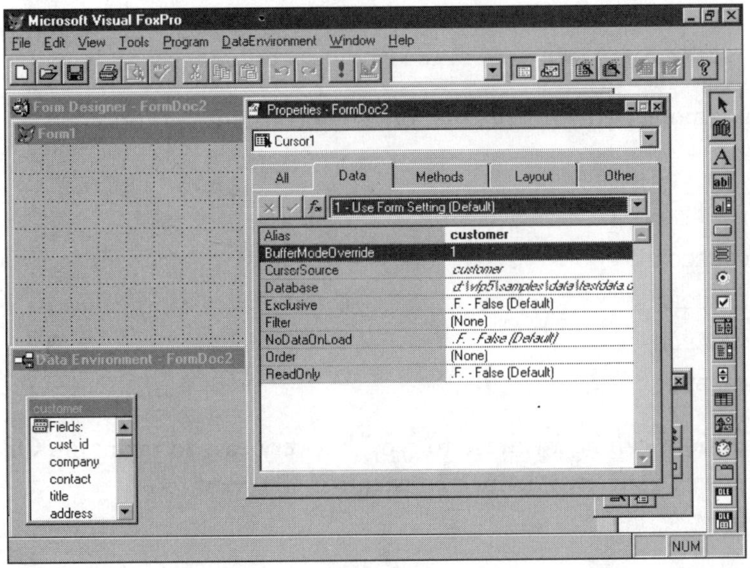

FIGURE 8-2

The VFP BufferModeOverride *list box is available in the Data Environment's property sheet.*

buffering if you use the Data Environment in your forms. If you do not, then you need to set the buffering elsewhere using the `Cursorsetprop()` function.

Setting Buffering Programmatically

When you set buffering programmatically using the `Cursorsetprop()` function, you must specify the buffering mode as one of the parameters. For example, you can indicate a mode of pessimistic row locking by putting the parameter value 2 in the `Cursorsetprop()` function, as follows:

```
SELECT customer
= Cursorsetprop('Buffering', 2, 'customer')
```

The remaining values you can use are 1 to set buffering off, 3 for optimistic row buffering, 4 for pessimistic table buffering, and 5 for optimistic table buffering.

There's an easy way to bypass the need to remember these values. If you place `#INCLUDE Foxpro.h` in your code, you can use a set of defined constants in place of the numbers:

```
#INCLUDE \vfp5\foxpro.h
Select customer
= Cursorsetprop('Buffering', DB_BUFOPTRECORD, 'customer')
```

`FoxPro.h` contains, among many others, the following constant definitions:

```
*— Cursor buffering modes
#DEFINE DB_BUFOFF            1
#DEFINE DB_BUFLOCKRECORD     2
#DEFINE DB_BUFOPTRECORD      3
#DEFINE DB_BUFLOCKTABLE      4
#DEFINE DB_BUFOPTTABLE       5
```

These constant definitions can be awkward to type, but very easy to maintain. Of course, you can substitute your own defined constants if you want.

Common Actions on Multi-User Forms

The most common editing actions on a multi-user form are Add, Edit and Delete. A multi-user form with buffering enabled must deal with each of these modes.

Add

The Add mode is by far the least work. When the user adds a row, and buffering is enabled, VFP places the added row in the buffer and no other user can edit that row until the table is updated. Therefore, no multi-user conflicts are possible.

Edit

With optimistic buffering enabled, multi-user conflicts can arise when one user edits and updates a row while another user is editing. This kind of conflict is possible only under optimistic buffering, not pessimistic. With this kind of conflict, VFP allows the second user's application to trap the conflict and query the user whether to overwrite the row or re-edit it.

Delete

Conflicts arising from deletion are a bit more complex. It's unlikely, but possible, that two users will try to delete the same row at the same time. Because they both want to do the same thing, this conflict isn't really a problem. It's quite possible, however, that one user might try to delete a row that another user is editing. The best policy here is to let the delete button detect that someone else has changed the row, and consequently refuse to perform the delete.

Building a Multi-User Form

This section steps you through the creation of a sample multi-user form, one that you can use to test the consequences, error handling, and user messages required for the type of buffering you would like to use. This form is restricted to the Edit mode, and by running multiple instances of the form, you can simulate multi-user conflicts among two or more users. This way, you can dynamically test optimistic and pessimistic buffering options at the row and table level. Figure 8-3 shows what your result should look like in design mode.

NOTE: The form you develop in this section is on the accompanying CD-ROM in the Chapter 8 subdirectory.

Here are the steps to follow:

1. Start Visual FoxPro and set your default to the `\vfp5\samples\data` subdirectory. Open the `Testdata.dbc` database.

2. Create a new form named `MultiFrm`, short for *multi-user form*. Right-click the form surface, then choose Data Environment. In the Data Environment, add the customer table from the Testdata database.

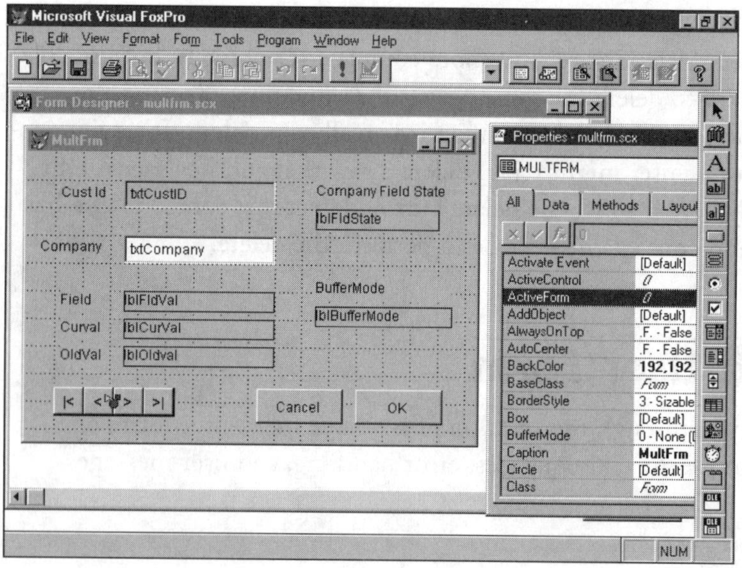

FIGURE 8-3

The sample multi-user form in design mode shows the controls used to display multi-user information.

(These instructions will be easier to follow if you make sure that you have the Standard and Form Designer toolbars active.) Next, choose Include from the Form menu. Select the \vfp\foxpro.h include file, so you can assume the defined constants in the form's methods. In the Property sheet, set the form's `Caption` property to **MultiFrm**.

3. In order to run multiple instances of the form, you need to make sure that each instance of the form has a private data session. In the Property sheet, go to the form's `DataSession` property and change it to **2 – Private Data Sessions.**

   To guarantee that buffering is enabled when the form starts up, and also to be able to identify the current data session on the caption of the form, open the form's `Init()` method and type the following:

```
Set Multilocks On
Thisform.Caption = Thisform.Caption+'
'+Alltrim(Str(Thisform.DataSessionID)-1)
```

   This takes the form's data session ID, which starts at 2, and subtracts 1 from it so that the form's caption shows multiple instances starting with 1.

4. Next, build the text and label controls. Drag the `cust id` and `company` fields from the Data Environment onto the form design surface. Change the `Name` property of the `cust_id` field to **txtCustId,** and the `Name` property of `company` to **txtCompany.** On the form, place `txtCustId` above `txtCompany`, and add one label object next to each field. On the label next to `txtCustId`, change its `Caption` property to **Cust Id.** Similarly, on the label next to `txtCompany`, change its `Caption` property to **Company.**

5. In this demo form, you only need the company name column to be editable, so set the `ReadOnly` property of `txtCustID` to **True.** In order to see resulting changes to the company name immediately in the rest of the form, enter the following in the `LostFocus()` method of `txtCompany`:

```
Thisform.Refresh()
```

6. Now, add labels that will show you the results of the current field, `Curval()`, and the original value, `Oldval()`. Underneath the two

fields, place three labels vertically that have their `Caption` properties set to **Field**, **Curval**, and **Oldval**, respectively. (You never need to refer to these labels, so their `Name` properties can remain the defaults.)

7. Now, show the results of these functions next to the labels by adding three more labels to the right of them. The new labels will contain the results of the functions in their captions. Give each label's `Caption` and `Name` properties **lblField**, **lblCurval**, and **lblOldval**, respectively, so that you can refer to them from other methods and see their variable names on-screen during design.

    In the `Init()` method of the `lblField` label, add the following:

```
this.Caption = company
```

    In the `Init()` method of the `lblCurval` label, add the following:

```
this.Caption = Curval('company')
```

    In the `Init()` method of the `lblOlcval` label, add the following:

```
this.Caption = Oldval('company')
```

    This causes the labels to display the function results on startup. You will insert other code in the form's `Refresh` method to change them. (You might want to stretch these labels to be as wide as the `company` field.)

8. You also need to see the result of the `Getfldstate()` function. Add two more labels to the right of the company field—one with `Caption` set to **Company field state**, and, below it, one with `Caption` set to **Getfldstate()**. For the latter, set the `Name` property to **lblGetFldState**, and in its `Init()` method, add

```
this.Caption = Alltrim(Str(Getfldstate('company')))
```

    to initialize the display of its value.

9. Finally, you need to see the current buffer mode displayed on the form. Add two more labels on the far right of the form: one with `Caption` set to **Buffermode**, and the other with `Name` and `Caption` set to **lblBufferMode**.

    In order to display the current buffer mode when the form starts up, add the following code to the `Init()` method of `lblBufferMode`:

```
Do Case
Case Cursorgetprop('buffering') = DB_BUFOFF
   This.Caption = 'None'
Case Cursorgetprop('buffering') = DB_BUFLOCKRECORD
   This.Caption = 'Pessimistic Row'
Case Cursorgetprop('buffering') = DB_BUFOPTRECORD
   This.Caption = 'Optimistic Row'
Case Cursorgetprop('buffering') = DB_BUFLOCKTABLE
   This.Caption = 'Pessimistic Table'
Case Cursorgetprop('buffering') = DB_BUFLOCKTABLE
   This.Caption = 'Optimistic Table'
Endcase
```

10. With all these objects defined, you now can put the following code in
   the form's Refresh event (this allows us to refresh all these objects on
   the form):

```
*— Refresh the function labels
Thisform.lblFldVal.Caption = customer.company
Thisform.lblCurVal.Caption = Curval('company')
Thisform.lblOldVal.Caption = Oldval('company')
Thisform.lblFldState.Caption = Str(Getfldstate('company'))


*— Refresh the buffer mode label
Do Case
Case Cursorgetprop('buffering') = DB_BUFOFF
   Thisform.lblBufferMode.Caption = 'None'
Case Cursorgetprop('buffering') = DB_BUFLOCKRECORD
   Thisform.lblBufferMode.Caption = 'Pessimistic Row'
Case Cursorgetprop('buffering') = DB_BUFOPTRECORD
   Thisform.lblBufferMode.Caption = 'Optimistic Row'
Case Cursorgetprop('buffering') = DB_BUFLOCKTABLE
   Thisform.lblBufferMode.Caption = 'Pessimistic Table'
Case Cursorgetprop('buffering') = DB_BUFOPTTABLE
   Thisform.lblBufferMode.Caption = 'Optimistic Table'
Endcase
```

11. To add navigation buttons, you can use the vcr class that comes with the VFP sample application. To activate the buttons class, enter the Form Designer Toolbar and click the View Classes button. Choose Add, and in the resulting dialog box, select \vfp5\samples\controls\buttons.vcx and click the Open button. Notice that the toolbar changes to show buttons for these classes. Find the vcr button, click it, and then drop the vcr control on the bottom of the form. Do the same for the cmdOk and cmdCancel buttons.

12. Now, you need to add logic to handle the error mesages that occur with optimistic row and table buffering. For optimistic row locking, a row will be updated automatically when the row pointer is changed, unless someone else has changed the row. So, you can simply try to move the pointer by letting the Click event on the vcr button occur, and then test for an error. In the vcr object's Error method, add the following code to manage conflicts for optimistic row locking:

```
If nError = 1585 AND Cursorgetprop('Buffering') = DB_BUFOPTRECORD
   LOCAL llOverwrite, llChanged, lnField, lcField
   llChanged = .F.
   llOverwrite = .F.
   *— Find whether anyone else has updated this row
   For lnField = 1 To Fcount()
      lcField = Field(lnField)
      If Curval(lcField) <> Oldval(lcField)
         llChanged = .T.
         Exit
      Endif
   Endfor
   *— If yes, dialog the user
   If llChanged
      lnResult = MessageBox("Someone else has also updated this row. ;
         Do you want to overwrite their changes?",
         MB_YESNO+MB_ICONEXCLAMATION, ;
         "Update Conflict!" )
      If lnResult = IDYES
```

```
        llOverWrite = .T.
     Endif
     *— Handle the update
     If llChanged And Not llOverwrite
        = Tablerevert()
     Else
        = Tableupdate(.F., .T.)
     Endif
Endif
Thisform.Refresh()
```

This code is simplified, and in a more fully developed application you might want to let the user know what the individual field changes were. You might even let them discard some of their own field changes.

13. In the cmdCancel button's `Click` method, add the following code to cancel any changes made with optimistic table locking:

```
*— Optimistic Table test
If Cursorgetprop('Buffering') = DB_BUFOPTTABLE
  =Tablerevert(.T.)
Endif
Thisform.Release()
```

14. In the cmdOK button's `Click` method, add the following code to manage conflicts for optimistic table locking:

```
*— Optimistic Table test
If Cursorgetprop('buffering') = DB_BUFOPTTABLE
  Local llOverwrite, llChanged, lnField, lcField, lnRec
  Go Top
  lnRec = Getnextmodified(0)
  *— Check each changed row
  Do While lnRec <> 0
    Goto lnRec
    llChanged = .F.
    llOverwrite = .F.
```

```
      *— Detect another's changes field by field
      For lnField = 1 TO Fcount()
         lcField = Field(lnField)
         If Curval(lcField) <> Oldval(lcField)
            llChanged = .T.
            Exit
         Endif
      Endfor
      *— If another has changed this, get user's choice
      If llChanged
   lnResult = MessageBox("Someone else has also updated this   ;
            row.  Do you want to overwrite their changes?", ;
            MB_YESNO + MB_ICONEXCLAMATION, ;
            "Update Conflict!" )
         If lnResult = IDYES
            llOverwrite = .T.
         Endif
      Endif
      *— If the user said no, revert the row, else update
      If llChanged and NOT llOverwrite
         = Tablerevert()
      Else
         = Tableupdate(.F.,.T.)
      Endif
      *— Get the next changed row
      lnRec = Getnextmodified(lnRec)
   Enddo
Endif
Thisform.Release()
```

Again, realistically, you probably want to give your users a dialog box to let them know what rows were changed by other users, and what the changes were field by field. The users then can make the best decision themselves. As with optimistic row locking, you might want to let the users discard some of their own field changes, and keep others.

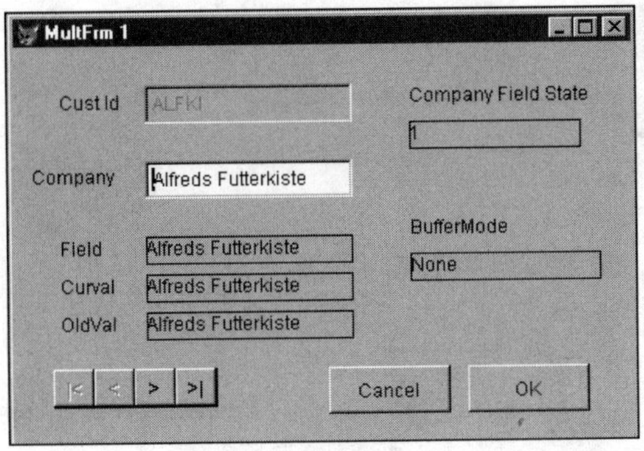

FIGURE 8-4

This is what your resulting form should look like when running.

15. Finally, change the background color of the form and all the labels to gray to improve their appearance. The resulting form should look something like the one shown in Figure 8-4 when you run it.

Exploring Multi-User Forms

When you explore the types of multi-user conflicts, the number of combinations can become quite complex. The following discussion assumes that you run with only two sessions of the form, and that each form instance uses the same buffering mode. (You can use two instances of the same form to simulate two separate users.)

Exploring Pessimistic Row Locking

To explore pessimistic row locking, follow these steps:

1. Enter the Form Designer.

2. Bring up the form MultFrm 1 created in the preceding section, and set the form's Data Environment buffering to Pessimistic Row.

3. Now, run two instances of the form by running the form twice without exiting it. Notice that each DataSessionID is shown in the form's caption. Each form also should show Pessimistic Row as the Buffer Mode, as you can see in Figure 8-5.

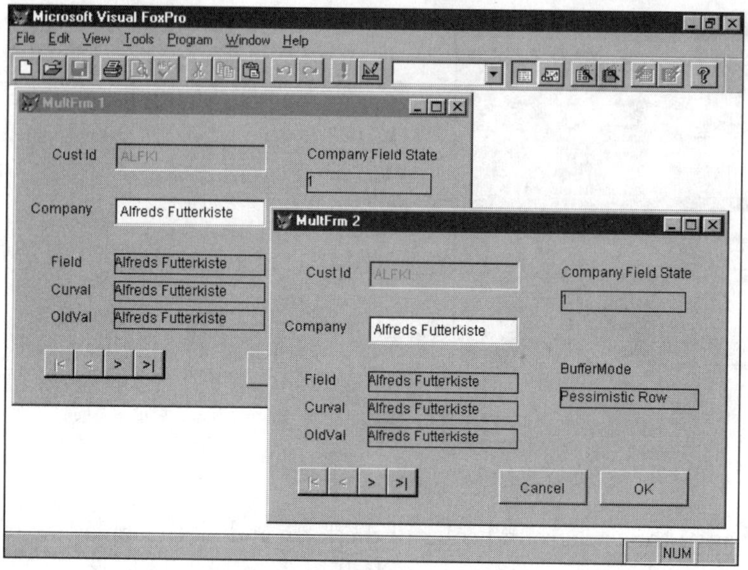

FIGURE 8-5

Two instances of the sample multi-user form can test multi-user conflicts.

4. If you separate the forms, you can enter values into one and then the other. Both forms should be on the first row in the customer table. In the first instance, insert a 2 at the beginning of the company name.

5. Now, try to insert a 3 at the beginning of the second form's company field, and note the error message. Table 8-4 shows a diagram of the events.

With row buffering, as soon as you move to another row, an update occurs and the row lock is released.

Table 8-4   Pessimistic Row Locking Events

	DataSession 1	**DataSession 2**
Action 1	Change row 1 (locks row 1)	—
Action 2	—	Attempt to change row 1 (lock denied)
Action 3	Move to row 2 (unlocks row 1)	—
Action 4	—	Change row 1 (locks row 1)
Action 5	Move to row 1	—
Action 6	Attempt to change row 1 (lock denied)	—

Exploring Optimistic Row Locking

To set the form to optimistic row locking, follow these steps:

1. Change the `BufferModeOverride` property of the Data Environment to **3**.

2. Run the two instances of the form as before, and verify that each instance states `Optimistic Row` for the Buffer Mode.

3. After you separate the forms on-screen, enter the first instance and insert a **1** at the beginning of the company name, then go to the second instance and insert a **2** at the beginning of its company name. Note the `CurVal` and `OldVal` values.

4. To cause an update, click the Next button of Session 2.

5. Go to Session 1 and click the form. Observe the `CurVal` and `Oldval` values.

6. Now, click Session 1's next button, and choose Yes in the dialog box. Table 8-5 diagrams what has happened.

Exploring Pessimistic Table Locking

To explore pessimistic table locking, follow these steps:

1. Change the buffering style to Pessimistic Table by setting the `BufferModeOverride` property of the Data Environment to **4**.

2. Run two instances of the form and check that each form's session displays correctly.

Table 8-5 Optimistic Row Locking Events

	DataSession 1	DataSession 2
Action 1	Change row 1 (no lock)	—
Action 2	—	Change row 1 (no lock)
Action 3	—	Move to row 2 (updates row 1)
Action 4	Attempt to move to row 2 (update conflict detected)	—

Table 8-6 Pessimistic Row Locking Events

	DataSession 1	DataSession 2
Action 1	Change row 1 (locks row 1)	—
Action 2	Change row 2 (locks row 2)	—
Action 3	—	Attempt to change row 1 (denied)
Action 4	—	Attempt to change row 2 (denied)
Action 5	Click the OK button (unlocks rows 1 and 2)	—
Action 6	—	Change row 1 (allowed)

3. In MultiFrm 1 insert a **1** at the beginning of the company name for both the first and second rows.

4. Now, try to insert a **2** in front of the MultiFrm 2 company field for both rows. Note the error message.

5. Click the OK button on MultiFrm 1 and then change the company field in row 1 in MultiFrm 2. Notice the result. Table 8-6 shows a diagram of the events.

Exploring Optimistic Table Locking

To explore optimistic table locking, follow these steps:

1. Change the form's buffering to Optimistic Table by setting the BufferModeOverride property of the DataEnvironment to **5**.

2. Run two instances of the form and separate them on-screen.

3. Enter MultiFrm 1 and insert a **1** at the beginning of the company name.

4. Click the Next button and insert another **1** at the beginning of the company field. Observe the CurVal and OldVal values.

5. Go to MultiFrm 2 and insert a **4** at the beginning of the company field in the first and second rows. Observe the CurVal and Oldval values, and observe the results. Table 8-7 presents a diagram of the events.

Table 8-7 Optimistic Table Locking Events

	DataSession 1	DataSession 2
Action 1	Change row 1 (no lock)	—
Action 2	Change row 2 (no lock)	—
Action 3	—	Change row 1 (no lock)
Action 4	—	Change row 1 (no lock)
Action 5	Click the OK button (update)	—
Action 6	—	Click the OK button (conflict detected)

Summary of Row and Table Buffering

The main advantage of buffering is clear: it gives you the ability to have your application directly edit data, as well as the ability to revert or cancel the changes with the `TableRevert()` function. Buffering makes it easy for you to use bound controls in forms. You no longer have to put your own buffering into your applications by having users edit memory variables and not data, because VFP now does the buffering for you.

The choice between optimistic and pessimistic locking is not as clear. If you simply cannot allow pessimistic locking, because users with locks can leave a row or table locked indefinitely (the "out to lunch" syndrome), then optimistic locking is for you. Once you start using optimistic locking, however, you must add code in your forms to arbitrate the potential conflicts, and this code can become quite complex. The tradeoff is clear: if you can abide the threat of your users going "out to lunch," you can adopt pessimistic locking and rely on VFP's default messages, and no multi-user conflicts will arise.

Using Transaction Processing

A database transaction is often defined as "a logical unit of work." VFP provides you with *transaction processing* to let you wrap sequences of database updates together and treat them as a unit of work. Then you can apply all or none of the changes.

VFP lets you define a transaction with the `Begin Transaction` command. Once this command is executed, all updates to your database are written not to the data, but to a transaction buffer. To commit the changes in the buffer, you must issue the `End Transaction` command. To revert or cancel them, you can issue the `Rollback` command. Because the changes are in the transaction buffer and not in the database, any time the user aborts (turns off the PC), an automatic rollback occurs.

You can apply transaction processing in VFP only to tables in a single database. That is, the transaction can apply only to one database and only to tables in the database. Changes to free tables are directly written, and therefore cannot be rolled back. This contrasts with buffering, which you can apply to tables outside of a database, but only to one table at a time.

Visual FoxPro transaction processing is similar, but not identical to, the transaction processing implemented in more fully relational databases. For a further discussion, see Chapter 10, "Creating a Visual FoxPro Database."

When Transactions are Needed

There is a severe limitation to the way you can update data in Visual FoxPro. When you update more than one data element at a time, it's possible for your update process to fail in the middle, leaving the database in an incomplete or inconsistent state. This is a limitation that has existed since FoxPro's origin.

There are many ways this can happen. To see how it might occur, try building the following single-table example that executes a series of updates in which one of the updates fails. Suppose that you want to change the Customer table's `Max-ordamt` value's three IDs ("ALFKI", "ANATR", and "ANTON"). If you're using optimistic table buffering, you can use the following program to update the table:

```
*_

* TranUpd1.prg Session 1

* A sample for transaction processing

* See the CD for this code

*_

Set Exclusive Off
Use Customer Shared
```

```
Set Multilocks On
Set Reprocess To 3
= Cursorsetprop("Buffering",5)
Update Customer Set Maxordamt = 1000 Where Cust_Id = "ALFKI"
? IIF(Tableupdate(), "Tableupdate Succeeded", "Tableupdate Failed")
Update Customer Set Maxordamt = 2000 Where Cust_Id = "ANATR"
? IIF(Tableupdate(), "Tableupdate Succeeded", "Tableupdate Failed")
Update Customer Set Maxordamt = 3000 Where Cust_Id = "ANTON"
? IIF(Tableupdate(), "Tableupdate Succeeded", "Tableupdate Failed")
```

To cause a conflict with another user, you can open a second instance of VFP that locks the second row that you're updating:

```
*—
* TranLock.prg Session 2
* Do this on a separate instance of VFP
* See the CD for this code
*—
Set Exclusive Off
Use Customer Shared
Locate For Cust_Id = "ANATR"
? Rlock()
```

Execute TranLock on one instance of VFP to secure the lock on the second update row. Then execute TranUpd1 on the other session and observe the output to the screen. Figure 8-6 shows how you can arrange your VFP instances to see the output in the VFP desktop.

Now, without some additional kind of buffering, there's no simple way to undo the first update if either of the other two fail. You could modify the above program to use a single Tableupdate() by switching to table buffering, as in the following program:

```
*—
* TranUpd2.prg Session 1
* A sample for transaction processing
* See the CD for this code
```

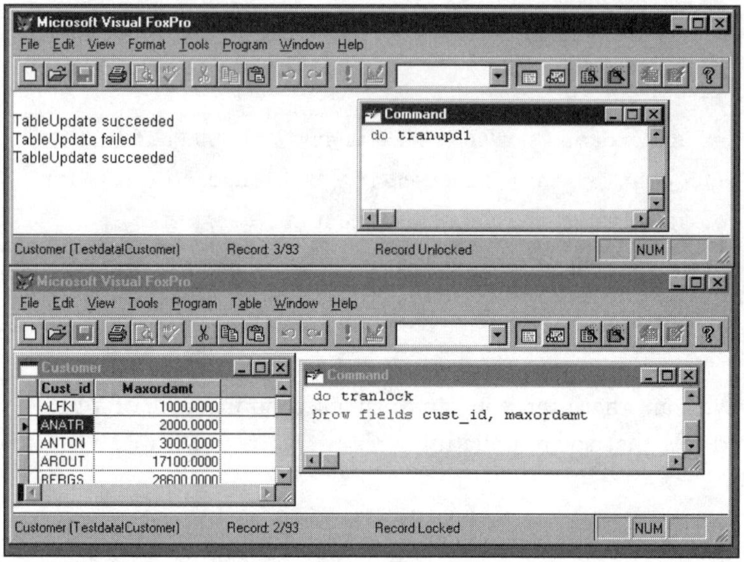

FIGURE 8-6

With two VFP instances running, the top instance shows the output of the transaction programs.

```
*_
Set Exclusive Off
Use Customer Shared
Set Multilocks On
Set Reprocess To 3
= Cursorsetprop("Buffering",5)
Update Customer Set Maxordamt = 1000 Where Cust_Id = "ALFKI"
Update Customer Set Maxordamt = 2000 Where Cust_Id = "ANATR"
Update Customer Set Maxordamt = 3000 Where Cust_Id = "ANTON"
? IIF(Tableupdate(1), "TableUpdate succeeded", "TableUpdate failed")
```

Still, you only get a partial update, as shown in Figure 8-7.

Once a `Tableupdate()` is finished, the changes have been written to the data. Unless you've buffered the old values elsewhere yourself, you can't restore them.

The problem extends to other kinds of multiple updates: updating a summary field in a parent table based on calculations in the child table, you need some way to group these updates together into a single unit, which Visual FoxPro lets you do with transactions.

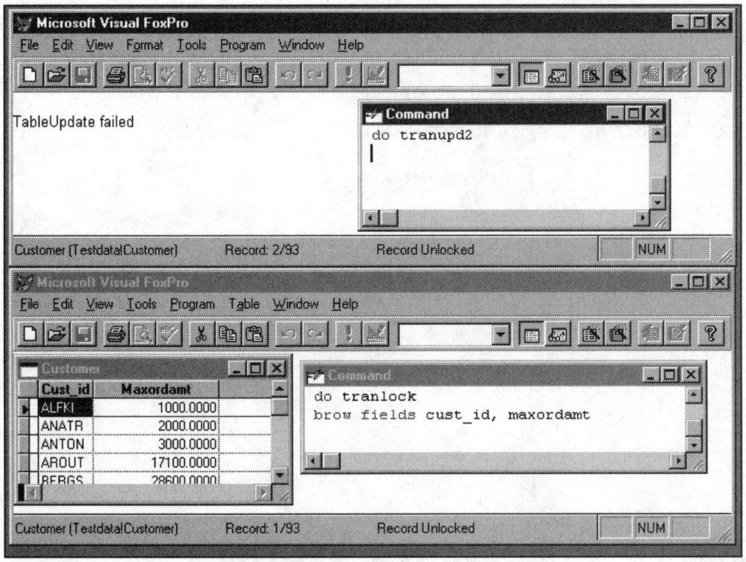

FIGURE 8-7

Switching to table buffering still only provides a partial update.

VFP's row and table buffering gives you the ability to cancel directly-edited data, but it still does not solve the problem of multiple updates. When you update one row of a table and a second update somewhere else fails, you cannot return to the initial row and revert it or cancel the changes.

With transaction processing, you can group together the changes as a logical unit, then commit them or roll them back in an all-or-nothing fashion. You can see how to use transaction processing in the following program. It applies the same updates to the customer table that you saw earlier in this section, but wraps Tableupdate() in a transaction.

```
*_
* TranUpd3.prg Session 1
* Sample using transaction processing
* See the CD for this code
*_
Set Exclusive Off
Use Customer Shared
Set Multilocks On
Set Reprocess To 3
```

```
= Cursorsetprop("Buffering",5)
Update Customer Set Maxordamt = 1000 Where Cust_Id = "ALFKI"
Update Customer Set Maxordamt = 2000 Where Cust_Id = "ANATR"
Update Customer Set Maxordamt = 3000 Where Cust_Id = "ANTON"
Begin Transaction
IF Tableupdate(1)
   ? "Commit"
   End Transaction
Else
   ? "Rollback"
   Rollback
Endif
```

How VFP Transaction Processing Works

Visual FoxPro implements transactions by adding a special transaction buffer which contains the changes you are making to your VFP database tables. When you are ready to commit, you issue End Transaction, and VFP writes your changes to the database. If you want to revert or cancel the changes, you issue Rollback. Every Begin Transaction command must be terminated with either End Transaction or Rollback.

The transaction buffer is an additional data buffer that VFP provides. It has no connection with any of the buffers created when you enable row or table buffering. In fact, when you issue the Tableupdate() command in a transaction, the update goes just to the transaction buffer, not to the actual table.

NOTE: There are a couple of differences between VFP transactions and other databases. In VFP, to commit your changes you must use the End Transaction command, instead of a Commit command as in other databases (and in SQL-92). Also, VFP's Rollback command does not really roll back data — it simply fails to update the data. This is because during a transaction, data is written to a buffer, and never to the database; hence, there's nothing to roll back.

If you have a failure during the outermost commit phase of a transaction, VFP will not roll back your data when you restart the application. VFP does make use of a transaction log, but not as a separate table. See Chapter 10, "Creating a Visual FoxPro Database," for more information.

It still is possible for a VFP transaction to fail so that you end up with partially written data. If you have an operating system or hardware failure during an End Transaction, only part of the transaction buffer might be written to the database. Unless the commit portion of your transactions is very time-consuming, this should seldom be a problem.

You also can nest transactions; that is, you can place a transaction within a transaction, for up to five levels. You can programmatically determine the transaction level by using the Txnlevel() function. When you nest transactions, none of the changes are actually written until the outermost level (level 1) transaction ends and its commit occurs.

WARNING: Be careful when you nest transactions. It is possible for one nested transaction to overwrite another nested transaction's data.

How to Code Transactions

When a transaction executes, it locks all updated rows in the tables for the duration of the update, then releases the locks when the transaction ends. The following sections explain how to adapt transaction coding for different situations.

Transactions with No Buffering

When you don't use any buffering, you can't use Tableupdate() or Tablerevert(). You may have to apply the traditional methods of writing to data using the Insert, Update, and Delete SQL commands. Or, you may use the older Append, Gather, and Replace commands. The implicit row locks that VFP applies translate into explicit row locks for the duration of the transaction. The following pseudocode illustrates how to code a transaction with no row or table buffering:

```
* Remove all transactions
* Begin transaction
* Repeat for all rows:
* Make changes to first row
* Attempt table update with error capture
* If not successful
*    Test for errors
*    Rollback
* Endif
* If not rolled back
* End Transaction
* Endif
```

Because you're not using row or table buffering in this example, you must individually test each action and then act accordingly. For example, the following program inserts three rows into the customer table:

```
*_
* TranUpd4.prg Session 1
* Sample using transaction processing
* See the CD for this code
*_
Local llTranOK, lnUpdates
llTranOK = .T.
lnUpdates = 3
Set Exclusive Off
Set Multilocks On
Set Reprocess To 10
Use customer Shared
Begin Transaction
Do While Not llTranOK
  If !DoUpdate("ALFKI")
    llTranOK = .F.
```

```
      Exit
   Endif
   If !DoUpdate("ANATR")
      llTranOK = .F.
      Exit
   Endif
   If !DoUpdate("ANTON")
      llTranOK = .F.
      Exit
   Endif
Enddo
If llTranOK
   End Transaction
Else
   Rollback
   = MessageBox("Update failed.  Please resubmit", ;
   "Transaction error")
Endif
*— End of program

*—
* DoUpate: Update the tables based on the primary key
* Assumes the customer table is open
*—
Function DoUpdate
LParameters tcKey, tnValue
   Local llSuccess
   llSuccess = Seek("&tcKey.")
   If llSuccess
      Update customer Set maxordamt = tnValue Where cust_id = &tcKey
   Endif
Return llSuccess
```

In this code, if the key cannot be found, the transaction is aborted and all the changes canceled.

Transactions with Row Buffering

When you use row buffering, you still have to individually update your changes with a `Tableupdate()`. Since any of the changes could fail, you still need to wrap all of them in the transactions. The following pseudocode illustrates VFP transactions when you're using row buffering:

```
* Remove all transactions
* Enable table buffering
* Begin transaction
* Repeat for all rows:
* Make change to first row
* Attempt table update with error capture
* If not successful
*     Test for errors
*     Rollback
* Endif
* If not rolled back
* End Transaction
* Endif
```

Transactions with Table Buffering

When you use table buffering, you can make your changes and apply the update in one command with the `Tableupdate()` command. That means you only need to wrap one command in the transaction. The following pseudocode illustrates VFP transactions when you're using table buffering:

```
* Remove all transactions
* Enable table buffering
* Accumulate changes to data
* Begin transaction
* Attempt table update with error capture
* If not successful
* Rollback
* Test for errors
* Else
```

```
*  End Transaction
*  Endif
```

Notice that the `Rollback` command is placed right after testing for failure of the `Tableupdate()`. This way, you can place dialog boxes in the error handling without worrying about keeping the transaction's locks active.

Summary of Transaction Processing

The best time to use transactions is with multiple-row or multiple-table changes in a database. The extra protection of transaction processing is vital when sensitive data is written in several places. The ability to bundle it all into a single unit of work is invaluable.

On the other hand, single-row updates do not need a transaction wrapper— especially if you use row buffering—because you can test the results of the `Tableupdate()`. If you do not use buffering, however, you can easily benefit from transaction processing for even a single row.

Because transactions execute implicit locks, there are a number of points to keep in mind. First, it's best to keep all transactions as brief as possible. One way to do this is to keep commands to a minimum between `Begin Transaction` and `End Transaction` (or `Rollback`). Do not insert any user dialog boxes or queries. Also, only put changes into a transaction if they really need to be there, and if they really fit together into a unit of work. If some of the changes do not depend on each other, remove what you can to make separate transactions.

Second, don't use explicit row locks inside a transaction. You can rely on the implicit locks and VFP's automatic locking during transactions. Any explicit locks you make must be explicitly unlocked, because a transaction never unlocks them after you end it.

Third, avoid deadlocks. A *deadlock* occurs when one transaction has a lock on a row, and seeks another row lock that currently is held by a different transaction, which in turn seeks a lock on the row that's locked by the first transaction. As an example, imagine that the following code fragment is run by a user:

```
*— Deadlock 1.prg (on the CD)
Begin Transaction
```

```
Update customer Set maxordamt = 1000 Where cust_id = "ALFKI"
* synch point
Update customer Set maxordamt = 2000 Where cust_id = "ANATR"
End Transaction
```

Now, the following code fragment is run by another user simultaneously:

```
*- Deadlock 2.prg (on the CD)
Begin Transaction
Update customer Set maxordamt = 3000 Where cust_id = "ANATR"
* synch point
Update customer Set maxordamt = 4000 Where cust_id = "ALFKI"
End Transaction
```

User 1 gets the lock on "ALFKI" and then tries to get the lock on "ANATR" which user 2 already has. So user 1 waits. . . . In the meantime, user 2 is seeking the lock on "ALFKI" which is impossible because user 1 already has it. VFP will not arbitrate a deadlock for you, so you have to do it yourself by careful coding. You can prevent this by always coding your forms to access the affected tables in the same order. There might only be a problem when you provide the user two different forms that can update the same tables.

Summary

You have seen that multi-user conflicts are unavoidable once you expose your data to many users. Fortunately, Visual FoxPro has many useful tools to help you arbitrate such conflicts. First, there are traditional locking mechanisms—you can insert locking into an application so that no one else can write to the locked data while your user is editing it. Visual FoxPro also offers you the ability to buffer your edits to tables and rows, and lets you decide whether to use pessimistic or optimistic locking. Finally, Visual FoxPro provides a set of invaluable transaction processing commands to protect multiple updates to your data.

Chapter 9

Creating
Development Tools

Introduction

For all that the Visual FoxPro *integrated development environment (IDE)* offers in terms of features, it does not contain everything a developer will require over the long term. Fortunately, Microsoft has exposed the IDE to allow developers to create their own tools, and to integrate them into the IDE. These tools generally are known as *builders*, because they help the developer automate the process of building application components. Most of what a builder does is make property settings to a single control or multiple controls. Instead of having to negotiate the Properties window for every control, a builder sets the required property values for various controls in one step. When a developer is engaged in either rapid prototyping or rapid application development (RAD), productivity—and getting it right the first time—is the name of the game. Builders empower the developer to be as productive as possible. During the course of this chapter, you will explore how builders work and how to construct a builder. In addition, you will explore how to create your own developer shortcut menu that contains ready access to all your tools. Finally, you will learn how to create and use add-ins for the Class Browser. *Add-ins* are programs that you write which can be called from within the Class Browser. These add-in programs extend the functionality of the Class Browser.

Understanding Visual FoxPro's Open IDE

What does it mean to say that Visual FoxPro's integrated development environment (IDE) is *open*? Simply put, it means that Microsoft has left hooks in the development environment that allow you to interact with your objects and classes at design time in the same way you do at runtime. As you know, Visual FoxPro is an object-oriented environment. Objects exist not only in the context of a running application, but also at design time. In short, just about everything in the Form and Class Designers is an object, in that it has some exposed properties and methods. You can manipulate these properties and methods if their current state will not suffice. This manipulation is often done through the Properties window interface. Working directly with the Properties window can sometimes be cumbersome, especially when dealing with many objects, or a containership hierarchy with many levels. This section will examine how to expose properties and methods of objects during a design session. It should be noted that while an example may be illustrated in either the Class Designer or Form Designer, the techniques will work in both designers, because they're essentially the same.

Understanding the `Aselobj()` Function and Creating Simple Builders

At the heart of every builder is the `Aselobj()` function. This function takes any selected object and creates an array that holds object references to the selected object.

The function takes two arguments:

- The first argument, which is required, is the name of the array that will hold the object references to the selected controls.

- The second argument, which is optional, determines whether the form or the data environment is being analyzed. Its possible values are:

    1: A one-dimensional array is created that holds an object reference to the container of the selected control. For example, if a command button directly contained on a form is selected, the container of the command button is the form. Therefore, if you pass the value 1 as the second argument, the resulting array will contain an object reference to the form. If no objects are selected, the current design form is assumed to be the container.

    2: A one-dimensional array is created that holds an object reference to the Data Environment of the current design form.

If an array is not created, the `Aselobj()` function returns 0. Otherwise, it returns the number of selected controls. In the case that either 1 or 2 is passed as the second argument, the value 1 is returned by the function, indicating that an array has been created.

Now that you know technically how `Aselobj()` works, consider the scenario shown in Figure 9-1.

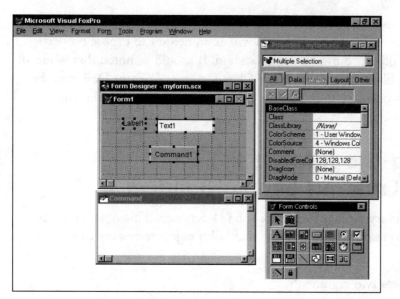

FIGURE 9-1

This form design session has three controls selected.

In this sample form in the Form Designer, three controls have been selected: a label, a text box, and a command button. Consider the following code:

```
Aselobj(laObjects)
```

If you issue this code in the command window, an array named `laObjects` is created. Displaying the contents of the `laObjects` array yields the following:

LAOBJECTS	Pub	A	
(1)	O	TEXTBOX	
(2)	O	LABEL	
(3)	O	COMMANDBUTTON	

You get the following results if you pass 1 or 2, respectively, as the second argument:

```
Aselobj(laForm,1)
```

LAFORM	Pub	A	
(1)	O	FORM	

```
Aselobj(laDataEnvironment,2)
```

| LADATAENVIRONMENT | Pub | A |
| (1) | O | DATAENVIRONMENT |

Because the array contains references to the objects, the objects' properties and methods can be manipulated.

Consider what happens, for example, when you issue the following in the command window:

```
laObjects[1].FontName = "Times New Roman"
laForm[1].BackColor = Rgb(255,0,0)
laDataEnvironment[1].AutoCloseTables = .F.
```

The `FontName` property of the text box changes to Times New Roman, the `BackColor` property of the current design form changes to red, and the `AutoCloseTables` property of the Data Environment changes to False.

All you have achieved at this point is the ability to manipulate properties. In fact, though, you also can use builders to automate the process of writing method code. Assume in your sample form that you need to place some datasession-specific `Set` settings in the `Load()` method. To automate this task, you can employ the following steps:

1. Establish a variable to hold a carriage return and line feed.

2. Establish a variable to hold new method code.

3. Read any existing code in the `Load()` method.

4. If no existing code exists, insert a call to the class's `Load()` in order to preserve inheritance. If code does exist, append your code to what is already contained in the `Load()` method. Also, you can assume that the previous code already contains a scope resolution operator to preserve inheritance. In this example, there is no existing code. You can, however, write the code to account for those situations where code already exists.

Before going any further, establish a variable in the command window to hold a carriage return and line feed. The following code is broken down according to the steps listed above. (When writing the code, be sure to omit the step numbers. They're listed here only for the sake of clarity.)

Now, onto writing the code. Create a program named MYBUILD and type in the following:

Step 1:

```
lcCRLF = CHR(13) + CHR(10)
```

Step 2:

```
lcMethod = "Set Multilocks On" + lcCRLF + "Set Deleted On" ;
+ lcCRLF + "Set Talk Off"
```

Step 3:

```
lcCode = laForm[1].ReadMethod("load")
```

Step 4:

```
If Empty(lcCode)
    lcNewMethod = laForm[1].Class+"::Load()" + lcCRLF + lcMethod
Else
    lcNewMethod = lcCode + lcCRLF + lcMethod
Endif

laForm[1].WriteMethod("load",lcNewMethod)
```

At this point, you have manipulated properties and have written method code through the use of Aselobj(). You also can add and remove objects to and from containers via object references created by Aselobj(). For example, if you want to add another text box to your design form, based on the TextBox class and named Text3, all you need to do is issue the following code:

```
laForm[1].AddObject("Text3","TextBox")
```

To further build upon the example listed above regarding the Data Environment object reference, you can add a cursor object as follows:

```
laDataEnvironment[1].AddObject("Cursor1","Cursor")
```

Using builders can overcome some of the limitations in not being able to visually subclass the Data Environment and its associated cursor and relation objects. By subclassing these items programmatically, you can add them to form objects via the `Aselobj()` function.

Conversely, you also can remove objects with `Aselobj()`. Assume that you want to remove the text box from the form, and the cursor from the Data Environment. Here's the code to accomplish these tasks:

```
laForm[1].RemoveObject("Text3")
laDataEnvironment[1].RemoveObject("Cursor1")
```

If you feel comfortable with what has been discussed so far in regards to `Aselobj()`, then you understand all that is required to create your own builders. Now, turn your attention to how builders and Visual FoxPro interact.

How Builders and Visual FoxPro Interact

As stated previously, builders and the Visual FoxPro IDE are integrated. The question now is, "How are they integrated?" Up until now, your simple builders have been stand-alone procedures. Often, you want your builders to coexist with the builders that ship with VFP. Sometimes, you want your builders to replace the VFP default builders. In other instances you always want to use a VFP default builder. By understanding how builders are integrated with the VFP IDE, you decrease the difficulty of integrating your builders with the default VFP builders.

How Visual FoxPro Calls Builders

Visual FoxPro has a system memory variable named _Builder. By default, _Builder points to an application named BUILDER.APP that resides in the root of the VFP directory. You can point the _Builder variable to your own program, just as you can point the GenMenu variable to an alternative program such as GENMENUX.PRG. When you do something in VFP to execute the builder application, the program specified by _Builder is called and is passed two arguments. The first argument is an object reference upon which the builder will act.

Table 9-1 Visual FoxPro **Builder** Values

Argument 1	Argument 2	Definition
Object Reference	TOOLBOX	The builder was called while placing a control on the form while the Builder Lock button was clicked.
Object Reference	RTMOUSE	An object was right-clicked in either the Form or Class Designer, and then Builder was chosen from the shortcut menu.
Object Reference	QFORM	The Form Builder button was clicked on the Form Designer toolbar.
Null String	RI	Referential Integrity was chosen on the Database menu.
Null String	RI	A relation object was double-clicked in the Database Designer, and then the Referential Integrity button was clicked in the resulting dialog box.
Null String	RI	The Database Designer was right-clicked, and then Referential Integrity was chosen from the shortcut menu.

The second argument is a character string denoting where the builder was called. Table 9-1 summarizes the possible values passed to the _Builder program by Visual FoxPro.

To demonstrate how you can create your own hook into the VFP builder call, try creating a program named MYBUILD.PRG. Here's the code:

```
Lparameters toObject,tcFrom
Local lcFrom,lcMsg
Store Space(0) To lcFrom,lcMsg
Do Case
   Case tcFrom = "TOOLBOX"
      lcFrom = "You called the builder while picking a control ;
      from the Form Control's Toolbar."
   Case tcFrom = "RTMOUSE"
      lcFrom = "You called the builder while clicking the right ;
      mouse key."
```

```
  Case tcFrom = "QFORM"

     lcFrom = "You called the builder while picking a control ;
     from the Form Designer Toolbar."

  Case tcFrom = "RI"

     lcFrom = "You called the builder while attempting to run the ;
     RI Builder"

Endcase

Messagebox(lcFrom,38)

If Isnull(toObject)

   lcMsg = "There is no object reference to report on"

Else

   lcMsg = "The name of the object is " + toObject.name

Endif

Messagebox(lcMsg,38)

If Messagebox("Do you wish to proceed to the default builders?",36) = 6

   Do (Home()+"Builder") With toObject,tcFrom

Else

   ** Run our custom builder code

Endif

Return
```

To see the MYBUILD program in action, you must issue the following in the command window:

```
_BUILDER = "mybuild.prg"
```

Now, when you choose to invoke a builder, your own builder program is called. Depending on how you respond to the dialog box, the default VFP builder, BUILDER.APP, may or may not be called. At this point, it should be apparent that, depending on where _Builder has been called from, you may choose what is executed. For example, you may elect that when the _Builder program is executed by a right-click, your builder program is executed by default—in all other circumstances, the default VFP builder is executed. Or, as is the case in the above sample code, you can choose which builder programs to run. Finally, because an object reference is passed, different builders can be executed for different classes. When you right-click a Grid object as opposed to a TextBox object, a different builder interface is presented. Therefore, when you create your own classes, you can also create builders that are customized to those classes just by testing the `Class` property of the passed object reference.

Fortunately, you aren't limited to just calling your builders in the ways listed above. In fact, most of the time, custom builders are called directly from a toolbar that is present during a form/class design session. You'll create such a toolbar containing three builders later in this chapter.

Now that you have done some basic work with builders, and understand how they're integrated and can be called in the VFP IDE, it's time to create and examine more complex builders.

Creating Complex Builders

Perhaps one of the most challenging aspects of writing robust builders is dealing with the containership hierarchy that can exist in forms. For instance, suppose that you have a form that has a pageframe within a pageframe within a pageframe. How do you effectively deal with the contained objects at the various levels in the hierarchy? Of course, the level of containership is a dynamic variable. In some forms, the levels may be two. Others may be five or six levels deep of containership. The issue then is how to write code that is flexible in handling any level of containership, and can be used by any builder that requires its services.

What you need to design is a class whose sole job is to traverse the containership hierarchy and obtain object references to every object in the hierarchy, so that the objects can be acted upon. In the `BUILDER.VCX` file that accompanies this book is a class definition named `traverse`. The `traverse` class is a custom class that accepts two arguments. The first is the object reference the class will traverse. The second is a numeric value denoting how many columns the array of resulting object references needs to possess. Remember, you need to design this class to be used by other builders, and if necessary, by another application component. The following is a code listing of the `Traverse` class from the Class Browser:

```
DEFINE CLASS traverse AS custom
    Height = 17
    Width = 110
    PROTECTED incounter
```

```
incounter = 0
PROTECTED inlevel
inlevel = 0
PROTECTED incols
incols = 2
Name = "traverse"
DIMENSION iaobjects[1,2]


* This method takes care of traversing objects in a pageframe class
PROTECTED PROCEDURE pageframe
    Lparameters toObject
    Local lncount,lncount2
    STORE 0 TO lncount,lncount2
    This.incounter = This.incounter + 1
    DIMENSION this.iaobjects[this.incounter,This.inCols]
    This.iaObjects[This.incounter,2] = This.inLevel
    This.iaObjects[this.incounter,1] = toObject
    For lncount = 1 to toObject.PageCount
       This.CheckIt(toObject.Pages(lncount))
    Endfor
    Return
ENDPROC


* This method takes care of traversing objects in a container class
PROTECTED PROCEDURE container
    Lparameters toObject
    local lncount
    store 0 to lncount
    this.incounter = this.incounter + 1
    dimension this.iaobjects[this.incounter,This.inCols]
    This.iaObjects[This.incounter,2] = This.inLevel
    this.iaobjects[this.incounter,1] = toObject
    For lncount = 1 to toObject.ControlCount
       This.checkit(toObject.Controls(lncount))
```

```
     endfor
     Return
  ENDPROC


  * This method takes care of traversing objects in a optiongroup class
  PROTECTED PROCEDURE optiongroup
     Lparameters toObject
     This.incounter = This.incounter + 1
     DIMENSION this.iaobjects[this.incounter,This.inCols]
     This.iaobjects[this.incounter,1] = toObject
     This.iaObjects[This.incounter,2] = This.inLevel
     For lncount = 1 to toObject.ButtonCount
        This.CheckIt(toObject.Buttons(lncount))
     Endfor
     Return
  ENDPROC


  * This method takes care of traversing objects in a commandgroup class
  PROTECTED PROCEDURE commandgroup
     Lparameters toObject
     This.incounter = This.incounter + 1
     DIMENSION this.iaobjects[this.incounter,This.inCols]
     This.iaobjects[this.incounter,1] = toObject
     This.iaObjects[This.incounter,2] = This.inLevel
     For lncount = 1 to toObject.ButtonCount
        This.CheckIt(toObject.Buttons(lncount))
     Endfor
     Return
  ENDPROC


  * This method takes care of traversing objects in a grid class
  PROTECTED PROCEDURE grid
     Lparameters toObject
     This.incounter = This.incounter + 1
     DIMENSION this.iaobjects[this.incounter,This.inCols]
```

```
      This.iaobjects[this.incounter,1] = toObject
      This.iaObjects[This.incounter,2] = This.inLevel
      For lncount = 1 to toObject.ColumnCount
         This.CheckIt(toObject.Columns(lncount))
      Endfor
      Return
ENDPROC

* This method takes care of traversing objects in a column class
PROTECTED PROCEDURE column
      Lparameters toObject
      local lncount
      store 0 to lncount
      this.incounter = this.incounter + 1
      dimension this.iaobjects[this.incounter,This.inCols]
      this.iaobjects[this.incounter,1] = toObject
      This.iaObjects[This.incounter,2] = This.inLevel
      For lncount = 1 to toObject.ControlCount
         This.checkit(toObject.Controls(lncount))
      endfor
      Return
ENDPROC

* This method takes care of calling the appropriate traversing
* method depending on the base class of the passed object
* reference. This method also keeps track of the containership
* level an object is contained within.
PROTECTED PROCEDURE checkit
      lParameters toObject
      Do Case
         Case Upper(toobject.baseclass) == "PAGE"
            This.inLevel = This.inLevel + 1
            This.Page(toObject)
            This.inLevel = This.inLevel - 1
```

```
      Case Upper(toobject.baseclass) == "FORM"
         This.inLevel = This.inLevel + 1
         This.Form(toObject)
         This.inLevel = This.inLevel - 1
      Case Upper(toobject.baseclass) == "COMMANDGROUP"
         This.inLevel = This.inLevel + 1
         This.CommandGroup(toObject)
         This.inLevel = This.inLevel - 1
      Case Upper(toobject.baseclass) == "GRID"
         This.inLevel = This.inLevel + 1
         This.Grid(toObject)
         This.inLevel = This.inLevel - 1
      Case Upper(toobject.baseclass) == "OPTIONGROUP"
         This.inLevel = This.inLevel + 1
         This.OptionGroup(toObject)
         This.inLevel = This.inLevel - 1
      Case Upper(toobject.baseclass) == "COLUMN"
         This.inLevel = This.inLevel + 1
         This.Column(toObject)
         This.inLevel = This.inLevel - 1
      Case Upper(toobject.baseclass) == "PAGEFRAME"
         This.inLevel = This.inLevel + 1
         This.PageFrame(toobject)
         This.inLevel = This.inLevel - 1
      Case Upper(toobject.baseclass) == "CONTAINER"
         This.inLevel = This.inLevel + 1
         This.Container(toobject)
         This.inLevel = This.inLevel - 1
      Otherwise
         This.incounter = This.incounter + 1
         Dimension This.iaobjects[This.incounter,This.inCols]
         This.iaobjects[This.incounter,1] = toobject
         This.iaObjects[This.incounter,2] = This.inLevel
   Endcase
```

```
      Return
ENDPROC


* This method takes care of traversing objects in a form class
PROTECTED PROCEDURE form
   Lparameters toObject,taArray,tnRow
   local lncount
   store 0 to lncount
   this.incounter = this.incounter + 1
   dimension this.iaobjects[this.incounter,This.inCols]
   this.iaobjects[this.incounter,1] = toObject
   This.iaObjects[This.incounter,2] = This.inLevel
   For lncount = 1 to toObject.ControlCount
      This.checkit(toObject.Controls(lncount))
   endfor
   Return
ENDPROC


* This method takes care of traversing objects in a page class
PROTECTED PROCEDURE page
   Lparameters toObject
   local lncount
   store 0 to lncount
   this.incounter = this.incounter + 1
   dimension this.iaobjects[this.incounter,This.inCols]
   This.iaObjects[This.incounter,2] = This.inLevel
   this.iaobjects[this.incounter,1] = toObject
   For lncount = 1 to toObject.ControlCount
      This.checkit(toObject.Controls(lncount))
   endfor
   Return
ENDPROC
PROCEDURE Init
   Lparameters toObject,tnCols
```

```
      If Type("tnCols") # "N" Or tnCols < 2
         This.inCols = 2
      Else
         This.inCols = tnCols
      Endif
      This.CheckIt(toObject)
      Return
   ENDPROC
ENDDEFINE
```

NOTE: The `Traverse` class definition is contained on the accompanying CD-ROM in `BUILDER.VCX`.

The way this class works is quite simple. The code continually "drills down" into the hierarchy. As you can see, nothing is hard-coded. If a pageframe is encountered, all pages in the pageframe are negotiated. If another pageframe is encountered, those pages are negotiated as well. This process continues until there are no more objects in the master container to evaluate.

This class has a member array named `iaObjects`. This array by default has two columns. The first holds the object reference, and the second contains a numeric value indicating the level in the containership hierarchy at which the object is contained. For a demonstration of how to use this class, create a form like the one shown in Figure 9-2.

In this example, we have a form that contains two pageframes, one nested within the other. On the first page of the nested pageframe is a command button. Enter the following code in the command window:

```
Set Classlib To Builder Additive
Aselobj(laForm,1)
_Vfp.Addobject("traverse","traverse",laForm[1])
Acopy(_Vfp.Traverse.iaObjects,laObjects)
Display Memory Like laObjects To mem.txt Noconsole
Modify Command mem.txt
```

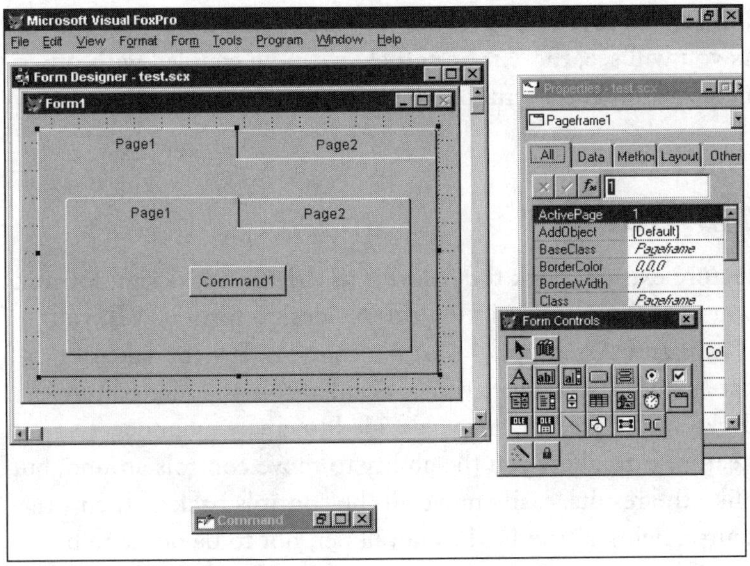

FIGURE 9-2

This form design session shows the outermost pageframe container selected.

Figure 9-3 shows the contents of `MEM.TXT`.

As you can see, the form itself is contained in the first level of containership, and the first pageframe is at the second level. The command button is contained in the fifth level of the hierarchy. Even if the hierarchy were ten or twenty levels deep, it would not make a difference. The above code is totally data-driven and could handle such a circumstance if it arose. The key points to take away from

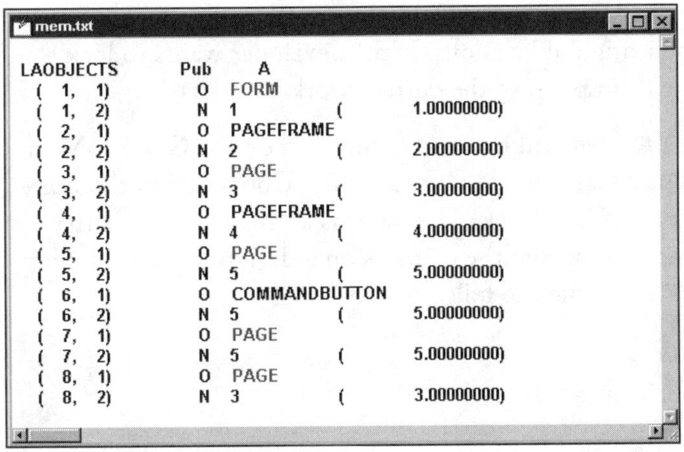
mem.txt

```
LAOBJECTS            Pub    A
   (  1,  1)          O   FORM
   (  1,  2)          N   1            (        1.00000000)
   (  2,  1)          O   PAGEFRAME
   (  2,  2)          N   2            (        2.00000000)
   (  3,  1)          O   PAGE
   (  3,  2)          N   3            (        3.00000000)
   (  4,  1)          O   PAGEFRAME
   (  4,  2)          N   4            (        4.00000000)
   (  5,  1)          O   PAGE
   (  5,  2)          N   5            (        5.00000000)
   (  6,  1)          O   COMMANDBUTTON
   (  6,  2)          N   5            (        5.00000000)
   (  7,  1)          O   PAGE
   (  7,  2)          N   5            (        5.00000000)
   (  8,  1)          O   PAGE
   (  8,  2)          N   3            (        3.00000000)
```

FIGURE 9-3

The `MEM.TXT` file here shows the contents of the `laObjects` array.

this discussion and the remainder of this section are the design aspects of the Traverse class. As you will see, the Traverse class can be coupled with other classes to form some powerful and useful builders.

The Lock Controls Builder

In Visual Basic, a feature exists to lock the controls of the current design form in place. Basically, if you lock the controls in the current design form in VB, you cannot change the Left and Top properties of the controls. For the sake of this example, assume that as a VFP developer you've decided this is a nice feature—and, because VFP lacks such a feature, you've decided to create a builder. The key benefit of this feature is to allow you the ability to move controls around, but then, if you do not like the results, easily move all the controls back to their original locations. Of course, being a true FoxPro developer, not to be outdone by another development platform, you are going to make the Visual FoxPro version of this feature a bit more flexible.

For starters, in VB, it's an all-or-nothing proposition. Either all your controls are locked, or none are. In your VFP solution, you want to allow the developer to either select all controls (as in VB) or select a specific control to lock. There essentially are two steps required to gain this functionality:

1. Have the ability to traverse the containership hierarchy to record the starting Top and Left properties of the contained objects. You already have this requirement satisfied with the Traverse class.

2. Give the developer the ability to unlock the controls, thereby moving them back to their original locations. If the developer wants to lock a new location, she'll simply save the current work.

To access these builders, a toolbar will be used. Contained on the CD-ROM in BUILDER.VCX is a ToolBar class named tbrBuilder. Contained in the tbr-Builder class is a class named chkLock. The latter is a CheckBox class that will take care of locking and unlocking the controls on a design form. In order to instantiate the ToolBar class, issue the following code:

```
Set Classlib to Builder Additive
oToolBar = CreateObject("tbrBuilder")
oToolBar.Show()
```

NOTE: The `Lock Controls` class definition is contained on the accompanying CD-ROM in BUILDER.VCX.

The following is a code listing from the Class Browser on the `chkLock` class:

```
DEFINE CLASS chkLock AS checkbox
   Height = 27
   Width = 78
   Caption = "Un-Locked"
   Value = .F.
   Style = 1
   ToolTipText = "Stores current Top and Left Properties of objects ;
   in selected container"
   Name = "chklock"
   PROTECTED PROCEDURE lock
      Set Classlib To Builder Additive
      Local loTraverse,lnCount,loObjRef
      Local Array laForm[1],laObject[1]
      Aselobj(laForm,1)
      Aselobj(laObject)
      If Type("laObject[1]") = "O" And !Isnull(laObject[1])
         loObjref = laObject[1]
      Else
         If Type("laForm[1]") = "O" and !isnull(laForm[1])
            loObjref = laForm[1]
         Else
            loObjref = .NULL.
         Endif
      Endif
      If !Isnull(loObjref)
         This.Parent.AddObject("traverse","traverse",loObjRef,4)
         For lnCount = 1 To Alen(This.Parent.Traverse.iaObjects,1)
```

```
            If Type("This.Parent.Traverse.iaObjects[lnCount,1].Top") = "N"
                This.Parent.Traverse.iaObjects[lnCount,3] = ;
                This.Parent.Traverse.iaObjects[lnCount,1].Top
                This.Parent.Traverse.iaObjects[lnCount,4] = ;
                This.Parent.Traverse.iaObjects[lnCount,1].Left
            Endif
        EndFor
        This.Caption = "Locked"
    EndIf
ENDPROC
PROTECTED PROCEDURE unlock
    Local Array laForm[1]
    Aselobj(laForm,1)
    For lnCount = 1 to alen(This.Parent.Traverse.iaObjects,1)
        If Type("This.Parent.Traverse.iaObjects[lnCount,1]") = "O" ;
        And !Isnull(This.Parent.Traverse.iaObjects[lnCount,1])
            If Type("This.Parent.Traverse.iaObjects[lnCount,3]") = "N"
                This.Parent.Traverse.iaObjects[lnCount,1].Top = ;
                This.Parent.Traverse.iaObjects[lnCount,3]
                This.Parent.Traverse.iaObjects[lnCount,1].Left = ;
                This.Parent.Traverse.iaObjects[lnCount,4]
            Endif
        Endif
    Endfor
    If Type("laForm[1]") = "O" And !Isnull(laForm[1])
        laForm[1].BackColor = laForm[1].BackColor
    Endif
    This.Parent.RemoveObject("traverse")

    This.Caption = "Un-Locked"
ENDPROC
PROCEDURE Click
```

```
      If This.Value && Lock the Top and Left Properties
        This.Lock()
      Else && Unlock the Top and Left Properties
        This.UnLock()
      Endif
      Return
    ENDPROC
    PROCEDURE When
      Local Array laForm[1]
      Aselobj(laForm,1)
      Return Type("laform[1]") = "O" And !Isnull(laForm[1])
    ENDPROC
ENDDEFINE
```

In the `Lock()` method, take note of this code:

```
This.Parent.AddObject("traverse","traverse",loObjRef,4)
```

The value 4 passed as the second argument denotes the number of columns you need in the `Traverse` object's `iaObjects` array. Why the additional two columns? You're going to use these new columns to keep track of the `Top` and `Left` properties of each object while the controls are locked.

After you have instantiated the toolbar, create a test form and then add some objects to the form. Now, making sure that no item is selected on the design form, choose to lock controls. Notice that the caption on the graphical check box now reads `Locked`. Next, move the controls around the form. Finally, click again to unlock the controls. Voila! The items are returned to their original locations.

The central points to keep in mind here are the design considerations in creating these tools. The `Traverse` class, thanks to how it's written, can be utilized by other programs and classes. If you want to record the states of additional properties such as `FontSize` or `FontName`, it's merely a case of passing a larger value as the second argument when instantiating the `Traverse` class. With the additional columns available, you just need to record the relevant properties in the `Lock()` method, and write code in the `UnLock()` method to restore the font attributes.

The HelpContextID Recorder Builder

The next builder to look at also makes use of the previously described Traverse class to "surf" the containership hierarchy. The sole purpose of this builder is to fetch the HelpContextID property values from any control that has an assigned value. For controls that do have a HelpContextID value, a DBF file is created that holds four pieces of information. HelpContextID is recorded in the first field, the Caption property of the design form is stored in the second field, the Name of the object is contained in the third field, and the Comment property is contained in the fourth field.

The resulting DBF file can be used either as a basis for a DBF-style help file, or as a point of reference when creating graphical help. The process of creating an integrated help system is discussed in Chapter 14, "Deploying and Distributing Your Applications."

NOTE: The HelpContextIDRecorder class definition is contained on the accompanying CD-ROM in BUILDER.VCX.

Here is the code listing of the HelpContextID Recorder builder:

```
DEFINE CLASS cmdhelpcontextidrecorder AS commandbutton
    Height = 27
    Width = 151
    Caption = "HelpContextID Recorder"
    Name = "cmdhelpcontextidrecorder"
    PROTECTED PROCEDURE gethelpcontextid
        Set Classlib To Builder Additive
        Local loTraverse,lnCount
        lnCount = 1
        Local Array laForm[1]
        Aselobj(laForm,1)
        If Type("laForm[1]") = "O" And !Isnull(laForm[1])
```

```
This.Parent.AddObject("traverse","traverse",laForm[1],5)
For lnCount = 1 To Alen(This.Parent.Traverse.iaObjects,1)
   If Type("This.Parent.Traverse.iaObjects[lnCount,1].Top") ;
   = "N"
         This.Parent.Traverse.iaObjects[lnCount,3] = ;
This.Parent.Traverse.iaObjects[lnCount,1].HelpContextID
         This.Parent.Traverse.iaObjects[lnCount,4] = ;
         This.Parent.Traverse.iaObjects[lnCount,1].Name
         This.Parent.Traverse.iaObjects[lnCount,5] = ;
         This.Parent.Traverse.iaObjects[lnCount,1].Comment
   Endif
EndFor
If lnCount >= 1
   lcDBF = Putfile("","","DBF")
   If !Empty(lcDBF)
      If File(lcDBF)
         lnAction = Messagebox("Do you wish to overwrite ;
the file. If you choose No, new records will be ;
appended.",36)
      Else
         lnAction = 7
      Endif
      If lnAction = 6 Or !File(lcDBF)
         lcOldSafety = Set('Safety')
         Set Safety Off
         Create Table (lcDBF) Free ;
            (HelpID I(4),Form C(50),Name C(50),Comment C(254))
         Set Safety &lcOldSafety
         Else
         If !Used(lcDBF) And File(lcDBF)
            Use (lcDBF) In 0 Share
         Endif
      Endif
```

```
            For lnCount = 1 To Alen(This.Parent.Traverse.iaObjects,1))
                m.Helpid = This.Parent.Traverse.iaObjects [lnCount,3]
                m.Name = This.Parent.Traverse.iaObjects [lnCount,4]
                m.Comment = This.Parent.Traverse.iaObjects [lnCount,5]
                m.Form = laForm[1].Caption
                Insert Into (lcDBF) ;
                    From Memvar
            Endfor
        Endif
    Endif
    This.Parent.RemoveObject("traverse")
    Endif
ENDPROC


PROCEDURE Click
    This.GetHelpContextID()
ENDPROC
ENDDEFINE
```

As you can see, the same basic call is made to the Traverse class that you saw earlier in the chapter. In this builder, the HelpContextID, Name, and Comment properties have been gleaned from each object in the hierarchy. If you need to gather other information, it's only a matter of increasing the value of the column argument passed to the Traverse class in the CreateObject() call, then filling the additional array columns with the appropriate information. In this example, the use of the builder technology has been extended beyond the bounds of the design form. It should be fairly apparent at this point that there are unlimited uses for builders.

The DB Reset Builder

When dragging and dropping objects from the Data Environment in Visual FoxPro 5.0, you'll find several changes from version 3.0. First, when dropping a field onto a form, a label is automatically created, with its Caption property set to the Caption property contained in the DBC. In addition, any TextBox controls dropped onto the form have their `Width` property reflect the width of the underlying field width.

While this flexibility is nice, what happens if you make changes to the width of the field or the associated label caption, then later decide that you need to restore the original state of the objects? If you choose to restore the default values in the Properties window, you revert to the defaults in the class from which the controls were subclassed, not what was defined when the controls were dropped onto the form from the Data Environment.

Assuming that the controls dragged from the Data Environment were based directly on the VFP base classes, a label's `Caption` property would revert to "Label*x*" and a text box's `Width` property would revert to `100`. It would be nice in such situations to restore the settings that were established when the controls were first added to the form from the Data Environment. Although this functionality does not exist natively in VFP, you can get the job done via a builder.

> **NOTE:** The DB Reset class definition is contained on the accompanying CD-ROM in `BUILDER.VCX`.

The following is the builder code to restore the DB default property values:

```
DEFINE CLASS cmdreset AS commandbutton
    AutoSize = .T.
    Height = 27
    Width = 175
    Caption = "Reset DB Objects To Default"
    ToolTipText = "Properly sizes bound TextBoxes and resets ;
    caption on associated Labels"
    Name = "cmdreset"
    PROCEDURE Click
        Local lcDbc,loObject,lnCount,lcControlSource,lcOldError, ;
        lnError,lcTable
        Local lcType
```

```
Local Array laObjects[1],laForm[1]
lcOldError = On("Error")
On Error lnError = Error()
lnError = 0
Aselobj(laObjects)
Aselobj(laForm,1)
If Type("laObjects[1]") = "O" And !Isnull(laObjects[1]) And ;
   Type("laForm[1]") = "O" And !Isnull(laForm[1])
   lcDbc = Iif(Empty(Dbc()),Getfile("DBC"),Dbc())
   If !Empty(lcDbc)
      If Dbused(lcDbc)
         Set Database To (lcDbc)
      Else
         Open Database (lcDbc) Shared
      Endif
      For lnCount = 1 To Alen(laObjects,1)
         With laObjects[lnCount]
            .ResetToDefault("FontName")
            .ResetToDefault("FontSize")
            .ResetToDefault("FontBold")
            .ResetToDefault("FontItalic")
         Endwith
         If Upper(laObjects[lnCount].BaseClass) = "TEXTBOX"
            lcControlSource = laObjects[lnCount]. ControlSource
            lcTable = Substr(lcControlSource,1, ;
            At (".",lcControlsource)-1)
            If !Empty(lcControlSource)
               Dbgetprop(lcTable,"Table","Comment")
               If lnError = 0
                  lcType = "TABLE"
               Else
                  lcType = "VIEW"
               Endif
               If !Used(lcTable)
```

```
          If lcType = "TABLE"
              Use (lcTable) In 0 Again
          Else
              Use (lcTable) In 0 Again NoData
          Endif
      Endif
      With laObjects[lnCount]
          .Format = Dbgetprop(lcControlSource, ;
          "Field","Format")
          .InputMask = Dbgetprop(lcControlSource, ;
          "Field","InputMask")
          .Width =  Txtwidth(Replicate ;
          ("U",Len(Eval(lcControlSource))), ;
          .FontName,.FontSize, "N")* ;
          Fontmetric(6, .Fontname,.FontSize,"N")
      Endwith
      lcCaption = Dbgetprop(lcControlSource, ;
      "Field","Caption")
    Endif
  Else
    If !Empty(lcCaption)
        laObjects[lnCount].Caption = lcCaption
    Endif
  Endif
Endfor
Endif
laForm[1].BackColor = laForm[1].BackColor
Endif
On Error &lcOldError
ENDPROC
ENDDEFINE
```

The functionality of the DB Reset builder is quite simple. When scanning through the selected objects, you first determine if a text box is selected. If so, then its `ControlSource` property is examined, and the specific properties are fetched via a call to Dbgetprop(). If the text box has an associated label, that label becomes the next object in the array. When the properties of the text box were fetched, the Caption property was stored to a variable named lcCaption. The contents of that variable are assigned to the Caption property of the label. In terms of sizing, the Txtwidth() function is used in conjunction with the Fontmetric() function to determine what the overall width of the text box needs to be (based on its font) to accommodate data entry.

Creating Your Own Development Menu

One of the biggest improvements made in Visual FoxPro 5.0 is the ability to produce *right-click menus*. (These are also known as *context-sensitive menus* or *shortcut menus*.) While you can right-click just about anywhere in VFP and get a menu, no such menu exists when you right-click the main screen. This is the perfect opportunity to create a shortcut menu that contains ready access to your development tools, as well as to the most commonly executed VFP functions. The sample development menu included on the CD-ROM is named DEVMENU. The following is a code listing of the menu program (the menu was generated using the VFP menu builder):

```
*      ************************************************************
*      *
*      *                    Setup Code
*      *
*      ************************************************************
*
* This menu will only function if the mouse is positioned
* over the main VFP Screen. If the mouse is not positioned
* over the main VFP screen, we return.
LOCAL loObject
loObject = Sys(1270)
IF TYPE('loObject') = 'O' AND !ISNULL(loObject)
```

```
    IF loObject.Name <> "Screen"
       RETURN
    ENDIF
ENDIF

*     **********************************************************
*     *
*     *                  Menu Definition
*     *
*     **********************************************************
*

DEFINE POPUP shortcut SHORTCUT RELATIVE FROM MROW(),MCOL()
DEFINE BAR 1 OF shortcut PROMPT "\<Class Browser"
DEFINE BAR 2 OF shortcut PROMPT "\<Debug Window"
DEFINE BAR 3 OF shortcut PROMPT "\-"
DEFINE BAR 4 OF shortcut PROMPT "Display \<Status"
DEFINE BAR 5 OF shortcut PROMPT "Display \<Memory"
DEFINE BAR 6 OF shortcut PROMPT "\-"
DEFINE BAR 7 OF shortcut PROMPT "Modify \<Form ..."
DEFINE BAR 8 OF shortcut PROMPT "Modify C\<lass ..."
DEFINE BAR 9 OF shortcut PROMPT "\-"
DEFINE BAR 10 OF shortcut PROMPT "\<Builder Toolbar"
ON SELECTION BAR 1 OF shortcut Do (_browser)
ON SELECTION BAR 2 OF shortcut Activate Window Debug
ON SELECTION BAR 3 OF shortcut loObject.ActiveForm.Caption = ;
Str(Seconds())
ON SELECTION BAR 4 OF shortcut ;
   DO _rcx1cl4of ;
   IN LOCFILE("BUILDER\DEVMENU" ,"MPX;MPR|FXP;PRG" , ;
   "WHERE is DEVMENU?")
ON SELECTION BAR 5 OF shortcut ;
   DO _rcx1cl4si ;
   IN LOCFILE("BUILDER\DEVMENU" ,"MPX;MPR|FXP;PRG" , ;
```

```
            "WHERE is DEVMENU?")
ON SELECTION BAR 7 OF shortcut Modify Form ?
ON SELECTION BAR 8 OF shortcut Modify Class ?
ON SELECTION BAR 10 OF shortcut ;
    DO _rcx1cl4tu ;
    IN LOCFILE("BUILDER\DEVMENU" ,"MPX;MPR|FXP;PRG" , ;
    "WHERE is DEVMENU?")


ACTIVATE POPUP shortcut


*    ********************************************************
*    *
*    * _RCX1CL4OF  ON SELECTION BAR 4 OF POPUP shortcut
*    *
*    * Procedure Origin:
*    *
*    * From Menu:  DEVMENU.MPR,        Record:    8
*    * Called By:  ON SELECTION BAR 4 OF POPUP shortcut
*    * Prompt:  Display Status
*    * Snippet:    1
*    *
*    ********************************************************
*
PROCEDURE _rcx1cl4of
Display Status To _stat.txt NoConsole
Modify Command _stat.txt
Erase _stat.txt


*    ********************************************************
*    *
*    * _RCX1CL4SI  ON SELECTION BAR 5 OF POPUP shortcut
*    *
*    * Procedure Origin:
*    *
```

```
*     * From Menu:   DEVMENU.MPR,          Record:    9
*     * Called By:  ON SELECTION BAR 5 OF POPUP shortcut
*     * Prompt:   Display Memory
*     * Snippet:    2
*     *
*     ************************************************************
*
PROCEDURE _rcx1cl4si
Display Status To _mem.txt NoConsole
Modify Command _mem.txt
Erase _mem.txt
*     ************************************************************
*     *
*     * _RCX1CL4TU   ON SELECTION BAR 10 OF POPUP shortcut
*     *
*     * Procedure Origin:
*     *
*     * From Menu:   DEVMENU.MPR,          Record:    14
*     * Called By:  ON SELECTION BAR 10 OF POPUP shortcut
*     * Prompt:   Builder Toolbar
*     * Snippet:    3
*     *
*     ************************************************************
*
PROCEDURE _rcx1cl4tu
Public _oToolbar
Set Classlib To Builder Additive
_oToolbar = CreateObject("tbrBuilder")
If Type("_oToolbar") = "O" And !IsNull(_oToolbar)
  _oToolbar.Show()
Endif
```

In the setup of the menu, a test is conducted to make sure that the mouse is positioned over the main VFP screen. If it is, then your new custom shortcut

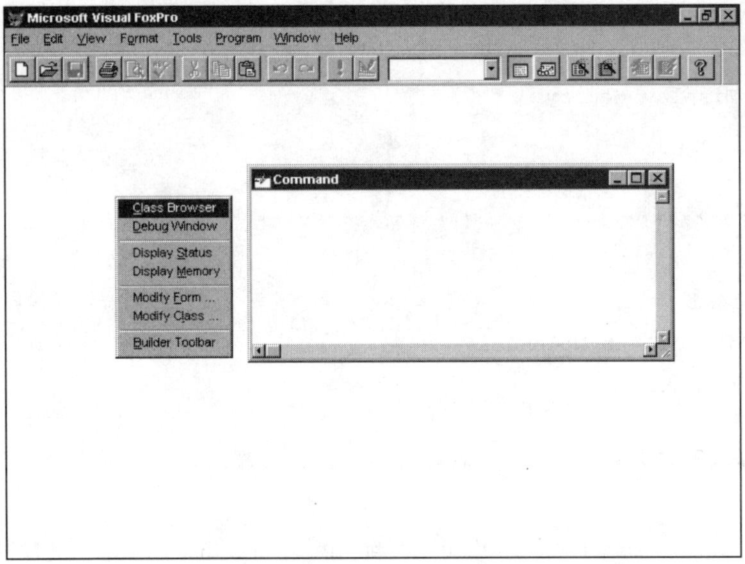

FIGURE 9-4

The custom development shortcut menu has been activated by right-clicking the screen.

menu activates. Otherwise, when there's a native VFP right-click menu, that menu is made available to the developer. To make the new development menu available, issue the following code:

```
On Key Label RightMouse Do devmenu.mpr
```

Figure 9-4 shows the development menu in action.

If the developer right-clicks the command window, for example, then the setup code in DevMenu determines that the custom menu shouldn't activate; instead, the native right-click menu associated with the command window activates. This illustrates how your own development tools can be seamlessly woven into the VFP IDE.

Class Browser Add-Ins

This section deals with the topic of add-ins for the Class Browser. The Class Browser is by far one of the most powerful tools in Visual FoxPro. An entire book could be devoted to nothing but the Class Browser. At the moment, though, we'll consider just one specific feature of the Class Browser: add-ins.

An *add-in* is an external program that can be called from the Class Browser as if it were a native component of the Class Browser. If you deal extensively with the Class Browser in your development efforts—and you should—then you may know about the capability to drag and drop classes from the Class Browser onto the main VFP Screen. (For more detailed information on the Class Browser, consult the online help file.) This helps you to quickly test and debug classes. Unfortunately, there's no native way to remove the object instances from the screen when you need to return to the Class Designer, as you cannot modify classes in use. Just as you can augment the functionality of the Class and Form Designers with builder programs, you can augment the functionality of the Class Browser with add-in programs.

Assume that you're testing your `HelpContextID` builder by dropping the class directly on the VFP screen. The name of the class is `cmdHelpContextIdRecorder`. Therefore, when an object instance is created on the screen, the name of the object is `cmdHelpContextIdRecorder1`. In order to remove this object, you would have to type the following:

```
_SCREEN.RemoveObjects("cmdHelpContextIdRecorder1")
```

You may not remember the full name of the objects. More importantly, you may have more than one instance on the screen. How can you determine the name of each instance? It would be nice if you could position the mouse over the object, and have it removed automatically. The following code, contained in a program named `Remove`, does the trick:

```
*Remove.prg
*
Lparameters toClassBrowser
Local lcParent
Wait Window "Move mouse over object to remove"
loObject = Sys(1270)
If Type("loObject") = "O" and !Isnull(loObject)
   If loObject.Name <> "Screen"
      If Type("loObject.Parent") = "O" and !Isnull(loObject.Parent)
```

```
      lcParent = Upper(loObject.Parent.Name)
      If lcparent = "SCREEN"
        lcCommand = "_Screen.RemoveObject ;
        ('"+loObject.Name+"')"
        &lcCommand
      Else
        Wait Window "The object's parent container must be ;
        the Screen." Timeout 1
      Endif
    Else
      Wait Window "The object's parent container must be the ;
      Screen." Timeout 1
    Endif
  Else
    Wait Window "The Screen cannot be removed." Timeout 1
  Endif
Endif
Return
```

When you take advantage of the Sys(1270) function, the task of removing the object becomes simple: place the mouse over the object, then click with any of the mouse buttons.

The public object variable referencing the Class Browser is named _obrowser. In order to register this add-in, you need to invoke the AddIn() method of the Class Browser. The AddIn() method accepts two arguments:

- The first is the prompt that will appear on the Add-Ins menu.
- The second is the name of the program to be executed.

The following code registers the Remove program as an add-in:

```
_obrowser.AddIn("\<Remove Object from Screen","remove.prg")
```

It is important to note that the _obrowser object variable is available only when the Class Browser is active.

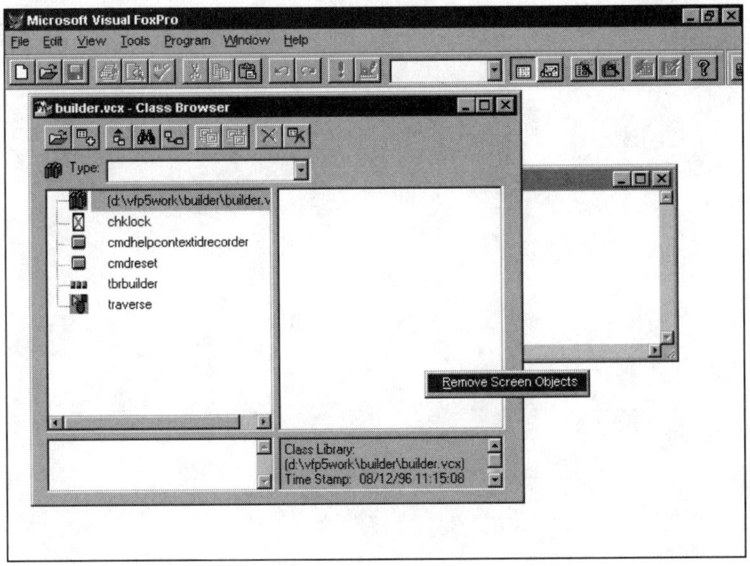

FIGURE 9-5

The Add-Ins shortcut menu in this example shows only one option, an add-in for removing objects from the screen.

To access the Add-Ins menu, right-click the Class Browser and choose Add-Ins from the shortcut menu. Another shortcut menu appears, listing the defined add-ins for your installation. The option for removing objects from the screen is shown in Figure 9-5.

Summary

As you have seen in this chapter, the real power of Visual FoxPro lies in its open architecture. This open architecture allows you to augment the base integrated development environment (IDE) with your own tools. The most common of these tools are builders. In addition to builders, you also have the ability to create your own development utility menu and add-ins for the Class Browser. The upfront time you spend creating a set of development tools can save you hundreds of hours of work in the long term, thanks to increased productivity.

PART III

Database Development

Chapter 10

Creating a
Visual FoxPro Database

Introduction

Visual FoxPro basically gives you two ways to access your data, and two ways to organize it. The two ways you can access your data are: traditional record-by-record navigation, or the newer, SQL-based relational access methods. The two ways you can organize your VFP data are into stand-alone tables, or into a VFP database. If you leave them as stand-alone tables, you lose a fair amount of control over the data.

It's important to be familiar with all these options, because each has its advantages, and you can mix and match them as well. In this chapter, you will explore all four options in the core technology of Visual FoxPro database development. In the latter half of the chapter, you will focus on VFP's native database structure and on using relational access methods.

VFP's Navigational and Relational Paradigms

VFP incorporates two major paradigms of database access: navigational and relational. Since you can often use the two methods interchangeably, it is helpful to be fully aware of both styles of access and when each is appropriate.

Navigational access makes references to the physical or logical order of the data, traversing the data from a beginning point to an end point, or vice versa. You position a record pointer somewhere within the data file, and then access the data in that record. When you are ready to deal with other data, you move to the record where that data is located.

Navigational access favors the use of the terms *file*, *record*, and *field*. That's because in navigational and flat-file systems, you store each table as a separate file, and you navigate the file record by record, from top to bottom and back. Within each record, there are fields that contain the data. Navigational language inherits much from COBOL applications and is still widely used, even by people working with relational databases.

Relational access refers to data by its values only, and treats data in sets, with no underlying physical order assumed. Instead of positioning yourself within a file, you apply operations to an entire set of data. The standard language for relational access is SQL (see Chapter 11, "Using SQL in Visual FoxPro Applications," for a thorough treatment of VFP's SQL).

Relational access uses the terms *table*, *row*, and *column*. In a relational system, how the data is stored on disk is hidden from you. You simply refer to the table, and then the rows and columns of the table store the data. Since relational access does not use navigational methods, you do not need to know anything about the position that a particular row physically has in a table.

In Visual FoxPro, you will see the terminology for navigational and relational access intermixed. You will see this in VFP's own documentation, as well as in books and articles. It's better, however, to stick to the relational terminology, because doing so will help you understand other databases and books on relational design more easily.

This chapter will refer to tables, rows, and columns unless the context demands otherwise. Recall the scene in *The Wizard of Oz* where Dorothy and The Tin Man are going through the forest, singing about "lions and tigers and bears"? Feel free to replay that scene in your mind: "tables and columns and rows—oh, my!"

VFP uses these two methods of data access because of an accident of history. Beginning with the navigational method of data access, VFP later added a relational access method. To show how and why this happened, the following sections take a look at the types of databases and when they developed.

Types of Databases

The variety of database software can be a little bewildering. The architectures vary greatly depending upon the age of the design, as well as the hardware and software platforms on which they reside. It's important to distinguish between database systems that originated on mainframe or UNIX systems, and those that began on PC desktops. Since PC databases took their lead from the existing database software of the time, it's useful to examine the types of databases in existence when PC databases were first produced.

Hierarchical, Network, and Relational Databases

When PCs became popular for database storage, it was common to classify large database systems into three major categories: hierarchical, network, and rela-

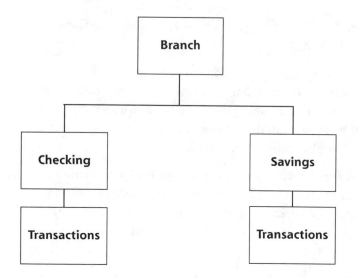

FIGURE 10-1

The hierarchical data model has a tree structure.

tional. A fourth type, object-oriented databases, came into being later (these will be discussed later in the chapter).

Hierarchical database systems organize data into a tree structure of files, where each node of the tree contains one type of data. For example, you might organize a bank's data in a hierarchical format as shown in Figure 10-1.

In this figure, each bank has branches. Each branch has checking accounts and savings accounts, and each account has transactions. As you proceed down the tree, any given node is usually in a one-to-many relationship with the nodes below it. In a hierarchical database system, you access each node by beginning with the root node, then following pointers down to the desired level. You navigate the system record by record, following pointers embedded in the records in order to get to related data.

While hierarchical systems had good performance, they often introduced redundant data, had difficulty implementing many-to-many relationships, and the need to access all data through the root node was clumsy. Hierarchical database systems such as IBM's IMS/VS are among the oldest database systems in existence, and originated on mainframe computers.

In the early 1970s, a group named CODASYL released a specification for *network* database systems. In this type of system, you store data and access it a bit more independently than with hierarchical systems. There is no longer any need for a single root node, though network systems still store data using pointers from parent nodes to sets of child records.

Unlike hierarchical database systems, network systems can implement many-to-many relationships easily. However, network databases tend to be complex and require a lot of programming. They also use record-by-record navigation based on embedded pointers. Network database systems gained popularity throughout the 1970s on minicomputer as well as mainframe systems.

Relational database systems have removed the need for complex navigation by presenting data to the user or programmer as independent sets of data. You represent these data sets as tables, often called *R-tables*. R-tables have no duplicate rows and no multi-valued data in columns. Relational databases have replaced record navigation with a relational algebra, a group of set-like operations on the tables. As a result, the user or programmer never sees any embedded pointers.

E.F. Codd, who first formulated the *relational model*, based it on applied set theory, giving it a much more solid theoretical foundation than its competitors. The relational model quickly gained acceptance as theoretically superior to the other models, even though there were no commercially available systems until the 1980s. Since that time, almost all new database products have been relational—or have claimed to be relational—until the introduction of object-oriented databases in the 1990s. The great majority of database products actually in use today follow the relational model.

Origin of Visual FoxPro's Navigational Paradigm

Visual FoxPro has a complex genealogy. It descends from a number of products dating back to dBASE II, as you can see in Table 10-1.

In early 1982, as microcomputers based on the CP/M operating system were just gaining popularity, a small company named Ashton-Tate introduced dBASE II, with "Assembly Language Relational Database" splashed on the manual cover.

Like the relational model, dBASE II stored data in independent tables with no embedded pointers visible to the user. Ashton-Tate chose DBF, short for "database file," as the file extension for the data files that stored tables. To manage the data, however, dBASE II used record-by-record navigation commands that at first relied on the physical ordering of the tables. These navigational commands

Table 10-1 VFP Genealogy

Product	Year (approx.)	Operating System	Company
dBASE II	1982	CP/M	Ashton-Tate
dBASE III	1985	MS-DOS	Ashton-Tate
dBASE III+	1986	MS-DOS	Ashton-Tate
FoxBase+	1987	MS-DOS	Fox Software
FoxPro 1	1990	MS-DOS	Fox Software
FoxPro 2	1991	MS-DOS	Fox Software
FoxPro 2.6	1993	MS-DOS, Windows, Mac	Microsoft
Visual FoxPro 3.0	1995	Windows, Mac	Microsoft
Visual FoxPro 5.0	1996	Windows, Mac	Microsoft

made reference to a *record pointer*, a marker the software keeps to a particular record in the data file. Then, when you wanted to process any data, you just positioned yourself to the proper record and invoked the necessary commands. This record navigation made dBASE II much more of a flat-file processing system than a relational database.

In addition, dBASE II introduced a way of linking two open tables together so that movement of a record pointer in one table caused appropriate movement in another, related table. The command to do this was (and still is) Set Relation. Based simply on this command, many users began to call dBASE II a relational database system. The fact that this record pointer synchronization had nothing to do with a database being relational only came to light later. dBASE II was a tremendous innovation in microcomputer software, and dBASE II and its successors have been very popular PC products.

Soon Nantucket produced the Clipper compiler, effectively cloning dBASE III+, and Fox Software produced its FoxBase+ clone. All these PC database products became known first as "dBASE software" and then later as "xBase software." Most of the evolution of dBASE and its clones consisted of enhancing the navigational commands and capabilities of the software. All the while, the data storage continued to consist of independent DBF files.

At the same time that dBASE II and its progeny were spreading throughout the PC world, IBM developed the SQL language as a method for querying relational data. (See Chapter 11, "Using SQL in Visual FoxPro Applications," for a thorough treatment of SQL.) SQL provided some very efficient query commands that PC database developers soon came to desire in their own tools.

The next significant forward leap for Fox developers occurred in the early 1990s when Fox Software provided an implementation of the SQL `Select` command in FoxPro 2.0. FoxPro programmers and users suddenly had a choice between record navigation and relational access to data. Since then, much effort has gone into furthering the implementation of SQL in FoxPro.

As a result, in Visual FoxPro you can use two kinds of access to data. You can use a relational kind, based on the SQL language as it has evolved since 1980 or so. You also can use a record navigation kind, which has been in the desktop database world since dBASE II.

Recently, Visual FoxPro introduced the concept of the *database container*. This is a very significant addition of relational functionality to the DBF file structure. The database container gives developers many features, such as referential integrity and views, that are standard in relational databases. You will learn about the database container in more detail later in this chapter.

Desktop versus Server Databases

There are other ways to classify databases. These days, a way to distinguish relational database products is to classify them as "desktop databases," as opposed to "server databases" (or "backend databases"). *Desktop databases* place the database engine in the PC running the software, whereas *server databases* put the processing engine on a separate server computer. Of course, just to show this scheme is not complete, some of the server database companies are now marketing scaled-down versions of their backend products. They call them *desktop server databases*, and they run on the user's PC. Table 10-2 shows some sample database product names.

Object and Object-Relational Databases

In the 1990s, a new type of database, the object-oriented database, has gained attention. *Object-oriented (OO) databases* actually store methods—and, in some cases, persistent objects—from classes in the database as an attempt to provide

Table 10-2 Database Products and Types

Desktop Databases	Server Databases	Desktop Server Databases
Access	Informix	Personal Oracle
Paradox	Microsoft SQL Server	Sybase SQL Anywhere
Rbase	Oracle	
Visual dBASE	Sybase SQL Server	
Visual FoxPro		

a seamless integration between data storage and object-oriented programming languages.

Additionally, a hybrid variety of database, called the *object-relational (OR) database*, has emerged recently. These are actually relational databases with significant extensions to handle many things previously reserved for OO databases.

Michael Stonebreaker, a prominent database author, has proposed another classification of databases that includes the OO and OR versions. Figure 10-2 depicts his view of the current state of affairs.

In this figure, File Processing refers to flat files accessed in navigational fashion, as with Basic or COBOL.

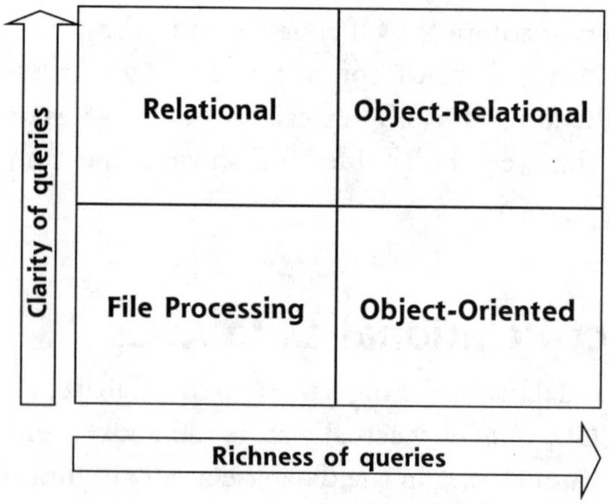

FIGURE 10-2

This is a look at object-oriented and object-relational databases.

Where Visual FoxPro Fits as a Database

Visual FoxPro straddles the File Processing and Relational categories, depending on how you choose to store your data and access it. If you make use of VFP's database structure, which you learn about in this chapter, and you use the relational aspects of VFP's SQL language, then you are working with a mostly relational database. Under the best conditions, VFP does not have as many relational features as the standard relational databases, but it does have quite a few of them. The trend in new versions of FoxPro and Visual FoxPro over the past several years has been to increase the relational features of its database engine and data access language.

Even though Visual FoxPro does have an object-oriented programming language, its data model is still firmly rooted in the relational model, and does not have OO or OR features. It's therefore important for you to gain an understanding of the relational model in order to understand the origins and functions of VFP's database container.

The Relational Model

What makes a database relational (beyond the fact that the maker of the database engine calls it so)? Adherence to the relational database model is the criterion most often applied to determine whether a database is relational. Sometimes rather picky debates go on about what it takes for a database to be relational. E.F. Codd, who first articulated relational theory in the early 1970s, initially proposed a set of 11 rules that a product would have to follow in order to qualify. He later expanded the number of rules to 67, making qualification something of a moving target!

Codd supplies a brief way to state the criteria in what he calls "Rule Zero":

> *For any system to be advertised as, or claimed to be, a relational database management system, that system must be able to manage databases entirely through its relational capabilities, no matter what additional capabilities the system may support.*

By "relational capabilities," Codd means the manipulation of relational data by relational operators. When you step from relational theory into the practical world of actual relational database products, you find varying degrees of support for the relational model. Most relational databases allow you the option of keeping your data in a strictly relational format, or deviating from it in a number of ways. This makes it all the more important to understand what the relational model requires.

Characteristics of a Relational DBMS

Among the many implications of Codd's Rule Zero, perhaps the most important one concerns the data itself. In a fully relational *database management system (DBMS)*, all data should appear to the user as organized into one or more special sorts of tables called R-tables. An R-table is a table of data with unique rows and single-valued columns. Therefore, an R-table allows neither duplicate rows nor repeated data in its columns.

This is a very fundamental rule, and all relational databases make it possible to enforce this rule on your tables. They also make it possible, however, for you to violate the rule, because with most—perhaps all—relational databases you can store duplicate rows in your tables. The point is that it's up to you to make your databases relational or not, based on how you implement your design.

A relational DBMS must, according to Codd, provide the ability to retrieve, insert, update, and delete rows. While many alternative ways of doing this have been proposed, the winner and still champion in the database world is the SQL language. SQL uses the `Select`, `Insert`, `Update`, and `Delete` commands to access data. These SQL commands operate on the data as entire tables, and have no positional reference in them—they do not rely on record navigation.

Another important characteristic of relational DBMSs is that they preserve the consistency of their data by providing transaction capabilities. One or more operations on the data can be placed within a transaction, so that the entire group of operations takes place completely or not at all. If the transaction fails, the database can recover into a stable state.

Relational DBMSs must also provide support for concurrent access—that is, locking methods. Operations on the data by many users must not cancel each other out, and the database must provide a consistent view of the data to each user.

Finally, there are two other requirements. A relational DBMS must support a set of tables about the data, usually called a *catalog*, which stores data about the database. It also must support *views*, which are derived tables based on the R-tables.

So how do you get your data into R-tables? Codd invented the method of normalization to handle that process.

Normalization

When Codd introduced his relational model, it was common in most databases of the time to store data redundantly. Many of the tables stored in hierarchical and network databases therefore did not qualify as R-tables. It was not always clear how to get them into the appropriate state. Further, designers needed a set of rules to keep their design relational. So Codd came up with a series of steps called "normal forms" to assist people in achieving fully relational organization of their data.

The steps involved in *normalization* are an attempt to take R-tables and prevent what are called "update anomalies." These anomalies are situations where you might end up with inconsistent data due to redundancies in the data.

You take a set of data stored in one or more *unnormalized* R-tables, and then *normalize* them in a series of steps. The steps are called *normal forms*, so the results of your efforts are the various stages in the process: first normal form, second normal form, and so on. The process culminates in third normal form for most tables. For tables with compound primary keys, there are a number of other, more exotic steps to the process. In this chapter, we will discuss only the first three normal forms.

Codd based the process of normalization on the idea of *functional dependency*, sometimes abbreviated as *FD*. The essence of a functional dependency is this: one column of a table functionally depends on one or more other columns if its values are normally determined by the others. In other words, A functionally depends on B if A is a function of B. For example, in the customer table, the name of the customer functionally depends on the customer ID, because the ID determines the name. Select an ID, and you get some name.

The goal of the normalization process is to get all your FDs in order. That is, in every R-table, all columns in the table other than the primary key should functionally depend on the primary key of that table. The other columns should not depend on each other or on any other key.

First Normal Form

A table is in *first normal form (1NF)* if and only if its columns are single-valued (sometimes called *atomic*) and fixed. This means a 1NF table cannot have repeating groups in its columns.

When you look at raw data, all sorts of redundancies and disorganization can occur. Before the normalization process can even begin, you must get the data into the R-table format.

To do that, you need to make sure that there is some way, within the data, of uniquely identifying rows. Record numbers will not work, because they are not criteria in the data values. You can even use the sum total of all the columns in the table. Most people, however, like to settle on one or two columns.

The column or columns that uniquely identify a row are called a *candidate key*. Any table can have more that one candidate key, because you might be uniquely identifying each row in more than one way.

The candidate key you select to be the key that other tables use to refer back to any given row of the table is called the *primary key*. When that key is used in other tables to refer back to the table it came from, it's called a *foreign key*. In the following example, cust_id is a primary key in the Customer table, but is a foreign key in the Orders table:

> Customer (<u>cust id</u>, name)
>
> Orders (<u>order id</u>, cust_id, order_amt)

Table Notation

The convention used in this chapter for defining a table with its columns is to state the table name, followed with the columns in parentheses, with the primary key underlined. For example, the following notation describes a table named OrderLines with order_id and line_no serving as the primary key:

> OrderLines (<u>order id, line no</u>, cust_id, company)

Unnormalized Data

Now, consider a table that is not an R-table, and put it into proper shape. Here's the table:

OrderLines (<u>order id</u>, lines (`line_1`, `line_2`, and so on), `cust_id`, `company`)

Figure 10-3 shows a sample view of the data.

Notice that the line numbers repeat in the lines column, separated by commas. This makes the lines column non-atomic, and therefore the data is not an R-table, so it is not a relation according to Codd's definition.

An R-table Not in First Normal Form

You could expand those line numbers into separate columns of their own, hoping therefore to normalize the OrderLines table:

OrderLines (<u>order id</u>, `line1`, `line2`, `line3`, `line4`, `product1`, `product2`, `product3`, `product4`, `product5`, `cust_id`, `company`)

This makes the table a relation, as shown in Figure 10-4, because the values are all atomic. However, it is still containing a repeating group of data, so it's not yet in first normal form.

Getting to First Normal Form

To get the OrderLines table into first normal form, you can just condense the lines columns into one `line_no` column and repeat the rows, not the columns. That is, instead of making repeating groups of order line columns, make the

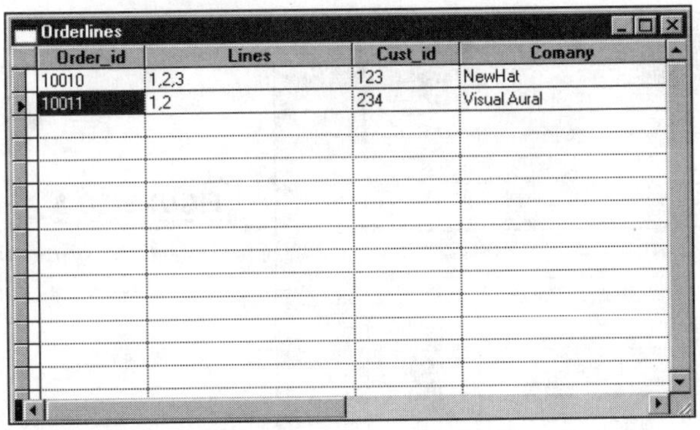

Order_id	Lines	Cust_id	Comany
10010	1,2,3	123	NewHat
10011	1,2	234	Visual Aural

FIGURE 10-3

A table with non-atomic values is not an R-table.

Orderlines

Order_id	Line1	Line2	Line3	Cust_id	Comany
10010	1	1	1	123	NewHat
10011	1	1		234	Visual Aural

FIGURE 10-4

A table with repeating groups in columns is still not in first normal form.

repeating values rows instead, by adding a row to the table for each line number:

OrderLines (<u>`order_id, line_no`</u>, `cust_id`, `company, product_id`)

Now you have a compound primary key in OrderLines, because each row is uniquely identified by the combination of `order_id` and `line_no`, as shown in Figure 10-5.

Whenever you find yourself with tables that have repeating groups, it's a good idea to either fold the repetition into the current table, or remove the repeating groups to a separate table. The reason is that without atomic values in a composite column, searches and updates will be slow and complex. Also, for repeating columns, there is much wasted space and you have to place an artificial limit on

OrderLines

Order_id	Line_no	Cust_id	Company	Product_id
10000	1	FRANS	Franchi S.p.A.	17
10001	1	MEREP	Mère Paillarde	25
10001	2	MEREP	Mère Paillarde	40
10001	3	MEREP	Mère Paillarde	59
10001	4	MEREP	Mère Paillarde	64
10002	1	FOLKO	Folk och fä HB	31
10002	2	FOLKO	Folk och fä HB	39
10002	3	FOLKO	Folk och fä HB	71
10003	1	SIMOB	Simons bistro	18
10004	1	VAFFE	Vaffeljernet	29
10004	2	VAFFE	Vaffeljernet	63
10005	1	WARTH	Wartian Herkku	62
10006	1	FRANS	Franchi S.p.A.	13
10006	2	FRANS	Franchi S.p.A.	50

FIGURE 10-5

OrderLines is now in first normal form.

the number of repetitions in the group. Now, take the same table and move on to the next step.

Second Normal Form

A table is in *second normal form (2NF)* if it's in 1NF and all the column values depend on the whole primary key, not just part of it. If a table has a single column as the primary key, your normalization process just skips this step. The example from the last section does have a compound primary key, so look to see if it can be moved into 2NF.

Looking at the table, notice that `cust_id` and `company` repeat for each line, but really only depend on `order_id`, which is just part of the primary key. You can remove those attributes and put them into a table of their own, resulting in two tables. To illustrate this process, you can look at the two equivalent tables in the VFP `testdata` database:

Orders (<u>order id</u>, cust_id, company)

OrderLines (<u>order id, line no</u>, product_id)

Figure 10-6 shows the results in two VFP browses.

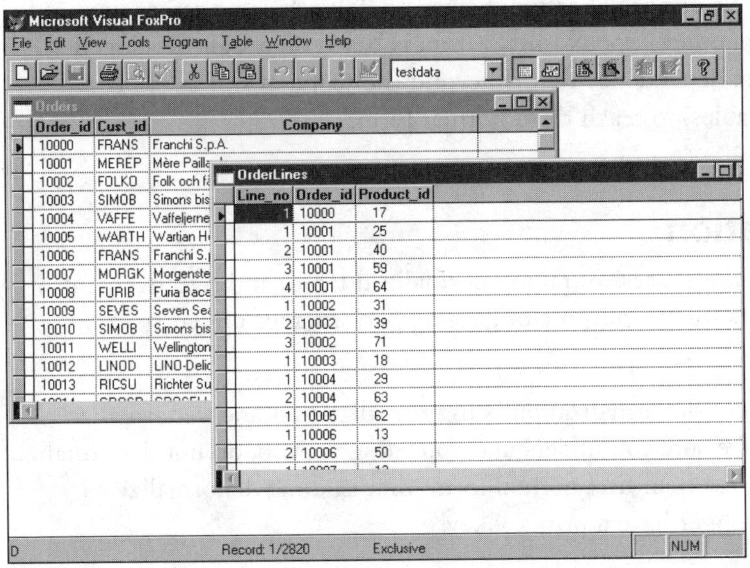

FIGURE 10-6

The OrderLines table now has been resolved into two tables: Orders and OrderLines.

Third Normal Form

A table is in *third normal form (3NF)* if it's in 2NF and all the column values depend on only the primary key. In other words, there are no transitive dependencies. Take a look at the Orders table:

> Orders (<u>order id</u>, cust_id, company)

Notice that the company value really depends on the cust_id value, and that the cust_id value is a function of order_id. This means that there's a transitive dependency between company and order_id. The solution that moves this into 3NF is to create a new table containing company with cust_id as the primary key.

The final results of our normalization effort are the following three tables:

> Customer (<u>cust id</u>, company)
>
> Orders (<u>order id</u>)
>
> OrderLines (<u>order id, line no</u>, product_id)

These tables minimize the redundancy or repetition of data between tables, and therefore eliminate update anomalies. In the OrderLines table, the product_id column is a function of the whole compound key, so that table is already in 3NF. It does not have any transitive dependencies.

There are more levels of normalization, having to do with some rather involved problems with compound keys. Normalization is based on a well-developed theory of functional dependency that is beyond the scope of this book. It is enough, for most tables, to reach third normal form.

Denormalization

Denormalization is the process of taking normalized tables and selectively introducing redundancies for the purpose of gaining performance or clarity in the database.

The best advice about denormalization is to normalize first and denormalize later, only after you're sure you understand your design. Also, do not denormalize back to something less than first normal form; that is, don't denormalize so much that you no longer have a primary key!

The following types of denormalization are offered as examples of when denormalization can help the performance or clarity of a database.

Aggregate Values

You might want to add a column to a table that includes an *aggregate value*. For example, you might include an order total calculated column in the Orders table, which sums up all the amounts in the OrderLines table for each order. In doing so, you'll establish a functional dependency that goes beyond the primary key of the Orders table, and violates relational rules, so it's advisable to be careful.

Vertical Splitting

If you find you have very wide tables (lots of columns in a table), and performance is taking a hit, you might want to consider a *vertical splitting* of the table. For example, an employee table might have a lot of information about each employee, stored in a large number of columns:

Employee (<u>emp id</u>, emp_name, department, phone, address, city, state, zip, home_phone, . . .)

If an important component of the application must execute fast searches or Select commands from the employee table for a company directory—let's say, to get the employee's phone number—you might split the table into two tables that are related in a one-to-one fashion:

Employee (<u>emp id</u>, emp_name, department, phone)

Employee_info (<u>emp id</u>, address, city, state, zip, home_phone, . . .)

With the split tables, you can access the narrower Employee table faster because the index file is smaller, and the data can be loaded from disk faster.

Horizontal Splitting

You often will find a single table carrying information about different types of data, with some columns applying to only one of the types. In this case, you end up with a lot of empty columns because the data in that row is of another type. For example, the employee table contains information about several types of employees, such as full-time, part-time, and contract. You might consider a *horizontal splitting* of the table into a supertype employee table that's in one-to-one relationships:

> Employee (<u>emp id</u>, emp_type, emp_name, department, phone)
>
> Emp_Full (<u>emp id</u>, address, city, state, zip, home_phone, ...)
>
> Emp_Part (<u>emp id</u>, duration, ...)
>
> Emp_Contract (<u>emp id</u>, company, rate)

In this scheme, the Employee table collects all information that is held in common for all employees, and the other tables are *subtype tables* that hold information specific for that type. In this example, it's assumed that the subtypes are exhaustive and exclusive—that is, every employee must belong to one of the subtypes, and no employee can belong to more than one subtype.

Columns for Duplicating Data

If you find you have an important query that involves several joins across many tables just to get a single column of data, you might consider duplicating that column in order to shorten the query. For example, if each employee in the Employee table belongs to a department, and every department belongs to a division, you can copy the division value into the Employee table. Then you no longer have a three-table join in order to access employees of a particular division:

> Employee (<u>emp id</u>, emp_type, emp_name, department, division, phone)

Columns for Calculated Data

If you have a query that must produce a calculation, and the query is very lengthy, you can consider adding a calculated column. For example, consider the case where you must query the orders in the OrderLines table, and calculate an extension of number of parts sold times unit price. If the table is large, your results set is large, and the data is seldom (if ever) updated, you might gain some performance improvement by adding a calculated column named extension that keeps the calculation per row:

> OrderLines (<u>order id, line no</u>, product_id, quantity, unit_price, extension)

Data Warehousing and Data Mining

An important application for denormalization is the ability to access static data rapidly. The term *data warehouse* describes static data that is rebuilt periodically but is thoroughly denormalized. For example, a simple data warehouse of the World Wide Shoes application might look like the following:

> WWShoes (`order_id`, `line_no`, `emp_id`, `emp_name`, `emp_phone`, `cust_id`, `cust_name`, . . .)

You might build this sort of table overnight, index it on all the relevant columns to have fast queries, and then leave it static throughout the day. *Data mining* is the term for techniques you develop for accessing parts of the data warehouse.

Primary Keys

One of the most important decisions you can make when designing a table is choosing the primary key, distinguishing it from other candidate keys, and keeping it simple.

When you choose the column or columns to be the primary key, you are deciding which of the columns will reliably identify each row, whether the reference is from inside this table or from another table. For example, suppose that in the Customer table, as follows, you have both a customer ID and a customer name. Both are candidate keys.

> Customer (`cust_id`, `name`, `address`, `city`, `state`, `zip`, `phone`, `fax`)

Which column, between `cust_id` and `name`, should be the primary key? First of all, look at the functional dependency. Is `name` a function of `cust_id`, or vice versa? If you permitted duplicate company names, then there would be no question that the name depended on the ID. If they are both candidate keys, however, then either can be used as the primary way to refer to the rows.

Now, think of how you will search the table for unique rows, either in this table or from other tables. In the Orders table, do you want to store the customer ID or the company name as the reference back to the original table? Surely you want the customer ID, because it's simpler, shorter, and more reliably typed by people. Therefore, `cust_id` is the logical choice to be the primary key.

Once you have chosen a primary key, you should use the primary key—and only the primary key—in other tables as a foreign key. In other words, even though `name` is a candidate key, in all other tables that refer to the customer rows, make the foreign key `cust_id`, not `name`.

Avoid Meaningful Primary Keys

The best type of primary key is a simple key, perhaps just an incrementing integer. When you make more complex and meaningful primary keys, you can get into trouble.

Look, for example, at the customers table from the VFP samples and Tastrade databases, a table originally from the Microsoft Access Northwind traders sample database. The table has the following elements:

> Customer (<u>cust_id</u>, company, contact, title, address, city, region, postalcode, country, phone, maxordamt)

Now, take a look at the underlying data shown in Figure 10-7.

Compare the customer ID values with their company values. What is wrong with this picture? Even though `cust_id` is the primary key, its structure depends on the actual name. What happens if the company name changes? Do you then have to change the primary key? The dependency is backward: if `cust_id` is going to be the primary key, then its value should not be a function of the name. The following example adds a primary key named `cust_key`:

Customer_id	Company_name	Contact_name
ALFKI	Alfreds Futterkiste	Maria Anders
ANATR	Ana Trujillo Emparedados y helados	Ana Trujillo
ANTON	Antonio Moreno Taquería	Antonio Moreno
AROUT	Around the Horn	Thomas Hardy
BERGS	Berglunds snabbköp	Christina Berglur
BLAUS	Blauer See Delikatessen	Hanna Moos
BLONP	Blondel père et fils	Frédérique Citea
BOLID	Bólido Comidas preparadas	Martín Sommer
BONAP	Bon app'	Laurence Lebih
BOTTM	Bottom-Dollar Markets	Elizabeth Lincol
BSBEV	B's Beverages	Victoria Ashwort
CACTU	Cactus Comidas para llevar	Patricio Simpson
CENTC	Centro comercial Moctezuma	Francisco Chan
CHOPS	Chop-suey Chinese	Yang Wang

FIGURE 10-7

Here's a table where the primary key actually depends on the name!

> Customer (cust_key, <u>cust id</u>, company, contact, title, address, city, region, postalcode, country, phone, maxordamt)

Then you can keep the cust_id if the user needs it, or you can drop it. The important thing to remember is to keep the key values independent of any other columns in the table.

Another problem that can occur with primary keys is choosing a number for a key and then letting ranges of the key indicate the type of entity. For example, suppose that in the Customer table, you choose a primary key cust_id to be a four-digit number.

> Customer (<u>cust id</u>, company)

You then assign the following ranges to this primary key:

1001–2000	Northeast
2001–3000	Mid-Atlantic
3001–4000	Southeast
4001–5000	South
5001–6000	Midwest
6001–7000	Southwest
7000–8000	Rocky Mountain
8001–9000	Northwest
9001–9999	Other

What is wrong with this scheme? Well, the major problem arises from trying to encode something meaningful, namely a region, into the key. If the bulk of your customer's sales are in the Midwest, you probably will run out of keys! Also, what happens if you need to add new regions? To avoid these problems, use an incrementing number for the key and add a separate column for the region:

> Customer (<u>cust id</u>, region, company)

Surrogate Keys

Encoding meaningful information into a key can cause real problems. Some developers like to avoid meaningful information completely, and instead make a primary key for each table that the user never sees, calling it a *surrogate key*. For example, in the World Wide Shoes database that comes on this book's CD-

ROM, all the tables have surrogate keys. The user never sees or modifies a table's primary key.

Surrogate keys can be a real advantage for tables like a parts inventory, where the user sees the part code, but the primary key of the table is actually a surrogate key:

> Parts (<u>part key</u>, part_code, part_name)

You then can store part_key in other tables as a foreign key. If the manufacturer ever changes the part code, or someone makes a mistake entering the part code, you can change part_code in one table without having to change part_key in other tables.

Consistent Reference to Primary Keys

When using primary keys, make sure that you use the primary key's column name when referencing it as a foreign key in other tables. Do not, for example, give the same name to every primary key in every table. A legendary example of what not to do is that the popular and useful Codebook 2.6 for FoxPro put a surrogate key in each table, and gave each key the same name. In that scheme, you could end up with tables like the following:

> Parts (<u>cid</u>, part_code, part_name)
>
> Invoices (<u>cid</u>, invoice_total)

What is the problem here? Well, you've got the Parts primary key named cid, as well as the Invoices primary key named cid. Therefore, when you're in another table, and want to use those primary keys as foreign keys, you have to rename the foreign keys something like part_cid:

> Orders (<u>invoice cid, line no</u>, part_cid)

You now have to refer to the same data element, the part key, by two names: cid in Parts, and part_cid in Orders.

A better way is to create a surrogate key in each table with a unique name, and then use the same name as both primary and foreign key:

> Parts (<u>part cid</u>, part_code, part_name)
>
> Orders (<u>invoice cid, line no</u>, part_cid)
>
> Invoices (<u>invoice cid</u>, invoice_total)

With consistent naming, you can keep your system simple and easy to remember. This pays off when the number of tables you have grows larger.

Database Design

Of the many ways to design relational databases, by far the most popular is the *Entity-Relationship (ER)* technique. Developed by Peter Chen in the late 1970s, this method identifies entities, attributes of the entities, and relationships between the entities in a graphical fashion. The entities map to tables, the attributes map to columns, and the relationships may map to referential integrity constraints. This is a very useful approach when you have a pretty good idea of what your tables must look like, and how you will reach third normal form. The ER method assumes that you do the normalization yourself, because the ER tool will not do it for you.

Figure 10-8 shows an example ER diagram of the World Wide Shoes tables using Logic Works' ErWIN/ERX.

You identify entities by the blocks in the diagram. The entities have their attributes listed inside. The primary key is listed at the top of the entity.

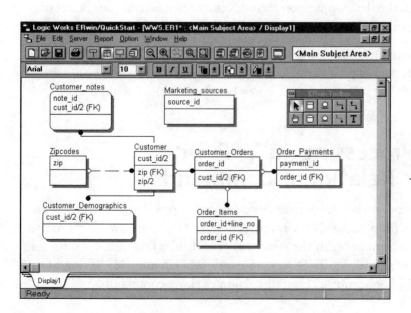

FIGURE 10-8

The Entity Relationship diagram for World Wide Shoes shows the entities graphically.

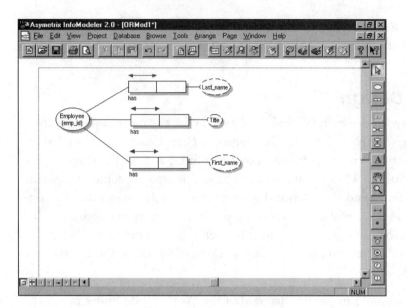

FIGURE 10-9

An ORM diagram shows object relationships in greater detail.

A new type of database modeling called *Object-Role Modeling (ORM)* has recently come on the scene. It is a type of diagramming that will do normalization for you, and guarantee fully normalized tables. It comes with Asymetrix's Infomodeler, and the desktop version includes drivers for FoxPro tables. Figure 10-9 shows a partial ORM diagram of the Employee table using Infomodeler.

This type of diagramming is more verbose than ER, but also more accurate. Because it writes the scripts for creating fully normalized tables, it's well-suited for complex modeling when you don't know how your tables should look.

Navigational Processing in VFP with Corresponding Relational Commands

Visual FoxPro supports so many commands for data access, it can be difficult to distinguish them from each other. In this section, you can see how VFP's navigational commands compare with the relational commands. This chapter assumes that you are familiar with VFP's SQL commands (see Chapter 11, "Using SQL in Visual FoxPro Applications," for a discussion of those commands).

Work Areas

When dBASE II was first introduced, it contained the rather revolutionary innovation (for the time, on microcomputers) of supporting two DBF data files open at the same time. It also came with a set of navigational commands to manipulate the data. However, the commands assumed an open file without distinguishing which file it was. To allow the programmer to change from one open table to the other, dBASE II created a context called a *work area*. The work area determined to which of the two open tables the commands would refer.

These days, Visual FoxPro has considerably enhanced the notion of a work area, but the basic concept still survives. You can see how complex work areas have become by looking at the syntax of the Use command. When you open a DBF file with the Use command, by default the file is opened in whatever the current work area is:

```
Use customer
```

You can tell VFP to find a new, empty work area with the In 0 qualification:

```
User customer In 0
```

You can also tell VFP which work area you want, by specifying the work area number:

```
Use customer In 3
```

This is not useful very often, because it's easier to let VFP just find a new area on its own.

Visual FoxPro has introduced a fundamental enhancement to the work area concept with the notion of a *data session*. Normally, every work area with its tables is visible to all parts of an application, as long as the file is open. This is called a *public data session*. Other parts of the application can see all aspects of the work area.

You can protect a work area from other applications, however, by making the data session private. When you issue the command that a particular work area should have a *private data session*, then other parts of the application with their own data sessions cannot see or manipulate the protected work area or its properties.

Relational Commands

SQL commands do not explicitly open tables, and they process tables with no positional reference. Therefore there's no need to navigate the table before applying any operations.

Navigating a DBF File

Once you have a DBF file opened in a work area, you navigate the file one record at a time. It's assumed that you start at the top of the file, and to act on other records in the DBF file, you must navigate to them. Here is an example of a number of navigational commands in sequence:

```
Use customer       && Open the DBF file
? Recno()          && Displays the record number 1
Skip               && Move to the next record
? Recno()          && Displays the record number 2
Skip 10            && Move to the previous record
? Recno()          && Displays the record number 12
Goto Bottom        && Move to the last record
? Eof()            && Displays .F. because not at the end of the file
Skip               && Skip past the end of the file
? Eof()            && Displays .T. because at the end of the file
Skip -1            && Skips back to the last record
Goto Top           && Move to the first record
? Bof()            && Displays .F. because not at the beginning
Skip -1            && Move previous to the first record
? Bof()            && Displays .F. because prior to the first record
Skip               && Moves to the first record
? Recno()          && Displays the record number 1
```

In the above sequence, you can see how VFP's navigational logic works. When you first use a DBF file, you are positioned at the first record—provided the file has records—and you are not using an index. If the file has no records, then you cannot navigate it. If it has records and you set an index order, then you navigate according to the index (you'll learn more about that later in this chapter).

You can move back and forth in the file with the Skip command, or you can go directly to the top or bottom with the Goto command. (This is VFP's only use of the Goto command. You cannot use Goto to move to labels in a program, as you can in BASIC.) If you use Goto Bottom, you are placed on the last record. If you try to skip past the last record, you are placed on what has been euphemistically called the "phantom record," because VFP returns a record number even though there's nothing there. At any rate, when you are one past the end, the Eof() function, short for "end of file," becomes True. There is no Bottom() function to tell you that you're at the last record.

When you use Goto Top, you move to the first record—again, there is no Top() function to tell you that you're there. If you do Skip -1 while on the first record, then the Bof() function becomes True.

Visual FoxPro provides ways to programmatically loop so that you can step through a group of records. The most important construct is the Scan command, which automatically takes care of moving the record pointer:

```
*— Scans the customer file from top to bottom
Use customer
Scan
   ? cust_id
Endscan
```

Much of the time, you do not want to navigate a file based on its physical order. To provide fast access based on key values, VFP provides the ability to create indexes on fields or expressions within the DBF file. These indexes are called *tags* and are essentially lists of field values with record locations. You then can seek a particular value in the table, and VFP scans the index rather than the DBF itself. This can make for very fast seeks, and VFP also uses these indexes to optimize its SQL commands.

You access an index by using the Order option on the Use command or in a Set command. For example, you can activate the cust_id index tag of the Customer file with the following code:

```
Use Customer
Set Order To cust_id
Seek "10010"
```

If the value is found, the Found() function returns True and you are positioned at the record that matches the value. It's important to note that these indexes do not guarantee uniqueness—they permit duplicates.

> **WARNING:** When building an index, watch out for the Unique qualifier. It does not prevent duplicate values of a key in a table; it simply makes it so you cannot see them. The duplicates seem to disappear, but they're in the file. The Unique qualifier is seldom useful.

When you activate an index, the top and bottom records of the file become the first and last records of the index, respectively. When you have an index order set, record numbers do not follow the physical order of the file.

Relational Commands

When you use SQL commands, there is no need to explicitly open tables; VFP automatically does that for you. Also, you cannot use SQL commands to position yourself anywhere in a table. Instead, to see all the customer IDs in a temporary table called a *cursor*, for example, you just issue the command:

```
Select cust_id from customer
```

As you can see, this is a much simpler command than the Scan command used earlier. There are times when you may find it useful to scan a table from top to bottom, but if you're just looking for certain values, the SQL commands are simpler and more powerful.

Adding and Changing Data in a DBF File

Once you have used a file, you can use a number of navigational commands to add, change, or delete its data.

To add new records with a navigational command, use the Append Blank command to add a new record at the end of the file. Then, to put data values into the record, use the `Replace` command. The following example illustrates these two commands:

```
*— Program to add a new record and fill with couple values
Use customer
Append Blank
Replace cust_id With "10011", name With "Sudso Cleanser"
```

In this example, the `Replace` command assumes that you're over the top of your desired record, then changes the values you specify. There are many other options for the `Replace` command, but all those variations assume that you know what records you're dealing with.

```
*— Program to update a record with a couple values
Use customer
Locate For cust_id = "10011"
Replace name With "Sudso Cleanser"
```

NOTE: FoxPro some years ago introduced the `Scatter` and `Gather` commands to do quick replaces.

Relational Commands

The programs just presented to change data all make assumptions about record position. The SQL commands to add new rows or to change existing data (`Insert` and `Update`, respectively) do not make assumptions about the position of the data. Generally, the SQL commands are simpler and easier to understand.

```
Insert Into Customer (cust_id, name) Values ("10011", "Sudso Cleanser")
Update Customer Set name = "Sudso Cleanser" Where cust_id = "10011"
```

Because the SQL commands make no assumptions about position, they operate on entire tables at once.

Deleting Data

To delete a record in VFP's navigational paradigm, you position yourself on the record, then issue the `Delete` command:

```
Use Customer
Locate For cust_id = "10011"
Delete
```

What VFP does is to mark the record for deletion, but not physically remove it from the file. To get the deleted record removed, you have to issue the `Pack` command. When you pack the database, the file is rewritten without any of the records that have been deleted. Since `Delete` delays the physical removal of a deleted record, you can undelete a record by issuing the `Recall` command before you issue `Pack`.

Relational Commands

VFP also has a SQL `Delete` command:

```
Delete From customer Where cust_id = "10011"
```

The VFP SQL `Delete` also marks a record for deletion, rather than physically removing it. While this deletion method makes a number of programming tricks possible, it does deviate from the way the `Delete` command works in most relational databases. It also makes it possible to have hidden duplicate primary keys, as you will see in the next section. This is a case where the implementation of the SQL command shows the underlying navigational structure. No `Pack` command should really be necessary after a SQL `Delete`.

Set Relation To

The keystone of navigational processing—introduced by dBASE II and still used in Visual FoxPro—is the `Set Relation` command. This command sets up a coordination or linkage between the record pointers of two open DBF files. Then, when there is a match between the values, you can reference the values from both tables. For example, look at the following program, and then its results as shown in Figure 10-10.

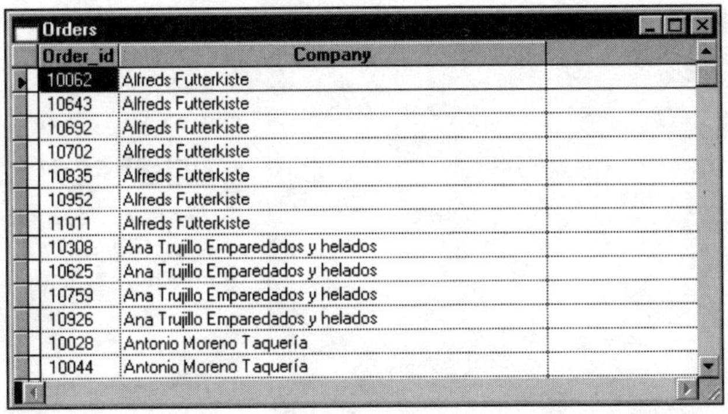

FIGURE 10-10

The Set Relation *command can allow you to browse across two tables.*

```
*— Program to browse two tables
Use Customer In 0 Order cust_id
Use Orders In 0 Order cust_id
Select Orders
Set Relation To cust_id Into Customer
Browse fields Orders.order_id, Customer.company
```

In this program, you open both tables, each with an index on the customer ID. Then, as you browse the Orders table, the customer name corresponding to the customer ID in the Orders record will show in the name column. This is really a coordinated synchronization of the record pointers. This kind of Set Relation is usually considered a many-to-one, because the customer ID can have repeated values in the Orders table, but only one value in the Customer file.

This can break down sometimes when you try to go one-to-many. Look at the results of the following program, shown in Figure 10-11.

```
*— First attempt at One to Many linkage
Use OrderLines In 0 Order order_id
Use Orders In 0 Order order_id
Select orders
Set Relation To order_id Into OrderLines
Browse fields Orders.order_id, OrderLines.line_no
```

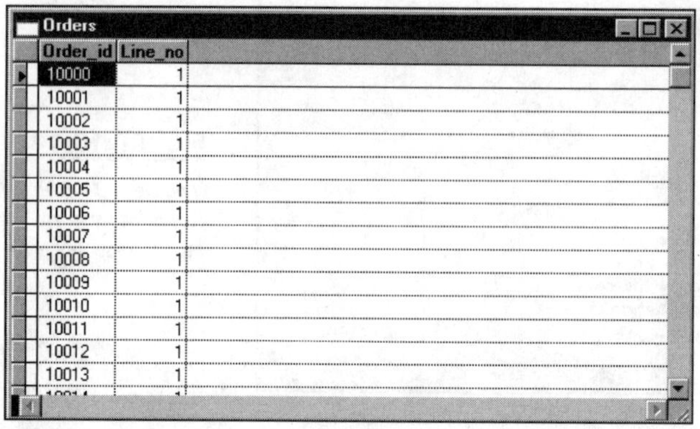

FIGURE 10-11

The Set Relation *command cannot by itself do a one-to-many browse.*

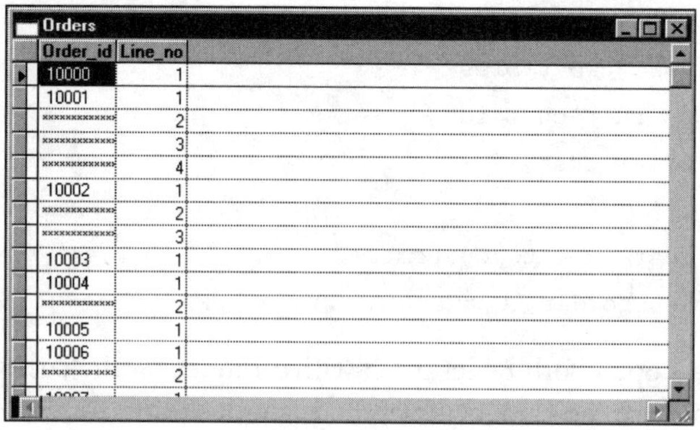

FIGURE 10-12

The Set Skip *command can cause a one-to-many browse.*

The intention here is to browse each order with all its lines, but because Set Relation is many-to-one, only one line number shows for each order.

To remedy this, you can use the Set Skip To command to make the linkage one-to-many. Look at the results of the following version of the program, shown in Figure 10-12.

```
*- Successful one to many linkage
Use OrderLines In 0 Order order_id
Use Orders In 0 Order order_id
Select Orders
Set Relation To order_id Into OrderLines
Set Skip To OrderLines
Browse fields Orders.order_id, OrderLines.line_no
```

Relational Commands

The Set Relation command looks very similar to the join conditions of the SQL Select command. However, Select can accomplish the one-to-many linkage much more easily:

```
Select o.order_id, l.line_no
  From Orders o, Orderlines
  Where o.order_id = l.order_id
```

In this case, the relational processing clearly is simpler and easier to program.

> **NOTE:** It is unfortunate that this command is named Set Relation To. It would be better to call it Set Linkage To or something similar, and get rid of the word "relation." In the relational model, the term "relation" means a set of values which can be represented as a table. At the worst, you'd think that this command might be named Set Relationship To, because that's what it's doing. Regardless, the command is named what it's named, and this one little command has been the source of much developer confusion!

Object-Property Navigation with Visual FoxPro

Microsoft's Visual Basic, Access, and Visual Basic for Applications also use navigational commands for processing data. Rather than work areas, however, they reference an object that is the opened table, and then reference properties of that object. In Visual Basic, for example, you could move around a Jet database table in the following way:

```
' Set up the database and table
Dim Ws As Workspace
Dim Db As Database
Dim Tbl As Recordset
Set Db = Ws.OpenDatabase("C:\Access\Samples\Northwind.MDB")
Set Tbl = Db.OpenRecordSet("Customers",dbOpenTable)
' Move to the first record
```

```
Tbl.MoveFirst
' Move to the next record
Tbl.MoveNext
' Move to the 11th record
Tbl.Move 10
' Move to the last record
Tbl.MoveLast
```

You can duplicate this *object.property* way of navigating a table by using VFP's classes and defining your own properties and methods. In the following program, you see how to define a class that opens a table and navigates it:

```
*_
* Program to illustrate using object-dot-property notation when
* navigating a VFP Table
*_
oCust = CreateObject("OpenCust")
? Recno()
oCust.Skip(10)
? Recno()
oCust.Skip(-1)
? Recno()
oCust.GoTop()
? Recno()
oCust.GoBottom()
? Recno()
oCust.Destroy()

Define Class OpenCust As Custom
Procedure Init
   If !Used("Customer")
      Use Customer In 0
      Select Customer
   Else
      Select Customer
      Goto Top
```

```
    Endif
Endproc
Function Skip
  LParameters lnSkipAmt
  If Type("lnSkipAmt") <> "U" And Not IsNull(lnSkipAmt)
    Skip lnSkipAmt
  Else
    Skip
  Endif
EndFunc
Function GoTop
  Goto Top
EndFunc
Function GoBottom
  Goto Bottom
EndFunc

EndDefine
```

The syntax of the method calls in VFP differs from that of VB, but the upshot is the same.

When to Use Relational versus Navigational Methods

There occasionally are situations where the navigational system can do something with ease that the SQL commands cannot. Suppose that you want to copy the date in an Orders record into each of its OrderLines records. You could do the following:

```
*— one to many linkage and copy of data
Use OrderLines In 0 Order order_id
Use Orders In 0 Order order_id
Select Orders
Set Relation To order_id Into OrderLines
Set Skip To OrderLines
Replace All OrderLines.order_date with Orders.order_date
```

Because VFP's SQL Update command cannot reference another table, this is very difficult to accomplish using SQL commands. In a case like this, the navigational system can still be useful.

It is generally true, however, that the relational SQL commands are simpler and more direct than the navigational commands. It makes sense to try to use relational methods first in your programming, and then use navigational commands only if the SQL commands cannot easily do the job.

VFP's New DBF Format

One of the problems standard DBF files face when exchanging data with other databases is that of incompatible data types. It's easy to lose data or have a difficult conversion if you don't match the data types.

In response to this need, Visual FoxPro has given you a variety of new data types in the DBF file. In doing so, though, VFP has established a new format for its native DBFs. This format is upwardly compatible with traditional DBFs. However, DBFs in the new VFP format cannot be read by versions of FoxPro prior to Visual FoxPro.

Another problem for older DBFs is that of missing information. In the new VFP DBF, you can explicitly declare a field to be empty by giving it a *null value*.

In this section, you learn how VFP stores data in a DBF, what the traditional data types are, what the new data types are, and how the addition of null values can affect your programming.

How a DBF Stores Your Data

All your application's data in Visual FoxPro are stored in disk files with DBF as the file extension. You actually can use different extensions on files that have the DBF format, but using the DBF extension is far more convenient.

Normally your data tables have the DBF extension, but FoxPro can read a file with any extension if the file has a DBF format. Your project file, for example, is stored in a DBF format, and can be opened and read like any other DBF, even though it has a PJX extension. This extends to many other file types in Visual FoxPro, including the database container discussed later in this chapter.

A file in DBF format consists of two components: a header record that contains a list of the columns in the table, followed by a variable number of data records as long as the header record specifies. All the data records are the same length.

Physically, a DBF file is stored as a simple stream of bytes. If you imagine a DBF as a ribbon, then the header record starts at the beginning of the ribbon and extends for a finite distance. This distance varies depending upon the number of fields in the DBF. Once the header record ends, the data part begins, where each record is a fixed length.

Logically, the DBF is like a table in which the first row may be wider or narrower than the others, but where all the rows from the second row through the end of the table are the same width.

Figure 10-13 offers a comparison of the physical and logical views of the DBF.

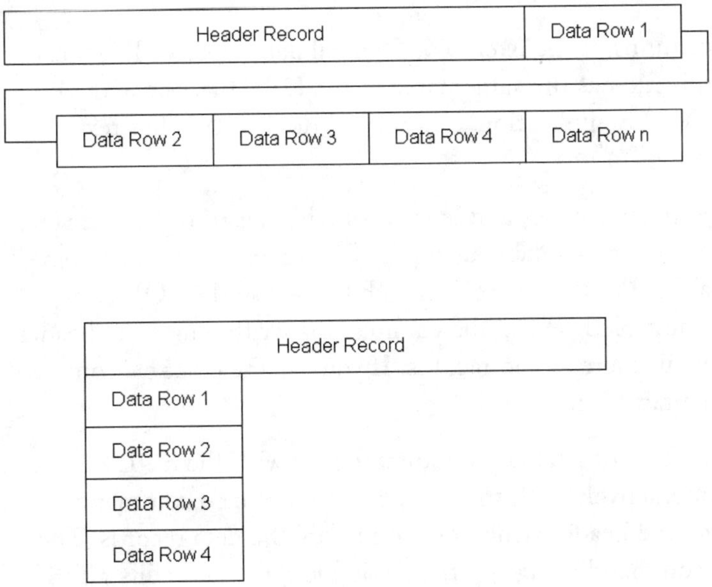

FIGURE 10-13

The hierarchical data model has a tree structure.

The DBF Header Record

The DBF *header record* is a beginning sequence of bytes that varies in length, depending upon the number of fields it has to list. This header record contains information about the DBF file itself and the data held in the file. It contains, for example, information about the following:

- Whether this file is a DBF file
- Whether a structural index file is associated with this DBF
- Whether a memo file is associated with this DBF
- What code page is associated with this DBF
- How many data records are in this file
- The field name, type, and length of each field in this file

The header record varies in length because the number of fields or columns in the data can vary. All the columns in a DBF file must be listed in the header record.

If your DBF has a structural index file, this has the same name as the DBF file, but with a CDX extension. In the WWS example, customer.DBF has the index file customer.CDX.

If your DBF has any columns of the Memo or General data type, VFP creates a file to hold that text; this file has the same name as the DBF file, but with an FPT extension. In the WWS application, customer_notes.DBF has text stored in customer_notes.FPT.

You determine the field names, types, and lengths of a header record when you first create a table. You can create a table using the SQL Create Table command or the traditional FoxPro Create command. If you use the SQL command, the schema for the table listed in the command is written into the header of the DBF, and by default there are no records. If you use the Create command, you can build the table interactively.

You can change the structure of a table programmatically with the SQL Alter Table command, or interactively with the Modify Structure command. Both commands change the header structure and rewrite the data records. The Modify Structure command brings up the Table Designer and edits a DBF file's header, as shown in Figure 10-14.

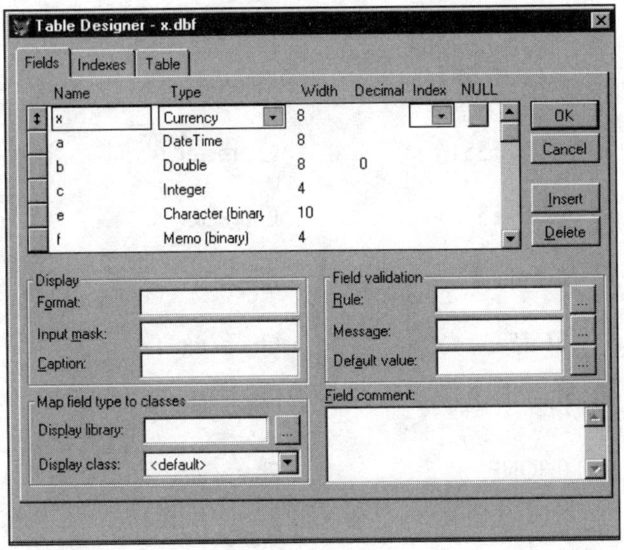

FIGURE 10-14

The VFP Table Designer shows the structure of a DBF table's header.

The DBF Data Rows (Records)

After the header record, the DBF file contains data. The data are stored in a variety of formats, depending upon the data type, but one thing you can count on is that all the rows have a fixed length. You can determine this length by issuing the Display Structure command. For the WWS Customer table, for example, the result is the following:

Structure for table: C:\VFPBOOK\WWS\PRIMA\CHAP3\SOURCE\CUSTOMER.DBF

Number of data records: 2

Date of last update: 08/06/96

Code Page: 1252

Field	Field Name	Type	Width
1	CUST_ID	Character	10
2	CUSTOMER_NO	Character	10

3	LAST_NAME	Character	30
4	FIRST_NAME	Character	25
5	ADDRESS1	Character	30
6	ADDRESS2	Character	30
7	CITY	Character	25
8	STATE	Character	2
9	ZIP	Character	10
10	PHONE	Character	12
11	FAX	Character	12
12	E_MAIL_ADDRE...	Character	50
13	SOURCE_ID	Character	6
14	ADDDATE	Date	8
		** Total **	261

This table has two data records, and a code page of 1252, which is the standard Windows ANSI code page.

Notice that the total of the field lengths is actually 260, but the data record length reported by VFP is 261. That's because one byte is reserved at the beginning of each DBF data record for a deletion marker. When you delete a record, an asterisk (*) is written into its first byte. Only when you pack the table using the Pack command is the record physically removed from it.

One of the reasons access to data in DBFs is fast is that VFP can calculate exactly where in a DBF a particular record is. Once it knows the width of the header record, and the width of all the data records, it can calculate exactly what sequence of bytes must be read in a DBF in order to fetch any particular record.

Also, DBF files do not have "hot spots." In databases that store their tables together in one file, the locking must be done by pages, usually 2K in length.

Because they lock pages and not records, it's possible that one user appending data to the end of a table will lock out other users until the editing is finished.

In VFP, when you append a new record to a DBF, VFP locks the header record just for the instant required to increment the record counter in the header. Then VFP unlocks the header and locks the newly appended record. This frees up the file so that another user can come in and add a new record with no performance penalty. (For more information about locking, see Chapter 8, "Multi-User Development Techniques.")

This basic structure of the DBF file has been constant for a long time.

VFP Data Types

One main reason that the VFP-format DBF differs from the traditional-format DBF is that native VFP DBFs support new data types. In this section, you briefly review the traditional data types, see what the new types are, and learn how the new types affect your data.

Traditional DBF Data Types

For years, the standard FoxPro data types have been the ones shown in Table 10-3.

The Character data type stores strings of bytes, of a maximum length determined by the header, not to exceed 254 bytes total. You can enter printable as well as non-printing characters, including upper-order character sets.

Table 10-3 Traditional FoxPro Data Types

Data Type	Symbol
Character	C
Date	D
Logical	L
Numeric	N
Memo	M
General	G

The Numeric data type stores a number as a string of digits in the file. You determine the overall length of the number, including the decimal point if needed, and how many decimal digits there should be within that length. To store the number 99.99, for example, you need to specify **N(5,2)**: a length of five including the decimal, then two digits beyond the decimal point. By contrast, to store the number 9999, all you need is **N(4)**, because there is no storage of the decimal. VFP stores the number as a character string of digits, with a maximum length of 20.

VFP also provides, for compatibility with dBASE IV, a Float data type. It's the same as the Numeric data type, so you're better off just using Numeric.

The Logical data type is stored as one byte, with a value of the single character T or F in the actual file.

The Date data type is stored as eight characters, all digits: four characters for day and month, and another four digits for the year. January 1, 1997, for example, is stored as the string 01011997 in the table. However, when you manipulate a date within VFP, you must always format it with a delimiter like a slash (/), as in {01/01/1997}. Also, you can drop the century part of the year if the year is in the current century. (For issues concerning the year 2000, see the next section.)

The Memo field stores binary and text data, with the maximum length determined by available memory resources. The General field stores a reference to an OLE object. Both data types are actually stored in the DBF as four-byte pointers to locations in the accompanying memo file. The structure of a memo file is beyond the scope of this chapter.

VFP's New Data Types

To bring the DBF data storage more in line with backend relational databases, Visual FoxPro has added a number of new data types to the DBF. Table 10-4 lists these new types.

The Currency data type stores numeric data with four decimal digits in a binary format. The integer part of the number can range to 15 digits, and the number can be positive or negative.

Table 10-4 New Visual FoxPro Data Types

New VFP Data Type	Symbol
Currency	Y
Datetime	T
Double	B
Integer	I

VFP introduced the Datetime data type in order to become more compatible with ODBC data sources, such as Microsoft SQL Server and the Jet database, but also to provide a way of inserting a date and time stamp into your data.

The Double data type is a way to store numeric data in floating point format. It has a much broader range than the Numeric data type, ranging from roughly 10 to the 323rd power on the high side, to roughly 10 to the −307th power on the low side.

The Integer data type stores an integer number in a binary format, with a range of +/− 2^32 (roughly 2 billion). It takes up four bytes in the DBF, and matches the Integer data type in ODBC and Microsoft SQL Server.

In addition to the new data types already mentioned, Visual FoxPro allows you to specify Character and Memo fields with no code page translation. This means that when you change the language support from Windows ANSI, VFP puts a marker in the header of the DBF. This way you can designate that the Character fields should store characters according to whatever language you specify, such as German or French. You might, however, have Character and Memo fields that should not change their values across languages, and you can specify that with the data types shown in Table 10-5.

Table 10-5 Data Types for Language-Specific Fields

Data Type	Symbol
Character (binary)	C
Memo (binary)	M

An Arithmetic Anomaly

Beware of combining numbers from opposite sides of their ranges. For example, if you issue the command

```
? 1000000000000000000.1 + .0000000000000000001
```

in VFP, you'll get

```
1000000000000000000.000000000000000000
```

So, what happens to the `.1`? It drops off, because VFP has an internal limit of 20 for the width of the Numeric data type. Adding the second number put the value over the top.

If you shorten the combined width, as in

```
? 100000000000000.1 + .1
```

then VFP regains its accuracy.

This can lead to odd results. For example,

```
? (1000000000000000000.1 + .0000000000000000001 -
1000000000000000000) = 0
```

returns True. These or similar arithmetic anomalies occur in all computer numeric systems, not just VFP's. There is always some limit to the width of the numbers they can store.

Having all these new data types means that the header record of a VFP DBF will store new values. There are probably hundreds of software products that can read the traditional DBF format, but cannot recognize these new data types. Therefore, VFP has placed a marker in the DBF header, giving this new format a special code. Not even Microsoft Excel, for example, can read the new VFP-format DBFs. You have to use the VFP ODBC driver, or else export the DBFs into the traditional DBF format, a process that translates the new data types into the older format.

Data Type Translation

Often you must translate data from one data type to another. Visual FoxPro provides conversion functions for each of the VFP data types. To convert a Character string to a Date, for example, you use the CTOD() function:

```
? CTOD("01/01/1997")
```

There are a total of 10 data types in VFP, so the number of conversion functions required is quite large; some of them, however, make no sense. For example, there's no point in converting a logical to a number — at least not in VFP.

You can determine the data type of a column or memory variable with the Type() function. Remember to include the argument in quotes, as in the following:

```
? Type("cust_id")
```

The Type() function returns a single character symbol indicating the data type.

Automatic Data Type Translations

Visual FoxPro does not hold all the data types in memory variables the same way that it stores them in a table. For example, the Numeric data type always uses eight bytes in memory, and appears to be a floating point, whereas in a table it's a string between 1 and 20 digits in length. Table 10-6 shows you how VFP translates its data types into memory.

Notice that in the traditional DBF data types, VFP converts the Memo data type to Character type in memory. The Character type in memory can be longer than 254 characters, and therefore can hold the Memo's data.

In the new VFP data types, notice that the Type() function returns N for Integer. The storage in memory of Integer data copied from a DBF is also Numeric.

> **NOTE:** There is no way to determine with the Type() function whether a particular data element in a DBF table is an Integer or Double data type. The function returns N for each of these types.

Table 10-6 VFP Data Type Translations

DBF Formats	Field Type Name	Type ( ) Function	Memory Data Type
All	Character	C	C
All	Numeric	N	N
All	Logical	L	L
All	Date	D	D
All	Memo	M	C
VFP only	Currency	Y	Y
VFP only	Datetime	T	T
VFP only	Double	N	N
VFP only	Integer	N	N
VFP only	Character (binary)	C	C
VFP only	Memo (binary)	M	C

Date and Datetime

The purpose of the Datetime data type is to store a date and a time together in one data element. The date stored is a regular VFP Date, and the time is in the same format as the Time() function: hours, minutes, and seconds.

The Datetime data type is useful for storing the time and day that a row was last updated. It becomes less useful, however, if you need to manipulate or query the table based on time or date, because you must use a conversion function that can complicate the logic and slow down the query.

The Datetime data type has the same range as VFP's Date data type, which is 01/01/0100 through 12/31/9999. This seems like a nice, wide range, but watch out, because other databases do not store the same range of dates. (For a further discussion of data type translation between VFP, ODBC, and other databases, see Chapter 12, "Client/Server Database Development with Visual FoxPro.")

You can accommodate the year 2000 by showing the century portion of dates with the following command:

```
Set Century On
```

WARNING: Watch your arithmetic when working with the Datetime data type—you add seconds, not days, whenever you add a number to the data element. For example, adding 1 to 10/10/1997 in Datetime format with

```
? CTOT("10/10/1997") + 1
```

gives a result of `10/10/1997 12:00:01 AM`.

With the Date data type, adding 1 to the same date with

```
? CTOD("10/10/1997") + 1
```

gives a result of `10/11/1997`.

This way, you always let the user see the century on forms and grids. This is better than assuming a certain century as the default.

Converting from VFP to Fox2x Tables

It often will be necessary for you to get your VFP data into a format that can be read by other applications. For example, you might need to export your data so that Excel can read it. In pre-VFP FoxPro, this was no real problem. Many applications can read either the FoxPlus or Fox2x style of DBF file. However, other applications cannot directly read the new VFP-format DBF tables, regardless of whether or not they're in a database. Those applications can read VFP-format DBF tables if they use the Visual FoxPro ODBC driver which comes with VFP 5.0.

You can export your data into the older DBF format by using the Copy command with the `Type Fox2x` qualifier. The following command, for example, exports the World Wide Shoes Customer table to the older format:

```
Use customer
Copy To custold Type Fox2x
```

VFP automatically translates the new VFP data type values into an equivalent Fox2x format, as you can see in Table 10-7.

Table 10-7 VFP Data Type Translation

Data Type	Type() Function	Fox2x Type	FoxPlus Type
Currency	Y	F	N
Datetime	T	D	D
Double	N	F	N
Integer	N	N	N

The FoxPro 2.x format differs only slightly from the FoxPlus format. Actually, they're equivalent, because the Float and Numeric data types are equivalent.

It's important to note that you can lose information when you export to prior versions of the DBF format. The copy of a Double value to Fox2x format preserves the value, because it's stored in a Float data type. The copy of a Double to the FoxPlus format, however, does not preserve the value, because the Numeric data type does not have the range of the Double data type. Your Double data are truncated or garbled by the copy to FoxPlus.

You lose any times stored in Datetime columns when you export to either format.

Null Values

Visual FoxPro allows *null values* in the VFP-format DBFs so you can record the fact that a value is missing from a data element—that the data element has no value at all. With pre-VFP DBFs, there is no way to tell if a zero value in a Numeric column or a blank value in a Character column is there because someone has entered a zero or blank, or simply because no one has entered anything. The situation is even worse with Logical data types, because only two values are possible, and the false value, .F., is the default.

When you define a VFP table, one of the options along with the name and data type for each column is whether to allow null values in the column. In this section, you find out about null values and how they work.

Null Values in a Nutshell

The null value is a value, not a data type of its own. You assign a null value by using the keyword `Null`, as in the following command:

```
m.cust_id = Null
```

The data element retains its data type, but gets a value of `Null`.

> **NOTE:** Null values were requested by the VFP community in order to communicate more successfully with backend server databases, which have had null values for a long time.

There are a couple of minor commands related to null values. You can set the default behavior for how null values are handled by the SQL `Insert`, `Create Table`, and `Alter Table` commands with the `Set Null On` or `Set Null Off` command. `Set Null On` will default to allow null values, in the definition of the table, unless you override it. You can set the way null values are displayed in browsers, grids, and form objects with the `Set NullDisplay` command.

The way to determine whether a value is null is with the `IsNull()` function:

```
? IsNull(m.cust_id)
```

A handy function for returning the non-null value out of two values is the `Nvl()` function. Here's an example of its use:

```
? Nvl(m.cust_id, "hi there")
```

If `m.cust_id` is null, the function returns the string. If `m.cust_id` is non-null, the function returns the value of `m.cust_id` (this generalizes to: if both arguments are non-null, the function returns the first value). If both arguments are null, then the function returns `Null`. The `Nvl()` function behaves the same way as SQL Server's `IsNull()` function.

You can use `Nvl()` to update a master table from a change table. Assume that the change table has the same structure as the master table. All the changes in the change table have non-null values, and should overwrite the values in the master table. The null values in the change table should not overwrite anything in the master table. For each field, you could issue the following `Replace` command (in this case, it's for the `name` field):

```
Select Master
Set Relation To cust_id Into Change
Replace master.name With Nvl(master.name, change.name)
```

Using the SQL `Update` command is normally preferable to `Replace`, but you can't issue VFP's SQL `Update` command across two tables.

The Null Value Controversy

There's quite a controversy surrounding the use of null values. The two major authorities in relational databases, E.F. Codd and C.J. Date, split on whether null values are helpful.

Codd writes that there really are two fundamental kinds of null values: data that are appropriate but missing, versus data that are inappropriate. In other words, you might have columns in a table, let's say a Customer table, that apply only to certain kinds of customers and not to others. For those other customers, a null value might simply mean that a value is inappropriate.

C.J. Date writes that there are many more kinds of missing information, as well as information you might want to nullify. In fact, there are too many kinds of null values, according to Date, so it's better to avoid null values entirely. Date suggests, instead, that you use default values for every data element in place of nulls.

If Codd is correct, then there are two major kinds of null values. Most or all relational databases, however, including VFP, use just the single value `Null`. There's no way to tell which of the two meanings belongs to a null value. If Date is correct, and there are more than two kinds of meanings, then you're in even worse shape with null values.

You might find Date's advice most useful here. It would be nice if, when you defined a table, you could disallow nulls in every column and also specify default values. Well, you *can* do that if the table is in a database, as you'll see in the next section.

Checking for Null Values

You can use the `Set Null` command to manage null values. If you have issued `Set Null Off`, the `Insert` command will provide default blank or zero values for the columns not mentioned in the `Insert` command. For example, the following successfully inserts a new row into the Customer table:

```
Set Null Off
Insert Into Customer (cust_id, last_name) Values ("10010","Hanson")
```

This assumes that none of the columns will allow null values. The following command sequence for the same table, however, does not work:

```
Set Null On
Insert Into Customer (cust_id, last_name) Values ("10010","Hanson")
```

It fails because VFP attempts to insert null values. You get the `Field <field name> does not accept null values` error message.

There is yet another problem with null values, this time with variables. No matter what you've set using `Set Null`, you cannot prevent any variable value from being null. It's often necessary to test whether a variable has the correct data type. For example, the following code segment tests a parameter input to a function to see whether the passed parameter is of the correct data type:

```
*— Function that tests a parameter data type
Function MyFunction
Lparameters tnValue
Local lnX
lnX = 1
If Type("tnValue") <> "N"
   Messagebox("Numeric parameter required")
Else
   Do Case
   Case tn = 1
```

```
      lnX = lnX + tnValue
      ? lnX
   Endcase
Endif
EndFunc
```

The problem here is that you can call the function and pass it a Numeric variable with a null value. If you do pass a null value, the variable lnX ends up with a null value.

You must add some defensive measure to test for a null, perhaps like the following:

```
*— Function that tests a parameter data type and for null value
Function MyFunction
Lparameters tnValue
Local lnX
lnX = 1
Do Case
Case Type("tnValue") <> "N"
   Messagebox("Numeric parameter required")
Case tnValue = Null
   Messagebox("You cannot pass a null value to this function")
Otherwise
   Do Case
   Case tn = 1
     lnX = lnX + tnValue
      ? lnX
   Endcase
Endif
EndFunc
```

You want to exercise control over your code, and assure that you do not use null values in your variables. Otherwise, you need to test for a null value in every calculation.

VFP's Relational Database

In addition to the SQL relational access methods, and the more relational DBF format, Visual FoxPro also allows you to organize your tables into a database. In this section, you get an introduction to VFP's database features, in the perspective of the relational model.

After you see VFP's new database capabilities, you then see them applied to three fundamental data integrity problems. These problems are parts of the relational database model that traditional DBF files cannot supply. These problems concern entity (primary key) integrity, column integrity, and referential integrity.

VFP's solution to these problems consists of the database container and its supporting tools. With the database container, VFP now has most of the features required of a relational database.

The VFP Database Container

The *database container* is a disk file in DBF format with DBC as its extension, along with a supporting memo file and index file. This table contains supplementary information about the database tables, and contains database objects such as relationships, views, stored procedures, triggers, and long filenames and field names. A VFP database is the combination of the database container files and the accompanying DBF, memo, and index files.

> **NOTE:** FoxPro programmers requested for many years that future versions of FoxPro contain a *data dictionary*; that is, some way of ensuring data integrity in the database structure itself. For this reason, you will see many writers refer to the database container as a "data dictionary." In fact, the term "data dictionary" is a murky term in database theory, and most writers focus on what they call a "catalog," which is usually a set of tables of meta-data about the database tables. While the DBC might qualify as a mini-catalog, it's better to just refer to it as a "database container."

The Database Container Files

The purpose of the database container is to bind your data tables and the database objects in a way that makes them a whole database. Then you can use VFP's interactive tools and new database commands to create and manage a database. Once you have identified the database, these interactive tools and new commands let you manage the database without having to make specific reference to your data file locations.

It's important to understand that, unlike Jet or Microsoft SQL Server, a VFP database is not one disk file. It actually consists of two sets of disk files. The first set consists of the database container files, and the second set consists of the registered or "contained" DBFs, along with their memo and index files. The DBC data file does not hold any of your application data; rather, it contains supplementary data and certain database objects.

For example, the WWS example database on the CD-ROM that accompanies this book consists of the files listed in Table 10-8.

The database container itself is just three files: the DBF data file, the DCT memo file, and the DCX index file.

Since the database container data table is in DBF format, you can use it and explore it. For example, if you issue

```
Use wws.dbc NoUpdate
Browse
```

from the command line, you see something similar to Figure 10-15.

Objectid	Parentid	Objecttype	Objectname
1	1	Database	Database
2	1	Database	TransactionLog
3	1	Database	StoredProceduresSource
4	1	Database	StoredProceduresObject
5	1	Database	StoredProceduresDependencies
6	1	Table	customer
7	6	Field	cust_id
8	6	Field	customer_no
9	6	Field	last_name
10	6	Field	first_name
11	6	Field	address1
12	6	Field	address2
13	6	Field	city
14	6	Field	state

FIGURE 10-15

You can browse a VFP database container.

Table 10-8 World Wide Shoes Database Files

File	Explanation
wws.DBC	Database container in DBF format
wws.DCT	Database container memo file
wws.DCX	Database container index file
customer.DBF	Customer data table
customer.CDX	Customer indexes
customer_notes.DBF	Customer notes data table
customer_notes.FPT	Customer notes memo file
customer_notes.CDX	Customer notes indexes
customer_demographics.DBF	Customer demographics data table
customer_demographics.CDX	Customer demographics index file
customer_orders.DBF	Customer orders data table
customer_orders.CDX	Customer orders index
marketing_sources.DBF	Marketing sources data table
marketing_sources.CDX	Marketing sources index file
order_payments.DBF	Order payments data table
order_payments.CDX	Order payments index file
order_items.DBF	Order items data table
order_items.CDX	Order items index file
zipcodes.DBF	ZIP codes data table
zipcodes.CDX	ZIP codes index file

WARNING: Since the database container file contains compiled and binary information, there is always the danger that by directly editing it, you could destroy some important information. It's a good idea not to use it directly unless you add the Noupdate qualifier.

The objects in the DBC table are arranged in a tree structure. Each object gets a unique ID and a parent ID to which it belongs. The first object is the Database, which belongs to itself, making it the root node of the tree. All the remaining objects have this as their parent, or else derive from this parent.

FIGURE 10-16

The Project Manager is a safer tool for inspecting a database container.

For example, the Customer table, which has object ID 6, has the Database as its parent. Each of the columns that belongs to the Customer table has a 6 as the value in its `parentid` column.

A clearer and certainly safer way to inspect the objects in a database is to add the database to a project, and then use the Project Manager to explore the components. If you expand the Data tab of the WWS project, you see the objects shown in Figure 10-16.

Here, you see all the objects that can belong to a database. The data tables are first, followed by local views, remote views, connections, and stored procedures. Let's deal with each of these objects.

Managing Database Objects

A VFP database can contain the following objects:

- Long filenames and column names
- Connections
- Views
- Stored procedures

- Persistent relationships
- Triggers

If you register the database with a project, you can drill down with VFP's Project Manager and see these objects in a list format. From the Project Manager, you can reach the Database Designer by clicking the database name (wws) and then clicking the <u>M</u>odify button. You also can reach the Database Designer by opening the database from the command line, then issuing the `Modify Database` command:

```
Open Database wws
Modify Database
```

When you bring up a populated database for the first time, the tables and views will probably not be arranged the way you want them. You need to drag and stretch to get the appearance you like. After you do that, VFP saves the settings in your resource file. In order to put that database on a client computer and have those settings stay with your database, you also have to provide them with a resource file.

NOTE: This chapter assumes that you can operate the Database Designer. For a tutorial on using the Database Designer, see Chapter 3, "Collecting Tables into a Database," in the Visual FoxPro *User's Guide*. For a survey of the new VFP commands and functions for database management, see Chapter 6, "Creating Databases," in the Visual FoxPro *Developer's Guide*.

To get a list of the objects in a database, you can use VFP's `Adbobjects()` function to return the relevant data in an array. For example, to determine which tables are in the WWS database, you can issue the following:

```
Open Database wws
= Adbobjects(laTables,"Table")
Display Memory Like laTables
```

This is the main way to determine programmatically the database objects. Other arguments for the functions are `Connection`, `Relation`, and `View`.

To detect and set the properties of selected database objects, you can use the Dbgetprop() and Dbsetprop() functions.

Long Filenames and Column Names

Once you add a table to a database, Visual FoxPro allows you to assign alternative names for both the DBF and its fields.

You may find the disk filename too short and cryptic, so you can set an alternative filename which VFP will store in the database container. Once you have chosen that longer name, you must still use the short name as the alias for the table in your program, but you can reference the longer name on the Use command.

> **TIP:** You are better off using the built-in support for long filenames in Windows 95 or NT, rather than this feature of VFP.

In the Visual FoxPro DBF format, column names are still limited to 10 characters in the header record of the DBF. You can get around this limit by entering longer, more descriptive names for the columns in the VFP Table Designer. When you do this, VFP still keeps a unique short name in the DBF. VFP will add a tilde (~) followed by a number to the end of the DBF header's column name if it has to, in order to keep the name unique. The long name is registered in the DBC data table, taking the place of the short name.

Long column names can be very useful, but they have an attendant risk. When you use a long column name, it's really an alternative name that exists in the DBC data table and not in the DBF data table. Therefore, if the link gets broken between your DBF and its DBC, you lose the long column name and see only the short, cryptic name. You therefore should use long column names with care (see "Managing Database Tables," later in this chapter).

Connections

A *connection* is how VFP registers a communications method with an external data source via ODBC. These connections make forming remote views easier.

The connection row in the DBC holds a lot of information that you can read and set with the `Dbgetprop()` and `Dbsetprop()` functions.

When using a connection with an external data source that requires a password, if you put the password into the connection, it makes the formation of remote views much easier. This, however, exposes the password—anyone who can read the DBC connection record, or use the `Dbgetprop()` function, can read the password.

Therefore, for sensitive connections, do not include the password. The user will be prompted for the password when the connection is activated.

Views

Views are cursors or temporary tables that VFP builds dynamically. You can make them updatable by selecting the appropriate check boxes. Figure 10-17 shows an example of the View Designer.

A common mistake is to miss the Send SQL Updates box. You have to specify not only the individual columns of the view you want updated, but also mark the small box in the lower-left corner.

Be careful with updatable views. If you make them so denormalized that you can no longer determine a primary key, you will not know which source rows are being updated by the view. If you must have a view that is significantly denormalized, then do not make it updatable.

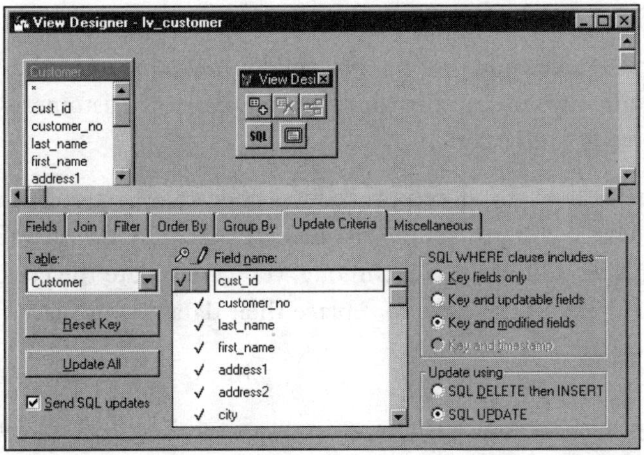

FIGURE 10-17

The Update Criteria tab in the View Designer is where you specify a view's update characteristics.

For more information about remote views, see Chapter 12, "Client/Server Database Development with Visual FoxPro."

Persistent Relationships

You can record permanent relationships in the DBC. You do this by drawing the relationship in the Database Designer, or by using the `Foreign Key References` clause in the `Alter Table` command. VFP puts the label `Relation` in the persistent relationship's DBC row.

VFP uses persistent relationships as the basis for referential integrity, and as default settings for join conditions in views and queries. VFP also uses persistent relationships as the basis for navigational relationships in a form's data environment.

These persistent relationships register the foreign keys for tables, and their cardinality. They match the relationships drawn in an ER diagram. The possible cardinality is either one-to-one or one-to-many.

You will learn more details in the "Referential Integrity" section later in this chapter.

Stored Procedures

VFP stores source and executable code associated with the database in the DBC. One row contains the source, and a second row contains the object code. You code column and referential integrity rules in the stored procedures. VFP automatically compiles them and places the resulting object code in the Code column of the `StoredProceduresObject` row.

You can delete the source code part of your validation code out of the DBC and it will still run. This way you can distribute your DBC to a customer without having to expose your source code.

You can also place calls in the stored procedures code to an external library located with the DBC, and just supply the object code. The World Wide Shoes example works this way. Using this technique, you can update the compiled code on your customer site, and not have to replace their database or place the VFP compiler on the customer's machine.

The ODBC Driver

You need to be careful about the commands you use in stored procedures. If you are confident that only your application will be accessing the data, then you can code screen messages and object-oriented constructs into your stored procedures.

If, however, you need to expose your data to external applications through the VFP ODBC driver, then you need to trim down the commands that you use. The VFP ODBC driver has a help file that lists the VFP commands that the driver will, and will not, recognize. VFP installs an icon for this in your ODBC program group, labeled `Visual FoxPro ODBC Driver`.

Fortunately, the relational database engine is completely available in the ODBC driver. Missing from the VFP ODBC driver are interactive command-window commands, screen-messaging commands, and object-oriented constructs.

Therefore, use OOP constructs in your stored procedures only if you do not plan to expose your data via ODBC.

Column and Row Rules and Triggers

Column rules are validations per column that enforce column integrity. *Row rules* are a further validation at the row level. *Triggers* enforce referential integrity for any insert, update, or delete action against the table. You do not have to use the SQL `Insert`, `Update`, or `Delete` command for a trigger to fire. VFP assists you in building triggers with the Referential Integrity builder. You place the code for rules and triggers in stored procedures.

You will learn more about column/row rules in the upcoming "Column Integrity" section, and about triggers in the upcoming "Referential Integrity" section.

Managing Database Tables

You can classify VFP DBF tables as two kinds: free tables and database tables. *Free tables* are VFP DBFs that are not in a database. *Database tables* are included in some database. A given database table can exist in only one database at a time. VFP writes a special marker into the header record of a database table, referencing the database to which it belongs.

There is no way to tell from the name or extension of a DBF file whether it's a database table or a free table. You can use the `Indbc()` function to determine whether a given table is in a database, as in the following lines:

```
Open Data wws
? Indbc("customer","Table")
```

You can use the `Cursorgetprop()` function to determine what database a table belongs to, as in the following line:

```
? Cursorgetprop("Database")
```

This returns the full filename and path of the database container data table, such as `C:\WWS\WWS.DBC`.

When you transfer tables in and out of a database, you have to be careful. There are two commands that act on a table, `Remove Table` and `Free Table`. `Remove Table` takes a database table and makes it a free VFP-format table, and removes all references to it, as well as objects referring to it, from the database. It's a clean removal.

`Free Table`, however, just makes a database table into a free table, and does not affect the DBC. Therefore you should only use the `Free Table` command in emergencies, when you have lost the database container or the DBC is unrecoverable.

You can add a free table to a database with the `Add Table` command. When you add a Fox2x or FoxPlus DBF to a database, VFP prompts you for confirmation, because you're making that file unreadable to applications other than VFP or those using the VFP ODBC driver.

Three Data Integrity Problems

As you have seen, Visual FoxPro descends from a long line of products. The navigational commands in VFP have been developed over many years and many revisions of prior products. All those navigational commands were meant to deal with data stored in DBF files. However, DBF files have three fundamental problems with data integrity.

The first problem concerns the lack of *entity integrity*. In standard DBF files, there is no way you can specify a truly unique key in a table in order to prevent duplicate key values. Hence there is no way you can guarantee that your table would stay a relational table (see the prior discussion of R-tables). Even if your application always checks to make sure that no new rows in a table duplicate the primary key, you cannot prevent someone else from using the file and adding the duplicates, thus making your table no longer an R-table.

The second problem concerns *column integrity*—namely, constraining column values in a table. There is no way, in the traditional DBF, to constrain a value of some column to a certain range, format, or list. Just as with primary keys, it's all up to your application.

The third problem concerns constraining values between tables, or *referential integrity*. Traditional DBF files have no intrinsic relationship to each other. The only way you can assure data integrity between standard DBF data tables is to program it into your application. For example, if you wanted to make sure that only valid customer keys could ever be entered into a `customer_orders` file, you could do that in your application. If someone else edited the data outside your application, or there was a bug in your data integrity code, then your rules would be violated, and there would be nothing in the DBFs to prevent it.

As discussed earlier, VFP has added the database container as a solution to the problem of data integrity between tables. If you register your tables as part of a VFP database, you can specify, for example, that the `customer_orders` table must always have customer keys that are validated against the `customer` table.

Entity Integrity

Visual FoxPro solves the problem of a lack of entity integrity by adding two new kinds of indexes: candidate key and primary key indexes.

A *candidate key index* acts to prevent duplicates on the index key expression. There can be more than one candidate key in a DBF. The key's expression can be any legal VFP index expression. The candidate key is available on all VFP-format DBFs, whether they are part of a database or not.

A primary key is simply one of a DBF table's candidate keys with a special status. In order to have a primary key, your DBF must be part of a database. There can only be one primary key per table. The primary key is used in the database to establish foreign key references and persistent relationships between tables.

You establish a primary key in the Table Design dialog box, when the table is part of a database (recall the earlier discussion of managing databases). The addition of a primary key in VFP lets you specify that a table should be a relational table (R-table). With a primary key in place, VFP guarantees that duplicate values cannot be added; however, the quality of the primary key can vary.

Some VFP programmers put a `For Not Deleted()` clause on the primary key, making it ignore deleted rows. Remember that deleted rows remain in a DBF table until you issue the `Pack` command. With that clause, the deleted rows are ignored in the primary key expression. The reason for keeping deleted rows around is to use them later instead of inserting new rows. You also can reuse the primary keys because VFP will not detect duplicate keys in the deleted rows. Some developers like to blank out the primary key, so that all deleted rows have a blank or equivalent in the primary key column.

This strategy, however, has its risks. It violates the entity integrity of the table. Even if you issued `Set Deleted On`, so that now the user cannot see the deleted rows, they are still in the table and the integrity of the primary key is gone. If the user can issue `Set Deleted Off`, either interactively or through a bug in your code, then he or she can see the deleted rows.

Moreover, you really should not try to reuse deleted rows. It's much clearer and simpler to use the SQL `Insert` command to insert a new row. To recycle deleted rows, your program must issue `Set Deleted Off`, then use a sequence of navigational commands in order to find the deleted row and give it a new primary key.

If there is more than one blank deleted record, you'll be unable to use the SQL `Update` command to get new data in the table, because you won't be able to tell one blank row from another in the `Update` command's `Where` clause.

The reason VFP programmers recycle deleted rows is primarily for performance improvement. Unless you have millions of rows in a table, this technique will not gain you any advantage.

Rather than let deleted rows remain in the table, you should periodically `Pack` your application's tables (see the "VFP Database Administration" section later in this chapter). Also, if you use an incrementing primary key, there's no need to recycle deleted rows (see the "Avoid Meaningful Primary Keys" section above, and the "Default Values" section below).

Column Integrity

Column integrity refers to your ability to impose rules in the database concerning allowable values in columns, during actions on a row. Visual FoxPro provides you with several ways to impose these rules.

Column Validation

VFP calls the first type of validation *field validation*. You will also see it called *check constraint* in database writings. You can see the appropriate place to put a call to a validation rule in the Field Validation/Rule box in the Table Designer, as shown in Figure 10-18.

You also can enter column-level validation rules with the `Alter Table` and `Create Table` commands. You only need to enter a logical expression, something that evaluates to True or False. For example, if you want to ensure that `customer_name` in the WWS database will never be blank, you can put the following in the Rule text box.

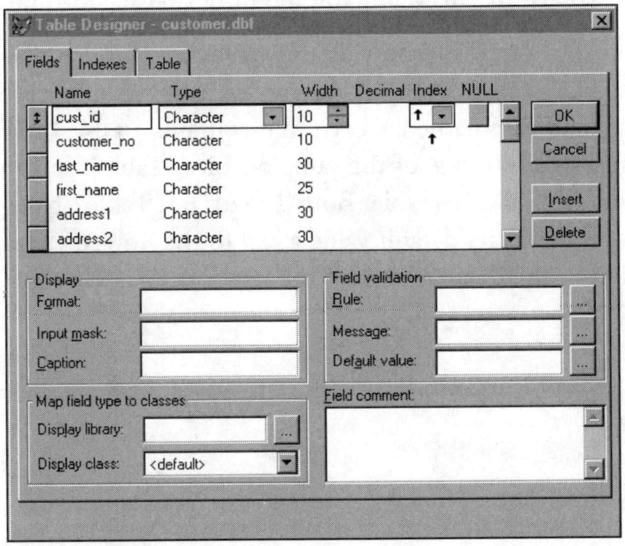

FIGURE 10-18

You can enter column validation rules in the Table Designer.

```
Not(Empty(customer_name))
```

Alternatively, you can issue the `Alter Table` command as follows:

```
Alter Table customer Alter Column customer_name Set Check ;
Not(Empty(customer_name))
```

In this example, the check constraint is just a brief expression. You also could put in a function call to a stored or external procedure. In addition, you could specify message text to be returned if the check constraint fails.

Default Values

In the same box, but with a very different meaning, you also can enter default values for each column in a table. Default values are initial values that VFP will give to a column when it is first inserted, if no other values are specifically mentioned for it. The default value must consist of an expression that evaluates to the same data type as the column. That expression can, as in column validation, be a function call.

Default values can be very helpful. For example, if you do not allow null values in your columns, but you do not want to force users to spell out values for every column in their `Insert` statements (which makes for complex and error-prone statements), just specify default values for the columns. You do not have to do this if `Set Nulls Off` is in effect, but you might not have control over that.

Another use for default values is to provide the values for surrogate keys. You have an example of this in the `\VFP\Samples\Solutions` subdirectory. There you can find a small database named `NewId` that contains a table of IDs. Each time a new ID is inserted into one of the sample tables (Table1 or Table2), VFP retrieves a new value from the Ids table. Both Table1 and Table2 have a primary key named `id`, which has as its default value a call to the `newid()` function. This function, found in the database's stored procedures area, is as follows:

```
FUNCTION NewID(tcAlias)
  LOCAL lcAlias, ;
        lnID, ;
        lcOldReprocess, ;
        lnOldArea
```

```
lnOldArea = SELECT()

IF PARAMETERS() < 1
   lcAlias = UPPER(ALIAS())
ELSE
   lcAlias = UPPER(tcAlias)
ENDIF

lcOldReprocess = SET('REPROCESS')

*- Lock until user presses Esc
SET REPROCESS TO AUTOMATIC

IF !USED("IDS")
   USE newid!ids IN 0
ENDIF
SELECT ids

IF SEEK(lcAlias, "Ids", "table")
   IF RLOCK()
      lnID = ids.nextid
      REPLACE ids.nextid WITH ids.nextid + 1
      UNLOCK
   ENDIF
ENDIF

SELECT (lnOldArea)
SET REPROCESS TO lcOldReprocess

RETURN lnID
ENDFUNC
```

This function uses some navigation logic to seek and increment the relevant ID. It also sets the Reprocess value so that the user will see a status message while a record lock is being attempted. Once the record is locked, the program increments the ID and returns the value found in the table. Thus, the table always stores the next available ID, not the last one assigned. The id column is of the Integer data type, so its maximum value is just above 2 billion.

A more relational way to write this function is to drop the navigational logic and add transactions. Look at this version from the wws database:

```
Function NextID(tcAlias)
  Local lcAlias, ;
            lnID, ;
         lcOldReprocess, ;
         lnOldArea

  lnOldArea = Select()

  If Parameters() < 1
    lcAlias = Upper(Alias())
  ELSE
    lcAlias = Upper(tcAlias)
  ENDIF

  lcOldReprocess = Set('Reprocess')

  *- Lock until user presses Esc
  Set Reprocess To Automatic

  Begin Transaction
  Update ids Set nextid = nextid + 1 Where ids.table = (lcAlias)
  If TableUpdate()
    Select nextid From ids Where ids.table = (lcAlias) Into Array laId
    If _Tally > 1
      lnID = laId[1] - 1
      End Transaction
    Else
      Rollback
      * error
```

```
   Endif
Else
   Rollback
Endif
Select (lnOldArea)
Set Reprocess To lcOldReprocess

   Return lnID
Endfunc
```

Notice that the relational approach is somewhat simpler, yet the effect is the same. Both programs lock the appropriate row in the Ids table so that no other users will get the new ID. The second program uses table buffering and transactions.

Row Validation

In addition to column-level check constraints, VFP allows you to apply a check constraint to an entire row. The VFP Table Designer identifies this *row validation* as `Record Validation` in its Table tab. Figure 10-19 shows an example.

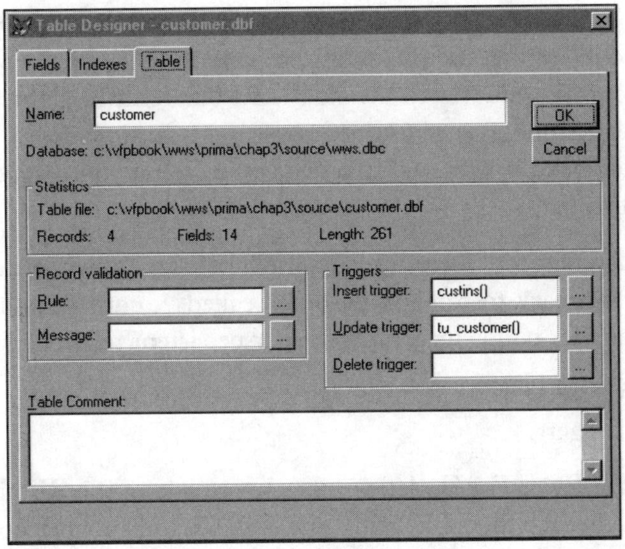

FIGURE 10-19

The Table Designer's Table tab allows entry of row-level validations.

Row validation is useful when you need to impose constraints across column values, such as validating one column on the basis of another.

Referential Integrity

VFP applies referential integrity through the use of triggers. That is, VFP guarantees the integrity of a foreign key by the use of triggers. Triggers are really a special class of stored procedures, and come in three flavors. Any table can have up to three triggers: one each for insert, update, and delete. The insert trigger for a table fires when an `Insert` is done into the table, the update trigger fires after the `Update` command, and the delete trigger after the SQL `Delete From` command.

VFP also fires a table's trigger when the appropriate parallel navigational command executes. For an insert trigger, `Append Blank` fires it as soon as the record pointer moves off the record. For an update trigger, the relevant navigational command is `Replace` or `Gather`, and again the trigger fires as soon as the record pointer moves to the next record.

An exception for trigger firing concerns buffering. When table buffering is enabled, the triggers fire after `TableUpdate()`, not the record pointer movement.

The VFP RI Builder

One of the nicest utilities that comes with Visual FoxPro is the *Referential Integrity (RI) builder*. You can use this utility to build triggers for the most common kinds of situations. One way to invoke the RI builder is by right-clicking the Database Designer design surface, then choosing Edit Referential Integrity. The resulting dialog box presents an attractive way to select your triggers, as shown in Figure 10-20.

You select the dialog tabs for insert, update, or delete triggers, while the grid holds the tables in primary-to-foreign key order, called `Parent` and `Child` in the grid. The RI builder builds its grid from your persistent relationships.

The RI builder gives you three options for update and delete triggers, and two options for insert triggers.

When you select the Rules For Updating tab, you are asking the RI builder to write an update trigger for the table being updated. The table being updated is the parent table in the grid. The RI builder finds the parent table by examining

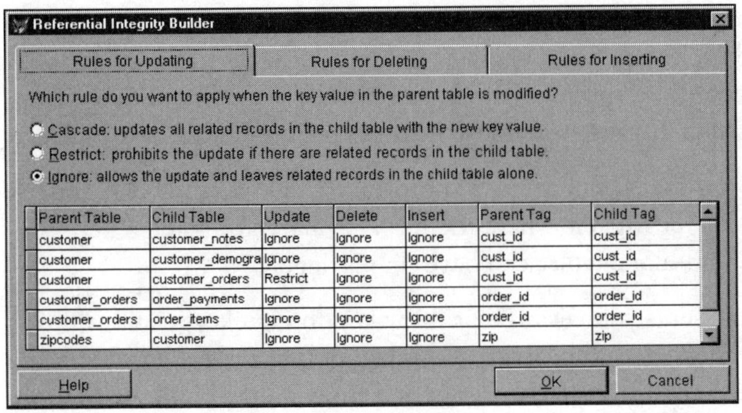

FIGURE 10-20

The Referential Integrity Builder form lets you select most triggers.

the database for its persistent relationships, and bringing up every one-to-many and one-to-one relationship to be listed in the grid.

The settings you can make for update actions specify what to do if the user updates the primary key in the parent table. The options are to cascade the changed key throughout the child table, restrict the change if the child table has instances of that key, or ignore the change (allowing it in the parent but taking no action in the child table).

The delete options are similar to the update options. If the primary key is deleted in the parent table, you can cascade the delete into a delete of all the child rows with the same key, restrict the delete if there are child rows with that key, or ignore the delete (allow it and take no action).

The insert option is a little different. This time, you are writing an insert trigger for the child table, not the parent. The options are to restrict the insert if the foreign key has no match in the parent table, or ignore and let the insert proceed if there is no match.

There is no simple rule for determining what the best choices are. You have to take a look at your particular application and the nature of the data you're working with to determine what to do in the RI builder.

Once you have made your selections, the RI builder generates code and inserts the code into the stored procedures of the database. The code is compiled right away and the object code goes into the stored procedures object row.

The RI builder marks the beginning and end points of the code with special comment lines, and each time you commit your builder changes, it overwrites whatever was between those special markers. It generally is unwise to tamper with the generated code, because you'll lose it the next time you run the builder.

You should not rely on the RI builder as a complete trigger writer. It only presents you with options for triggers where there is a primary key-foreign key relationship. Yet even stand-alone tables can have three triggers.

Also, even when it presents you with the primary key-foreign key relationships, it covers update and delete on the parent, and insert on the child. However, there are really six triggers here, three on the parent and three on the child. So the builder is ignoring, per relationship, the insert trigger for the parent, and the update and delete trigger on the child table. Yet the RI builder does manage to capture most of the possibilities. In addition, a table that is a child in one relationship may be a parent in another.

Do not read the parent/child relationships in the RI builder as meaning one-to-many. The RI builder lists one-to-one relationships as "parent" and "child," as well.

There are a number of other limitations in the RI builder:

- The RI builder does not offer all the actions you might want to take. For example, if a parent key is deleted, you might want to nullify or blank out the instances of the foreign key in the child table. The RI builder lacks this option.

- The RI builder does not produce correct code when you have a composite key in the child table.

- You might find it difficult to follow the code generated by the RI builder. This code is not documented especially well, and the naming conventions are rather odd.

Generally, though, the RI builder does its limited job well, and you'll probably like its interface. Realistically, you should look upon it as a way to "jumpstart" your triggers, in the same way you might use the Form Wizard to create an initial form which you then refine and recode. The fact is that in any complex application, you'll have to customize your triggers, because you might have to do more than just check for RI in a given trigger. In addition, the keys might be so complex or the business rules sufficiently unique that you simply cannot use the generated code to do the job.

So, how do you write triggers of your own? That's the next topic.

Writing Your Own Triggers

In order to write your own triggers, you need to use some kind of matrix like that found in the RI builder, so that you can determine what your options are. Table 10-9 shows a sample matrix for the World Wide Shoes database. In the table, PK stands for primary key, and FK stands for foreign key.

Once you have decided your options, you can set about writing the trigger. For example, try writing the update trigger in the Customer table for changes to the cust_id primary key. You do not want to allow such changes—in other words, want to restrict them—if there are customer IDs in the Customer_Orders table. To handle this, look at the following pseudocode:

```
* Declare variables
*
```

Table 10-9 A Sample Referential Integrity Matrix

Parent Table	Child Table	What conditions should be placed on PK changes in the parent table?			What conditions should be placed on FK changes in the child table?		
		Update Parent PK	Insert into Parent	Delete from Parent	Update Child FK	Insert into Child	Delete from Child
Zipcodes	Customer	Restrict	Ignore	Restrict	Restrict	Restrict	Ignore
Customer	Customer_Notes	Restrict	Ignore	Restrict	Restrict	Restrict	Ignore
Customer	Customer_Demographics	Restrict	Ignore	Restrict	Restrict	Restrict	Ignore
Customer	Customer_Orders	Restrict	Ignore	Restrict	Restrict	Restrict	Ignore
Customer_Orders	Order_Items	Restrict	Ignore	Restrict	Restrict	Restrict	Ignore
Customer_Orders	Order_Payments	Restrict	Ignore	Restrict	Restrict	Restrict	Ignore

```
* Get the current cust_id
* If it is a change from the old value
* If there are rows in the child table with the old customer id
*    Set return value to false
* Else
*    Set return value to true
* Endif
* Endif
```

What you need to do is to somehow determine, within the trigger and before the update occurs, whether the key value has changed. One way to implement that code is as follows:

```
Function tu_customer
Local llRetVal, lcCurVal, lcOldVal, laMin
llRetVal = .F.


lcCurVal = cust_id
lcOldVal = OldVal("cust_id")
* If it is a change from the old value
If lcCurVal <> lcOldVal
   * If there are rows in the child table with the old customer id
   Select min(cust_id) from orders a ;
     Where a.cust_id = lcOldVal ;
   Into Array laMin
   If _Tally > 0
     * Set return value to false
     llRetVal = .F.
   Else
     * Set return value to true
     llRetVal = .T.
   Endif
Else
   llRetVal = .T.
Endif
Return llRetVal
```

It turns out that you cannot completely avoid navigational features when writing a trigger. You have to depend on the fact that VFP positions itself on the row when it does the update. This also extends to delete.

Notice a few things about this code. First, there's a naming convention for the trigger function. It's good to have some kind of convention so you can tell which functions are triggers. In this case, there's a tu_ prefix (meaning "trigger, update") and then the table name.

Second, all variables are declared locally in order to not disturb any executing program's variables. The results of the SQL Select are sent to an array so that no cursor is created, which might disturb the user's work areas.

Third, there is no error handling. This is something that must be added, but would complicate the example here. The RI builder produces code to handle errors.

Last, the trigger uses relational access methods wherever possible. It's not complete, but just using the SQL Select instead of navigating the child table greatly clarifies the code.

VFP Database Administration

Along with freedom comes responsibility. Now that Visual FoxPro gives you most of the capabilities of a relational database, you also have the responsibility of maintaining one. In this section, you get a brief tour of some of the things you have to consider and do in order to meet this responsibility.

Security

Security is a sensitive issue for VFP databases. When you expose your data across an enterprise, you must face the possibility of unauthorized tampering.

When your data consists of traditional pre-VFP DBFs, security of your data is identical to the security of the LAN environment. To let a user run your application, that user must have read and write access to the portion of the LAN that contains your data. Once they have those rights, though, they can read and write that data using other software products that do not respect the business rules you've built into the application. The more sensitive the data, the more serious this exposure becomes.

The new VFP-format DBF adds a small layer of security, in that VFP DBFs are only readable through the VFP ODBC driver. Also, with free VFP DBFs, you can enforce candidate key integrity. If your application consists of free VFP DBFs, however, you still must grant all your application users read and write access to the data. If an unauthorized user does not have the VFP ODBC driver, or their application does not use ODBC, then they cannot read or write to it.

Adding your VFP DBFs to a database secures your data somewhat more than free DBFs. If an unauthorized user accesses your database via ODBC, the VFP ODBC driver will enforce the primary key, column, and referential integrity that you have encoded into the database.

Still, VFP lacks a certain number of features, making your VFP data, by comparison with backend server SQL databases, vulnerable to unauthorized tampering.

The most serious problem is that you normally must grant users read/write access to your data on the LAN so that they can use your application. That means the user can interactively, via their operating system, delete application data files. If you could put a second login in your application, and then have the application log out, perhaps you could get around this.

Backend server databases like Microsoft SQL Server operate as a service on the LAN operating system. As a result, the user does not need read/write access to the data in order to get the data through SQL Server. Then you can impose further security constraints within the database server.

Another missing feature of VFP databases is the lack of a password. There's no "open database" event to which you can tie a request for a user login ID, to try to keep unauthorized users out of the data. Of course, once a user opens a VFP database, they can read any table that is not used exclusively by another user.

Security is one issue that sharply contrasts VFP databases with the backend SQL relational databases.

Maintenance Issues

Maintenance is not a new issue for VFP programmers, for you've always had to face issues of backup and reindexing; however, the VFP database structure raises some new and interesting issues.

Backup

You've always had to back up your data, and perhaps the simplest way of doing this is the best. You copy the data, using a backup program, to a backup device such as tape or disk.

Unfortunately, there are some limitations to this. Standard backup software like that in Windows NT will not back up files that are in use. If anyone is using any of the tables in your database, then part of the database does not get backed up. This can present a problem during a restore, if you cannot restore all the data to the same backup time period. Some data might be later than others, thus making the database inconsistent.

In the case of a database, you need a consistent snapshot of the data, a time slice such that all the data is from the same moment. One way to do this is to take control of the situation in your application, and run a program that opens the database exclusively. This prevents other users from changing any data, thus making it safe to copy the database to a backup location. The data in the backup location then can be backed up using standard backup software.

The following program uses VFP's gendbc utility to accomplish the VFP backup:

```
*—
* Backup.prg
* Backs up a database to a specified subdirectory
* Make sure you add filenames
*—

Close All
Clear All
Set Safety Off

*— Open the wws database exclusively
cd \wws
Open Data wws Exclusive

*— Make sure no tables are open
```

```
Close Tables

*- Generate a programmatic image of it
Do \vfp5\tools\gendbc\gendbc With "wws"

*- Copy the programs to the backup directory
Copy File wws.prg To \wwsbak\wws.prg
Copy File wws.krt To \wwsbak\wws.krt

*- Compile and run the image of the database
cd \wwsbak
Compile \wwsbak\interm.prg
Do \wwsbak\wws.prg

*- Open the backup database and append the original's data
Open Data \wwsbak\wws
* Get a list of data
lnTables = Adbobjects(laTables,'Table')
* Step through the tables and copy them
For lnX = 1 To lnTables
   lcTableName = laTables[lnX]

   *- Copy the data table first
   Copy File &lcTableName..dbf To \wwsbak\&lcTableName..dbf

   *- Copy the memo file next
   If File("&lcTableName..fpt")
     Copy File &lcTableName..fpt To \wwsbak\&lcTableName..fpt
   Endif

   *- Copy the index file last
   If File("&lcTableName..cdx")
     Copy File &lcTableName..cdx To \wwsbak\&lcTableName..cdx
   Endif
Endfor
```

NOTE: This is a simplified version of the program—in production you would want to add error handling, as well as special cases for your application.

You also would probably want to add a loop for the exclusive opening of the database. This would make sure that if other users had tables open, the backup program would continue to wait until they let go. An obvious potential problem is that if a user left for home at night with the database open while your application was running, the backup program might never be able to get exclusive access.

This program opens the database exclusively so that you can be sure that nobody else is accessing it. Then it makes sure that no tables are open, and copies the database tables, memo files, and index files to the backup directory.

Disaster and Recovery

Disasters come in many flavors. Here are a few, with some suggestions for recovery.

Missing Files Due to Accidental Deletions

When you have missing files, you have no choice but to restore from a backup. However, if your application is at all complex, you should restore an entirely consistent database. That means you should not just restore the missing files, but the whole database, unless you're fairly certain that the missing file or files did not get changed since the last backup.

If you are restoring any of the database container files, you need to make sure that nobody is using the database at the time. You might have to work with the LAN administrator to remove everyone else's access to your data directory.

Corrupt Database Container

You will find that database containers occasionally become corrupt, due to users aborting at critical times, bad file transfers, or perhaps a media failure.

One kind of corruption is easy to duplicate. Bring up the database container index file in an editor, and change the first few bytes. Normally that invalidates it, and when you try to open the database, VFP reports that the index file is invalid. A very nice feature of VFP is that it will recreate a database container index file automatically. All you need to do is delete the DCX file, and the next time you open the database, VFP creates a proper index.

Other kinds of corruption occur when you have mismatches between the columns in the database tables and the database container. You can use the Validate Database command to recover the database:

```
Open Database wws
Validate Database Recover
```

Corrupt DBF or Memo Files

When DBF files or their companion memo files become corrupt, you can either restore from a backup copy or attempt to fix the file. Before spending much time trying to fix it, read the file using the VFP editor—but not as a DBF. For example, you can just issue Modify File from the VFP command window:

```
Modify File customer.fpt
```

Then see if the data looks coherent. It's always possible that a bad disk write somewhere has made the data so bad that the file is not worth trying to recover; in that case, you must go to a backup version.

Corrupt Index Files

Fortunately, when index files become corrupt, all you need to do is reindex. You will not have any data loss. If, however, you do not restore the index file the way the VFP database expects to see it, you will get an error. The program file generated by the gendbc utility contains index expressions for all the tables in the database. They are located at the bottom of each of the Create Table statements, and you can use pieces of the resulting program to reconstruct the entire index file.

Reindexing

Even though Visual FoxPro keeps all its index files up-to-date dynamically, it's a good idea to recreate those indexes on a regular basis. For heavily used applications, or applications with lots of data activity, you can reindex overnight or on weekends.

Beware of deleting all the tags in a table with the `Delete Tag All` command. The primary key is an index, and if you delete it, any relations making reference to it are also deleted, so you might lose some referential integrity constraints.

Primary and foreign keys, therefore, should just be reindexed. You can delete and recreate other tags. Recreation of a tag can improve the spatial organization of the index file.

Summary

Visual FoxPro provides you with the capability to store your data in a relational database. While you can continue to use navigational methods to access your data, VFP now provides a mostly complete set of relational SQL commands you can use in their place. Most impressively, you can embed stored procedures and triggers in your VFP database to protect your data's integrity and consistency. With VFP, you now have a remarkably flexible and comprehensive set of tools for database access.

Chapter 11

Using SQL in Visual FoxPro Applications

Introduction

In Chapter 10, "Creating a Visual FoxPro Database," you learned about creating databases in VFP. Once you have defined the structure of your databases, you want efficient ways to change the structure of your database tables, and to access your data. This is where SQL comes in. *Structured Query Language (SQL)* is an ANSI (American National Standards Institute) standardized language used to create and query data from database applications. Its history dates to the 1970s when E.F. Codd wrote his initial papers on a subject known as *relational algebra*. This chapter will cover the techniques necessary to use SQL in your Visual Fox-Pro applications. This chapter is not meant to be a definitive coverage of SQL, but rather to familiarize you with the basics of SQL.

What is SQL?

In order to use SQL in your applications, you need to understand what SQL is and how it is structured. SQL is a standardized language that can be used to create and access data from databases. The language is similar to English, and lends itself to creating complex queries with very little code. One of the most important aspects of this language is its standardized approach to database access. SQL is a standard data access language found in many of the most powerful database systems on the market, including SQL Server, ORACLE, and DB2. Its syntax and structure are defined by ANSI, and are supported by dozens of different database packages.

Understanding SQL's Structure

SQL is a very robust language and supports numerous commands. These commands are broken into two distinct categories: a data definition language and a data manipulation language. The *data definition language (DDL)*, as its name conveys, is used to define databases and data tables. This language is used to create the structure, business rules, and relationships among tables found in a database application. The *data manipulation language (DML)* allows you to add, update, query, and delete data from your database tables. The use of the DDL occurs rather infrequently. You probably will use the DDL to create your initial database structure, and then use the DDL on an infrequent basis to alter the structure throughout your application's lifetime. The more commonly used category of SQL commands is the DML, because the entire purpose of a database application is to add and manipulate data within its structure.

Why Use SQL?

As you know by now, you can create and manipulate data tables using many of FoxPro's Xbase commands. Visual FoxPro includes many commands that you can use to alter the data found in your databases. The Replace command is provided to facilitate updates to data in your tables. You also can use the Copy and Seek commands to query data from your tables. These commands are pretty powerful, but to optimize them in your applications you need to have specific and detailed knowledge of your data tables. It takes a great deal of training and time to develop optimized applications. This is where SQL has a real advantage. By its nature, SQL is a *set-oriented language*, which means that it processes data in sets of records. The advantage of this approach is that by choosing your syntax carefully, you can create optimized queries with very few lines of code. Another advantage of SQL is its portability. If you want to manipulate data from client/server databases, you can use syntax that is supported on platforms other than FoxPro. A final advantage is SQL's natural, English-like syntax. As you will see, SQL is very similar to English, and better yet, follows the logic that you would expect to use when querying data. To summarize, SQL offers the following advantages:

- A set-oriented language to create optimized queries
- Multi-platform support
- English-like syntax

Using the Data Definition Language

The first step in creating a database application is to take your logical design and create physical tables from your design. This is the purpose of the SQL DDL, which is used to create tables and business rules attached to those tables. Visual FoxPro supports an active data dictionary that will enforce any rules that you establish using VFP's implementation of the DDL. This section covers the syntax necessary to create tables using the DDL.

Using CREATE TABLE

The first step in creating your database applications is to translate your logical database design into physical tables. This is where the CREATE TABLE command comes in. CREATE TABLE allows you to define your tables, as well as business rules associated with those tables. In this chapter, we'll use the organization and contact tables found in the World Wide Shoes example. For more information about World Wide Shoes, see Chapter 2, "Analysis, Design, and Prototyping."

When you want to create a table, the first thing to do is create the basic set of columns for that table. The following code demonstrates the creation of the basic structure of the organization table:

```
Close All
Clear All

Create Database WWS

Create Table organization ( ;
  org_id i Primary Key,  ;
  organization_name        c(50), ;
  organization_address1    c(50))
```

This code creates a table named organization that contains three columns: org_id, organization_name, and organization_address1. It also specifies the org_id column as the primary key for the organization table. For an explanation of primary keys, see Chapter 10, "Creating a Visual FoxPro Database."

The most important aspect of this piece of code is the syntax for defining each column. After you issue the CREATE TABLE command, you begin creating a comma-delimited list of columns with the following structure:

```
(fieldname1 datatypecode1 [datalength1], fieldname2 datatypecode2
[datalength2], . . .)
```

Each column creation line requires a set of three arguments. The first is the name of the column. This argument must conform to the column naming requirements found in the Visual FoxPro documentation. The second is a code indicating the data type of the column. Table 11-1 lists the codes for all the available data types.

Table 11-1 Visual FoxPro Data Types

Data Type Code	Data Type
C(n)	Character of width n
D	Date
T	Datetime
N	Numeric
F	Floating numeric
I	Integer
B	Double
Y	Currency
L	Logical
M	Memo
G	General

The last argument, which is optional, is the length of the column to be stored in the database. Some data types—such as Date, Memo, Integer, and Double—have pre-defined lengths. Other data types—such as Character and Numeric—allow you to specify the length of the column (and, in the case of Numeric, the number of decimal points).

The column definition syntax allows you to define other optional information, including:

- Default values
- Whether the column is the primary key for the table
- Whether the column supports null values
- Validation rules for the column
- Error message information for the column

The following code demonstrates the creation of the organization table with its business rules:

```
Close All
Clear All


Create Database WWS
```

> **NOTE:** The optional column information items listed above (with the exception of null values), are available only in tables attached to a database container (DBC). These arguments are not available with free tables. For more information on database containers, see Chapter 10, "Creating a Visual FoxPro Database."

```
*— Create organization table
*— This time with a primary key
Create Table organization ( ;
   org_id integer Primary Key Not Null, ;
   organization_name         c(50), ;
   organization_address1     c(50), ;
   organization_address2     c(50), ;
   organization_city         c(25), ;
   organization_state        c(2) Default "WA" ;
            Check g_isstate(organization_state)  ;
            Error "Incorrect state entered. Please re-enter.", ;
   organization_zip          c(5))
```

This code shows the full syntax for creating tables and attaching business rules to the columns in those tables. Here's a description of what this particular code specifies:

- The NOT NULL keyword on the org_id column prevents you from adding a record if the value in the org_id column is missing (not entered).

- The DEFAULT keyword on the organization_state column inserts the value WA into the organization_state column whenever a new column is added.

- The ERROR keyword on the organization_state column specifies that an Incorrect state entered. Please re-enter error message gets displayed if an invalid state is entered.

> **WARNING:** If you use the CHECK keyword and also want to use the ERROR keyword, you need to specify the keywords in that order. If you put ERROR following a keyword other than CHECK, you'll receive an error from Visual FoxPro.

- The CHECK keyword on the organization_state column calls the g_isstate() function to check whether or not the entered state is valid for entry.

Relating Tables Using the REFERENCES Keyword

Another feature of the CREATE TABLE command is its ability to create persistent relationships between different tables. You accomplish this by using the REFERENCES keyword, which requires two pieces of data. The first is the name of the table with which you want to create a relationship. The second is the name of the PRIMARY KEY index tag in the table with which you want to create a relationship. The following code creates the organization and contact tables, and establishes a relationship between the two using the REFERENCES keyword:

```
Close All
Clear All

Create Database WWS


*— Create organization table
*— This time with a primary key
Create Table organization ( ;
    org_id integer Primary Key Not Null, ;
    organization_name          c(50), ;
    organization_address1      c(50), ;
    organization_address2      c(50), ;
    organization_city          c(25), ;
```

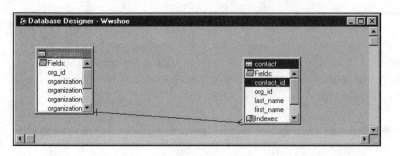

FIGURE 11-1

These are the database tables created and related using the CREATE TABLE *command in the preceding code example.*

```
organization_state c(2) Default "WA" ;
            Check g_isstate(organization_state)  ;
            Error "Incorrect state entered. Please re-enter.", ;
organization_zip   c(5))


*— Create related table
Create Table contact ( ;
   contact_id integer Primary Key, ;
   org_id integer References organization Tag org_id, ;
   last_name        c(30), ;
   first_name       c(25))
```

Figure 11-1 shows the final result of this table definition.

Using ALTER TABLE

Inevitably you will want to alter the structure of some tables found in your databases. This is where the ALTER TABLE command comes in. This command allows you to add or remove columns, business rules, relationships, and other table information. The following code shows how to add a phone_number column to your organization table:

```
Alter Table organization ;
   Add Column phone_number c(12)
```

If you use the VFP Table Designer to alter the structure and add a new business rule to a table, then by default the Table Designer makes sure that all records in the table correspond to the newly added business rule. The ALTER TABLE command provides a NOVALIDATE keyword that allows you to add a new business rule without having VFP validate all records against the new business rule. The following code demonstrates an ALTER TABLE command using the NOVALIDATE keyword:

```
Alter Table organization ;
   Alter Column organization_zip ;
   Set Check Val(organization_zip) > 0 ;
   Novalidate
```

As you can see, the ALTER TABLE command is quite powerful and useful. You can use it to automate structure changes in applications that you have distributed. These changes include adding, deleting, and renaming columns in VFP tables. The following code demonstrates testing to see if a particular column exists in a table, then adding the column if it doesn't exist:

```
Close All
Clear All

Use organization Exclusive

*- See if the column already exists
If Type("organization.organization_notes") = "U"

   *- If not, add it now
   Alter Table organization Add Column organization_notes m
Else
   Wait Window "Field Already Exists"
Endif
```

The key to this program is the TYPE() function, which returns the data type for a particular column or variable. If that variable does not exist, the function returns U (so that's what the code tests for).

> **TIP:** The ALTER TABLE command requires that the tables being modified can be opened exclusively by the workstation making the changes.

Using CREATE SQL VIEW

One of the more useful SQL commands is the CREATE SQL VIEW command. This command allows you to create queries that behave like tables. The CREATE SQL VIEW command has two components: the name of the view to be created, and the SQL query that will provide the data for the view. The following code creates a new SQL view and shows how to open it in a browse window.

```
Close All
Clear All

Open Database WWS Exclusive

Create SQL View view_organization ;
  As Select * ;
  From organization ;
Order By organization_name
```

> **NOTE:** The latter part of this CREATE SQL VIEW statement utilizes the SQL SELECT command, which is discussed later in this chapter.

Using DROP TABLE

The DROP TABLE command removes a table from a database container. The syntax is as follows:

```
DROP TABLE tablename [NORECYCLE]
```

Specifying NORECYCLE physically deletes the table from disk, circumventing the Windows 95 (or Windows NT 4.0) Recycle Bin.

Using DROP VIEW

The DROP VIEW command removes a view from a database container. The syntax is simple:

```
DROP VIEW viewname
```

> **NOTE:** Where the DROP TABLE command has the optional keyword NORECYCLE, DROP VIEW has no keyword because views are maintained inside the DBC file.

Using the Data Manipulation Language

After creating your tables, you can begin adding, editing, and deleting the data found within your databases. You perform this with the DML subset of SQL commands. The DML allows you to create new records using the INSERT INTO command, edit records using the UPDATE command, delete records using the DELETE command, and query records using the SELECT command. This section describes the use of these commands within your applications.

Using INSERT INTO

You can use the INSERT INTO command to add new records to your database. The syntax is as follows:

```
INSERT INTO tablename (comma-delimited column list)
VALUES (comma-delimited value list)
```

The following code demonstrates adding data to the organization table found in the World Wide Shoes example:

```
Close All
Clear All

Use organization

Insert Into organization (org_id, organization_name, ;
organization_zip) ;
   Values (1, "Microsoft Corporation", "99999")

Insert Into organization (org_id, organization_name, ;
organization_zip) ;
   Values (2, "Computer Associates", "99999")

Insert Into organization (org_id, organization_name, ;
organization_zip) ;
   Values (3, "Borland International","99999")
```

The INSERT INTO command also provides two alternative methods of adding records to a database. These are the ability to insert the contents of an array using the FROM ARRAY keyword, and the ability to insert data into a table using the FROM MEMVAR keyword. These keywords insert data into your table, substituting variables found in memory into columns with similar names.

> **TIP:** One of the easiest ways to optimize your VFP applications is to convert all APPEND BLANK/GATHER MEMVAR commands to their respective INSERT INTO commands. This is because whenever you add a blank record with the APPEND BLANK command, then GATHER the data, VFP performs two updates of the indexes attached to the table. The INSERT INTO command performs this operation only once.

Using SQL UPDATE

The DML is also responsible for updating data, which is done using the SQL UPDATE command. This command is divided into two sections. The first section consists of the table and columns within the table to update. The second section is a filter that specifies the set of records on which the update will be performed. The following command, for example, updates all the records where organization_state equals "WA" by converting the value of organization_name to uppercase.

```
Close All
Clear All

Use organization

Update organization ;
   Set organization_name = Upper(organization_name) ;
   Where organization_state = "WA"
```

Note that the WHERE keyword can be used to filter records. (The WHERE keyword is explained later in this chapter, in the "Using SQL SELECT" section.)

The SQL UPDATE command is limited to updating data in a single table. You cannot update records using a join condition. A *join condition* is defined as a relationship between two tables commonly using a primary and a foreign key. There is a trick, however, that will allow you to update data based on values in another table—you can do so with the SEEK() function. The following code changes the company column to uppercase for each record where the customer has at least one order:

```
Update customer ;
   Set company = Upper(company) ;
   Where Seek(customer.cust_id,"orders","cust_ID")
```

This statement updates all customers with at least one order. What if you want to add more conditions to the *join* you are performing? You can do this by using the SEEK() function in conjunction with the IIF() function. The following code shows how to update information in the customer table using information from the orders table:

```
Update customer ;
  Set company =  ALLTRIM(company ) + "***" ;
  Where Iif(Seek(customer.cust_id,"orders","cust_ID"), ;
  orders.order_net > 1000,.f.)
```

This works because VFP evaluates the IIF() and SEEK() functions as a single unit.

Using SQL DELETE

Another function of the DML is the ability to delete records from tables. The SQL DELETE command is very similar to the SQL UPDATE command, with the exception that the only set of information specified in SQL DELETE consists of a table and an optional filter of records to be deleted. The following command deletes the set of records in the organization table for which the organization_state value equals "WA":

```
Use organization

Delete From organization ;
  Where organization_state = "WA"
```

NOTE: The SQL DELETE command behaves exactly like VFP's procedural DELETE command. It does not physically delete records, but instead marks them for deletion. A PACK command must be performed to physically remove the records.

WARNING: The SQL DELETE command is limited to deleting data in a single table. With it, you cannot update records based on related data. You can, however, use the same techniques that were described for the SQL UPDATE command in the preceding section.

Using SQL SELECT

One of the most powerful features of Visual FoxPro and SQL is the SQL SELECT command. This command is used to query data from database tables, and is very useful for the creation of both simple and complex reports.

The SQL SELECT statement has two distinct components. The first is the creation of a set of records. The second is a set of actions that can be performed on the set of records created by the first part of the statement. The remainder of this chapter is dedicated to a look at how to use the SQL SELECT statement in your applications.

Creating a Set of Records

The first step in using the SQL SELECT statement is to create a set of records for the query. The simplest set you can create is to select all rows from a single table. The following code selects all records from the organization table:

```
Select * ;
  From organization
```

The FROM keyword specifies the table from which information will be extracted. In most queries, you'll want to limit the number of columns returned from the query. The following code extracts the org_id and organization_name columns from the organization table:

```
Select org_id, organization_name ;
  From organization
```

Another feature of the SQL SELECT statement is its ability to combine multiple columns into a single column presented in the query. The following code combines the organization_city, organization_state, and organization_zip columns into a single column:

```
Select organization_city + "," + organization_state ;
    + " " + organization_zip ;
  From organization
```

Keep in mind, however, that VFP creates a name automatically for the combined column expression. In the preceding query, VFP returns exp_1 as the column name. This has two disadvantages: first, exp_1 is not a very descriptive column name, and second, the name created is not always predictable. To account for this, the AS keyword allows you to specify the name of the created column. The following code alters the preceding query to specify the name full_address for the combined column:

```
Select organization_city + "," + organization_state ;
    + " " + organization_zip As full_address ;
  From organization
```

So far, you've always selected all the records from the organization table for addition to your query. In practical applications, though, you usually don't want all records to show up in your queries. The WHERE keyword allows you to filter the set of records presented by a query. The following code returns only those records from the organization table in which the value of organization_state equals "WA":

```
Select * ;
  From organization ;
  Where organization_state = "WA"
```

The WHERE clause supports valid Boolean directives such as AND and OR in its syntax. The following code, for example, returns all records in which the value of organization_state equals "WA" or "CA":

```
Select * ;
  From organization ;
  Where organization_state = "WA" ;
    Or organization_state = "CA"
```

The WHERE clause is also used to perform the operation of creating relationships between tables using a *join*. In order to create a join condition you need to specify two (or more) tables in the FROM clause of your SELECT statement. After you have specified the tables, you need to specify an expression in the WHERE command that instructs the VFP query engine how to join the tables. This expression evaluates the columns that are common among the tables. The following code, for example, links the organization and contact tables:

```
Select organization_name, last_name, first_name ;
```

> **WARNING:** It's very important to specify a join condition in your WHERE clause whenever you specify two or more tables in the FROM clause. If you don't, then VFP creates a set of records known as a *Cartesian product*. Essentially, VFP matches every record in the first table with every record in the second table. For example, if you have 1,000 records in each table, then your result set holds 1,000,000 records. Be careful.

> **NOTE:** Visual FoxPro 5.0 provides the ability to select the TOP *n* or TOP *n* PERCENT of a certain set of records. This is useful for constructing queries to get, let's say, the top 15 sales people for a month, or the top 10% of your customers.

```
From organization, contact ;
Where organization.org_id = contact.org_id
```

The preceding query presents all records from the organization table that have matching records in the contact table. What happens, however, when an organization has no contact records? More often than not, you'll still want to list it. Fortunately, VFP 5.0 now supports the OUTER JOIN keyword.

How to Perform an Outer Join

One thing that you'll quickly notice is that when you join two or more tables, the set returned is limited to the set of records that exist in each table linked by the WHERE clause. This is fine for queries where you only want records that exist in both tables. It doesn't work, however, if you need records from one side of the join that do not exist in the other side of the join. For instance, what if you want to select all customers and the number of orders for each customer? You can use the following SELECT statement:

```
Select customer.cust_id, customer.company, customer.contact, ;
orders.order_id
   From customer, orders ;
```

```
Where customer.cust_id = orders.cust_id ;
Into Cursor c_orders
```

This query is fine for customers who have orders, but fails to pick up customers who have no orders. This is where an *outer join* is useful. In VFP 3.0 you could perform an outer join using a UNION query and a sub-select—the following code shows how this was done:

```
Close All
Clear All
Use customer In 0
Use orders In 0

Select customer.cust_id, customer.company, customer.contact, ;
orders.order_id ;
  From customer, orders ;
  Where customer.cust_id = orders.cust_id ;
  Union All ;
Select customer.cust_id, customer.company, customer.contact, ;
Space(6) as order_id ;
  From customer ;
  Where customer.cust_id Not In (Select Distinct cust_id From orders) ;
  Into Cursor c_orders
```

As you can tell, this created some very large, unwieldy code to maintain. That is why VFP 5.0 has added the OUTER JOIN keyword to the SQL SELECT command. Now, if you want to create an outer join, you can use the following syntax:

```
Select customer.cust_id, customer.company, orders.order_id ;
  From customer Left Outer Join orders ;
  On customer.cust_id = orders.cust_id ;
Into Cursor c_temp
```

The first thing to notice about this new syntax is the keyword string LEFT OUTER JOIN ON added to the FROM section of the SQL SELECT statement. The valid syntax for using OUTER JOIN is as follows:

```
FROM table1 INNER|LEFT|RIGHT OUTER JOIN table2 ON
table1.keyfield = table2.keyfield
```

Notice that you choose between two types of outer joins: RIGHT and LEFT. Using LEFT OUTER JOIN selects all records from *table1*, and returns the contents of the joined records. If a record in *table1* has no match in *table2*, then null values are returned in place of the columns selected from *table2*.

Using RIGHT OUTER JOIN has the opposite effect. All records from the right-hand portion of the join expression (*table2*) are returned, and null values are returned from *table1* wherever the join condition fails.

Using INNER allows you to perform *self joins*. Self joins are useful when you want to use two different rows in the same table as criteria for a search. An example is if you want to select all customers who have ordered blue and green shoes. You use the INNER keyword to find this information.

Omitting the LEFT and RIGHT keywords makes VFP use its normal join behavior, which is to leave out non-matching records.

How to Perform a Sub-Select

One of the lesser known abilities of Visual FoxPro is its ability to use *sub-selects* in the SQL SELECT statement. The normal way to select data from two tables is to use a join condition in the WHERE clause. What if you don't care about a join condition, though, and simply want to do a lookup in another table? In this case, you can use a sub-select. The outer join example shown in the preceding section contains a sub-select statement, and the following code demonstrates using a sub-select to select all orders where the customer lives in Washington:

```
Select order_id, order_date ;
  From orders ;
  Where cust_id IN (Select cust_id From customer Where
  customer.region = "WA")
```

Notice that this query does not use a join condition, but instead uses two distinct queries to accomplish the required selection.

Optimizing Your SQL SELECT Commands

No discussion of SQL would be complete without a discussion of optimization. Visual FoxPro now provides two new methods of optimizing queries. The first is the Sys(3054) function. The second is the FORCE keyword that can be used in the FROM clause. The FORCE keyword allows you to tell VFP to process the joins in your FROM clause in order. Using this keyword removes any decision-making from the SQL optimizer, relying instead on your knowledge of your tables. This keyword has limited usefulness, as the optimizer generally does a good job. To better understand how the optimizer really works, you need to explore the Sys(3054) function in detail.

Using Sys(3054)

Visual FoxPro 5.0 includes a new function, Sys(3054), that you can use to optimize your SQL SELECT commands. The Sys(3054) function has a single parameter. Passing 1 to Sys(3054) turns on the SQL SELECT analyzer, and passing 0 turns off the analyzer.

The Sys(3054) function returns the level of optimization that VFP uses when it is processing a query. The value returned is one of the following: None, Partial, or Full. Take a look at the following SQL SELECT commands with the analyzer on:

```
Close All
Clear All

Use Customer Exclusive
Delete Tag region
Delete Tag deleted
Clear

Erase txt3054
Set Alternate To TXT3054.txt
Set Alternate On
? Sys(3054)

? "NONE"
*— No optimization here
Select * ;
   From customer

Select * ;
```

```
From customer ;
Where customer.region = "WA"
```

The analyzer returns the following:

Rushmore optimization level for table customer: none

Rushmore optimization level for table customer: none

The analyzer can only partially optimize due to the lack of any optimizable indexes being present. The next set of SELECT statements is partially optimizable thanks to the creation of a region tag and the existence of a tag on the cust_id field:

```
*- Partial optimization here
? "PARTIAL"
Select customer
Index On Region Tag Region

Select * ;
  From customer ;
  Where customer.region = "WA"

Select * ;
  From customer ;
  Where Cust_id = "ANTON"
```

The analyzer returns the following:

Using index tag Region to rushmore optimize table customer

Rushmore optimization level for table customer: partial

Using index tag Cust_id to rushmore optimize table customer

Rushmore optimization level for table customer: partial

Now that the table has an index tag on region and cust_id, the analyzer begins using those tags. As you can see, the analyzer mentions which tags are being used to optimize. You might wonder, however, why these SELECT statements did not receive full optimization. The reason is that SET DELETED is ON.

This means that the SELECT statements need to process the results in order to remove deleted records. Adding a tag on DELETED() fully optimizes the SELECT statements, as shown below:

```
*- Full optimization here
? "FULL"
Select Customer
Index On Deleted() Tag Deleted

Select * ;
   From customer ;
   Where customer.region = "WA"

Select * ;
   From Customer ;
   Where Cust_id = "ANTON"
```

The analyzer returns the following:

> Using index tag Region to rushmore optimize table customer
>
> Using index tag Deleted to rushmore optimize table customer
>
> Rushmore optimization level for table customer: full
>
> Using index tag Cust_id to rushmore optimize table customer
>
> Using index tag Deleted to rushmore optimize table customer
>
> Rushmore optimization level for table customer: full

Now that the tag on DELETED() has been added, the analyzer can fully utilize the tags on the customer table, providing the best performance possible. You should strive to achieve full optimization of your queries whenever possible.

The last option to look at involves optimizing join conditions. If you call the Sys(3054) function using 11 as the parameter, VFP shows you optimization information for your join conditions:

```
? "JOIN"
Sys(3054,11)
```

```
Select * ;
  From Customer, Orders ;
  Where customer.cust_id = orders.order_id
```

The analyzer returns the following:

> Sql Showplan is enabled with join optimization
>
> Using index tag Deleted to rushmore optimize table customer
>
> Rushmore optimization level for table customer: full
>
> Rushmore optimization level for table orders: none
>
> Joining table customer and table orders using index tag Order_id

Processing a Set of Records

The previous sections demonstrated the syntax for creating sets of records. This section concentrates on what you can do with a set of records once it has been created.

The first possibility is to sort the records. The SQL SELECT command allows you to specify a sorting order for your set of data by using the ORDER BY clause. The following code selects the organization_name and organization_city columns from the organization table, and sorts them by the organization_name column:

```
Select organization_name, organization_city ;
  From organization ;
Order By organization_name
```

You also can specify whether the column is sorted in ascending or descending order. The default behavior is to sort records in ascending order. The following code demonstrates selecting the organization_name and organization_city columns from the organization table, and sorting them by both organization_city and organization_name, with organization_city in descending order:

```
Select organization_name, organization_city ;
  From organization ;
```

```
Order By organization_city Desc, organization_name
```

Along with the ability to sort records, you can group records using the GROUP BY keyword. The following code demonstrates grouping records by state, and presenting a count of the records for each state:

```
Select organization_state, Sum(1) as state_count ;
  From organization ;
Group By organization_state
```

If you want to filter your query further using the results of a GROUP BY statement, you can use the HAVING keyword. The following code shows selecting all states with more than 10 organizations:

```
Select organization_state, Sum(1) as state_count ;
  From organization ;
Group By organization_state ;
  Having state_count > 10
```

After you finish your query, you can send its output to a number of external data sources. With the INTO command, you have the choice of sending your data to any of the following types of external data sources:

- A data table
- An array
- A read-only cursor

NOTE: *Cursors* are temporary tables created by Visual FoxPro that are erased upon being closed. They generally are not updatable when created by a SQL SELECT command. Cursors created using the CREATE CURSOR command, on the other hand, may be edited.

Summary

As you can see, it's possible to use SQL commands to create simple queries that accomplish the same results that might require dozens (or even hundreds) of lines of code without the use of SQL commands. Using SQL in your applications can provide some great functionality without the need for extensive lines of code.

This chapter has served as a primer so that you can begin using SQL in your applications immediately. Certain other chapters in this book offer more detail about implementing queries and data table definitions in your applications. You might want to take a look at the following chapters:

- Chapter 10, "Creating a Visual FoxPro Database," discusses the creation of databases, including normalization techniques, validation rules, and other database concepts.
- Chapter 12, "Client/Server Database Development with Visual FoxPro," offers information on using VFP in the client/server world, which relies heavily on SQL to perform its tasks.

PART IV

Application Deployment

Chapter 12

**Client/Server Database
Development with
Visual FoxPro**

Introduction

Over the past few years, no doubt you have seen the rapid growth of client/server database development. Client/server databases descended from mainframe and minicomputer databases in the 1980s, but in the 1990s have also made their stamp on the PC world. Many of the new features in Visual FoxPro are a direct response to the impact of these relational databases.

The subject of client/server database development is huge and complex. You have to deal with two additional factors in your development: the backend database (normally not VFP) and the ODBC translation layer between your application and the server database. These additional factors can more than triple the complexity of your development, because you not only have to learn new database commands, but also have to deal with the complexity of new interfaces and their interactions with your application.

No single chapter, book, or even set of books can tell you everything you need to know to develop a client/server application using Visual FoxPro. The truth is, while these books often describe problems that other people have solved, in real life you're likely to hit things from time to time that no one else has solved. There is so much complexity that certain combinations of factors might be unique for your situation.

This chapter will give you an in-depth view of client/server database development, and show you how to use VFP as a client/server front end. It will get you started, but there is no substitute for your own experience. Along the way, you will deal with a series of questions:

- What does client/server database development look like from a VFP standpoint?
- What is the basis for deciding whether to go client/server with VFP, or stay file-server?
- What sorts of things must you face when dealing with a server back end?
- How does VFP programming fit into the client/server scene?
- How do VFP applications compete with non-VFP client/server applications?
- How can your VFP applications work with client/server databases?

This chapter builds on your knowledge of VFP's SQL implementation (see Chapter 11, "Using SQL in Visual FoxPro Applications") and the VFP database engine (see Chapter 10, "Creating a Visual FoxPro Database"). It also assumes that you are familiar with the material covered in Part 6, "Creating Client/Server Solutions," of the VFP *Developer's Guide*.

Client/Server from a VFP Viewpoint

Client/server database development is different from standard VFP application development. In this section, you will see what those differences are, and how VFP can fit into a client/server application; you will also get some pointers on how VFP applications can compete with rival client/server apps.

As you know, the client/server database development trend brought a slew of new buzzwords and terms to database development. One challenge is to make sense out of client/server itself. One way to do this is to see how it fits into database development.

Three Types of Database Applications

The term *client/server* implies a division of function between two components, a client and a server. You have seen the term applied to more than just database development.

For example, client/server applies to OLE: an OLE client application makes calls through the OLE interface to an OLE server (see Chapter 6, "Communicating with other Applications Using OLE"). The upshot is that there are two distinct software processes involved. You also might see the term applied to DDE, as well as XWindows (where the meaning shifts slightly).

Just as in the above examples, client/server database applications imply a division of function between two distinct applications, a client application and a server application. The client application usually resides on a user's computer, and the server application usually resides on a LAN server or special database server PC.

As a rule, when you share data in an enterprise, you put the shared database on a sharable PC or database server, not on users' PCs. On the users' PCs, you put a software application that can communicate with the database. Given this hardware division, it's easy to classify database applications.

In the 1970s, it was common to put all the database processing on the server mainframe or minicomputer, and none on the users' computers or terminals. We will call this a *host-based* database application architecture.

In the early 1980s, desktop PC databases put all the database processing on the users' PCs and stored the data on the LAN server. We will call this a *file-server* application.

In the early 1990s, when PCs and PC-based LANs became more powerful, it became possible to divide the processing between any given user's PC and the LAN database. This was the origin of *client/server* databases.

In this section, you will see how these kinds of database architectures work, and how VFP fits into the picture.

Host-Based Databases

Host-based applications place all the database processing in the host computer. Users run the application by connecting to a host from a "dumb" terminal or a PC acting as a terminal. When you see people running a mainframe or mini or UNIX application from a terminal, or from a PC emulating a terminal, they are running a host-based application. IBM's DB2 was one of the first host-based databases.

In a host-based application, all temporary data handling and all data validation are handled by the host database. The host database consists of the data store on the host machine, as well as a constantly running process on the host computer. This process is often called a *service*, because it handles requests for data, and feeds the data out to a calling application.

What is important is that the host computer does all the database processing. In mainframes, the actual database application may reside on controllers separate from the mainframe computer. If so, the mainframe database returns data to the controller, and the application on the controller actually shows the results to the user.

The user of a host-based application simply passes character strings to and from the host. Therefore, you can often run a host-based application using a simple ("dumb") terminal, or you can run it on any PC that emulates a terminal. Nevertheless, no matter how much CPU power you may have in your local computer, the database processing still takes place on the host computer.

Although many host-based systems in recent years have been downsized to client/server or file-server systems, a large number of them still—and will—remain in existence. There are some applications, such as airline reservation systems, that remain ideal host-based applications. New development of host-based systems is flat, however, mirroring the flatness in mainframe and minicomputer sales.

File-Server Databases

File-server applications place the database processing on the user's computer, but access shared data from a shared spot on a LAN server. All the desktop databases originated with this architecture. You can call VFP, dBASE, Access, and Paradox all file-server databases, because there is no database processing on the LAN server PC that stores the data.

Visual FoxPro is natively a file-server database. If you put your application on a user's PC, all the user has to do is load and run it. If the user has rights to the data subdirectory on the LAN, then the user can access the data. You might have the user load the application from the LAN, but then the entire VFP database engine will have to transfer down to the user's PC to execute. There is no instance of the VFP database engine running on the LAN PC.

In a file-server application, then, the shared database on the server is essentially just a set of files. You read and write to them directly, with no other intervention. Also, you typically must do administrative maintenance of the data (such as reindexing and packing) from a user's PC.

It's important to note that Microsoft's Jet database engine is also a file-server database. There are a number of separate DLLs that contain the Jet database engine, but they normally reside on the user's PC and definitely must execute on the user's PC. The Jet engine does not execute as a separate process just for the database.

Client/Server Databases

At this point, it's easy to define a client/server database. Client/server database applications separate the database processing into client (user) and server components. Client/server databases combine the best of both host-based and file-server databases.

From host-based computing, client/server databases borrow the idea of having a software process (a service) running on the server machine to maintain and protect the database. If that server is not running, the database cannot be accessed. This is the server application, which preserves the database rules.

From file-server databases, client/server databases take the idea of running an application with some database processing capability on the user's computer. This is the client application, which preserves business rules by validating data entry in any forms your database applications use.

The combination of the two allows you to balance processing power between the client and the server, to achieve maximum performance or other goals.

A new development in client/server database applications is the so-called *third-tier system*, where a middle-tier process runs on the server PC, separate from the database server, and encapsulates the business rules. Then the client software does not have to contain business rules. Three-tier technology, however, is not nearly as widespread as the standard two-tier technology, and so far is not proving any simpler.

The big players in the client/server database world are Oracle, Sybase SQL Server, Informix, and Microsoft SQL Server. Some lesser known databases are CA-Open Ingres, Centura, and Borland Interbase. They are often called *SQL databases* because their primary programming and maintenance language is SQL.

It is possible for you to put both the server and client components on a single computer, but that's a peculiar thing to do. If you put the client application on the server, you use up resources on your database server.

If you do not need to share the data, however, you can move the server part of a client/server application to the user's PC. You can do this in a couple of ways.

Many developers choose to run Windows NT on their development machines and then install the same database software that would normally reside on a dedicated database server. If you do this, you can develop an application in stand-alone mode that ultimately will become a shared application. If you corrupt the database or crash the database software, you only do it to your own machine.

Also, though, you might want to put a SQL database on the user's PC to manage local data. Both Oracle and Sybase make database server products that are meant to reside on a single user's PC or a small LAN. Oracle's Personal Oracle and Sybase's SQL Anywhere both can run under Windows 95 on a single PC. SQL Anywhere can serve as a department-level database.

We'll refer to these as *desktop server databases*, to distinguish them from backend server databases.

As you might expect, client/server applications come in a wide variety of flavors, mostly differing in how you balance the database processing between the client and the server. Some applications place all the processing on the server end, making them almost host-based applications. The client normally still processes forms and validates data entry, so they're not true host-based applications.

On the other hand, some applications make the validation of data and security on the server very weak, move almost all the database processing local, and have something very close to a file-server application. Nevertheless, no matter how weak the validation and security of the server database is, there's still a separate database process running on the server, so these are not true file-server applications.

Client/Server Advantages and Disadvantages

As you plan a new application, or revise an existing one, you may have to decide whether to design its architecture for client/server or file-server. This section discusses the factors you need to consider when making that decision.

Client/server architecture has gotten a lot of attention recently, because it can have some inherent advantages over the other two architectures. Because client/server divides the processing load between the server and client, it can increase performance and security, though it requires more maintenance. It has become one of the preferred ways to downsize aging mainframe applications.

Performance

Client/server network traffic can be less than file-server application traffic in situations where the user needs only a portion of data. The server database can execute a query and just send the results down the wire to the PC.

Revenge of the Host-Based Systems: The Internet

A lot of recent database development has occurred on the Internet, and especially the World Wide Web. There is an interesting parallel between host-based systems and the Web.

Most Web database development puts both a database and an HTML generator application on the Web server. When requests for data arrive, the server formats the results into an HTML text string to send back to the requester. You can see the similarity to a terminal/host system, which also sends text back and forth.

It's probably better to view Web databases as a form of client/server architecture, because the browsers require a fair amount of brainpower in order to paint the screens with graphics based on HTML text commands. In addition, it takes a local CPU to execute Java applets, ActiveX controls, or plug-ins.

For more information about using VFP for Web development, see Chapter 13, "Deploying Visual FoxPro Internet Applications."

This does not always work, however. If there are many queries—or the queries are complex—the server can get bogged down in them. In addition, server databases can get out of tune, and then performance can degrade until the database administrator tunes them again.

Security

Client/server applications can be more secure than file-server ones, and can have the same level of security as host-based systems. Because there is an actual server database program running, through which all applications must go to access data, client/server imposes security beyond just LAN security.

If the database server software is running, then even users who have read/write access to the application's LAN subdirectory cannot see, edit, or delete the data. They must log into the database first, either through the client application or some other database access method.

In a file-server application, however, the only security available is that enforced by the LAN administrator. If users have read/write access to the application's LAN subdirectory, then they can damage data without even running the application.

Maintenance

Client/server databases require fairly constant attention from a database administrator to ensure that their performance is optimized, and often that they don't run out of space. For example, with many databases, the database administrator must allocate space on the LAN server for the data. The database will essentially freeze if that space is filled up, even if there's lots of space left on the LAN drive.

Making the Client/Server Decision

So, should you choose client/server or file-server? The answer, as usual, is, "It depends."

From the security angle, client/server databases clearly can protect their data better than file-server systems. Of course, a database administrator must maintain the database security, and the customer must bear that additional cost.

There are other areas, however, where client/server is not apparently better than file-server applications.

For instance, some trade journals and industry watchers note that there are a very large number of failed client/server projects. They can be costly and still fail to deliver the promised performance.

Many more things have to go right with a client/server application for it to be considered successful. As a rule, client/server applications are more expensive to build than file-server applications. The advice of performance experts is needed throughout the design and implementation process, and the development tools can be very expensive.

Often there's no gain—and sometimes there's some loss—in client/server performance compared to file-server applications. LANs are getting faster, so a reduction in network traffic is becoming less important. In addition, file-server database engines such as Visual FoxPro can have very fast data seek times.

Sometimes one query runs faster on a client/server system than a file-server system, but with just a few parameters changed, the client/server query runs slower. Some industry observers claim that decision-support systems generally run faster on a file-server system.

Finally, client/server applications are more expensive to maintain than file-server applications, because you must more-or-less constantly tune the server database. File-server applications usually just need to be reindexed regularly to keep their performance tuned.

The bottom line is that if your application needs additional security, the customer can afford additional maintenance costs, and some potential losses in performance can be tolerated, then client/server is a good bet. But if your application doesn't meet these conditions, you should be cautious about committing to client/server.

The World of SQL Databases

In this section, the differences between Visual FoxPro and SQL databases will be examined from a VFP programmer's point of view. The discussion will refer to backend databases for the most part, and will take specific examples from Microsoft SQL Server.

General Differences

In Chapter 10, "Creating a Visual FoxPro Database," you saw how Visual FoxPro lets you store your data in a mostly relational format using the database container, in which you can put stored procedures and triggers. In addition, Visual FoxPro also gives you a new set of data types in VFP-format DBF tables. Both of these changes, along with enhancements to VFP's SQL language, bring VFP more into line with backend server databases.

Nevertheless, there are a great number of differences between VFP and backend server databases.

The Database Wall

The most immediate and profound difference between backend server databases and Visual FoxPro is the wall that backend servers put up between the programmer and the database. This wall makes contact with data in VFP seem immediate by comparison. In backend SQL databases, you must use server utilities and SQL commands to manage tables and databases. All maintenance and management tasks proceed via special utilities or SQL statements in the server's dialect; there's no command window in which to issue commands to manage data.

Many of the FoxPro data manipulation commands you probably take for granted are not available in backend servers. For example, in neither Sybase nor Microsoft SQL Server is there an equivalent to `Modify Structure`. Removing or rearranging a table column in those databases requires backing up and recreating the table in the new format.

In addition, server databases have special utilities (called `transfer` and `bulk copy`) to export and import data. These backend databases lack `Copy To` and `Append From` commands. As a final example, there is no online equivalent in backend SQL server databases to a `Browse`. You must issue a SQL `Select` command to see results.

Consequently, when you migrate to client/server you have to learn new administrative utilities, plus the SQL dialect of the database, just to manage the data. These things have the effect of increasing distance between the programmer and the data, while in VFP the contact is more immediate.

Fortunately, these server databases do have query utilities, where you can issue SQL commands and see results. This way you can test a command before putting it in a program, somewhat similar to what you would do in VFP using the command window.

Security

The same wall that backend SQL databases erect to distance the programmer from data makes it possible for the server to require permission to access, maintain, and manage tables and databases. Visual FoxPro DBFs and even database containers have, by comparison, little or no security.

Security procedures in VFP can easily become complex, and management can be time-consuming. By comparison, backend database security is well-tested and robust. For example, restricting users to certain subsets of data, something quite complex in VFP, is relatively straightforward in many backend server databases.

Installation

Visual FoxPro makes a number of assumptions for you at installation that back-end server databases do not. These server databases often require you to specify sort order, case sensitivity, and character set choices upon installation. These choices have far-reaching implications and must be carefully considered up-front. With Microsoft SQL Server, once you install a database, you cannot reverse these choices, and you cannot transfer a database from one format to another.

Surprisingly for Visual FoxPro developers, the backend server databases often require explicit device choices and allocations of disk space for each database. Their databases are not separate files, so they cannot dynamically expand as needed, something we take for granted in VFP.

Interface Differences

Any time you change your development platform, you have to face differences in programming techniques. Here are some of the differences between Visual Fox-Pro and SQL databases.

Character Data Storage

You can find most of the VFP data types in Microsoft SQL Server, and this makes data translation relatively easy.

One important difference, however, is with the varchar datatype. When you store character data in VFP, unless it's in a memo field, you always specify the exact length the character string will have in the DBF table. That's because the DBF stores data in a fixed-length format. SQL databases, as well as Jet databases, do not store data in fixed-length format, so they also allow variable character strings. The varchar data type is a variable length string, and only the maximum length is specified in the structure of a table.

In VFP, an empty string of length 12 characters is stored in a table as 12 blanks or a null. With a varchar data type, a truly empty string—one that does not contain any blanks—can be stored in the data table.

Variables

Variable usage in backend server databases might look odd to a VFP programmer. In both Sybase and Microsoft SQL Server, global variables are always preceded by @, and local variables are preceded by @@.

Database Storage Differences

Backend SQL databases give administrators a lot more control over how data is stored and accessed than does Visual FoxPro. Microsoft SQL Server, for example, stores its data in *allocation units*, each of which contains segments that are broken down into 2K pages. No table's row can exceed the size of a 2K page less some administrative bytes, making the maximum row size 1962 bytes! It does contain equivalents of a memo text data type (named Text) and the memo/general data type (named Image), and these are not part of the 1962-byte limit.

SQL Server administrators can experiment with data distribution by fine-tuning the distribution of data across pages and segments.

Meta-Data

All information about the data in a backend server database is stored in system tables in that database. A SQL database developer must become used to accessing those tables in order to know how the data is structured.

Indexes

Backend SQL database indexes work somewhat differently from Visual FoxPro's indexes. Because the former have no navigational commands, there are no Seek commands. Also, you may find that the backend server indexes cannot proceed in reverse order, and cannot contain expressions. Finally, unlike FoxPro, Microsoft SQL Server is limited to one index per table per query (unless there's an OR in the WHERE clause).

To force data to be stored in a particular order, Microsoft SQL Server requires the use of a special type of index called a *clustered index*. There is no corresponding feature in VFP; you usually can observe a physical order of records just by making all indexes inactive.

Differences in Database Implementations

There are several differences between VFP and backend SQL database implementations, including triggers and stored procedures, transactions and savepoints, and locking.

Triggers and Stored Procedures

You will find yourself at home with the concept of SQL default values and triggers if you have dealt with the Visual FoxPro database container. Even here, however, there are differences. In VFP, you edit a trigger or stored procedure using the VFP integrated development environment. Backend SQL databases often do not come with a development environment, so editing stored procedures and triggers is not as easy. Also, you are restricted to the backend database's SQL dialect in stored procedures and triggers.

Transactions and Savepoints

Transaction processing in backend SQL databases is more complex and flexible than in Visual FoxPro. In Visual FoxPro, for example, a transaction must be rolled back in its entirety, whereas in Microsoft SQL Server, you can roll back to a *savepoint*. A savepoint is a marker in the transaction process that you can name, and then later roll back to if something fails.

Locking

Locking capabilities vary widely in backend SQL databases. In keeping with Microsoft SQL Server's storage methods, its locking is by 2K pages, not by row (except under special conditions, where some inserts will lock just a row). Whenever a lock occurs, all the rows on that page are locked, no matter how many rows are part of the page. In addition, locking is accomplished quite differently: in order to write to a row, it must be locked exclusively, unlike in Visual FoxPro, where a record lock for writing does not prevent others from reading it.

NOTE: Oracle does provide true row locking, so not all backend SQL databases have this limitation.

For more information about locking in VFP, see Chapter 8, "Multi-User Development Techniques."

Optimization Differences: Performance and Tuning

In SQL Server, there is much more control over optimization than in Visual FoxPro. "Rushmore" optimization is essentially done automatically by the FoxPro engine, and is out of the hands of—and invisible to—the programmer.

SQL databases often reveal the exact plan for executing any given query. If the programmer does not like the plan, there are ways to override it and try other methods for better performance. VFP, on the other hand, hides its implementation of queries and its methods of optimization from the programmer. SQL databases need these optimization techniques because the upper limit on their size is in the hundreds of gigabytes. VFP, by contrast, is limited to 2 gigabytes per table.

Optimization in SQL databases is an administrative task that can be very exacting. Any site with a backend server database running must have someone available to tune and optimize it on a periodic basis. It's very difficult to leave a backend SQL database unattended.

Differences in SQL Syntax

As you have seen in prior chapters, you can use Visual FoxPro to handle data in a navigational way, or you can use its relational, set-oriented SQL commands. The ability to use either type of command as the need dictates makes VFP a very powerful tool.

SQL databases, which use SQL almost exclusively, do not have navigational commands. What they lack in that department, however, they make up for in extended SQL commands. All the backend server databases have more powerful implementations of SQL than VFP does.

Subqueries

VFP has a limit of one subquery in a Select command. SQL databases, however, have no theoretical limit on the number of subqueries. The following is legal in a full SQL implementation:

```
Select * from customer
```

```
Where cust_id In
  ( Select cust_id From Orders
    Where part_code In
      (Select part_code From Parts) )
```

In Visual FoxPro, this is not valid.

> **NOTE:** There are some important and subtle differences between SQL Server's implementation of SQL, and FoxPro's implementation. For example, listing an extra field in the `Select` clause can cause a `Group By` to fail in SQL Server, but not in FoxPro. On the whole, however, FoxPro programmers will find it easy adapting to SQL Server's SQL dialect.

Insert From

When you want to insert a group of rows into a table in VFP, you can use a command like this:

```
Use temp1
Append From temp2
```

In SQL databases, which do not use navigational commands, you use something like this instead:

```
Insert Into Temp2
  Select * From Temp1
```

This command would fail in VFP, because you cannot do an `Insert` from a table.

Update From

In Visual FoxPro, if you want to update an address from one table into another table, you have to use the navigational `Set Relation` command, as in the following:

```
Use Customer In 0 Order cust_id
Use Cust_temp In 0 Order cust_id
```

```
Select Customer
Set Relation to cust_id Into Customer_temp
Replace all customer.address with cust_temp.address
```

In Microsoft SQL Server, though, you can do this with one <u>Update</u> command:

```
Update Customer From Cust_temp
   Set customer.address = cust_temp.address
   Where customer.cust_id = cust_temp.address
```

Alter Table

Another example of the more powerful implementation of SQL on backend servers is the `Alter Table` command. In Visual FoxPro, if you want to add three new columns to the customer table, you must use three commands:

```
Alter Table customer Add Column temp1 C(10)
Alter Table customer Add Column temp2 C(10)
Alter Table customer Add Column temp3 C(10)
```

In Microsoft SQL Server, you can do this in one command:

```
Alter Table customer Add temp1 char(10) Null, temp2 char(10) Null,
temp3 char(10) Null
```

You need to be aware, however, that Microsoft SQL Server 6.5 can only add new columns that allow nulls.

How Visual FoxPro Accesses Remote Data

Visual FoxPro has a native access to DBF files, either to free tables or to tables registered with a database container. For connecting to data in other formats, VFP relies on the ODBC standard. When you use VFP to connect live to external data using ODBC, it's called *remote data*.

Microsoft built in two fundamental ways to connect to remote data. The easier, more developer-friendly way is with the *remote view*. This is a view that has a remote data source as its base table, rather than a local DBF. In addition, though, you can use a set of commands that expose much of the ODBC API, called *SQL pass-through commands* because with them you can send SQL strings to the host data source.

The tools in VFP that you use to access remote data can connect to backend SQL databases as well as file-server data.

In this section, you will see how to use remote views as well as SQL pass-through commands. You will see how to use them to contact both kinds of remote data sources. First, you need to understand how VFP uses ODBC.

How ODBC Works

ODBC stands for *Open Database Connectivity*. Originated by Microsoft, ODBC is a standard set of interface calls and data translation specifications for accessing disparate types of data. With it, an application that has one native data format can exchange data with an application that has a potentially different data format.

ODBC accomplishes this by presenting an interface to both sides. To permit ODBC access to a particular data format, a vendor writes an ODBC driver to be used by other applications. For example, Microsoft has written both the Jet ODBC driver and the Microsoft SQL Server driver. The Jet ODBC driver is automatically installed with Microsoft Office, and the Microsoft SQL Server driver is installed when you install Microsoft SQL Server.

Vendors write their ODBC drivers to a standard interface. In their drivers, they translate data between their native format and the ODBC format. In turn, your application calls the driver's functions and sends it data in the ODBC format. The driver translates between the two formats by using a third format, the ODBC data format.

ODBC may not store any data, but it is almost a database: it has data types and a standard SQL syntax. Your application, VFP, talks to the ODBC driver and sends it data in the ODBC format. Then the driver translates the data into a format that can be interpreted by the other data source.

In the case of file-server databases, the ODBC driver contains a good portion of the database engine. For example, both the VFP and Jet ODBC drivers are rather large, and they directly read and write to the data source in question.

> **NOTE:** You can spot the various ODBC drivers on your computer by inspecting the \System subdirectory of your Windows directory. Look for all DLL files beginning with odbc.

However, backend SQL database drivers just send appropriately formatted SQL statements to the database engine that's running on the database server. Then the actual database engine takes over and returns data to the driver.

The ODBC Interface

Managing ODBC on your PC can be rather confusing. You can bring up the ODBC Administrator program by finding its icon either in the Control Panel (usually listed as ODBC), or in its own ODBC group (with the title 32-bit ODBC Administrator). If you double-click the ODBC icon, you see a screen like the one shown in Figure 12-1.

In order to use ODBC, you have to identify which driver you want to use. When you first bring up the ODBC Administrator program, however, you see what it calls *data sources* rather than ODBC drivers. What is going on?

Well, the dialog box is presenting you with a set of pre-established data sources. A *data source name (DSN)* is a specific linkage of the ODBC driver with a particular database or server. Figure 12-2 contains a diagram of how DSNs work.

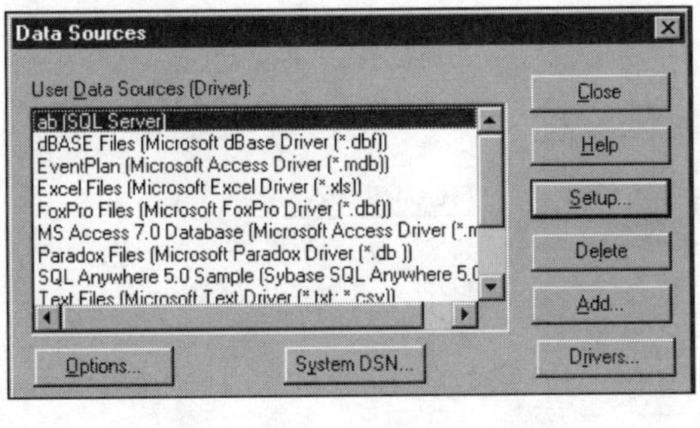

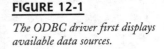

FIGURE 12-1

The ODBC driver first displays available data sources.

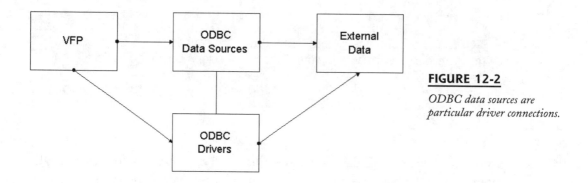

FIGURE 12-2

ODBC data sources are particular driver connections.

As you can see, VFP can use ODBC directly or through the data source name. What is confusing is that the ODBC Administrator dialog box puts you in contact with DSNs first, not the drivers.

This dialog box is actually rather complex. Take a look at the more important options.

Add

In order to make a new data source, you can click the <u>A</u>dd button. The resulting dialog box (see Figure 12-3) shows a list of all the ODBC drivers installed on your system, from which you must select one.

After you select a driver, the setup dialog box for that driver appears. These setup dialog boxes differ from each other somewhat. A file-server driver setup might ask only for a name, and let you choose a location or directory. A SQL database ODBC driver usually asks for a name and a server name. With some drivers, you also can specify a particular database.

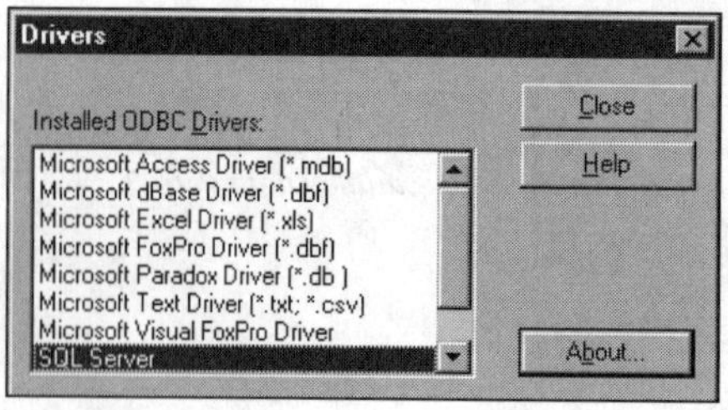

FIGURE 12-3

You have to drill down into the Data Sources dialog box to see the ODBC drivers.

> **TIP:** Be sure to specify a database name in the DSN if you can. If you do not, the user might have to choose one when connecting, or ODBC might default to the wrong one.

Setup

Setup here is equivalent to edit, and lets you change the various parameters for that data source name.

System DSN

If you click System DSN, you get another dialog box (see Figure 12-4), almost identical to the first one. Only the title seems different.

The functional difference is that under Windows NT, if you do not use a system DSN, the DSN you specify is available only to the currently logged-in user. A system DSN, however, is available to all users on that system.

Options

The Options dialog box lets you track ODBC calls in a log file. This can be helpful if you want to know exactly what commands your application is sending to the ODBC driver.

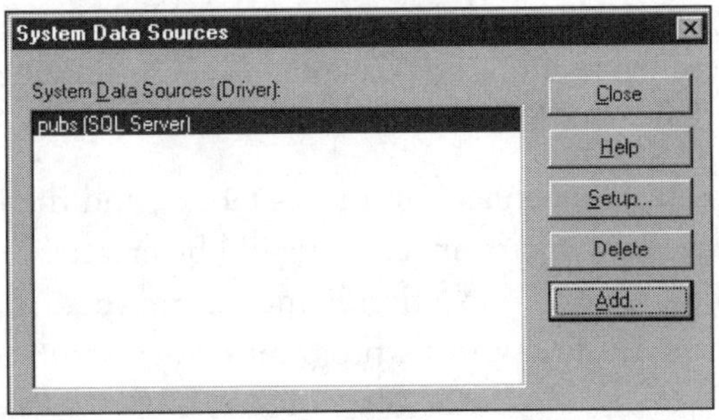

FIGURE 12-4

The System Data Sources dialog box is very similar to the initial dialog box.

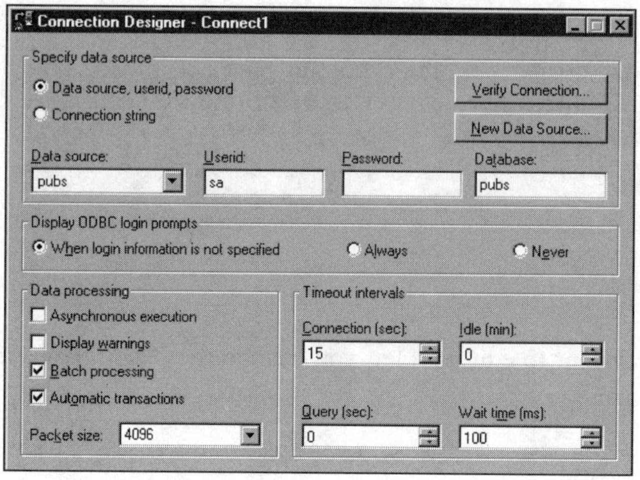

FIGURE 12-5

The VFP Connection Designer records ODBC parameters.

VFP Connections

In order to access any external data through ODBC, you must make a connection. Visual FoxPro allows you to store connections permanently in a database, or create them on the fly using the SQL pass-through commands.

When you create a connection in a database, VFP asks you for certain parameters, as shown in Figure 12-5.

Here you see that you can specify an existing DSN. VFP reads the available ODBC DSNs and gives them to you in a list, if you have the Data Source option button selected. If you select the SQL connection string option, then you have to fill in the string exactly as you want it.

The other options on the dialog box allow you to set various parameters affecting the connection. Normally, you can just use the defaults provided by VFP. For more information about these parameters, see Chapter 22, "Optimizing Client/Server Performance," in the VFP *Developer's Guide*.

An interesting exercise is to create a connection in a database, and then use VFP's gendbc program to see how the connection would be created programmatically. For example, if you create a connection named Connect1 in the wwshoes database, the gendbc utility writes a program named wwshoes.prg with the following code:

> **TIP:** Be sure to specify a database name in the connection dialog box. If you don't, then ODBC may default to the wrong one.

```
CREATE CONNECTION CONNECT1 ;
    DATASOURCE "Pubs" ;
    USERID "" ;
    PASSWORD ""

****
=DBSetProp('CONNECT1', 'Connection', 'Asynchronous', .F.)
=DBSetProp('CONNECT1', 'Connection', 'BatchMode', .T.)
=DBSetProp('CONNECT1', 'Connection', 'Comment', '')
=DBSetProp('CONNECT1', 'Connection', 'DispLogin', 1)
=DBSetProp('CONNECT1', 'Connection', 'ConnectTimeOut', 15)
=DBSetProp('CONNECT1', 'Connection', 'DispWarnings', .F.)
=DBSetProp('CONNECT1', 'Connection', 'IdleTimeOut', 0)
=DBSetProp('CONNECT1', 'Connection', 'QueryTimeOut', 0)
=DBSetProp('CONNECT1', 'Connection', 'Transactions', 1)
=DBSetProp('CONNECT1', 'Connection', 'Database', '')
```

Notice the `Create Connection` command in SQL syntax. The data concerning the connection are stored as a row in the database container, then the default parameters are written with that data.

> **NOTE:** VFP connections are not the same as ODBC connections. VFP connections are VFP database objects that specify an ODBC connection. To confuse matters further, backend SQL databases have their own instances of connections, which are not necessarily the same as ODBC connections. Each ODBC connection becomes a backend connection, but the database server may have more connections through other interfaces.

Remote Views

Visual FoxPro *views* are temporary tables created by permanently-stored SQL statements. VFP stores the SQL statement as an object in the database container, just like a connection. To create a view of remote data, all you need to do is base the view on a connection. There is a set of dialog boxes for creating views, which you can read more about in Chapter 8, "Creating Views," of the VFP *Developer's Guide*.

Be sure to select the Send SQL Updates check box on the Update tab of the View Designer; otherwise, VFP will not make the view updatable.

VFP defaults to making the primary key of your remote table not updatable; however, if the target table requires a non-null primary key, and it's not an auto-incrementing key, you will be unable to insert rows unless you can pass a value for the primary key.

You can run gendbc for views and see the parameters programmatically. For example, here are the results of a view named View1:

```
CREATE SQL VIEW "VIEW1" ;
   REMOTE CONNECT "Connect1" ;
   AS SELECT * FROM dbo.authors Authors


****

=DBSetProp('VIEW1', 'View', 'UpdateType', 1)

=DBSetProp('VIEW1', 'View', 'WhereType', 3)

=DBSetProp('VIEW1', 'View', 'FetchMemo', .T.)

=DBSetProp('VIEW1', 'View', 'SendUpdates', .T.)

=DBSetProp('VIEW1', 'View', 'UseMemoSize', 255)

=DBSetProp('VIEW1', 'View', 'FetchSize', 100)

=DBSetProp('VIEW1', 'View', 'MaxRecords', -1)

=DBSetProp('VIEW1', 'View', 'Tables', 'dbo.authors')

=DBSetProp('VIEW1', 'View', 'Prepared', .F.)

=DBSetProp('VIEW1', 'View', 'CompareMemo', .T.)

=DBSetProp('VIEW1', 'View', 'FetchAsNeeded', .F.)

=DBSetProp('VIEW1', 'View', 'ShareConnection', .F.)
```

```
*! Field Level Properties for VIEW1
* Props for the VIEW1.au_id field.
=DbSetProp('VIEW1.au_id', 'Field', 'KeyField', .T.)
=DbSetProp('VIEW1.au_id', 'Field', 'Updatable', .T.)
=DbSetProp('VIEW1.au_id', 'Field', 'UpdateName', 'dbo.authors.au_id')
=DbSetProp("VIEW1.au_id", "Field", "DataType", "C(11)")
* Continues for every field.
```

In this case, you can see the calls to DBSetProp() specifying the various update parameters.

SQL Pass-Through

Visual FoxPro makes accessing external data very easy for you through remote views, which you can treat just like VFP tables. When that isn't enough, or is too slow, you can pass a literal SQL string through to the backend server, via ODBC.

Executing: SQLExec()

You can pass backend SQL commands through to the SQL database using the SQLExec() function:

```
lnSuccess = SQLExec(lhPubs, "Select * From Authors", "mycursor")
```

VFP stores the results set in a cursor, in this case named mycursor because the command specified the name.

The SQLExec() function is the primary SQL pass-though command, because you can pass a literal string through to the back end, using the backend's SQL.

Be careful with SQLExec(). Sometimes ODBC intervenes with its own rules. For example, in both VFP and Microsoft SQL Server, if you insert a string longer than a character definition, the insert succeeds and the string is truncated. ODBC does not accept it, however, and returns an error.

Also in Microsoft SQL Server, unless you specify otherwise, single quotes may only be used for delimiting strings. This can cause problems with names like O'Leary.

Detecting Backend Tables and Columns

You can get a list of the tables on the target database by calling the `SQLTables()` function. Similarly, you can get a list of the columns in a table with the `SQLColumns()` function. You have to be careful, however, with `SQLColumns()` and user-defined data types.

You call the `SQLColumns()` function once you have a connection, and you can just specify the table. For example, you can select the employee table from the SQL Server `pubs` database, which has the user-defined data type of `empid`:

```
lhConnect = SQLConnect("connect2")

lnResult  = SQLColumns(lhConnect, "employee")
```

When you do this, the result is in a cursor named `Sqlresult1` that looks like Figure 12-6.

VFP defaults to showing you the VFP data types for the employee table, and VFP shows the data type as Character. This is how VFP will translate the data type in a remote view, but it's not showing you the SQL data types. To get those, you need to add the "native" parameter:

```
lnResult  = SQLColumns(lhConnect, "employee", "native")
```

Now, you get a lot more information (see Figure 12-7). In particular, though, notice that the type_name column of the VFP cursor indicates the user-defined data type, not the SQL data type.

Field_name	Field_type	Field_len	Field_dec
EMP_ID	C	9	0
FNAME	C	20	0
MINIT	C	1	0
LNAME	C	30	0
JOB_ID	I	4	0
JOB_LVL	I	4	0
PUB_ID	C	4	0
HIRE_DATE	T	8	0

FIGURE 12-6

The SQLColumns() function can show you data types from backend tables in their VFP equivalents.

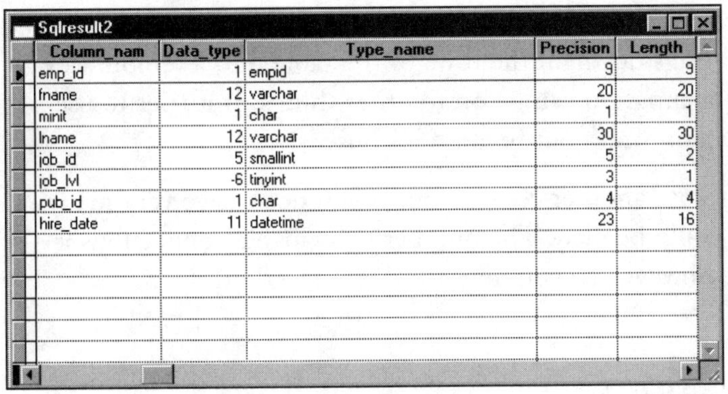

Sqlresult2

Column_nam	Data_type	Type_name	Precision	Length
emp_id	1	empid	9	9
fname	12	varchar	20	20
minit	1	char	1	1
lname	12	varchar	30	30
job_id	5	smallint	5	2
job_lvl	-6	tinyint	3	1
pub_id	1	char	4	4
hire_date	11	datetime	23	16

FIGURE 12-7

The `SQLColumns()` function can return the SQL backend table data types if you use the `"native"` parameter.

So, how can you find out that `empid` is really of Character type? In this case, refer to the Data_type column. It contains the value `1`, the same as the other Character columns.

The lesson here is that if the backend database allows user-defined types, you cannot trust the Type_name column when trying to determine the data source's data type. Use the numeric values in the Data_type column instead.

Detecting Errors

Visual FoxPro will detect ODBC errors and trigger your error routines if you use the `On Error` command. If you do not, VFP will present your user with a standard dialog box listing the error.

You can put the error into an array using the `Aerror()` command. VFP will populate the array with the appropriate ODBC error messages. ODBC errors are hard to pin down sometimes, because they return the error that ODBC found, not an error with the backend server.

Busy Connections

Visual FoxPro lets you share connections between various views or SQL pass-through commands. It is possible for a connection to be busy, thereby making other commands time out and produce error messages. This can be very frustrating to debug.

For example, if you have a remote view of a large table named rv_View1, and you use the view, VFP brings down all the rows of the table into a remote view. While that happens, your program can go on to other things. If it tries to use another view, the connection times out because it's busy.

You might be tempted to use another connection. If you don't have very many connections active, this could be okay. The number of available connections is limited on the backend, however, so you might not want to do this.

Dropped Connections

Occasionally a connection will fail, but you will get no error message. As far as VFP is concerned, the connection handle is okay. In that case, you have to reestablish the connection by disconnecting and reconnecting.

Data Translation

Visual FoxPro's remote views make working with external data quite easy. However, problems can crop up in your results if you are counting on certain data types. VFP has to translate your external data into VFP's own data types, and as you might guess, they do not always match.

In this section, you will see a method for finding out how VFP will translate your external data types, and some of the limitations that can occur as a result.

How VFP Translates External Data

When you deal with external data, there's a relatively easy way to determine exactly how VFP will translate your data. You build a table on the external database containing all the data types available, then build a VFP remote view of that data.

You can see a concrete example of this method in the following step-by-step instructions, which work with Microsoft's SQL Server 6.5.

1. Enter Microsoft SQL Server 6.5's ISQL/W window, with create table privileges to some database. Do not use the Master database. Instead, select some temporary database or the pubs database.

2. Copy the following script into the ISQL query window. (You can find this script on the CD-ROM as \chap12\dtypes.sql.)

```
/*
* Dtypes.sql
* A program to create a Microsoft SQL Server table
* containing all possible data types
*/
Create Table dtypes (
   cidentity integer identity,
   cbinary binary,
   cbit bit,
   cchar char (20),
   cdatetime datetime,
   cdecimal decimal (10,2),
   cfloat25 float(25),
   cfloat44 float(44),
   cimage image,
   cint int,
   cmoney money,
   cnumeric numeric (10,3),
   creal real,
   csmalldatetime smalldatetime,
   csmallint smallint,
   csmallmoney smallmoney,
   csysname sysname,
   ctext text,
   ctimestamp timestamp,
   ctinyint tinyint,
   cvarbinary varbinary,
   cvarchar varchar (25)
)
```

This script creates a table with all the user-available data types for Microsoft SQL Server 6.5. The reason for having the extra integer column (named `cidentity`) is to see whether remote views are affected by the `identity` property.

3. Execute the script by clicking the green arrow at the right of the window. The results window should appear next, with the message `This command did not return data, and it did not return any rows`. If you get error messages instead, make sure that your privileges allow you to create tables.

4. After you've created the table, leave ISQL/W and bring up Visual FoxPro.

5. In VFP, create a connection to the SQL database. Remember to put the database name in the connection dialog box.

6. Create a remote view against the dtypes table, and select all the fields in the remote view dialog box. Save the view with a name such as `rv_dtypes`.

7. Use the view from the command window, and list the structure to a text file:

```
Use rv_dtypes
list structure to dtypes.txt
modify file dtypes.txt
```

8. The resulting text file should look like this:

Structure for table: F:\TEMP\04740957.TMP

Number of data records: 0

Date of last update: / /

Memo file block size: 64

Code Page: 1252

Field	Field Name	Type	Width
1	CIDENTITY	Integer	4
2	CBINARY	Memo	4
3	CBIT	Logical	1
4	CCHAR	Character	20
5	CDATETIME	DateTime	8
6	CDECIMAL	Numeric	12

7	CFLOAT25	Double	8
8	CFLOAT44	Double	8
9	CIMAGE	General	4
10	CINT	Integer	4
11	CMONEY	Currency	8
12	CNUMERIC	Numeric	12
13	CREAL	Double	8
14	CSMALLDATETI..	DateTime	8
15	CSMALLINT	Integer	4
16	CSMALLMONEY	Currency	8
17	CSYSNAME	Character	30
18	CTEXT	Memo	4
19	CTIMESTAMP	Memo	4
20	CTINYINT	Integer	4
21	CVARBINARY	Memo	4
22	CVARCHAR	Character	25
	** Total **		193

You now can see how VFP will translate your external data into VFP data types. You do not have much choice in this matter, because VFP does not allow you to override the way it deals with the ODBC drivers.

You can use this procedure on other external sources, backend databases such as Oracle, or file-server databases such as the Access/Jet database.

This tells you some things about how VFP will translate external data into VFP format, but how about translating VFP data into an external format?

How VFP Translates VFP Data to an External Source

When you send VFP data to an external source, you actually have a fair amount of choice, because you can assemble the SQL statement you want sent to the external data source.

VFP does provide a default data translation using the Upsizing Wizard. The Upsizing Wizard is a series of dialog boxes that takes a selected set of VFP tables, creates parallel tables on your external database, and then uploads the data. (For more information about the Upsizing Wizard, see Chapter 20, "Upsizing Visual FoxPro Databases," in the VFP *Developer's Guide*.)

> **NOTE:** VFP 3.0's Upsizing Wizard does not work well with Microsoft SQL Server 6.5. It will add a timestamp column to all your tables, then attempt to insert a null value into this column. Make sure that for Microsoft SQL Server 6.5, you use VFP 5.0's Upsizing Wizard.

Table 12-1 shows how the Upsizing Wizard translates VFP data types. (The source for this table is the VFP *Developer's Guide*.)

Notice that there are not as many data types listed in VFP for upsizing as there are on the SQL side. Many SQL data types have no exact parallel in VFP. To see this, simply compare the above table and the earlier remote view listing.

Table 12-1 VFP Upsizing Wizard and Microsoft SQL Server Data Types

VFP Data Type Abbreviation	VFP Data Type Name	SQL Data Type
C	Character	char
Y	Currency	money
D	Date	datetime
T	Datetime	datetime
B	Double	float
F	Float	float
G	General	image
I	Integer	int
L	Logical	bit
M	Memo	text
M(binary)	Memo binary	image
C(binary)	Character binary	binary
N	Numeric	float

VFP and Microsoft SQL Server Data Translation Table

When thinking of data translation between Visual FoxPro and an external data source, you have to keep in mind that all the translation is done via ODBC, and ODBC also has its own data types. In fact, the VFP data types translate into ODBC data types, and from there into SQL Server data types.

Fortunately, the documentation for either Visual FoxPro or Microsoft SQL Server provides a listing of the translation into ODBC data types. All this information can be merged into a final table, Table 12-2, which is definitive about the translation of data between VFP and Microsoft SQL Server. The technique can be matched for any external database that documents the ODBC data types.

As you can see, the table is relatively straightforward on a few data types, but there are some surprises. For example, you can see that VFP upsizes both the Date and Datetime data types to the SQL datetime datatype, and the remote view translates both as VFP's Datetime.

Are there some mismatches between the data types? Yes, as you will see in the next section.

The Limitations of Data Translation

When you examine Table 12-2, you can see that sometimes data which goes up into Microsoft SQL Server from VFP does not come back down in the same format.

Character

VFP keeps character data in a fixed-length format, and the Upsizing Wizard translates it into fixed-length character format in SQL Server.

Notice that the Upsizing Wizard upsizes the VFP character binary data type into the binary data type in SQL. When it's seen via a remote view, it's translated into a Memo field.

Data that you keep in SQL as varchar is seen in a remote view as VFP's fixed-length character, padded with blanks.

Table 12-2 VFP and Microsoft SQL Server Data Types

VFP Data Type (Upsize)	SQL Server SQL Data Type	ODBC SQL Data Type	VFP Data Type (Remote View)
C Character	char	SQL_CHAR	C
	varchar	SQL_VARCHAR	C
C(binary) Char. binary	binary	SQL_BINARY	M
D Date T Datetime	datetime	SQL_TIMESTAMP	T
	smalldatetime	SQL_TIMESTAMP	T
B Double F Float N Numeric	f float(n) real	SQL_FLOAT (n=24–53) SQL_REAL (n=1–23)	B
	decimal	SQL_DECIMAL	N
L Logical	bit	SQL_BIT	L
G General M(binary) Memo binary	image	SQL_LONGVARBINARY	G
I Integer	int	SQL_INTEGER	I
	smallint	SQL_SMALLINT	I
	tinyint	SQL_TINYINT	I
Y Currency	money	SQL_DECIMAL	C
	smallmoney	SQL_DECIMAL	C
	numeric	SQL_NUMERIC	N
	sysname	SQL_VARCHAR	C
M Memo	text	SQL_LONGVARCHAR	M
	timestamp	SQL_BINARY	M
	varbinary	SQL_VARBINARY	M

> **WARNING:** Watch out for sending character strings through VFP to Microsoft SQL Server via ODBC. If you attempt to insert or update a SQL character column that has a maximum length of 25 with a character string length of more than 25, ODBC returns an error. This happens in spite of the fact that both VFP and SQL Server normally just truncate a string under the same circumstances!

Numeric

The VFP numeric data types, excluding the integer, are Numeric, Double, and Float. The VFP Upsizing Wizard translates them all into the SQL float data type. A remote view, however, sees all of them as the Double data type.

Integer

While Visual FoxPro has one integer data type, Microsoft SQL Server actually has three integer data types: tinyint, smallint, and integer. This can cause some problems.

The integer data type is roughly equivalent in both databases, ranging from −2,147,483,647 to +2,147,483,646 in VFP, and −2,147,483,648 to +2,147,483,647 in Microsoft SQL Server.

VFP has no equivalent, however, for the Microsoft SQL Server tinyint and smallint. A tinyint ranges from 0 to 255, and smallint ranges from −32,768 through +32,767. Therefore, when you are sending data to the back end, you must check the ranges of your integer data before inserting into tinyint and smallint SQL data types. If you do not, and try to insert a larger number than allowed, you get an ODBC error.

Logical

The Logical data type translates smoothly between these platforms.

Date and Time

Visual FoxPro contains the date data type, and a time string, and a datetime data type that mimics SQL Server's. However, VFP's datetime data type does not hold seconds, which means that you might lose time precision when you view SQL data from VFP.

SQL Server natively supports only a datetime data type, and neither date nor time by themselves. This causes some hardship on SQL Server developers. Functions must be used to extract the date or time portions of datetime data. You might want to query a table of orders, for instance, on a certain date—and the date only, excluding the time. In Microsoft SQL Server, you can use a function in the query string to extract the date, but this can cause a performance hit. You also can create an extra column in the table, to hold a character string translation of the date portion of the datetime, then index on that new column. Either solution is problematic. This is a very sore point in Microsoft SQL Server developer circles.

Currency

Visual FoxPro has one currency data type, but Microsoft SQL Server has two, money and smallmoney. Therefore, when you use a remote view to see SQL smallmoney, your view shows it as currency.

Just as with integers, however, you need to know whether you're translating data into a SQL smallmoney, and check to make sure that your data are within the range. If your data are outside the range of −214,748.3648 to +214,748.3647, you must reject the data or receive an ODBC error.

Other Data Types

Notice that many other Microsoft SQL Server data types come down into VFP as memo types: binary, text, timestamp, and varbinary. While that makes the storage easy for VFP, these data are then essentially unreadable.

The SQL Server Identity Property

Microsoft SQL Server's way of adding an auto-increment column to a table is to apply the identity property to a numeric data type. SQL Server developers often select integer for this type, but almost any numeric data type works. The VFP Upsizing Wizard allows you to add an `identity` property to a column, and this is no problem.

A problem arises, however, when you are adding a block of data to a table that has an identity column using VFP's SQL pass-through. Microsoft SQL Server does not allow you to insert values into the identity column.

If the identity column is the primary key of the table, it cannot be null. How do you get a value into it? Well, SQL Server automatically increments the id for you, so you just leave the column name out of the `Insert` statement.

Suppose that you have a set of values for the primary key in your local table, and you want to upload them all into a table named temp. Then, you want the `identity` property to increment the primary key, starting with the maximum number plus one. You can do this by sending the following command, on the same connection, before each insert:

```
lnResult = SQLExec(lnHandle, "Set Identity_Insert temp On")
```

This temporarily allows an insert with a value in the identity column.

Summary

Client/server programming is a large, complex topic, and one with a lot of pit-falls. In this chapter, you have learned how Visual FoxPro fits into the client/server database scene, and how SQL databases differ from VFP. Also, you have learned many of the factors that you need to consider when deciding whether to go client/server yourself, or to compete with client/server applications. Finally, you have seen many of the problems that arise when translating data between VFP and backend SQL databases, and how to resolve these problems. Despite the given difficulties, the benefits of more secure and relational databases become clearer as you continue to work with backend SQL servers.

Chapter 13

Deploying Visual FoxPro Internet Applications

Introduction

The Internet has taken the world by storm. Prior to 1994, the Internet was primarily the domain of government and educational institutions. Today, you cannot watch a television commercial or news broadcast without at least one reference to the Internet. Some say it's hype; some say it's substance. What are you going to do now to prepare for the day when your company or clients ask you for an Internet solution? In Chapters 6, "Communicating with Other Applications Using OLE," and 12, "Client/Server Database Development with VFP," you learned how to expose your data to other applications and front ends. The Internet is another method of "opening up" your applications. In this chapter, you will learn how to expose your VFP applications to the Internet. Some of the topics covered in this chapter include the following:

- Basic Internet terminology
- Basic HTML page construction techniques
- How to create HTML pages from your Visual FoxPro applications
- How to create your own browser with the Internet Control Pack
- How to use the VFP Internet Wizard
- How to modify the Internet Wizard to do some cool stuff

Basic Internet Terminology

With most new technology comes a new set of terminology—the Internet is no different. Before you can fully understand Internet technology, you need to understand the relevant terminology. Table 13-1 presents some essential terms.

Now that you have an understanding of some basic Internet terminology, you can begin developing your own Internet applications.

Basic HTML Page Construction

Your first step in developing Internet applications is to understand the language that is used to create Web pages. In this section, you learn some of the basic techniques used to create Web pages with HTML.

Table 13-1 Internet Terminology

Term	Meaning
Hypertext	The Internet as we know it today is a huge, networked *hypertext system.* Hypertext allows you to add a reference in a document, and users can then use that reference to "jump" to a different part of the current page, a different page, a completely different document, or a different Web server. Common hypertext systems that you might be familiar with include most modern help files.
Internet	This is the communications network upon which the World Wide Web resides. In the context of your company, the Internet resides in the outside world.
Intranet	This is an internal Internet environment that resides inside your company. Intranets are accessible to employees of the company, but not the outside world. These currently are being used to present formatted information to internal company users, to conduct meetings involving geographically distributed parties, and to provide better access to corporate information locked up in legacy systems.
TCP/IP	This is the networking protocol used as the backbone of the Internet and your intranets.
WWW (World Wide Web)	This is the cornerstone of today's Internet. The WWW is a technology that rides on top of the Internet. The WWW allows developers to create documents, known as Web pages, that are linked much like the threads on a spider web. It is the purpose of the WWW to facilitate access to these Web pages that contain the "valuable" content that Web users need.
Web page	Web pages are simply text files that contain HTML-formatted information, and possibly links to other Web pages.
HTML (Hypertext Markup Language)	This is the language you use to create Web pages. HTML operates much like the attribute tags that can be attached to selected text by most word processing programs, with the key difference that in HTML you see only the formatting codes in your document. It is the job of a Web browser to present the document with all its formatting applied.
Web browser	This is an application capable of reading a Web page and displaying it with correct formatting according to the HTML it contains. Currently, the most popular browsers are Netscape Navigator, Microsoft Internet Explorer, and Spyglass Mosaic.
Internet servers	These applications serve Web pages to the Internet.
CGI (Common Gateway Interface)	This is the protocol used to execute applications from within Web pages.

NOTE: Throughout the rest of this chapter, the term "Internet" is used. Please remember that "Internet" and "intranet" are interchangeable terms. You will be developing Internet components here, but the same techniques apply to developing intranet applications.

Creating a Basic Web Page

Whenever you create a new Web page, a set of very basic information is required. The following code demonstrates the minimum lines of text necessary to create a basic Web page that can be seen in a browser frame:

```
<HTML>
<HEAD>
<TITLE>Test Web Page</TITLE>
</HEAD>
<H1>World Wide Shoes </H1>
</HTML>
```

After you've created this Web page, you can go into your favorite Web browser and look at the document you've created. Figure 13-1 shows the HTML code above as presented in Netscape Navigator, a Web browser.

Here's how the code sample breaks down:

<HTML>	This tag specifies that this is a HTML Web page.
<HEAD>	This tag specifies that this is the header section of text.
<TITLE>	This tag specifies the title that is displayed in the title bar of a Web browser when this page is active.
<H1>	This tag specifies that this is a heading line which should be displayed in bold text.
</HTML>, </HEAD>, </TITLE>, </H1>	These are ending tags. Web pages consist of text surrounded by HTML *tag pairs*. Each tag pair consists of a beginning and ending tag. The ending tag is the beginning tag with a backslash pre-pended.

Now, it's time to learn about some code you can use to spruce up your Web page.

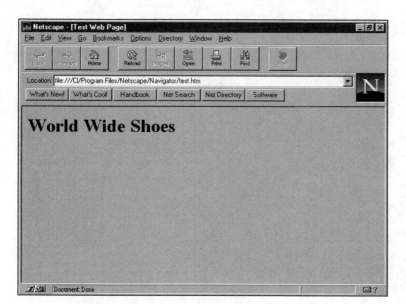

FIGURE 13-1

Netscape Navigator can be used to view the contents of the Web page specified previously.

NOTE: Not all HTML tags come in pairs. Some tags are *solo tags* that don't require an ending tag.

Adding Bulleted Lists

The following code creates a Web page with a bulleted list:

```
<HTML>
<HEAD>
<TITLE>Test Web Page</TITLE>
</HEAD>
<h1>World Wide Shoes </h1>
<UL>
<LI> North America
<LI> Europe
<LI> Asia
```

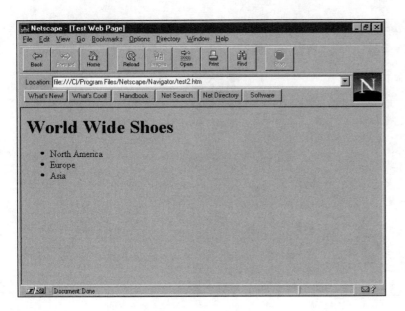

FIGURE 13-2

The bulleted list HTML code viewed in Netscape.

```
<UL>
</HTML>
```

Notice that this new code uses the `<UL>` and `</UL>` tag pair, and uses `<LI>` for each bulleted item. `<LI>` does not have an ending tag. Figure 13-2 shows a Web page that contains a bulleted list.

Adding Tables

The following code creates a table to be displayed by a Web browser:

```
<HTML>
<HEAD>
<TITLE>Visual FoxPro Table Creation Demo</TITLE>
</HEAD>
<BODY>
<TABLE Border>
<CAPTION>Test Table Creation</CAPTION>
```

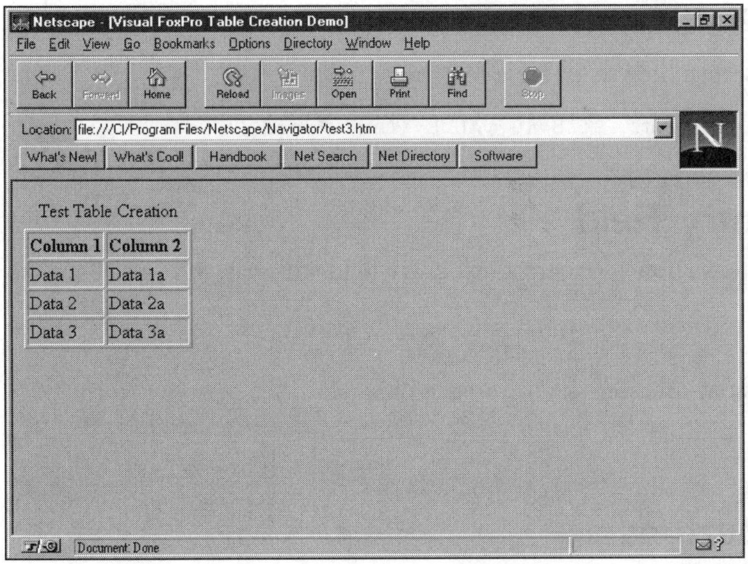

FIGURE 13-3

An HTML table presented in Netscape Navigator.

```
<TR><TH>Column 1<TH>Column 2
</TR><TR><TD>Data 1 <TD>Data 1a
</TR><TR><TD>Data 2 <TD>Data 2a
</TR><TR><TD>Data 3 <TD>Data 3a
</TR>
</TABLE>
</BODY>
</HTML>
```

This HTML text creates a formatted HTML table that can be viewed in a Web browser (see Figure 13-3).

Adding Controls

The following sections discuss tags that represent HTML controls that will look familiar to most Visual FoxPro developers. Each example simply shows the tag used to create a particular object. In order to display the object in a Web page, you still need to specify the other tags necessary to create a proper page.

Text Entry Field

This HTML tag shows how to create a text entry field:

```
<INPUT NAME="SearchParam" SIZE=40 VALUE="Text Field" >
```

Password Entry Field

This HTML tag shows how to create a text entry field with password capabilities:

```
<INPUT Type="Password" NAME="SearchParam2" SIZE=40 VALUE="" >
```

Password fields display an asterisk (*) for each character the user types into the field.

Command Buttons

These HTML tags show how to create command buttons, which are used to invoke actions from the user:

```
<INPUT TYPE="reset" VALUE="Reset Button">
<INPUT TYPE="submit" VALUE="Send To Server Button">
```

The first line creates a reset button and the second line creates a submit button. These two button types are commonly used for Cancel and OK buttons, respectively.

List Drop-Down Control

These HTML tags show how to create a drop-down control:

```
<SELECT Name="Selected-Report">
  <OPTION>Annual Sales
  <OPTION>Current Inventory
  <OPTION>A/R Aging
</SELECT>
```

List Box Control

These HTML tags show how to create a list box control:

```
<SELECT Name="Selected-Report" Multiple Size="3">
  <OPTION>Annual Sales
  <OPTION>Current Inventory
  <OPTION>A/R Aging
  <OPTION>Another report
</SELECT>
```

Radio Buttons

These HTML tags show how to create a group of radio buttons:

```
<INPUT TYPE="radio" Name="MY-RADIO"  Value="No"> Yes
<INPUT TYPE="radio" Name="MY-RADIO"  Value="Yes"> No
<INPUT TYPE="radio" Name="MY-RADIO"  Value="Maybe"> Maybe
```

Memo Editor

This HTML tag shows how to create a memo field editor:

```
<TEXTAREA Name="comments" Rows="5" Cols ="40">Memo Style
Field</TEXTAREA>
```

Check Boxes

This HTML tag shows how to create a check box object:

```
<INPUT TYPE="checkbox" Name="MY-CHECKBOX">
```

Figure 13-4 shows an HTML Web page with several HTML controls on it. Notice the similarity between VFP and HTML in terms of how these controls look.

When looking at the code that creates these controls, you need to be aware of some of the keywords used. The main items of interest are Name and Value. The Name keyword is the name of the variable that is handed to your Web server for processing. The Value keyword allows you to provide the default value for a specified control. You use these two keywords, respectively, to send and default information for your dynamic Web pages.

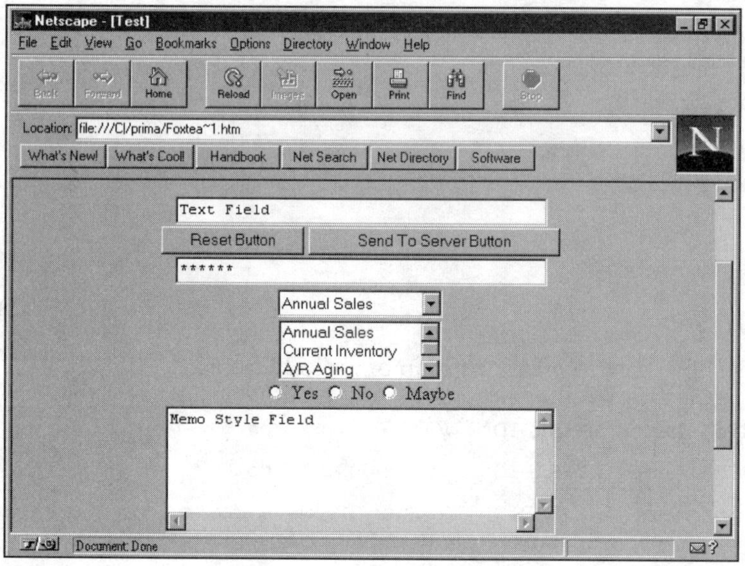

FIGURE 13-4

This HTML Web page contains many of the controls you'll want to use on your own pages.

Creating Web Pages from Visual FoxPro

Now that you understand some of the basics of Web page creation with HTML, you can begin looking at what it takes to create Web Pages from your VFP applications. For instance, assume that you want to create a Web page table from a VFP table. The following code creates a Web page containing an HTML table, so that the table can be populated with data from a VFP table:

```
Close All
Clear All
Use test

Set Textmerge To RODTEST.HTML
Set Textmerge On

\<HTML>
\<HEAD>
\<TITLE>Visual FoxPro Table Creation Demo</TITLE>
```

```
\</HEAD>
\<BODY>


\<TABLE Border>
\<CAPTION>Test Table Creation</CAPTION>
\<TR>
For X = 1 To FCOUNT()
\\<TH><<FIELD(x)>>
Endfor
\</TR>


Go Top


Scan
   \\<TR>
   For X = 1 To FCOUNT()
   \\<TD><<EVAL(FIELD(x))>>
   Endfor
   \</TR>


EndScan

\</TABLE>
\</BODY>
\</HTML>


Set Textmerge Off
Close All
```

Now, in keeping with the development standards for the FoxPro Foundation Classes, you should create a useful set of classes for creating Web pages. The following class, cHTML, assists in the creation of Web pages:

```
Define Class cHTML as Custom

*- Array for HTML Page Lines
Protected aPageLines[1]
```

```
Protected cTitle
Protected cCRLF
Protected nLines

Function Init
This.cTitle = ""
This.cCRLF  = CHR(13) + CHR(10)
This.nLines = 0

EndFunc

*- This method returns an HTML Web page. The plCGIPage
*- parameter specifies that the page should be returned
*- with proper CGI notation.
Function ReturnHTMLPage
Lparameters plCGIPage

Local lcRetVal
lcRetVal = ""

*- Add the footer
lcRetVal = lcRetVal + This.CreateHTMLHeader()
*- Traverse the page lines and create the text lines for the
*- Web page.
If This.nLines > 0
  Local lnKount
  For lnKount = 1 To This.nLines
    lcRetVal = lcRetVal + This.aPageLines[lnKount] + THIS.cCRLF
  EndFor
Endif

*- Add the footer
lcRetVal = lcRetVal + This.CreateHTMLFooter()


Return lcRetVal
```

```
EndFunc

*— This method creates the title of the Web page
Function CreateTitle
Lparameters pcTitle

*— Returns true or false depending on input type
Local llRetVal
llRetVal = .f.

If Type("pcTitle") = "C"
   llRetVal = .t.
   This.cTitle = pcTitle
Endif

Return llRetVal

*— This function creates a text line for an HTML Page
Function CreateTextLine
LParameters pcTextLine, plIncludeBreak
Local llRetVal
llRetVal = .f.
If Type("pcTextLine") = "C"
   llRetVal = .t.
Endif

This.AddTextLine(pcTextLine,.t.)

Return llRetVal

EndFunc


*— This method create a formatted HTML table.
*— You pass it the alias of the DBF file you are using
*— and the title of the table, and it creates the
*— information for generating an HTML table.
```

```
Function CreateTable
Lparameters pcAlias, pcTableTitle

Local lcRetVal, llRetVal, lcTblString
lcRetVal = ""
llRetVal = .f.

If Used(pcAlias)
  llRetVal = .t.
  This.AddTextLine("<TABLE Border>")

  *- If a table title was passed then create a table caption
  If Type("pcTableTitle") = "C"
    This.AddTextLine("<CAPTION>"+ pcTableTitle + "</CAPTION>")
  Endif


  Select (pcAlias)

  *- Create the column headers
  Local lnKount
  lcTblString = "<TR>"
  For lnKount = 1 To Fcount()
    lcTblString = lcTblString + "<TH>" + Field(lnKount)
  Endfor
  lcTblString = lcTblString + "</TR>"
  This.AddTextLine(lcTblString)

  Go Top

  *- Populate the fields with data
  Scan
    lcTblString = "<TR>"
    For lnKount = 1 To Fcount()
      lcTblString = lcTblString + "<TD>" + Eval(Field(lnKount))
    Endfor
```

```
        lcTblString = lcTblString + "</TR>"
        This.AddTextLine(lcTblString)
    Endscan

        This.AddTextLine("</TABLE>")
Endif

Return llRetVal


*- This method creates the title of the Web page
Function CreateHeaderLine
Lparameters pcHeaderText, pnHeaderNumber

*- Return true or false depending on input type
Local llRetVal
llRetVal = .f.

If Type("pcHeaderText") = "C" And Type("pnHeaderNumber") = "N"
    llRetVal = .t.

    *- Create the header line to add
    Local lcHeaderLine
    lcHeaderLine = ""
    lcHeaderLine = lcHeaderLine + "<h" + ;
    Alltrim(Str(pnHeaderNumber,10,0)) + ">"
    lcHeaderLine = lcHeaderLine + pcHeaderText
    lcHeaderLine = lcHeaderLine + "</h" + ;
    Alltrim(Str(pnHeaderNumber,10,0)) + ">"

    *- Add the line
    This.AddTextLine(lcHeaderLine,.f.)

Endif

Return llRetVal

EndFunc
```

```
*— This function returns creates the HTML Page header
Protected Function CreateCGIHeader

Local lcRetVal
lcRetVal = ""
lcRetVal = lcRetVal + "Content-Type: text/html" + This.cCRLF + ;
This.cCRLF

Return lcRetVal

EndFunc
*— This function returns creates the HTML Page header
Protected Function CreateHTMLHeader
Local lcRetVal

lcRetVal = ""

lcRetVal = lcRetVal + "<html>" + This.cCRLF
lcRetVal = lcRetVal + "<head>" + This.cCRLF
lcRetVal = lcRetVal + "<title>" + This.cTitle + "</title>" + ;
This.cCRLF
lcRetVal = lcRetVal + "</head>" + THIS.cCRLF
lcRetVal = lcRetVal + "<body>" + THIS.cCRLF
lcRetVal = lcRetVal + ;
[<FORM ACTION="vfpcgi.exe?IDCFile=FOXTEACH.IDC" METHOD="POST">]

Return lcRetVal

EndFunc


*— This function creates a text line for an HTML Page
Protected Function AddTextLine
LParameters pcTextLine, plIncludeBreak

Local llRetVal
llRetVal = .f.
```

```
If Type("pcTextLine") = "C"
  llRetVal = .t.
Endif


*- Add a new line to the HTML Array
If This.nLines = 0
  This.nLines = This.nLines + 1
Else
  This.nLines = This.nLines + 1
  Declare THIS.aPageLines[This.nLines]
Endif


THIS.aPageLines[This.nLines] = pcTextLine + ;
IIF(plIncludeBreak,"<br>","")


Return llRetVal
EndFunc


*- This function returns creates the HTML Page footer
Protected Function CreateHTMLFooter
Local lcRetVal
lcRetVal = "</body>" + THIS.cCRLF
lcRetVal = lcRetVal +  "</html>" + This.cCRLF


Return lcRetVal

EndFunc
Enddefine
```

Table 13-2 shows the basic definition of this class.

Take note of the fact that cHTML returns a string instead of creating an HTML page directly. The control does this so that it can provide the most flexible interface possible. The string returned might be written to an HTML file, shown directly in a browser, or even e-mailed to someone. Later in this chapter, you get a chance to use this class to alter the output of the Internet SERVER.APP program provided with VFP 5.0.

Table 13-2 The cHTML Class

Class name	cHTML
Description	This class is used to create HTML pages.
Parent class	cus
Classes used	cus
Public Properties	None
Private Properties	None
Public Methods	ReturnHTMLPage([lReturnCGI])—Returns a string representing an HTML Web page (the optional parameter specifies whether this page is to be returned by a CGI application) CreateTitle(cWebPageTitle)—Specifies the title of the Web page CreateHeaderLine(cHeaderText,nHeaderLevel)—Creates a new header line (cHeaderText specifies the text of the header line; nHeaderLevel specifies the numeric depth of the header: 1 signifies a top-level header to be displayed in a very large font) CreateTextLine(cTextLine,[lIncludeLineFeed])—Adds a new text line to the Web page (the first parameter specifies the text to be placed on the page; the second parameter, which is optional, specifies whether the line should include a linefeed tag) CreateTable(cAlias,[cHeaderTitle])—Adds an HTML table to the Web page (the first parameter is the alias of a currently open table, view, or cursor; the second parameter, which is optional, specifies a title to be displayed above the table)
Private methods	None

Creating Your Own Browser with the Internet Control Pack

Until now, you've been looking at Web pages through the window of a Netscape browser. You are not limited, however, to one of the commercially available browsers—you can create your own. This section shows you how to create your own browser using the Microsoft Internet Control Pack.

What is the Internet Control Pack?

The *Internet Control Pack* is a set of ActiveX controls created by Microsoft that enables developers to include Web-enabled forms in their Visual FoxPro forms. The Internet Control Pack includes the controls shown in Table 13-3.

As you can see, the Internet Control Pack allows you to do most things that robust Internet software applications can do. You can download the Internet Control Pack from Microsoft's Web site at **http://www.microsoft.com**.

Creating the Browser

After downloading the tools available in the Internet Control Pack, you can proceed to create your own browser. The ingredients for this browser are pretty simple, consisting of the following items:

- A single form from the VFP Controls class library
- A single text box from the VFP Controls class library

Table 13-3 Controls in the Internet Control Pack

Control Name	Description of Use
WinSock TCP control	A low-level control used for communicating between different machines using the TCP/IP protocol
WinSock UDP control	Another low-level control used for communicating between machines using the TCP/IP protocol
FTP Client control	Can be used to transfer files between machines using the FTP transfer protocol
HTTP control	Allows you to use Hypertext Transfer Protocol to gather Web page information
HTML control	Allows you to view Web pages designed using HTML
POP control	Allows you to set up Internet post offices using Post Office Protocol, version 3
SMTP control	Allows you to send e-mail using Simple Mail Transfer Protocol
NNTP Client control	Allows you to gather information using Internet newsgroups

■ A single HTML ActiveX control from the Internet Control Pack

■ A single line of code in the text box's `Valid()` method

To create your own browser you can create a new form based on the `frm` class provided in the FoxPro Foundation Classes provided with this book. Add the text box and the HTML control to the new Internet browser form. After adding these controls, add the following code to the `Valid()` method of the text box:

```
Thisform.ole_HTMLControl.RequestDoc(Thisform.txtURL.value)
```

Now, you're ready to use the Internet browser you've created. Run the form and type in the address for your favorite Web site. When you press Enter, the HTML form loads the default page from the Web server. In Figure 13-5, the browser shows a default Web page provided by the Microsoft Internet Information Server.

As you can see, it's pretty easy to create your own browser with the Internet Control Pack. After creating the basic framework, you can extend the browser to have additional capabilities. The following sections discuss further ideas for creating your own Web applications from VFP.

FIGURE 13-5

The custom Web browser created with the default page provided by the Microsoft Internet Information Server.

Using the VFP Internet Wizard

Now that you understand some of the basic techniques used to create Web pages from your Visual FoxPro applications, you can begin looking at creating interactive database applications using the VFP Internet Search Page Wizard. The wizard consists of three very important components:

- WWWPAGE.APP—A wizard that assists in the creation of a Web page
- VFPCGI.EXE—An executable program that's used by the wizard-generated Web page to send data to an Internet server
- SERVER.APP—A VFP application that processes Internet requests and returns a Web page as the result set for a query

Installing the Internet Search Page Wizard

The most difficult aspect of creating an Internet-integrated application is the installation of all the Web components. In order to create an interactive Web page using Visual FoxPro's Internet Search Page Wizard, you must have the following Microsoft products:

- VFP 3.0b or later
- VFP Internet Search Page Wizard
- Windows NT 3.51 running TCP/IP
- Internet Information Server

After successfully installing these applications, follow these steps to complete configuration of the Internet Information Server:

1. Copy the VFPCGI.EXE file that comes with the wizard into the wwwroot directory (or an equivalent directory).
2. Go into the Internet Server properties sheet and change the rights of the wwwroot directory to **Read** and **Execute**. Figure 13-6 shows how your Internet Information Server needs to be configured.
3. After creating the Web pages and associated files with the WWWPAGE application, copy them to the wwwroot directory.

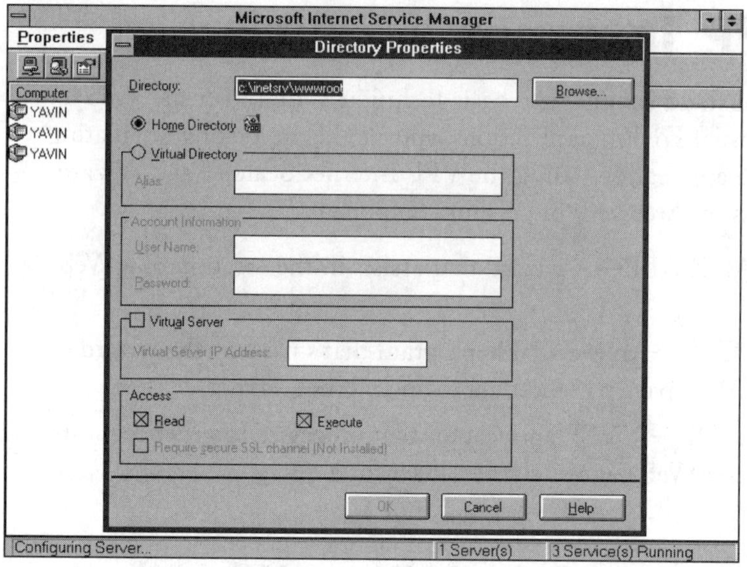

FIGURE 13-6

The Internet Information Server with the Directory Properties sheet shown.

4. Run the SERVER.APP program. You need to set the server options by clicking the Options button.

5. Next, enter the correct parameters for your server. Use the following settings (as shown in Figure 13-7): Scripts should be set to the scripts directory installed by your server applications; the HTTP directory should be set to wwwroot (or the equivalent); and the path should be set to the directory that includes the data files you want to query.

After configuring the server and all the appropriate files, you can generate a Web page using the Internet Search Page Wizard Web page generator. This wizard, which creates a Web page capable of querying a single table, takes you step by

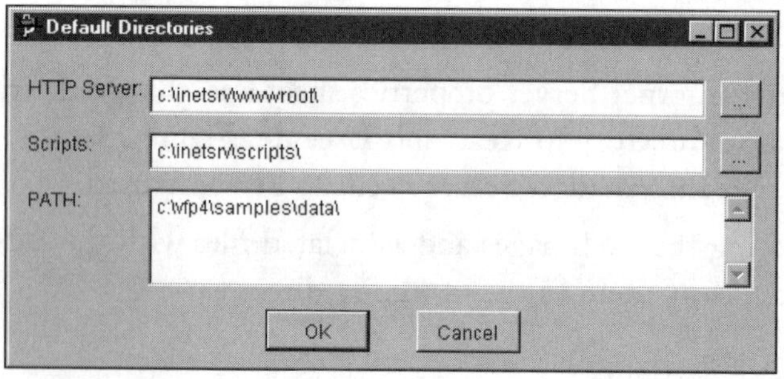

FIGURE 13-7

The SERVER.APP option screen with the proper script directory, root, and path set.

step through the criteria necessary to create the Web page. Follow these steps as you use the Internet Search Page Wizard:

1. Select a single table that you want to query (see Figure 13-8). The path to this table needs to be added to the SERVER.APP configuration screen.

2. Select a single indexed field that will be used for your selection criteria (see Figure 13-9). The Search Page Wizard is limited to selecting based on a single field. Later in this chapter, you can learn how to create your own more advanced queries.

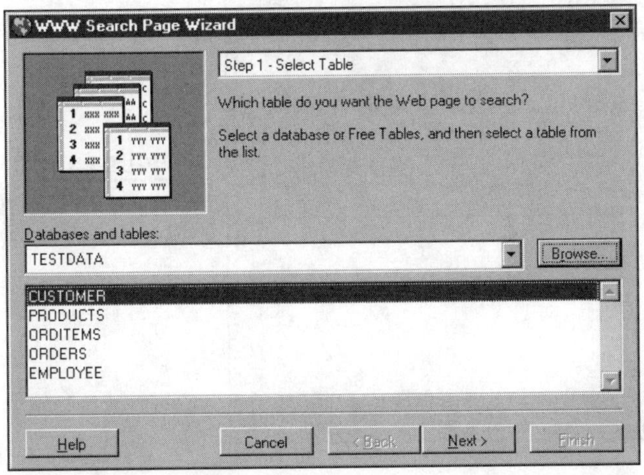

FIGURE 13-8

The Search Page Wizard here has the table selection screen active.

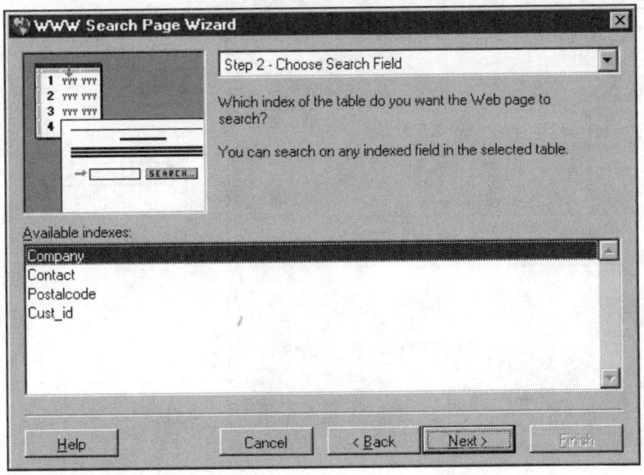

FIGURE 13-9

The Search Page Wizard here has the search key selection screen active.

3. Specify the title and text for your Web page (see Figure 13-10). Use this page to tell the users of your Web page what the topic or purpose of the Web page is.

4. Specify optional images (GIF or JPEG files) to be displayed on your search page (see Figure 13-11). This screen also allows you to configure a Web page that allows users to download the resulting query as a file.

5. Select the fields to be returned to your user (see Figure 13-12). You are limited to five. As with the problem noted in step 2 above, there's a

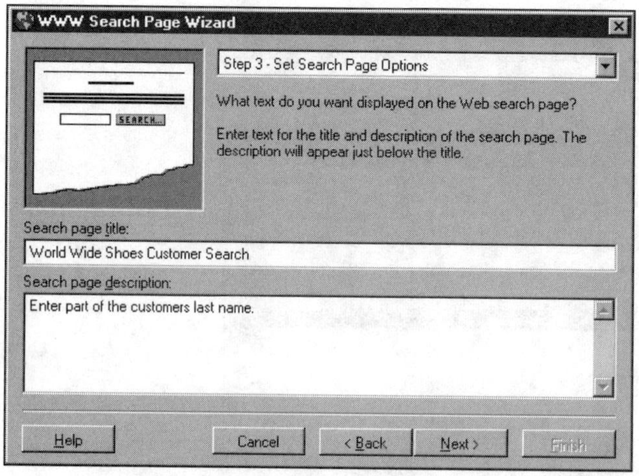

FIGURE 13-10

The Search Page Wizard here has the title and description screen active.

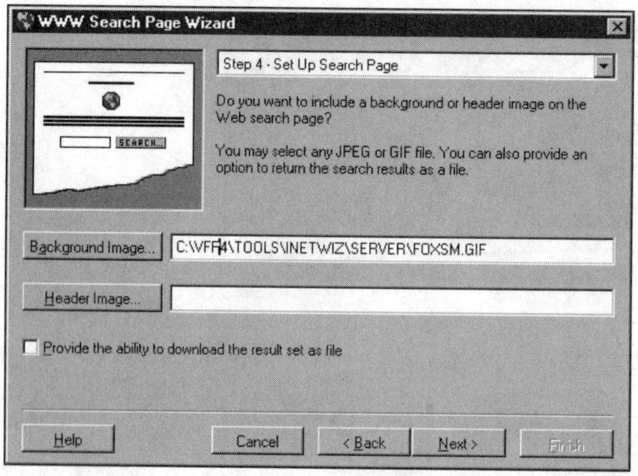

FIGURE 13-11

The Search Page Wizard here has the search page setup screen active.

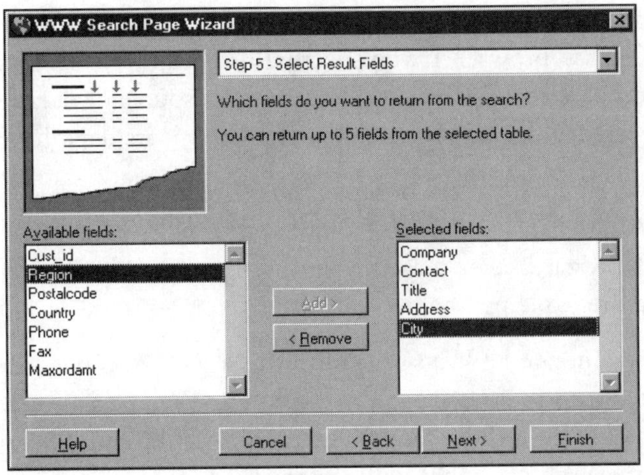

FIGURE 13-12

The Search Page Wizard here has the query results screen active.

technique by which you can modify the resulting Web page to return more than five fields.

6. The last set of options to specify are the results page options (see Figure 13-13). You can specify an optional background and header image file to be displayed; these can be in JPEG or GIF format. You also can limit the number of records to be returned. When you deal with the Internet, you might want to minimize the amount of data that is returned to the Web browser, because most people access Web pages using modems

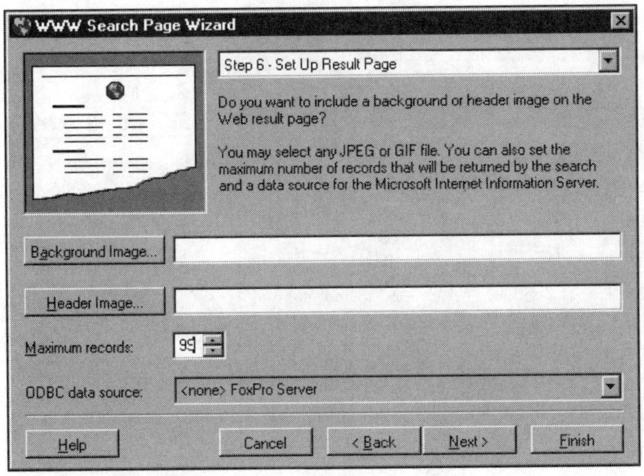

FIGURE 13-13

The Search Page Wizard here has the results page screen active.

that transfer data rather slowly. Another option you can specify is to have an ODBC browser. If you specify this option, the server application uses the ODBC data source as its source of data instead of going directly to the VFP data table (the latter is its default behavior).

After you finish working with these options, the wizard offers a finish line screen. When you click Finish, you are prompted to provide a name for your Web page files. The wizard saves these files using the name you specify and three file extensions that are explained below.

Now that you have generated a Web page with the wizard, you need to copy the files it has generated into the wwwroot directory. The Web page generator creates three files, which end in the following extensions: HTM, IDC, and HTX. The HTM file is the Web page that will be presented to your users. The HTX file is used to format the output of a Web page, and the IDC file is used to specify query information.

After copying these files to the appropriate directories, you can proceed to open the file in your Web browser. Figures 13-14 and 13-15, respectively, show the generated Web page and the results sent back from the server when it processes one of its requests.

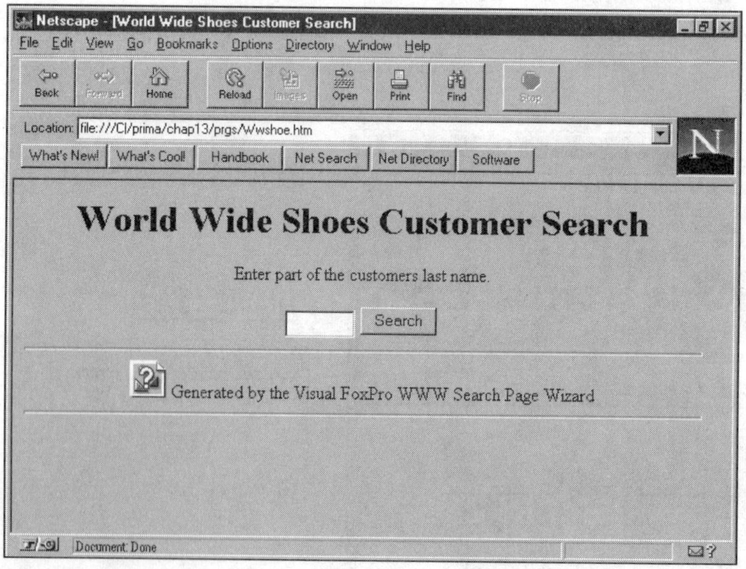

FIGURE 13-14

You can view the Web page created by the Internet Search Page Wizard.

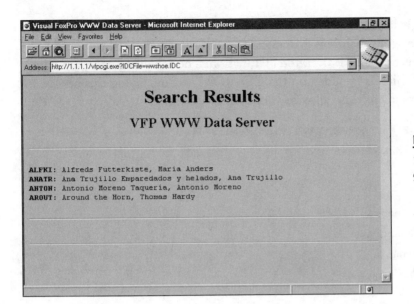

FIGURE 13-15

These are the results of a processed query.

Hacking the Visual FoxPro Internet Server

One of the nice things about the Visual FoxPro Internet Server is its openness. The developers of the Internet Wizard provide the source code to: 1) your generated Web pages, and 2) the SERVER.APP that processes requests and returns them to the server. This means that you can add or replace the capabilities of either side of your Internet application.

Tweaking SERVER.PRG

The entire SERVER.APP application centers around SERVER.PRG. This program takes the queries submitted by your Web pages, processes each query, and returns a Web page. You'll probably think that the returned Web page is too bland. It returns the results as a set of single lines, and is limited to only five columns. It would be nice to modify it to return your result set as an HTML table instead of a bunch of single lines. To perform this operation, you need to intercept the SERVER.PRG program before it generates its result set. To do this, you need to insert code after it calls its MakeData() function. The following code, a modified version of which is included on the CD-ROM accompanying this book, shows how to intercept this call with your own function:

```
lnRecordsReturned=RECCOUNT('TempResult')
IF lnRecordsReturned = 0
   CurrentRecord=0
ELSE
   CurrentRecord=1
   IF llReturnData
     =Cleanup()
     RETURN makedata()
   ENDIF
ENDIF

ENDIF

*****************************************
*- Call Custom Function
RETURN My_Server_Function("TempResult")
*****************************************

*Create HTML return page from .HTX and data

*Verify the existence of the Template (.HTX) file.
*It must be next to the .IDC file,
*pathed relative to the .IDC file, or in the Script root.
lcTmpFile=lcTemplate
```

In order to intercept the call from the server, you need to hand the name of the query result cursor set to your own function. This function needs to return a string representing the Web page to be returned to your browser. The following code demonstrates using the cHTML class to return a CGI page to a Web browser processing a request:

```
Function My_Server_Function
Lparamater pcAlias

*- This code assumes the presence of the cHTML classes developed
*- above.

Local loHTML, lcRetVal
lcRetVal = ""

loHTML = Createobject("cHTML")
loHTML.CreateTable(pcAlias)
lcRetVal = loHTML.ReturnHTMLPage(.t.)

Return lcRetVal
```

This change replaces the return value from the SERVER.APP file with a nicely
formatted Web page. Figure 13-16 shows the resulting Web page.

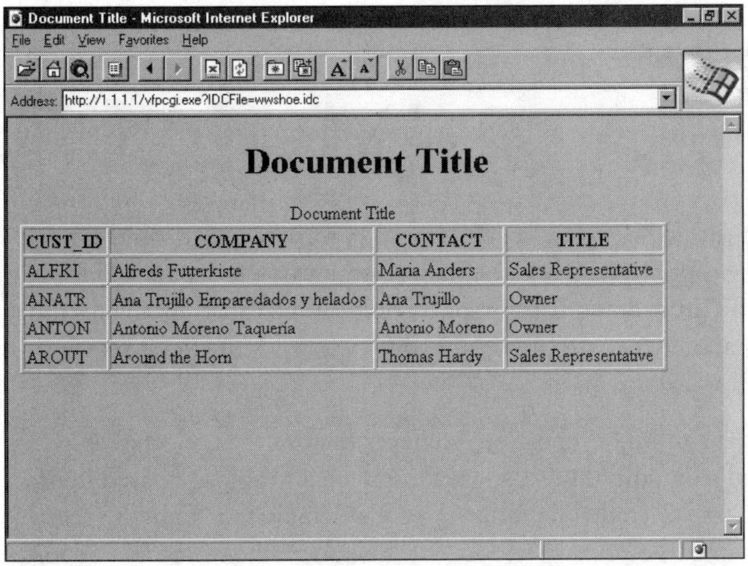

FIGURE 13-16

*The modified server application
returns the results in an HTML–
formatted table.*

Modifying the Internet Search Page Wizard

Now that you have modified the server application to return a different Web page, you can alter the query Web page to perform different tasks. To do this, you need to understand how the SERVER.PRG program processes a query.

Whenever SERVER.PRG receives a query, it takes a string passed to it from the server and creates an array with the options provided by the Web page. This array contains the parameters that have been input on the Web page. The following Web page has a few options on it:

```
<P>This demonstration shows how you can use Visual FoxPro as an
Internet server application.</P>

<FORM ACTION="vfpcgi.exe?IDCFile=FOXTEACH.IDC" METHOD="POST">

<INPUT NAME="SearchParam" SIZE=40 VALUE="" >

<INPUT TYPE="SUBMIT" VALUE="Search">

<br>


<!List dropdown control>

<SELECT Name="Selected-Report">

  <OPTION>Annual Sales

  <OPTION>Current Inventory

  <OPTION>A/R Aging

</SELECT>

<br>
```

The first option on this Web page is a TEXT input type. The TEXT input type field specifies a Name option, which is the name of the variable handed to the server. There is also a drop-down list of reports that can be called by the user. By intercepting these parameters, you can create your own types of stored requests and queries.

Suppose that you want to run a report on whatever the user has selected above. To do this, you need to modify SERVER.PRG to return a Web page based upon whatever your user has selected. The following code demonstrates how to search for the parameter named Selected-Report in the array, then process a report accordingly:

```
Function My_Server_Function2
Lparameters pcAlias, paArrayOfParameters
EXTERNAL ARRAY paArrayOfParameters

*- Declare our variables
Local lnReportParam, lcRetVal, loHTML

loHTML = Createobject("cHTML")

*- Store array element parameter here
lnReportParam = Ascan(paArrayOfParameters,"Selected-Report")

*- If we go to an element, then our parameter is the next element
*- So Add One and see what it is
If lnReportParam > 0
  lcReportToRun=Upper(Alltrim(paArrayOfParameters(lnReportParam+1)))
  Do Case
  Case lcReportToRun = "ANNUAL SALES"
    loHTML.CreateHeaderLine("Annual Sales Report")
  Case lcReportToRun = "CURRENT INVENTORY"
    loHTML.CreateHeaderLine("Current Inventory Report")
  Case lcReportToRun = "A/R AGING"
    loHTML.CreateHeaderLine("Accounts Receivable Aging Report")
  OTHERWISE
    loHTML.CreateHeaderLine("Report Not Found! ")
  Endcase
Else
    loHTML.CreateHeaderLine("Report Not Found! ")
Endif

lcRetVal = loHTML.ReturnHTMLPage(.t.)

Return lcRetVal
```

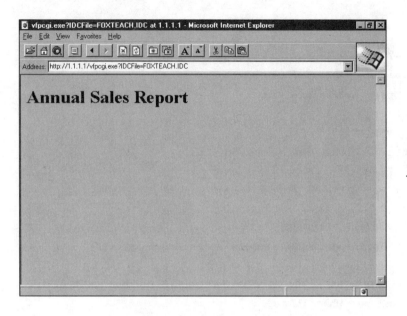

FIGURE 13-17

The results of the report processing feature added to the SERVER *application.*

Figure 13-17 shows the results of the changed Web page. It should be apparent now how to create your own stored procedures using the above techniques.

Information from the Web

The Internet is a very large subject that in no way can be handled by this chapter alone. You can check the following Web sites for more information to assist in your Web application development:

- **http://www.microsoft.com/vfoxpro**—Microsoft's official Web site; contains the latest news about VFP, new utilities, and links to other Web sites
- **http://www.sbtcorp.com/**—FoxPro accounting software company
- **http://www.hentzenwerke.com/**—Whil Hentzens' home page (Whil is a renowned Fox developer)
- **http://www.pinpub.com/**—Pinnacle Publishing's Web site

Summary

Integrating Visual FoxPro with the Internet is a very basic task, using some simple VFP techniques and tools. You can create your own Web sites, create Web pages dynamically, save data gathered from Web users, and create your own Web browser. This can help you add the following capabilities to your applications:

- Provide customers with access to data
- Schedule appointments across the Web
- Take orders for products
- Collect marketing information across the Web
- Gather research data on the Web
- Mail-enable your applications to use Internet e-mail

Chapter 14

Deploying and Distributing
Your Applications

Introduction

The time has arrived for you to distribute your application. The long hours of analysis, design, programming, and testing are finally going to pay off. Maybe.

While you might be 99% of the way there, it can be argued that despite the importance of design and testing, the time you spend deploying and distributing your application makes up the most crucial 1% of the entire project. Even if you have developed the best class designs, the tightest bulletproof code, or the fastest queries possible, they won't mean a thing if the application cannot be installed and run. This is the point in the development life cycle where many applications fail. Why? Usually because the developer, while competent with most of Visual FoxPro's tools, does not fully understand what is required to distribute an application.

The purpose of this chapter is to arm you, the Visual FoxPro developer, with all the tools necessary to confidently distribute your applications. This chapter will discuss what is involved in creating an executable (EXE) file, making sure that all files are accounted for in your installation disks, and finally, creating a help system for your application.

This chapter will be divided into four principal sections:

- Creating an EXE file
- Using the Setup Wizard
- Common problems with distributed applications
- Integrating help in an application

Creating an EXE File

Being an intermediate to advanced Visual FoxPro developer, it is assumed you have a good working knowledge of how the VFP Project Manager operates. Creating an executable file in VFP 5.0 is very much the same as in version 3.0 and earlier. There are, however, some nice features of the Project Manager in version 5.0 that merit special attention.

As you can see in Figure 14-1, the primary interface of the Project Manager has remained the same in version 5.0. The only notable difference is the use of the TreeView control in lieu of the Outline control for the listing of items in the

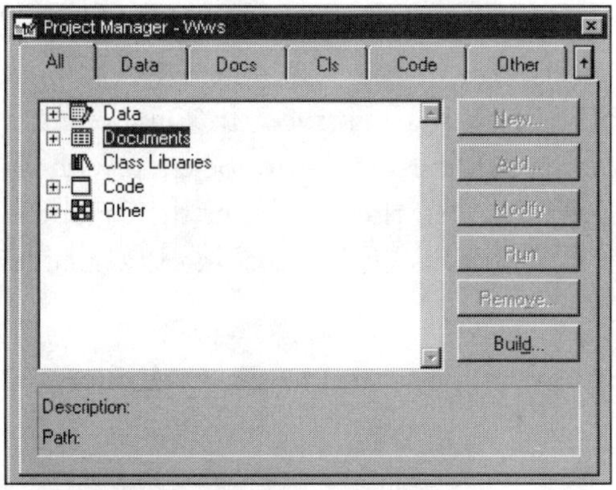

FIGURE 14-1

The VFP 5.0 Project Manager offers some very useful features.

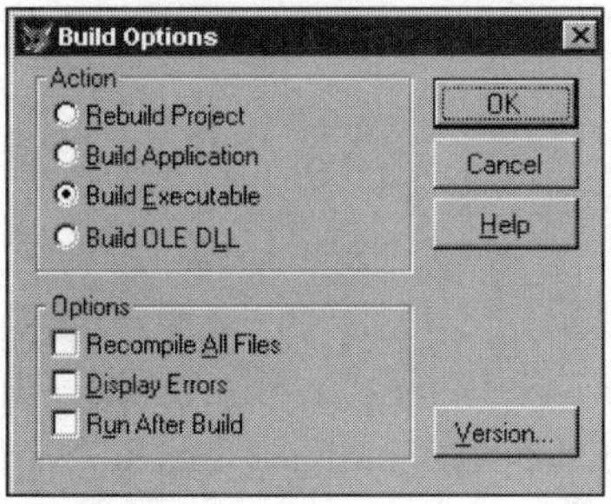

FIGURE 14-2

The Build dialog box contains a new option for building DLLs.

Project Manager. The new features become apparent when you click the Build button, as shown in Figure 14-2.

New to version 5.0 is a Version button in the lower-right portion of the Build Options dialog box, which leads to the dialog box shown in Figure 14-3.

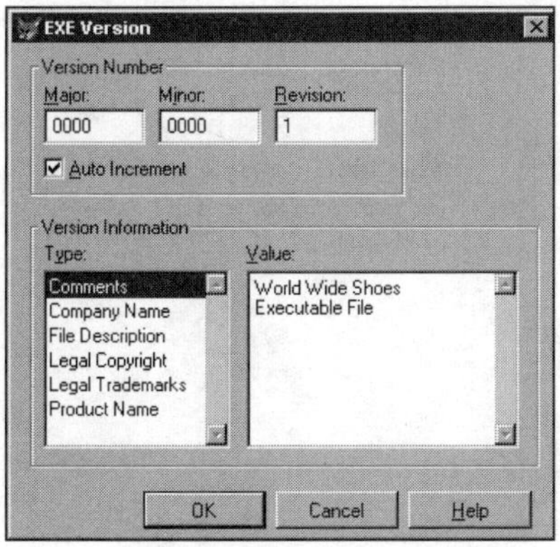

FIGURE 14-3

Version numbering is a feature that's new to VFP.

Beginning with Windows 95, when applications are right-clicked in Explorer, a dialog box is presented to the user. This dialog box has a series of page tabs, each containing information about the file being observed. In some cases, a page tab outlining version information is available. Keeping in lockstep with all the capabilities of Windows 95, VFP 5.0 has given the developer the capability of binding version information to the EXE file, as well as making it available to the end user of the developer's software.

The following version information can be bound to the EXE file:

- Comments
- Company name
- File description
- Legal copyright
- Legal trademarks
- Product name

The developer can maintain this information directly in the Version dialog box. Figure 14-4 shows the Version tab of the Properties dialog box in Explorer.

In addition to descriptive information, you also can maintain a version numbering system. VFP 5.0 uses the standard Major.Minor.Revision numbering scheme. For

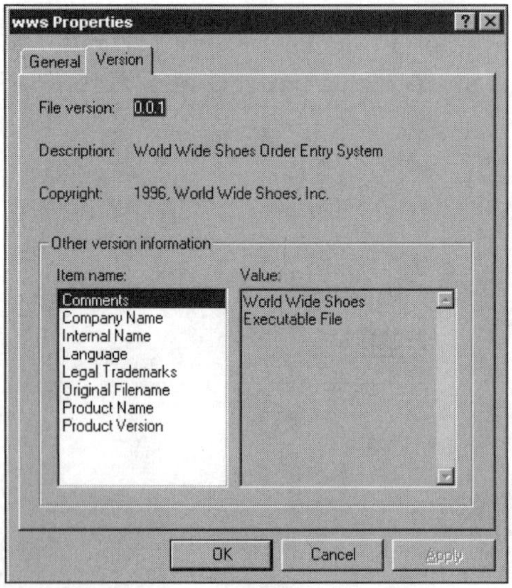

FIGURE 14-4

In addition to version numbering, copyright and author information can be embedded in the EXE file.

example, if the current build of an application represents the first build of the first maintenance release of the second version of the product, the version number reads as follows: 2.1.1. While you must manually maintain the incrementation of the Major and Minor numbers, VFP automatically increments the Revision counter every time an EXE is built (if the Auto Increment check box is selected). You are allowed up to 9,999 builds. Once this plateau has been reached, VFP stops incrementing the counter. In addition, when you manually set the Major and Minor numbers, you must manually set the Revision number to zero.

Once all your version information is correctly set, it's time to build the EXE file. This process is completed by clicking the OK button in the Build Options dialog box.

Using the Setup Wizard

With an EXE file created, it's time for you to place the application in the client's hands. The next task is to efficiently distribute the application. Whether the client is another department in your organization, or an external third-party entity, it's more than just important for the installation to work correctly—it's a drop-dead requirement. After all, if your application cannot be installed, it cannot be used.

Shipped with the Professional Edition of Visual FoxPro is an application named WZSETUP.APP. This is the Setup Wizard, accessed by choosing Wizards from the Tools menu (see Figure 14-5).

Prior to running the Setup Wizard, you should consider a few items in your final checklist, as explained in the following sections.

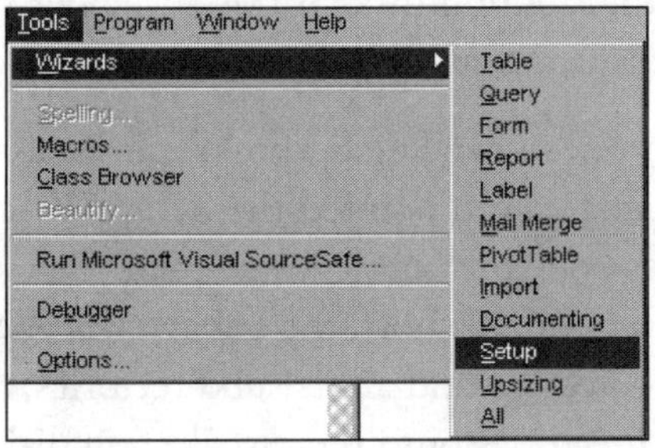

FIGURE 14-5

The Setup Wizard is accessed from the Wizards menu.

Are You Sure the Application is Ready for Distribution?

It's worth asking this question one final time. This is the last opportunity you have to prevent distribution of an application that might make your client call you at all hours demanding answers. Now is a good time to make sure that all elements of the application have been tested and debugged. It's also a good idea to ensure that the application is feature-complete. You and the client have previously agreed upon a set of specifications for the project; rest assured that the client will expect all these items to be included in the final delivery.

Create a Distribution Directory

Once you have the green light to cut the distribution disks, it's time to move the files that will be distributed into a *distribution directory*. A good naming convention to employ is a three-letter designation for the application at hand, plus the word DIST. In the World Wide Shoes example, our distribution directory is named WWSDIST. Files that need to be distributed include the following:

- The EXE file
- OCXs
- FLLs
- DLLs
- Data-related files (DBFs, DBCs, and so on)
- HLPs (help files)

The only additions to the above list are the VFP Runtime, ODBC, and MS Graph files. However, because the Setup Wizard is integrated into VFP, these files are added automatically to the distribution disks if the developer specifies that they should be included. You'll see an example of this later in the chapter.

Why should you create a distribution directory? The Setup Wizard asks which directory holds the files to be distributed. If you pointed the Setup Wizard to a directory that held both the EXE files and your source code, then your source code would be included on the distribution disks. In short, the behavior of the Setup Wizard is to recurse the distribution directory and all its subdirectories, then compress all the files contained in those directories onto the distribution disks.

Create a Disk Directory

Finally, you need a directory to hold the disk images that ultimately will be copied to floppy disks. Employing the same naming convention for the distribution directory, the disk directory is named WWSDISKS. Typically, both the WWSDIST and WWSDISKS directories are placed directly off the root. This is not a requirement, however, so use your best judgment and do what works best for you.

With your checklist complete, you're ready to begin the process of creating a setup of distribution disks. You start the process by choosing Wizards from the Tools menu, then choosing Setup.

The Setup Wizard is a powerful and simple tool to use, mostly because of its intuitive interface. The Setup Wizard has seven steps, which are described in the following sections.

Locate Files

The first step presents you with a dialog box for directing the Setup Wizard to the directory that contains the files to be distributed. In this example, as you can see in Figure 14-6, the directory is D:\WWSDIST.

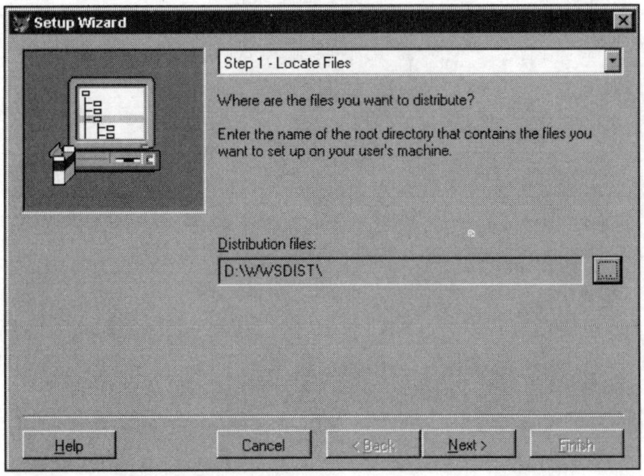

FIGURE 14-6

In step 1, you specify the location of the files to be distributed.

Specify Contents

This step serves two primary needs. First, you indicate whether the VFP Runtime files, MS Graph, ODBC Drivers, and OLE Server files are to be included in the distribution disk set. Second, you indicate the platforms on which your application can be distributed. As of VFP 5.0, only 32-bit platforms are supported. Therefore, Windows 95 and Windows NT are the only available choices, as shown in Figure 14-7.

All these files, in their uncompressed state, reside in the DISTRIB.SRC directory, which in turn resides directly beneath VFP's root directory. The DISTRIB.SRC directory contains two other directories: WINNT and WIN95. Each of these directories contains one file, CTL3D32.DLL. Because Windows NT 3.51 and Windows 95 have controls that differ in appearance, each has a different version of CTL3D32.DLL. As this book is being written, Windows NT 4.0 is very late in beta testing. One of the biggest features of NT 4.0 is its new look, abandoning the old Windows appearance in favor of a Windows 95 look. Perhaps when NT 4.0 is released, there will not be a need for two different DLL files.

For the moment, however, if you want both platforms included in the setup disks, then both versions of the DLL must be compressed. The platform on which the application is deployed determines which DLL is uncompressed at that time.

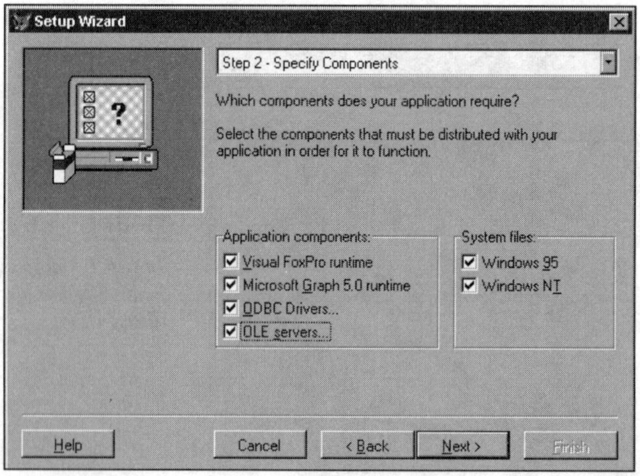

FIGURE 14-7

In step 2, you specify which components are included in the setup disks.

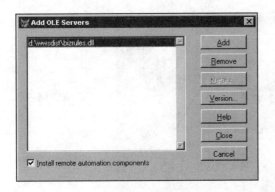

FIGURE 14-8

When specifying components, you must specify OLE servers that need to be registered on the target machine.

In addition to the VFP Runtime, ODBC, and MS Graph files, the Setup Wizard also accommodates a new class of files, OLE servers, as shown in Figure 14-8. These files require additional support files that are contained in DISTRIB.SRC. In addition, if you elect to have remote automation support, still more files are required.

The files that are included as a result of your choices in specifying components will be stored in the SYSTEM directory of the target machine's Windows directory.

Create Disk Image Directory

In this step, you tell the Setup Wizard where to place the compressed disk images that ultimately will be copied to floppy disks (see Figure 14-9). Currently, there are three options to choose from: 1.44 MB 3.5-inch, 1.2 MB 5.25-inch, and Netsetup. Hardly anyone still utilizes 5.25-inch disks, so that option doesn't merit further discussion. For the 3.5-inch option, at a minimum, you'll use four disks if the VFP Runtime files are included. Remember that the contents of the DISTRIB.SRC files alone are over 9 MB in size. If you elect to include MS Graph, all the ODBC drivers, and an OLE server in addition to the VFP Runtime files, then your distribution set will be at least six disks. And we have not compressed one file of our application yet!

The Netsetup option creates one large compressed file that resides on a network, and in turn can be used to install the application on client workstations. This option is particularly useful for those developers who have to deploy applications

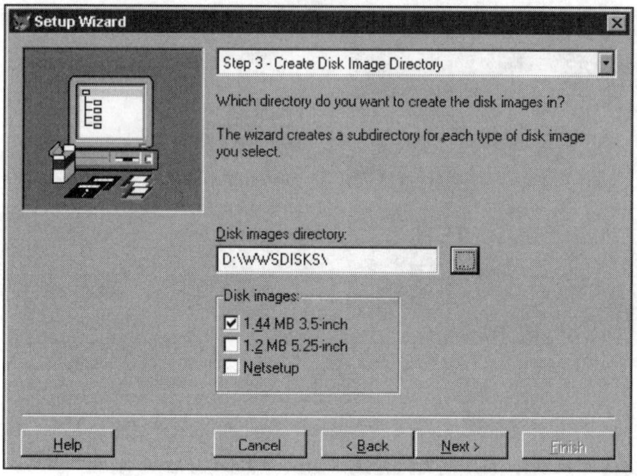

FIGURE 14-9

In step 3, you specify both the type of disk images and the directory in which the disk images are created.

on many workstations. Using this option, the setup files can be centrally located, the common login script of the affected workstations can be modified, and installation is basically complete. The next time the workstations are logged in, the installation process can start.

When the disk images are created, a subdirectory below the disk image directory is created for each option chosen. For example, a directory named DISK144 is created if the 1.44 MB 3.5-inch option is chosen. Under this directory is a directory for each disk. For example, the image for Disk 1 resides in a directory named DISK1. The DISK1 directory also contains the files required to carry out the installation. Among these files are SETUP.EXE and SETUP.INF. In addition to all these directories is one named COMPRESS. This directory contains the compressed versions of files that are contained in the distribution directory.

Specify Setup Options

This step allows you to specify a caption for the Setup dialog box, along with any copyright information that may be required (see Figure 14-10). In addition, a post-setup executable file can be run as soon as the setup is complete. Usually, this post-setup executable is a README.TXT file outlining key features of the release that was just installed.

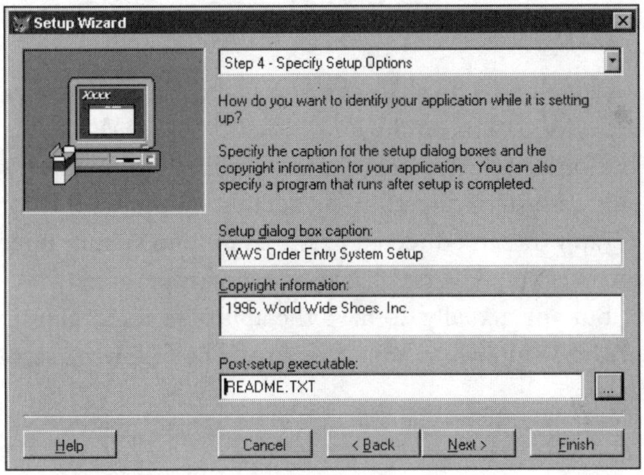

FIGURE 14-10

In step 4, you can specify options such as dialog box caption, copyright, and post–setup executable file.

Specify Default Destination

In this step, you specify the default destination directory. In addition, you specify the description for the program group. You decide whether to allow the individual installing the software to change the default destination directory, the program group name, or both (see Figure 14-11).

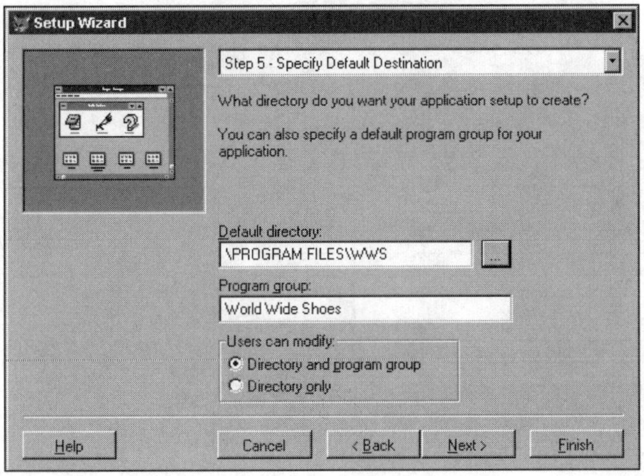

FIGURE 14-11

In step 5, you can specify the target directory and default Program Manager group to which your application will be installed.

Change File Settings

You're in the home stretch now. In this step, you make the Setup Wizard aware of some file-specific information, as shown in Figure 14-12. While many of the files in your distribution directory will go in the destination directory, some need to go into the Windows system directory. By default, all the VFP Runtime, ODBC, and MS Graph files are directed to the Windows system directory. This is all done behind the scenes. At first glance, it might appear that you do not have any flexibility, but you actually do have the ability to direct files to the default directory or the Windows system directory. The following section explains how to do so.

Target Directory

There are three directories to which you can direct application files:

- `AppDir`—The application's default destination directory (in this example, it's `\Program Files\WWS`)

- `WinSysDir`—The Windows system directory (files such as OCXs and DLLs usually are stored in this directory)

- `WinDir`—The Windows directory

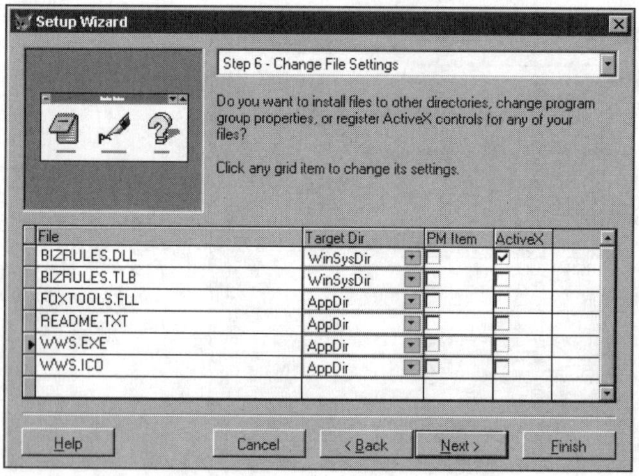

FIGURE 14-12

In step 6, you get a chance to change file attributes on a file-by-file basis.

Program Manager Item

When you select Program Manager Item, a dialog box is presented so that you can specify properties of the program file, as shown in Figure 14-13.

For the main program in an application—in this case, WWS.EXE—you need to specify the description of the program file, the command-line parameters, and, if you want, the program icon.

ActiveX

Lastly, if you have an ActiveX control, you can get the Setup Wizard to generate the necessary code to register the control in the Windows Registry. In addition, when you select ActiveX, the target directory automatically changes to WinSysDir.

Finish

You're done specifying all the necessary information. At this point, it's a good idea to run back through the steps to make sure that everything's in order. Once you're satisfied that everything's okay, click Finish (see Figure 14-14).

After you click Finish, the Setup Wizard begins the process of compressing the disk images. During the course of compression, the status dialog box shown in Figure 14-15 is displayed.

Once the disk images have been created, the dialog box shown in Figure 14-16 is displayed.

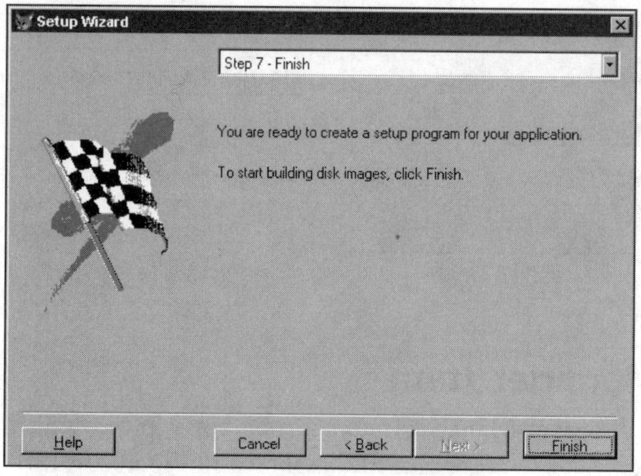

FIGURE 14-14

In step 7, you're now ready to build your setup disks!

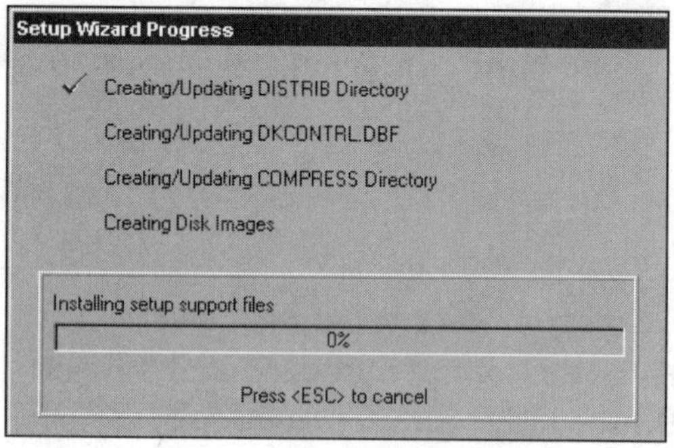

FIGURE 14-15

During the disk image build process, you're presented with a dialog box detailing what has been completed so far.

At this point, you know how many disks are required to distribute the application. In addition, you can print reports that outline exactly what has been compressed on each disk.

A Final Word on the Setup Wizard

For the developer who requires a simple, rudimentary setup installation process, the Setup Wizard is the perfect tool. For all its power and ease of use, however, it has limitations when you require an advanced installation process. For example, what if you have optional files that the user may or may not want to install? What if you desire a more customized look and feel to your installation process?

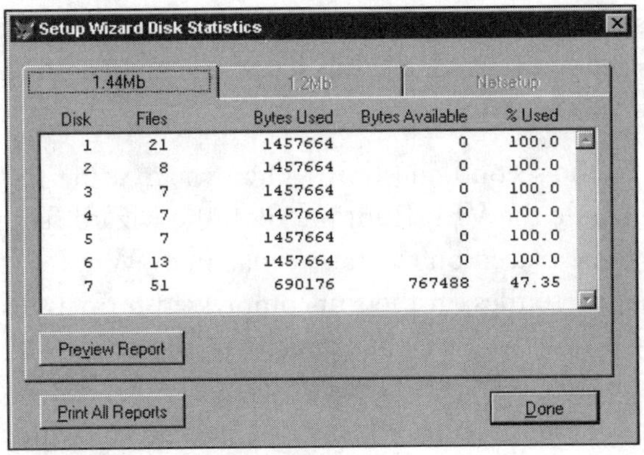

FIGURE 14-16

At the conclusion of the disk image build process, you're presented with a dialog box detailing how many disk images were created, and the size of each disk.

When you install disks created by the Setup Wizard, you find references to Microsoft Corporation in the first screen of the setup—what if you don't want that? What if you need to require the user to enter a name and company? Finally, what if you have files other than ActiveX controls that need to have entries in the Windows Registry?

If you have any of these advanced requirements, then the Setup Wizard is not robust enough to meet your needs. The following sections help you find an alternative.

InstallShield

InstallShield from InstallShield Corporation is the *de facto* standard in software installation. In fact, most software distributed today makes use of InstallShield, and it's likely that you've used InstallShield yourself. This software provides a rich scripting language that allows you to customize your installation process in almost any way imaginable. For the World Wide Shoes installation process, a customized setup has been created to demonstrate how easy it is to incorporate such third-party tools in the distribution of a VFP application.

When you resort to a third-party solution, two questions come to mind:

1. How do I use the new tool?

2. How do I retain needed functionality that exists in the old tool?

To answer the first question, InstallShield includes many examples of how to use the tool. In addition, to get you started, a setup script is included on the CD-ROM that accompanies this book.

There is also an answer to the second question. When you're using the Setup Wizard, and decide to include the VFP Runtime files, the wizard figures out which files are required to be placed on the target machine's Windows system directory. Remember that these files, in their uncompressed format, reside in the DISTRIB.SRC directory below the VFP root directory. The only required file that does not reside in the DISTRIB.SRC directory is VFP500.DLL (which is located in the Windows system directory). Just as we needed to created a distribution directory for the Setup Wizard, so too must we create such a directory for InstallShield. The only difference is that the VFP Runtime files, as well as any required ODBC or OLE files, must also be included in the distribution directory—and each of these files must be directed to the Windows system directory.

A Closer Look at InstallShield

The main script file that you write to tell InstallShield what to do is known as a *rule file* (its extension is RUL). Usually, this file is named SETUP.RUL. Like any program, this file needs to be compiled. Be forewarned that the InstallShield compiler is very unforgiving. If you declare a variable as a string type, it must remain a string type. Attempting to store a numeric to the variable somewhere in the code would result in a compile error. Also, all variable references are case-sensitive. If you declare a variable in all uppercase letters, you must refer to it in uppercase in all areas of the rule file; otherwise, a compile error results. Finally, InstallShield has a number of built-in functions. Many of these functions have mixed-case names. This mixed-case nomenclature must be respected throughout the rule file for a clean compile. If you have ever programmed in C or Pascal, you should feel right at home.

In the sample provided on this book's CD-ROM, the setup can be one of three choices:

- *Typical*—The source code for the World Wide Shoes Order Entry system is installed, as well as all the compiled application files.

- *Compact*—Only the compiled application files (plus any required OCX and DLL files) are installed.

- *Custom*—The user has the opportunity to install the VFP Runtime files.

Already, it's clear that your installation has much more flexibility when using a tool such as InstallShield.

Look at the structure of the WWS distribution tree and its contents when using InstallShield:

- \WWSDIST—This is the root of the distribution directory. Contained directly in the root is a file named BUILD.BAT. This DOS batch file is responsible for both compiling the SETUP.RUL file and compressing the distribution files onto disk images.

- \WWSDIST\SETUP—Among the files contained in this directory are any BMP files required by the setup process, and the SETUP.RUL file.

- \WWSDIST\DISK1...DISKx—Directly below the WWSDIST directory is a directory for each disk image. This is almost identical to the setup created by the Setup Wizard.

- \WWSDIST\DATA—This directory houses all the files that ultimately will be compressed onto the disk images.

- \WWSDIST\DATA\SOURCE—This directory contains all the source code for the WWS project.

- \WWSDIST\DATA\APPFILES—This directory contains all the compiled WWS application files.

- \WWSDIST\DATA\VFPRT—This directory contains the required VFP Runtime files that need to be placed in the Windows system directory.

By placing different types of files in various directories, it's a fairly easy task to associate choices the user makes in the installation process with certain files that need to be uncompressed. For example, if the user elects to have the VFP Runtime files installed, that fact is picked up on by code in the rule file that specifically looks to see if this choice has been made. When the code discovers that the choice has been made, the files contained in the VFPRT directory are installed.

In addition to choices the user can make, the WWS install process also contains a facility to collect the user's name and serial number. Moreover, generous use of graphics has been made throughout the installation process. Remember that the setup process you create is the first impression your users have of your work. The more appealing the setup is, the better. Using a third-party product like Install-Shield can make for a very professional installation.

A demo version of InstallShield is included on the CD-ROM accompanying this book. Definitely set aside some time to go through the samples, as well as the rule file created for the WWS example. InstallShield is going to integrate their product into Developer's Studio, a new Microsoft development platform. Since Microsoft has already stated that the next version of Visual FoxPro also will be integrated into Developer's Studio, it makes sense to get a headstart today in learning how to leverage the InstallShield technology in your VFP applications.

Common Problems with Distributed Applications

It is necessary to be aware of the common pitfalls developers can fall into when distributing applications. The goal of this section is to help you steer clear of these potential traps.

Beware of the Developer Machine Trap

Developers of VFP applications often have their machines optimally configured for the tasks that need to be carried out in the course of application development. Moreover, it's often the case that source code files (PRGs, SCXs, and so on) are located on the development machine. At the very least, the development machine usually has access to these files via a network connection. It's important to make sure that all your source code has been properly included in your distributed EXE. Testing on a development machine that has separate access to your source code files might give you a false sense of security. When testing your distributed application, follow these steps:

1. Make sure that a checklist of all functionality has been created, and is up-to-date.

2. Install the application from a setup of floppy disks to a machine that does not have any access to your source code files.

3. Ensure that all files have been included in the EXE file by running down your checklist of functionality.

The best test—and the only truly reliable one—is in an environment that exactly mimics the one in which the application will be deployed. You may be surprised at the issues that come into play when conducting this type of test. In the long run, thorough testing in a "real-world" setting might save you many hours of appeasing a disgruntled client.

Remember to Include Graphics Files

Make sure that any necessary bitmap and icon files (BMP and ICO, respectively) are included in your project file. While you may designate that a BMP or ICO file is used in a form, command button, or report, you cannot always rely on the Project Manager to ensure that these files are included. To be on the safe side, make sure to add these files manually to the project.

Remember to Include Your `CONFIG.FPW` File

If you are relying on a configuration file to make certain settings prior to the Visual FoxPro Engine starting, be sure to include this configuration file in the Other Files section of the Project Manager. If it's named CONFIG.FPW, then VFP will make use of it when your application is started. Beginning with version 5.0, you now have the ability to suppress the main VFP Screen entirely. The only place to do this, however, is in the configuration file with a Screen = Off directive. By including CONFIG.FPW in the project, you can be sure that your application will behave as expected on any target machine.

Make Sure to Include `DDEREG.EXE` for 16-bit DLL Calls

While 32-bit DLL calls can be made natively in VFP via the Declare...*DLL* command, 16-bit DLL calls must still be made through Foxtools.FLL. Unfortunately, the Setup Wizard does not automatically include the required file named DDEREG.EXE for making such calls. If you need to make 16-bit DLL calls in your application, make sure to add DDEREG.EXE to the root of your distribution directory prior to creating your disk images. This file is located in the VFP root directory.

Integrating Help in Your Applications

One of the most important features of a system, yet one of the most overlooked, is the help system. Building a help system is viewed by many as something that's done in the later stages of a project. Rather, building a help system is a process that should be undertaken from the moment the project commences. Just as planning is necessary for a project's success, planning is vital for a successful and useful help system.

The most useful help files are those that are jointly developed by the development team and the end users. After all, the users will be the primary beneficiaries of the help system. To be useful, the online help system must be written in language that is clear and understandable. Often, when users are questioned about the most useful aspects of their system, the online help system is mentioned. When asked why, many users say the help system saves hours of time by providing detailed information on how to accomplish a given task. As you will discover in the remainder of this chapter, integrating help into a VFP application is both fun and easy.

How Help Works in VFP

Visual FoxPro 5.0 and previous versions have always made implementing help very easy. The DOS version of FoxPro was light years ahead of any other development product with regard to help. The architects of VFP have recognized that supporting robust help systems is a baseline requirement. In keeping with a great tradition of FoxPro help capabilities, VFP 5.0 supports all the latest help features of Windows 95. The following sections closely examine how help works and how it's integrated in VFP.

Help File Styles

Visual FoxPro supports two types of help files: graphical and DBF-style. The DBF-style remains supported in the product for backward-compatibility. For more details on how to implement DBF-style help, consult the *Developer's Guide* that ships with VFP. In the following sections, you'll concentrate on creating graphical help, which has become the standard in Windows-based applications.

Help-Specific VFP Commands

The following commands are specific to invoking and supporting a help system in VFP:

- `Help`—Opens the help window
- `Set Topic To`—Specifies the help topic or topics to open when you invoke the VFP help system
- `Set Topic ID To`—Specifies the help topic to display when you invoke the VFP help system (the help topic is based on the topic's context ID)
- `Set Help On|Off`—Enables or disables VFP online help (with `Set Help On`, help is enabled; with `Set Help Off`, help is disabled)
- `Set Help To`—Specifies a help file

In addition to the commands listed above, VFP contains the following properties and methods to support the process of integrating help in an application:

- `HelpContextID` property—Specifies a context ID for a topic in a help file to provide context-sensitive help for an object
- `WhatsThisHelpID` property *—Specifies a help topic context ID to provide What's This help for an object
- `WhatsThisHelp` property *—Specifies whether context-sensitive help uses What's This help or the Windows help file that's specified with `Set Help`
- `WhatsThisButton` property *—Specifies whether or not the What's This button appears in a form's title bar

■ WhatsThisMode() method*—Displays the What's This help question
mark mouse pointer, and enables What's This help mode

As you can see, VFP fully supports the new Windows 95 help system. Now that
you understand what commands, properties and methods are available to support
help, it's time to discuss how a help system is created.

Creating a Help System

Creating a help system used to be a labor-intensive process. The help author was
required to memorize a series of *Rich Text Format (RTF)* codes. Today, just as
there are Web page authoring tools and templates, there also are tools for help
authoring. The most popular of these tools on the market today is ROBOHELP
by Blue Sky Software. In addition, VFP ships with a help authoring tool named
Help Workshop. This chapter will focus on using Help Workshop to create a
sample help file. The resulting help file then will be processed by the HTML
Tool Kit that ships with ROBOHELP. This utility takes existing help files and
creates HTML pages that can be accessed with a Web browser.

The Help File Creation Process

The following basic steps are employed to create a help file:

1. Create a DOC file in a word processor such as Microsoft Word.
2. Save the DOC file as an RTF file.
3. Create a help project (HPJ) file.
4. Compile the HPJ file with the help compiler.

Fortunately, the use of help authoring tools makes the process of putting together
the different pieces of a help file very simple, by providing a single interface. The
following sections describe in detail how to create a simple help file.

---

*Properties and methods specific to the new Windows 95 help system

Creating a DOC/Rich Text Format File

While the examples illustrated in this text use Microsoft Word, any word processor that supports RTF can be used. Before going further, however, it is important to understand that you cannot type text free-form into the word processor. Since the help project and RTF files will be compiled to create an HLP file, text must be typed into the word processor in a specific way. Think of writing this RTF as writing lines of code in a VFP program—there are some conventions you must employ to tell the help compiler what to do. They key to doing this with RTF files is something known as a *footnote code*. The following footnote codes are commonly encountered when writing RTF files for help systems:

- #—This symbol denotes the topic ID. The topic ID uniquely identifies this topic among all topics in a help system. Every topic defined in a help system must have a topic ID.
- $—This symbol denotes the title of a topic.
- K—This symbol is used for designating search keywords.

There are several other footnote codes, and the capability exists to create user-defined footnote codes. For more information, consult the Help Workshop documentation that accompanies VFP. For the purpose of this example, only the three codes listed above will be used.

The sample RTF file that will be created in this chapter contains three topics:

- A topic to describe the data entry form
- A topic to describe a data entry field in the form
- A topic to describe a command button in the form

To create the RTF file, follow these steps:

1. Open Microsoft Word.
2. Create a new blank document. Make sure that Normal is selected in the View menu.
3. Choose Footnote from the Insert menu.
4. In the Footnote and Endnote dialog box, choose Custom Mark and enter a dollar sign ($). Your dialog box should look like the one shown in Figure 14-17.

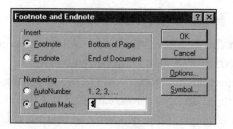

FIGURE 14-17

The Footnote and Endnote dialog box here has the $ (title) footnote entered.

Now that you have selected a footnote to enter, your Word document should be split into two sections, as shown in Figure 14-18.

5. With the mouse pointer positioned in the Footnote section, type **Customer Data Entry Form** next to the $.

6. Click the Close button in the Footnote section.

7. With the mouse pointer positioned at the top of the screen, repeat steps 3 and 4, using the # symbol instead of $.

8. Type **CUSTOMER_DATA_ENTRY_FORM** next to the #, the click the Close button.

9. Repeat steps 3 and 4, this time using the **K** symbol.

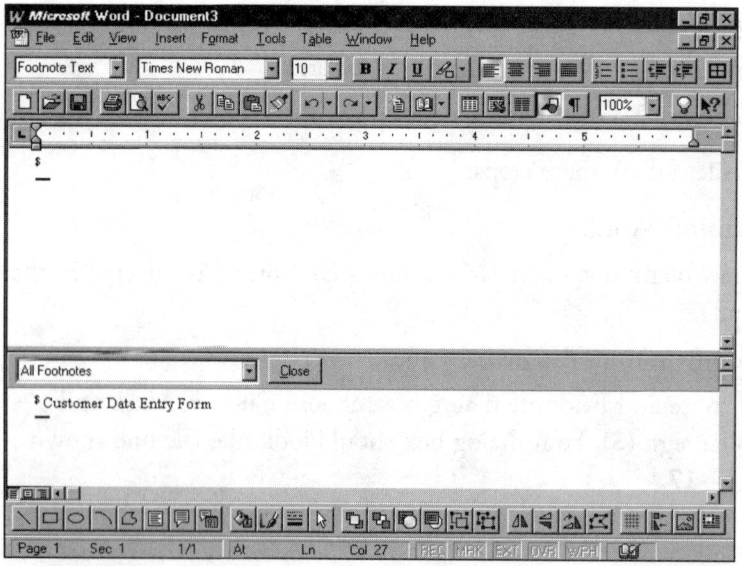

FIGURE 14-18

The lower panel specifies footnotes defined for text and graphics that appear in the upper panel.

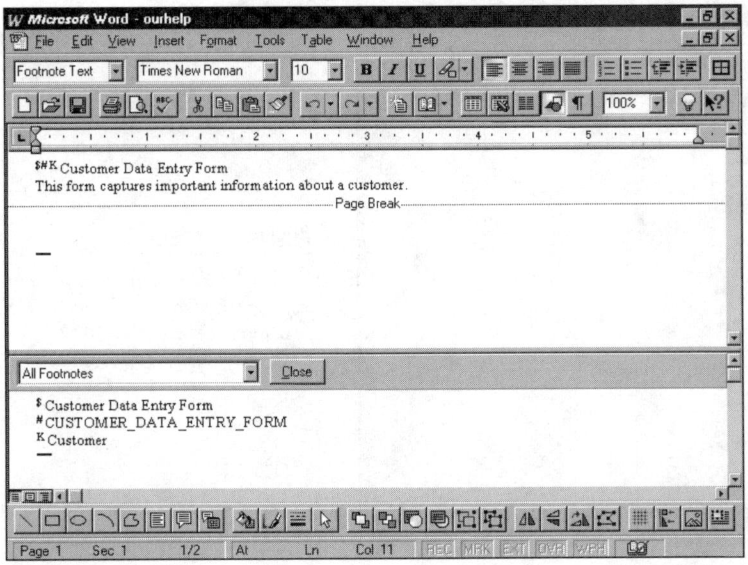

FIGURE 14-19

This RTF document in Word 95 has footnotes and text entered.

10. Type **Customer** next to the K. The Footnote section of your word document should look like the one shown in Figure 14-19.

11. Click the Close button.

12. With the mouse positioned at the top of the Word document, type **Customer Data Entry Form** and press Enter.

13. Type the following:
    This form captures important information about a customer.

14. Press Ctrl+Enter to force a page break. All topics in an RTF file used for help creation are separated with a hard page break. Your Word document now should look like the one shown in Figure 14-20.

At this point, you have done everything required to produce a help topic. Now, employing the steps above, create two more topics with the following information:

$ Customer Name

CUSTOMER_NAME

K   Customer;Name

Text   This field contains the name of the customer if the customer is an

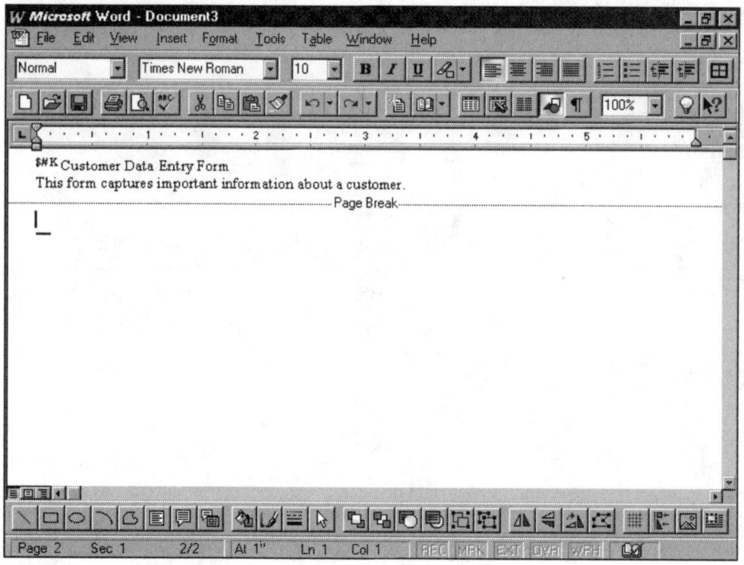

FIGURE 14-20

This RTF document has a forced page break placed at the end of the first topic.

individual. The name of the company is used if the customer is a business.

$	OK Button
#	OK_BUTTON
K	OK;Save
Text	Pressing this button will save changes made by user.

Your completed Word document should look like the one shown in Figure 14-21.

Now, save the file with the name OURHELP as an RTF file.

Using ROBOHELP to Create RTF Files

The preceding section demonstrated how to create an RTF file manually. Tools like ROBOHELP provide an interface over the word processor that shields the user from having to know the different footnote codes required to build an RTF file for a help system. Figure 14-22 shows an example of a ROBOHELP session in which a topic is created.

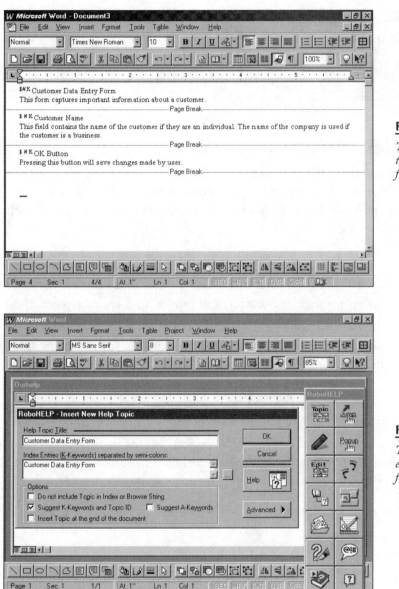

FIGURE 14-21

This RTF document contains three topics and associated footnotes.

FIGURE 14-22

The ROBOHELP interface eliminates the need to memorize footnote codes.

Notice that the ROBOHELP interface automatically creates the topic ID and search words, based on the topic title. When you save the information by clicking the OK button, ROBOHELP automatically takes care of creating the footnotes. A tool such as ROBOHELP makes complex jobs easy, thanks to its efficient interface.

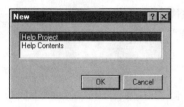

FIGURE 14-23

Creating a help file with the Help Workshop begins by creating a help project.

Create a Help Project (HPJ) File

With an RTF file created, it's time to create a help project with the Help Workshop. When VFP is installed, an icon for the Help Workshop is created. After activating the Help Workshop and choosing New from the File menu, you reach the dialog box shown in Figure 14-23.

When creating a Windows 95-style help system, there are two basic components:

- **Help project**—This is a collection of all the files that ultimately will come together through the compilation process to form a help file.

- **Help contents**—This file replaces the table of contents that was present in previous versions of Windows. The help contents constitute the first tab of a help system.

Following these steps will yield an empty help project:

1. Select Help Project from the dialog box.

2. Specify a directory and name for the project. In this example, type the name **ourhelp.hpj**. The Help Workshop should look like the one shown in Figure 14-24.

At this point, the RTF file can be added to the project:

3. Click the Files button.

4. Click the Add button in the Topic Files dialog box.

5. Add the previously created RTF file. Once the file has been added, click the OK button. The Help Workshop now should look like the one shown in Figure 14-25.

Next, because the HelpContextID Property in the VFP base classes is numeric, the character topic IDs in the RTF file must be mapped to numeric values. The following list shows the numeric topic ID that corresponds to each character topic ID:

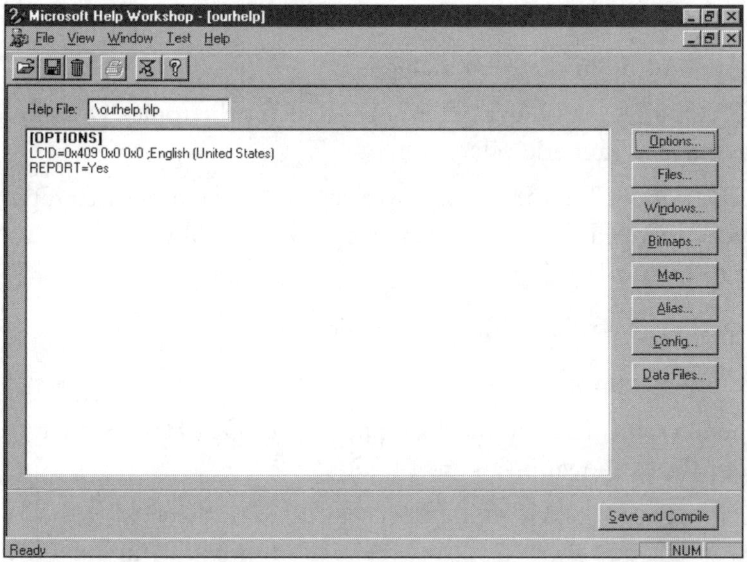

FIGURE 14-24

A help project is an INI file used by the help compiler to incorporate chosen attributes into the completed help file.

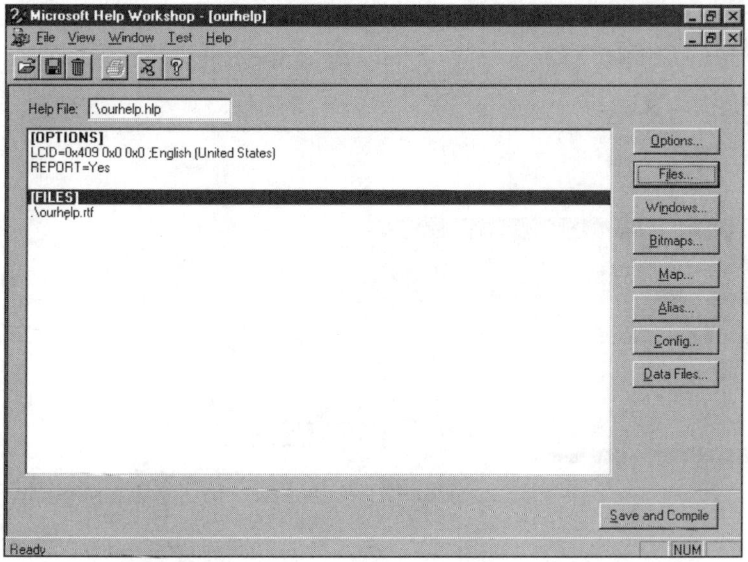

FIGURE 14-25

Files included in the help system are listed in the FILES section of the help project file.

Character Topic ID	Numeric Topic ID
CUSTOMER_DATA_ENTRY_FORM	100
CUSTOMER_NAME	110
OK_BUTTON	120

6. Click the Map button.

7. Click the Add button in the Map dialog box.

8. Enter **CUSTOMER_DATA_ENTRY_FORM** for the topic ID, and **100** for the mapped numeric value.

9. Click the OK button. Repeat the last two steps until the other two topic IDs have been mapped. The Help Workshop now should look like the one shown in Figure 14-26.

Finally, it's time to designate a title for the help window:

10. Click the Options button.

11. In the General tab of the Options dialog box, enter **Our Help System** for the help title, as shown in Figure 14-27.

12. The last step is to save and compile the project. Do so by clicking the Save and Compile button. When the project has finished compiling, the Help Workshop reports on the status of the compilation, as shown in Figure 14-28.

You have created OURHELP.HLP! Go into VFP and issue the following code:

```
Set Help To ourhelp.hlp
```

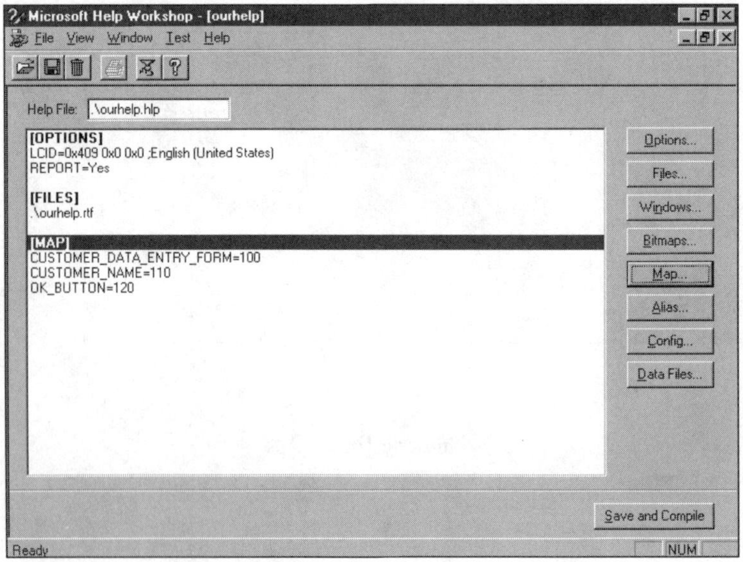

FIGURE 14-26

The MAP section of the help project file takes care of translating character topic IDs to numeric topic IDs that VFP can use.

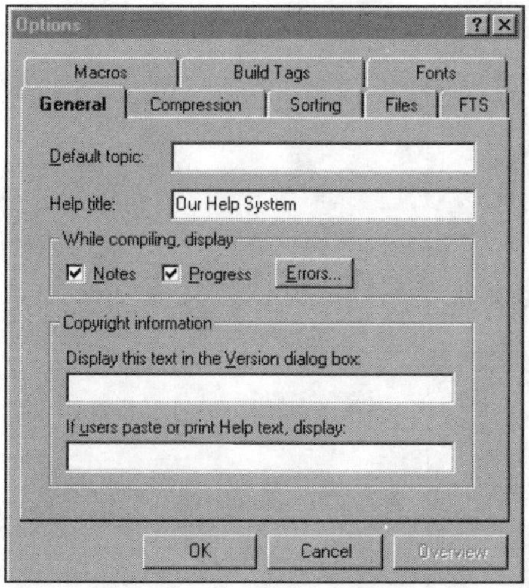

FIGURE 14-27

The Options dialog box gives you the opportunity to specify a title for the main help window.

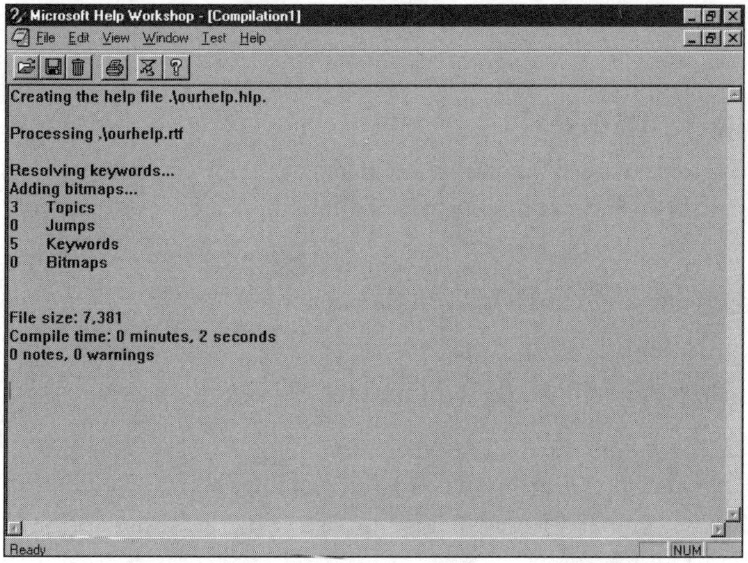

FIGURE 14-28

Once the help file has been compiled, a report is presented that outlines the results of the compilation.

Now, press the F1 key to invoke the help system. Figure 14-29 depicts the current state of the help file.

The only section missing from the help file now is the help contents.

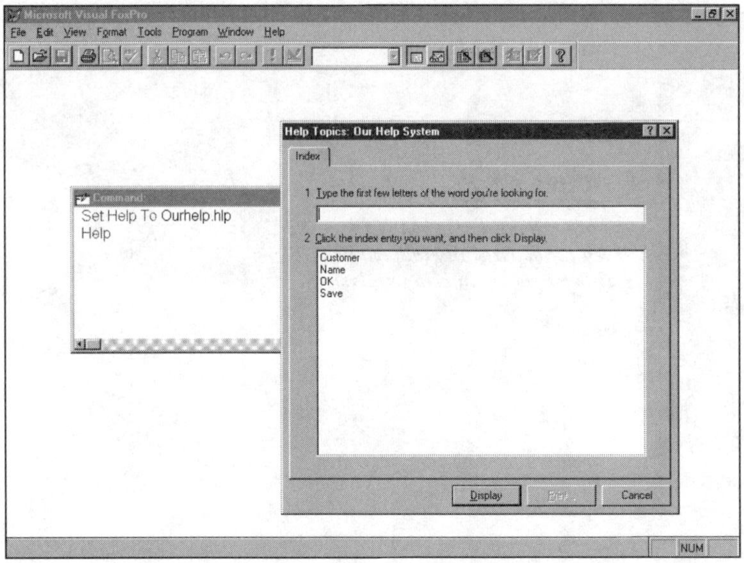

FIGURE 14-29

The new help file, although still incomplete, is fully functional in VFP.

Creating Help Contents

As stated earlier, help contents in Windows 95 replaces the table of contents from older versions of the Windows help system. Follow these steps for creating a contents file:

1. From the File menu in the Help Workshop, choose New.

2. Select Help Contents.

3. Enter **ourhelp** for the file name and **Our Help System** for a default title.

4. Click the Add Above button.

5. In the Edit Contents Tab Entry dialog box, select the Heading option and type **Our Help System**.

6. Click the OK button. You now should have something similar to the help system shown in Figure 14-30.

7. Click the Add Below button.

8. Leaving the selection at Topic, enter **Customer Data Entry Form** for the title, **CUSTOMER_DATA_ENTRY_FORM** for the topic ID, and **ourhelp** for the help file. Click the OK button.

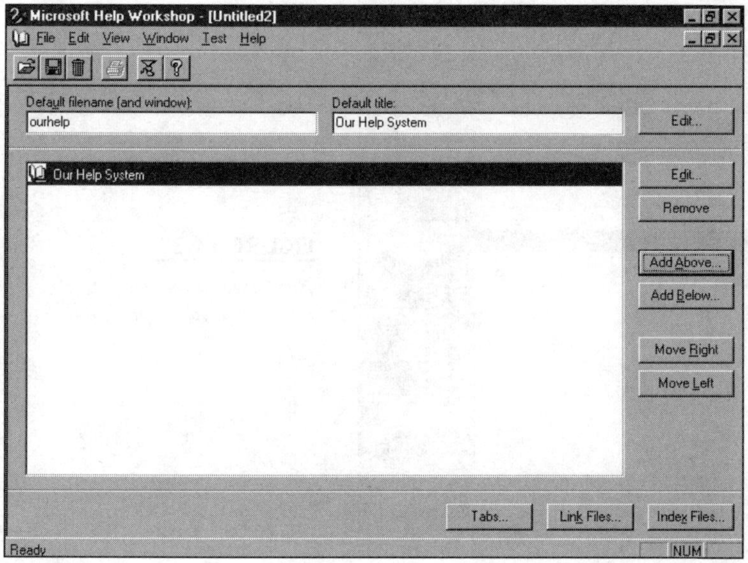

FIGURE 14-30

The Help Workshop also has the capability of creating a help table of contents.

9. Click Add Below again, then enter the information for the CUSTOMER_ NAME topic.

10. Repeat the last step, this time for the third help topic. Your contents file now should look like the one shown in Figure 14-31.

11. Save the contents file, naming it **ourhelp.cnt**. After saving the file, choose Close from the File menu. All that's required now is to link the help project and the contents file.

12. Click the Options button, then select the Files tab in the Options dialog box.

13. Assign the newly created contents file in the space provided, as shown in Figure 14-32.

14. Click the OK button.

15. Click Save and Compile to compile the help project. The newly modified help file now has a contents page, as shown in Figure 14-33.

Choosing any of the options in the contents page automatically selects the associated topic.

At this point, you have a fully functional help file. Now, try putting the file to work.

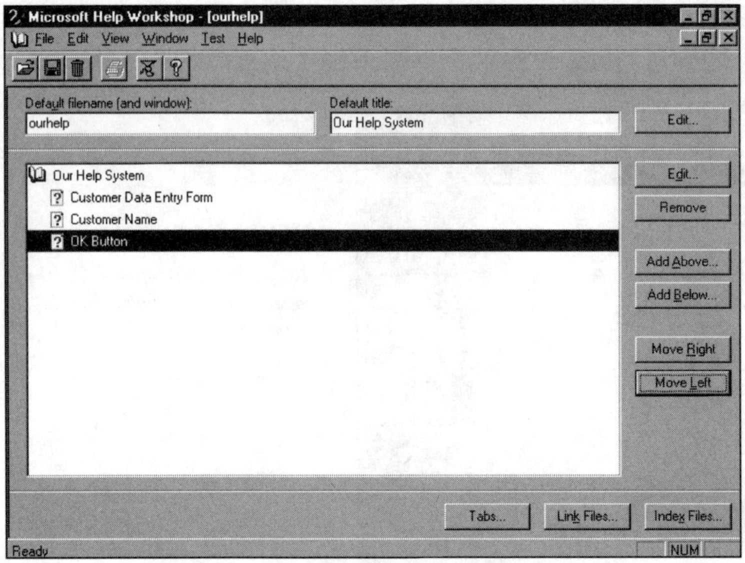

FIGURE 14-31

Each page in the contents file corresponds to a topic ID.

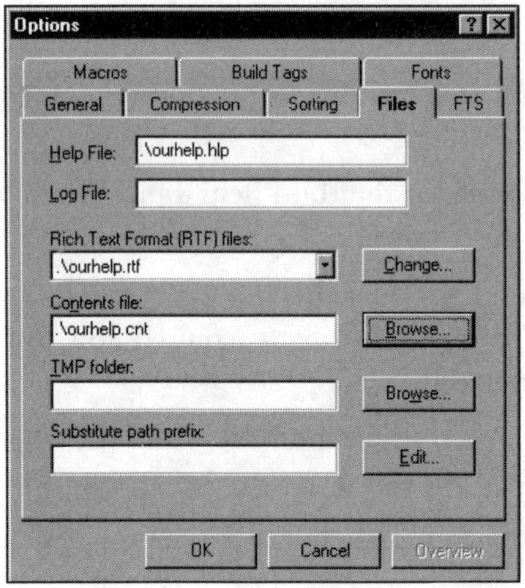

FIGURE 14-32

In order to link the contents file to the help system, you must specify the contents file in the Options dialog box.

Integrating OURHELP.HLP into VFP

By issuing a simple Set Help To command, you have made the help file immediately visible in Visual FoxPro. Of course, this is only a fraction of the help capabilities available in VFP 5.0. To fully illustrate these capabilities, a sam-

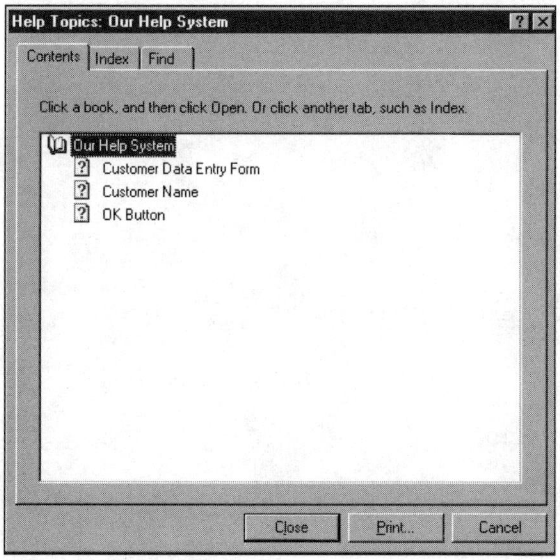

FIGURE 14-33

The new help system now is complete with a table of contents tab.

ple data entry form must be created. This form is pictured in Figure 14-34. Use the following code to create the form:

```
DEFINE CLASS form1 AS form

   Top = 0

   Left = 0

   Height = 119

   Width = 326

   DoCreate = .T.

   Caption = "Customer Information"

   MaxButton = .F.

   MinButton = .F.

   HelpContextID = 100

   WhatsThisHelpID = 100

   WhatsThisHelp = .T.

   WhatsThisButton = .T.

   Name = "Form1"


   ADD OBJECT label1 AS label WITH ;
```

```
         Caption = "Name:", ;
         Height = 17, ;
         Left = 24, ;
         Top = 27, ;
         Width = 40, ;
         Name = "Label1"


    ADD OBJECT text1 AS textbox WITH ;
         Height = 23, ;
         HelpContextID = 110, ;
         WhatsThisHelpID = 110, ;
         Left = 72, ;
         Top = 24, ;
         Width = 216, ;
         Name = "Text1"


    ADD OBJECT command1 AS commandbutton WITH ;
         Top = 72, ;
         Left = 121, ;
         Height = 27, ;
         Width = 84, ;
         Caption = "\<OK", ;
         HelpContextID = 120, ;
         WhatsThisHelpID = 120, ;
         Name = "Command1"

    PROCEDURE command1.Click
       Thisform.Release()
    ENDPROC

ENDDEFINE
```

With OURHELP.HLP as the current help file, clicking the button with the question mark (known as the What's This button) adds a question mark to the

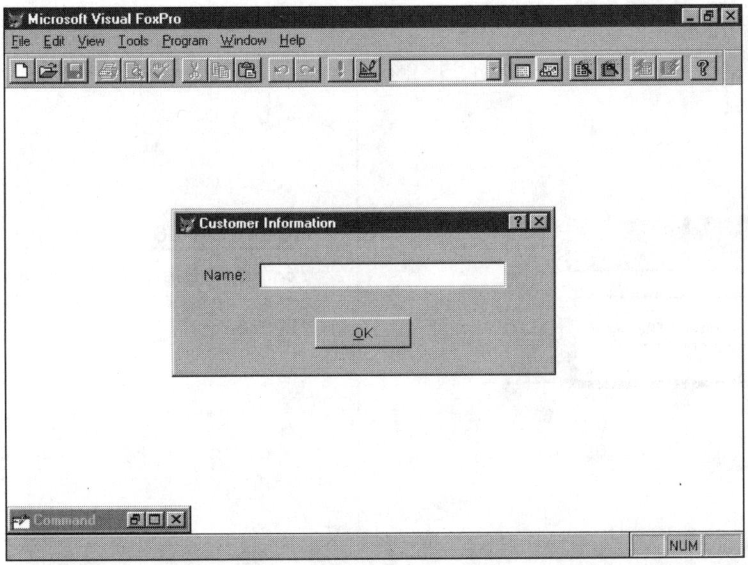

FIGURE 14-34

This is a sample data entry form to illustrate the new help features in VFP.

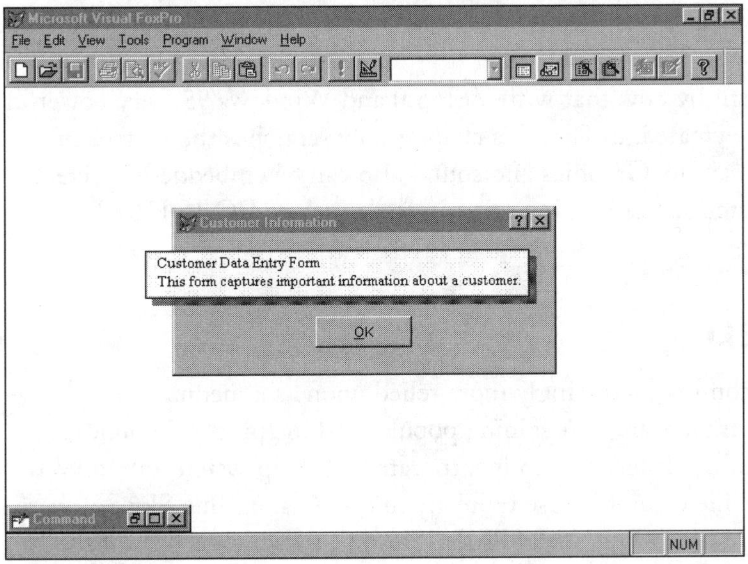

FIGURE 14-35

When you click the question mark in the upper-right corner of the form, then click the form, the new What's This help becomes visible.

mouse pointer. When you use this modified mouse pointer to click the form, the information shown in Figure 14-35 is presented.

If you click the What's This button, then click the text box, you see the information shown in Figure 14-36.

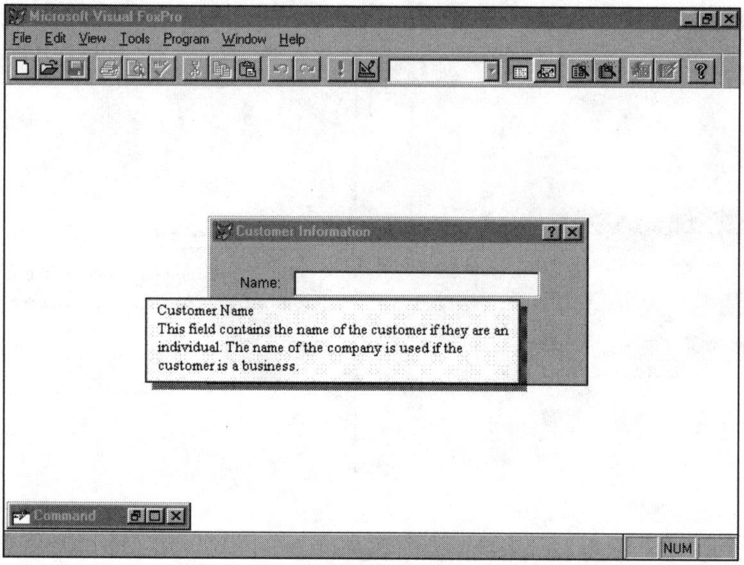

FIGURE 14-36

The help topic associated with the text box appears here in What's This format.

It should be apparent by now that with VFP 5.0 and Windows 95, very powerful help systems can be created; in fact, this chapter only scratches the surface of what help systems can do. Graphics and sound also can be embedded. To create the most robust systems, consider investing in tools such as ROBOHELP.

Help on the Web

The Internet is becoming increasingly more relied upon as a medium for conveying information. Intranets are also gaining popularity. One practical application to take advantage of the Internet is to incorporate your help system into a Web site. Since an HLP file cannot be used directly in a Web site, Blue Sky Software has created a utility named Help to HTML. This utility, which is part of the WinHelp Office 95 suite of tools (of which ROBOHELP is a component), automatically converts HLP files to HTML files. The resulting HTML files can be placed into a Web site. Figure 14-37 shows the contents page created earlier in this chapter, now converted to an HTML document.

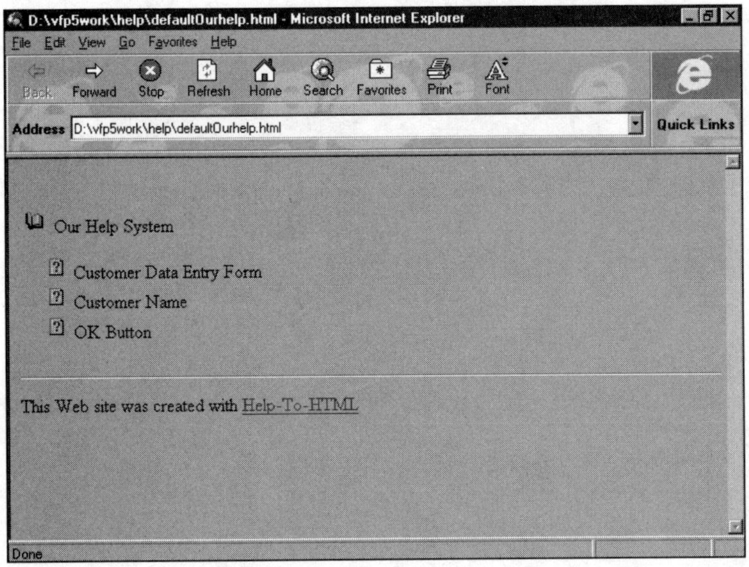

FIGURE 14-37

This help table of contents has been converted to a Web page.

Summary

While the native tools that ship with Visual FoxPro are good for creating some application help, third-party tools such as InstallShield and ROBOHELP allow you to go to a new level. It is important to be aware of what third-party tools are on the market, because someday you may find yourself in need of one or more of these tools.

This chapter has focused on issues regarding the deployment of your application and the creation of a help system. While this is the final chapter in the book, you should realize that planning how your application will be installed, and determining the contents and format of the help file, can never begin too early.

A good installation program takes the time to inform users about the latest (and greatest) features of your software, and to tell them how they can get in touch with you if they have a question. A good help file is one that is written in a clear, understandable style that helps end users do their jobs better. A help file always should be the result of a joint effort between the development team and the end users.

Appendix

What's on the CD?

The CD that accompanies this book contains the examples and source code from the book, including the code that serves as the basis of the World Wide Shoes order entry application. In addition, the CD contains tools and utilities to assist you with your FoxPro application development. You'll find barcode fonts, an OLE object browser, Windows utilities, and more.

Running the CD

To make the CD more user-friendly and take up less of your hard disk space, no installation is required. This means that the only files transferred to your hard disk are whichever ones you choose to copy.

WARNING: Significant differences between the various Windows operating systems (3.1, 95, and NT) sometimes render files that work in one Windows environment inoperable in another. 32-bit programs that run in Windows 95 and Windows NT cannot run in Windows 3.1, which is a 16-bit operating system. In addition, the length and case of filenames can make certain files invisible to one operating system or another.

Prima has made every effort to minimize this problem. It's impossible, however, to eliminate it entirely. You therefore might find that some files or directories appear to be missing from the CD. These files most likely are on the CD, but remain hidden from the operating system. To confirm this, view the CD contents using a different Windows operating system.

Windows 3.1

To run the CD, do the following:

1. Insert the CD in your CD-ROM drive.
2. From File Manager, choose File, Run to open the Run window.

3. In the Command Line text box, type **d:\primacd.exe** (where **d:** represents the correct drive letter of your CD-ROM drive).

4. Click OK.

Windows 95

Since there is no installation routine, running the CD in Windows 95 is a breeze, especially if you have autorun enabled. Simply insert the CD in your CD-ROM drive, close the tray, and wait for the CD to load.

If autorun is disabled, place the CD in your CD-ROM drive and then follow these steps:

1. From the Start menu, choose Run.

2. Type **d:\primacd.exe** (where **d:** represents the correct drive letter of your CD-ROM drive).

3. Click OK.

Prima's User Interface

Prima's user interface is designed to make viewing and using the CD contents quick and easy. The interface contains six category buttons, four option buttons, and a display window. Select a category button to show a list of available titles in the display window. Highlight a title in the window, then choose an option button to perform the desired action.

Category Buttons

- **Examples**—Examples and source code from the book
- **Developer Tools**—Things no developer's toolbox should be without
- **Utilities**—File and system utilities to help manage your system and improve its performance
- **Demoware**—Product demos from Azalea and InstallShield

Option Buttons

- **Install/Run**—If the highlighted title contains an installation routine, then choosing this option begins the installation process. If the title has no installation procedure, but contains an executable file, then the executable is run. If neither an install nor an executable file is present (as in the case of a graphics library), then the folder containing the information is shown. In the event that an application contains an executable file that will not run from the CD, the entire application is placed in a compressed zip file, which can be decompressed using WinZip (included on the CD).

NOTE: You can install some of the shareware programs that do not have installation routines by copying the program files from the CD to your hard drive, then running the executable (exe) file.

- **Information**—Choosing this option displays any available data about the selection. This information is usually in the form of a README or help file.
- **Explore**—Choosing this option allows you to view the folder containing the program files.
- **Exit**—When you're finished and ready to move on, choose this option.

The Software

The list below gives you a brief description of some of the software you'll find on the CD. As you browse the CD, you'll find much more, but this list describes a representative sampling:

- **CuteFTP**—Cute or not, it's a straightforward and easy-to-use FTP application.

- **VBA Companion**—This is an OLE object browser for Windows and Windows NT from APEX Software.

- **Vram**—Speed up your system performance with this 32-bit virtual RAM file system driver for Windows 95.

- **Web Graphics Locator**—Find graphics files anywhere on your system in a GIFfy with this utility.

- **Web Graphics Library**—You'll enjoy this collection of graphics from Blue Sky Software.

- **Windows Help Style Guide**—Blue Sky's style guide shows you how to create a help system the right way.

- **WinHelp Inspector**—Browse your help files and display statistics such as name, date, and size of a given help file, as well as keywords and fonts used in that file.

- **WinZip**—This is one of the leading file compression utilities for Windows 95, Windows NT, and Windows 3.1.

INDEX

Other books from Prima Publishing, Computer Products Division

ISBN	Title	Price	Release Date
0-7615-0801-5	ActiveX	$35.00	Available Now
0-7615-0680-2	America Online Complete Handbook and Membership Kit	$24.99	Available Now
0-7615-0915-1	Building Intranets with Internet Information Server and FrontPage	$40.00	Available Now
0-7615-0417-6	CompuServe Complete Handbook and Membership Kit	$24.95	Available Now
0-7615-0849-X	Corporate Intranet Development	$40.00	Fall '96
0-7615-0692-6	Create Your First Web Page in a Weekend	$24.99	Available Now
0-7615-0503-2	Discover What's Online!	$24.95	Available Now
0-7615-0693-4	Internet Information Server	$40.00	Available Now
0-7615-0815-5	Introduction to ABAP/4 Programming for SAP	$45.00	Available Now
0-7615-0678-0	Java Applet Powerpack	$30.00	Available Now
0-7615-0685-3	JavaScript	$35.00	Available Now
0-7615-0901-1	Leveraging Visual Basic with ActiveX Controls	$45.00	Available Now
0-7615-0682-9	LiveWire Pro Master's Handbook	$40.00	Fall '96
0-7615-0755-8	Moving Worlds	$35.00	Available Now
0-7615-0690-X	Netscape Enterprise Server	$40.00	Available Now
0-7615-0691-8	Netscape FastTrack Server	$40.00	Available Now
0-7615-0852-X	Netscape Navigator 3 Complete Handbook	$24.99	Available Now
0-7615-0751-5	NT Server Administrator's Guide	$50.00	Available Now
0-7615-0759-0	Professional Web Design	$40.00	Available Now
0-7615-0773-6	Programming Internet Controls	$45.00	Available Now
0-7615-0780-9	Programming Web Server Applications	$40.00	Available Now
0-7615-0063-4	Researching on the Internet	$29.95	Available Now
0-7615-0686-1	Researching on the World Wide Web	$24.99	Available Now
0-7615-0695-0	The Essential Photoshop Book	$35.00	Available Now
0-7615-0752-3	The Essential Windows NT Book	$27.99	Available Now
0-7615-0689-6	The Microsoft Exchange Productivity Guide	$24.99	Available Now
0-7615-0769-8	VBscript Master's Handbook	$40.00	Available Now
0-7615-0684-5	VBscript Web Page Interactivity	$35.00	Available Now
0-7615-0903-8	Visual FoxPro 5 Enterprise Development	$45.00	Available Now
0-7615-0814-7	Visual J++	$35.00	Available Now
0-7615-0383-8	Web Advertising and Marketing	$34.95	Available Now
0-7615-0726-4	Webmaster's Handbook	$40.00	Available Now

TO ORDER BOOKS

Please send me the following items:

Quantity	Title	Unit Price	Total
_____	_____	$_____	$_____
_____	_____	$_____	$_____
_____	_____	$_____	$_____
_____	_____	$_____	$_____
_____	_____	$_____	$_____

Subtotal $_____

7.25% Sales Tax (CA only) $_____

8.25% Sales Tax (TN only) $_____

5.0% Sales Tax (MD and IN only) $_____

Shipping and Handling* $_____

TOTAL ORDER (U.S. funds only) $_____

Shipping and Handling depend on Subtotal.

Subtotal	Shipping/Handling
$0.00–$14.99	$3.00
$15.00–29.99	$4.00
$30.00–49.99	$6.00
$50.00–99.99	$10.00
$100.00–199.99	$13.00
$200.00+	call for quote

Foreign and all Priority Request orders:
Call Order Entry department for price quote at
1-916-632-4400

This chart represents the total retail price of books only
(before applicable discounts are taken).

By telephone: With Visa or MC, call 1-800-632-8676. Mon.–Fri. 8:30–4:00 PST.

By Internet E-mail: sales@primapub.com

By mail: Just fill out the information below and send with your remittance to:

PRIMA PUBLISHING
P.O. Box 1260BK
Rocklin, CA 95677-1260

http://www.primapublishing.com

Name_____ Daytime Telephone_____

Address _____

City _____ State _____ Zip _____

Visa /MC# _____Exp. _____

Check/Money Order enclosed for $_____ Payable to Prima Publishing

Signature _____